Life of
Nathaniel Macon

Life of Nathaniel Macon

By William E. Dodd

Foreword by Dr. Clyde N. Wilson

©2017 The Scuppernong Press

First Printing

The Scuppernong Press
PO Box 1724
Wake Forest, NC 27588
www.scuppernongpress.com

Cover and book design by Frank B. Powell, III
Cover image from the collection of the U.S. House of Representatives

All rights reserved. Printed in the United States of America.

No part of this book may be reproduced or transmitted in any form or by any means, electronic or mechanical, including photocopying, recording, or by any information and storage and retrieval system, without written permission from the editor and/or publisher.

International Standard Book Number ISBN 978-1-942806-11-0

Library of Congress Control Number: 2017946963

THE LIFE OF

NATHANIEL MACON

BY

WILLIAM E. DODD, PH.D.
Professor of History in Randolph-Macon College

RALEIGH, N.C.
Edwards & Broughton, Printers and Binders. 1908

Foreword by Dr. Clyde N. Wilson

REPRINTED BY

The Scuppernong Press

Wake Forest, NC
www.scuppernongpress.com

TO MY WIFE, MATTIE JOHNS DODD,
whose encouragement and practical assistance have so much
aided in the completion of my undertaking,
THIS BOOK IS AFFECTIONATELY DEDICATED.

CONTENTS

Introduction iii
Foreword.. v
Preface... xi
Bibliography xii
I. The Macon Family 1
II. At College 5
III. North Carolina During the Revolution 9
IV. In the Army Again 17
V. In the General Assembly, 1781-1785 23
VI. Founding a Home 1782-1891 31
VII. The Adoption of the National Constitution 35
VIII. First Years in Congress, 1791-1795 43
IX. Leader of the North Carolina Delegation 59
X. Macon and the Federalist Supremacy 1797-1801 77
XI. The Revolution of 1800 113
XII. Republican Supremacy, 1801-1805 121
XIII. Macon and the "Quids," 1805-1808 143
XIV. Repeal of the Embargo, 1807-1809 157
XV. Macon a National Character, 1809-1812 175
XVI. Revolution in Congress and the War of 1812 197
XVII. In the United States Senate, 1815-1828 211
XVIII. In the United States Senate, 1820-1828 239
XIX. Macon's Last Years 267
Appendix 291
Index 341

INTRODUCTION

Welcome to the *Life of Nathaniel Macon*, who was one of the most fascinating of the many characters who made up our Founding Fathers. Almost unheard of and unknown to historians and the general public today, Macon stands as one of the most, if not the most, important figure in North Carolina's rich history.

We are pleased to bring the *Life of Nathaniel Macon* back to print so Macon may be known once again, not only in the present day, but to future generations as well. At this printing he is still the only North Carolinian to serve as speaker of the U.S. House of Representatives, which was during the presidency of Thomas Jefferson. Jefferson highly respected Macon and called him *"Ultimus Romanorum,"* the last of the Romans, which was high praise.

Macon thought of himself as a planter, which he was of course, but he was so much more. During his more than 40 years in public service he served in the North Carolina General Assembly, United States House of Representatives, U.S. Senate, and chairman of the North Carolina Constitutional Convention of 1835. He served as President Pro-Tempore of the U.S. Senate in 1826 and 1827. This is in addition to his service as a soldier in the Revolutionary War.

He became known as the "Father of States' Rights" and he fought hard for his "South Country" throughout his career. A young John C. Calhoun learned everything he knew about States' Rights from Macon. He knew of the sectional differences which were present from the founding of this country and foretold the coming War For Southern Independence which occurred 24 years after his passing. In an 1819 speech on the floor of the U.S. Senate Macon said, *"All the states now have equal rights and are content. Deprive one of the least right which it now enjoys in common with the others and it will no longer be content. ... The attempt to govern too much has produced every civil war that ever has been, and will, probably, every one that ever may be."*

He was totally selfless, not even wanting a grave marker. Instead, his final resting place would just be marked with a pile of rocks on the poorest land on his farm. His love for North Carolina and his "South Country" never wavered.

The Scuppernong Press is proud to produce this reprint of the *Life of Nathaniel Macon* for your learning and enjoyment. This edition has been completely reset in a modern typeface with only minor changes in typos, punctuation and some capitalization. Most of the capitalization does not meet modern standards, but it was left as the author intended it. The Index has been completely redone. In addition, photos and engravings have been added to enhance your reading experience.

And a special thanks to Dr. Clyde Wilson for his outstanding Foreword which starts on the opposite page.

We hope you enjoy our efforts.

— Frank B. Powell, III
Editor

FOREWORD

Nathaniel Macon is an important Founding Father almost unknown today. In his time Macon was widely admired as the perfect model of a (small "r") republican statesman. Thomas Jefferson called him "the last of the Romans," and he meant that as a high compliment — that Macon was a model of the selfless patriot and public servant. John Randolph of Roanoke, a close associate in the political battles of the early 1800s, while reminiscing in his last hours, said that Macon was the wisest man he had ever known. The city of Macon, Georgia, Randolph-Macon College, and counties in North Carolina, Alabama, Tennessee, and Illinois were named for him.

The American Founders much admired the heroes of Republican Rome — which is why we have "capitol" buildings and a statue of George Washington in a toga, and explains Jefferson's comment. Roman heroes like Cincinnatus, who was plowing his fields when they came to him and said the republic was in peril. He left home, took command of the army, defeated the enemy, and then returned home to his plowing. He sought nothing for himself, only to serve the people and maintain their liberties. He wanted the respect of his fellow citizens but sought no profit or glory for himself. This was the kind of republican hero that Macon represented to Americans of the early 19th century.

Macon was born in 1758 on a plantation in Warren County, North Carolina, which was his home all his life. When the American War of Independence broke out in 1775 he left Princeton and joined the fight. Characteristically, he refused a commission and the bounty paid for enlisting — true patriotism did not require pay. Near the end of the war he was elected to the North Carolina General Assembly while still in his twenties. He was identified with the Anti-Federalist position, and, significantly, his brother John Macon voted against the proposed federal Constitution in both ratifying conventions of the sovereign people of North Carolina.

When the federal government went into business in 1789, it became apparent that Northern interests were bent on turning it into a centralized power and a money-making machine for themselves by national banks, government bonds, tariffs, and other paper swindles which would be paid for out of the pockets of the farmers, who produced the tangible wealth of the country. To oppose such Hamiltonian schemes, Macon accepted election to the U.S. House of Representatives for the Second Congress.

He served in the House for 24 years and in the Senate for 13 years, representing North Carolina in Congress from 1791 to 1828, from the age of 33 to the age of 70, when he retired voluntarily. He was chosen by the Jeffersonian party to be Speaker of the House for six years, and willingly gave up that powerful office in principled disagreement with the party. He was chairman of the foreign relations committees in both the House and the Senate, and finally President Pro Tem of the Senate. He received numerous overtures to run for Vice-President and was twice offered Cabinet appointments, all of which he turned down. During all this time he never neglected his responsibilities as a citizen of Warren County. His last public service was to preside over the North Carolina Constitutional Convention of 1835, and he died two years later.

The offices Macon held are not the important thing. Today politicians scramble to get into office so they can have honor and importance as well as make money and flatter their vanity. But Macon, like Washington and Jefferson, was not important and respected because he occupied high office. He was elected to high office because he was honored and respected. He never campaigned. He never attended a party caucus. He never asked anyone to vote for him or promised them patronage. He was elected over and over again because of what he represented.

Macon was admired because he never changed from the principles with which he began. What were those principles?

1) The federal government should be tightly bound by the Constitution. It should not tax the people and spend money any more than was absolutely necessary to carry out its delegated tasks. By a few words in debate, Macon often stopped unconstitutional spending bills which had been proposed by someone on the grounds of "doing good."

2) Standing armies were invariably the enemies of liberty — a country with a just government would be defended by patriotic volunteers.

3) The government should not go into debt, which was just a way to make the taxpayers pay interest to the rich.

4) Eternal vigilance was the price of liberty. Power was always stealing from the many to the few. Office-holders were to be watched closely and kept as directly responsible to the people as possible by frequent elections — Macon opposed changing the state constitutional provision that established one-year terms for offices.

5) Politics should not be a profession. Politicians should make their own living just like everyone else. They were just citizens performing a temporary service who would soon return to private life and live under the laws they had made. Officials should not be glorified but reflect "republican simplicity."

Small "r" republicans believed history teaches the stronger and more centralized a government becomes, the less free are the people. The richer the government and its politicians and favoured clients become, the poorer are the people. Liberty had always been overturned in this way, but America, with governments created by and responsible to the people, had a chance to avoid the inevitable bad tendencies of governments in the past. Preserving that ideal, or dream, was what Macon's career was about and why he was admired and honored. As Dodd admiringly concludes, Macon "really believed in democracy."

Macon owned much land and many slaves and was a national hero. Yet he lived in "republican simplicity" in a rather remote location — so remote that I once spent a half-day driving around Warren County without finding it. He attended the Baptist church with his slaves. He left no cache of papers for future examination. He was, at his own direction, buried very unostentatiously. As far as I can find only one portrait was ever painted of him — the one customarily made of Speakers of the House. Americans had rebelled against hereditary aristocracy and future generations should continue to think for themselves and not worship ancestors. Macon's "republican simplicity" is a challenge for biographers.

William Edward Dodd (1869-1940), author of what is still the only substantial biography of Macon, was one of the first generation of American professionally-trained, academic historians — history before the late 19th century generally had been written and taught by gentleman scholars. A North Carolina native, Dodd, like many Americans of the period, went to Germany for advanced study and received a doctorate from the University of Leipizig in 1900. When he wrote the life of Nathaniel Macon he was a young professor at Randolph-Macon College. He left that institution in 1908 for the

University of Chicago and was thereafter less noted as a historian than as FDR's ambassador to Nazi Germany and a public activist and controversialist.

Dodd was the first professional, academic historian to proclaim himself a specialist in the history of the South. Interpretations of Southern history have cycled through many changes since he wrote. The viewpoint demonstrated in his works, except for the volume in hand, is long out-dated. Writing as a liberal in an era dominated by Big Business, Dodd wanted to rediscover a tradition of "democracy" in the early South — a democracy which he believed had been destroyed by the defense of slavery from the 1830s on. This is a rather simplistic notion of Southern history and underrates its continuity and the conservative nature of Macon's position. Dodd's *Life of Nathaniel Macon*, however, remains the only complete account of an important career.

Macon is a difficult subject for a writer because he deliberately left little documentation. His life has to be recovered from letters found amongst the papers of other people of his time, from scattered newspapers, and in nuggets of short speeches found here and there in the voluminous reports of Congressional proceedings. Nobody since Dodd has carried out the arduous research required for a full biography. The *Life of Nathaniel Macon* remains an important work of North Carolina and American history about a patriot who still has much to teach us.

As time went on, Macon realized that preserving republican principles was a losing cause. In his last years he spoke of the demise of "what was the Constitution," and of the fact the North was determined to exploit and rule the South. It is not surprising that when the sovereign convention of the people of North Carolina met in the spring of 1861 to unanimously ratify secession, Macon's son-in-law Weldon N. Edwards was in the chair.

Clyde N. Wilson
Emeritus Distinguished Professor of History
University of South Carolina

Nathaniel Macon
Collection of the US House of Representatives

PREFACE

The *raison d'etre* of a biography of Nathaniel Macon is to be found in the unique and also important role he played in our national life and in the great sectional contest which filled the first half of the nineteenth century. No comprehensive life of Macon has ever been attempted. A half dozen newspaper articles, and of recent years a few semi-scientific sketches of his career, have been published; and some letters of Macon with introductions and notes have appeared since the writer began his searches for materials. But none of these have given more than a glimpse of the able leader and astute politician who so long held the first place in the political affairs of North Carolina.

In the midst of the duties of a teacher of history, the author has tried to get together the scanty materials bearing on Macon's life, and to draw from these a picture of his rise to prominence in North Carolina during and just after the Revolution, of his activity as an ardent Jefferson republican, which brought him to the Speakership of Congress, of his long and determined opposition to Clay's American system, and finally of his share in the Jackson campaigns. How well this self-imposed task has been done, how accurately the picture of the real Macon has been drawn, is for the reader to determine. But one thing at least may be said of the work: it has been attempted, and with the attempt some of the materials of North Carolina's history have been collected and put within the reach of the public. In drawing the outlines of Macon's life a cursory review of the history of North Carolina has also been made, which will scarce be taken amiss by those who appreciate the present state of history writing in this section of the country.

Foremost among those who have lent valuable assistance in the collecting of the data for this work are Judge A. B. Hagner, of Washington, DC; Mrs. Walter K. Martin, of Richmond, Virginia; and Prof. Kemp P. Battle, of Chapel Hill, North Carolina, all of whom gave free access to collections of Macon letters in their possession. Mr. S. M. Hamilton, of Washington, was particularly courteous in making the collections of the Department of State so freely accessible. Senator Lodge, Henry Adams and Prof. J. F. Jameson took the trouble to put me in communication with persons who owned Macon letters and other data.

Josephus Daniels, Esq., of Raleigh, North Carolina, has manifested the greatest interest in the work from the beginning, and has given invaluable aid on several occasions. Capt. M.O. Sherrill, the efficient State Librarian of North Carolina, has at all times taken particular pains to render my use of the sources of information under his charge as easy and rapid as possible. Justices Walter A. Montgomery, Walter Clark and Charles A. Cook, of the North Carolina Supreme Court; General Matthew W. Ransom, of Garysburg; Col. H. C. Eccles, of Charlotte; Hon. Thomas M. Pittman and Col. Francis A. Macon, of Henderson, and Samuel L. Adams, Esq., of Elon College, North Carolina, have all lent generous assistance to my undertaking. Dr. Ulrich B. Phillips, of Wisconsin University, very kindly lent assistance in collecting Macon letters. To all of these, and many others who have given similar assistance, the author takes this means of expressing his hearty thanks.

My colleagues, Doctors E. W. Bowen and A. C. Wightman, and also Hon. H. G. Connor, Associate Justice of the Supreme Court of North Carolina, have very kindly assisted in the tedious work of proofreading, though they are in no way to be held responsible for errors and imperfections which the book doubtless contains. For this generous aid at a very trying season, the author desires here to express his hearty appreciation.

W. E. D.

RANDOLPH-MACON COLLEGE, VA., August 1, 1903.

NOTE : The recent appearance of volume 22 of the *North Carolina State Records* brings to light the journals of the General Assembly for the year 1790, which were supposed to have been lost. The author, at least, was unable to find them in the manuscript archives of the State Department.

These journals show that Macon returned to the Legislature as a member of the House of Representatives in 1790. He was very active and exerted great influence on the proceedings of the body particularly when matters of national concern were under discussion. It is too late now for any outline of this part of his life to be given. In general, however, it may be said that his efforts during this session were not inconsistent with those of his earlier course in the Assembly. Hence there is no need of reconstructing what has been written, or even of changing more than a single statement, and it is hoped that this explanation will satisfy those who might otherwise be astonished to find no mention of that part of Macon's career.

The error, if such it may be called, is one which could not well be repaired as the first part of the book had already been printed.

— AUTHOR.

SOURCES OF INFORMATION

1. Unpublished: The Macon Papers (a remnant of Macon's correspondence with Jefferson, Gallatin, Jackson and others); The Joseph H. Nicholson Papers; Yancey-Steele Correspondence; Warren County records; and the Jefferson and Monroe MSS. in State Department.

2. Published documents and correspondence; North Carolina Colonial and State Records; Annals of Congress; Benton's Abridgment of Debates in Congress; North Carolina Laws; Journals of North Carolina Assembly; Writings of Thomas Jefferson (Ford); Life and correspondence of James Iredell (McKee); Works of Washington (Sparks); Works of Madison (Congress Edition); The Leven Powell Correspondence (Branch Papers); Debates of the North Carolina Constitutional Convention of 1835; Life and Correspondence of Gallatin (Adams).

3. Newspapers and Periodicals: *Raleigh Register; Richmond Enquirer; National Intelligencer; Tennessee Democrat; The Nation; American Historical Review; Southern History Publications; William and Mary College Quarterly; Annual Register; The Sprunt Monographs.*

4. General and special accounts: Meade: Old Churches and Parishes; Wheeler: History of North Carolina; Cotten: Life of Nathaniel Macon; Moore: History of North Carolina; Fiske: Critical Period of American History; Schouler: History of the United States; Johnson: Life of Nathaniel Greene; Thomas: Character Sketches; Hudson: Journalism in the United States; Schenck: North Carolina, 1780-81; Hart: Formation of the Union; Garland: Life of John Randolph; Schurz: Life of Henry Clay; Peele: Distinguished North Carolinians; Channing: History of the United States.

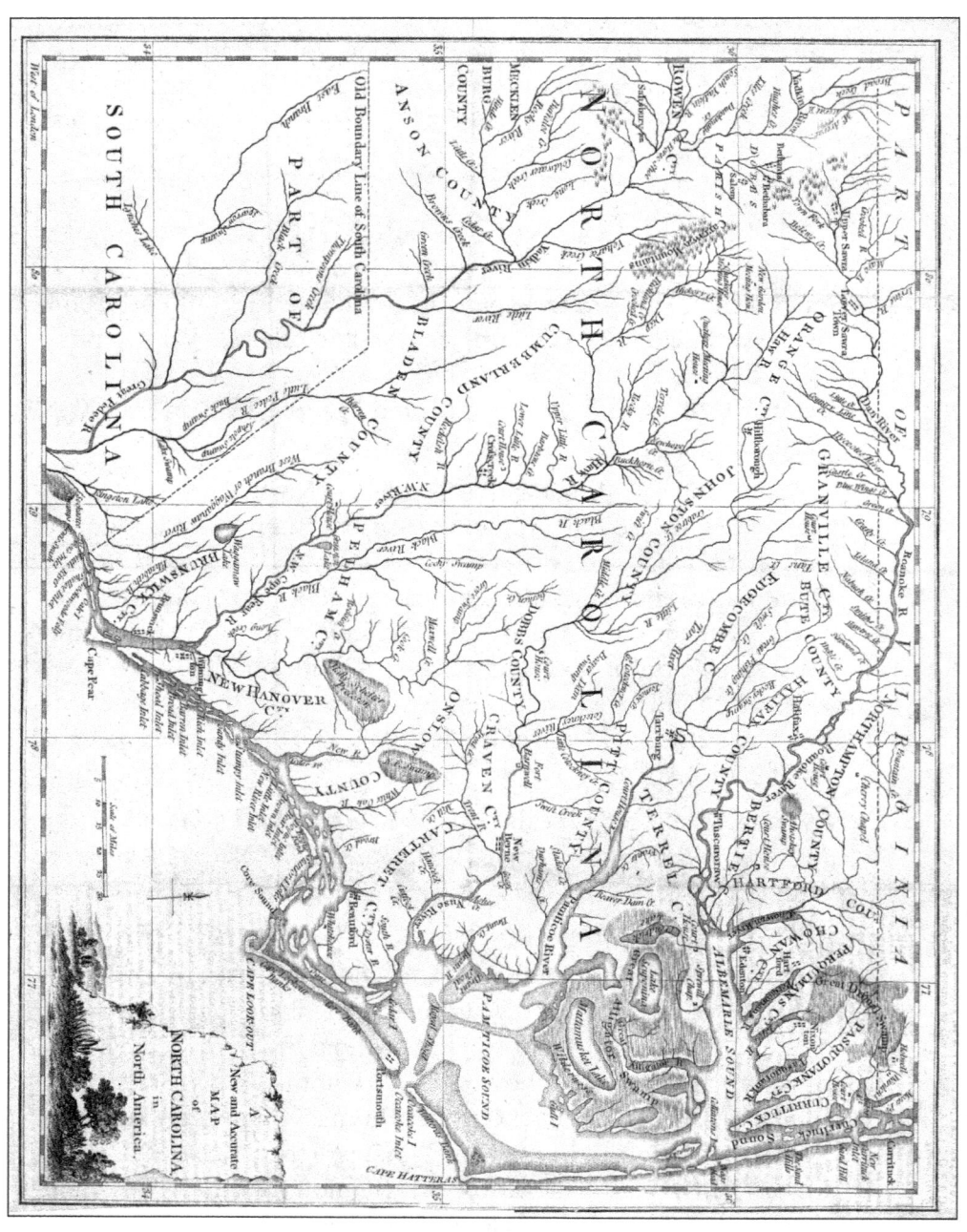

1779 map of North Carolina

CHAPTER I. THE MACON FAMILY.

The Macon family originated in France, in the Saone-Loire country. A certain "Jouserand de Macon" was knighted there, we are told, in the year 1321; Louis de Macon and Gabriel, his son, bore the title "de" and were masters of considerable estates. But just where they lived and what their connection with the American Macons was, are questions which can not be answered. There was a French Huguenot of some means who settled at Middle Plantation, in Virginia, in the second half of the seventeenth century, and who was a prominent tobacco planter and a vestryman in St. Peter's parish, New Kent County, in the year 1680.[1] This was Gideon Macon, and his estate, Prospect Hill, is still regarded as one of the fine old landmarks of Eastern Virginia. The second owner of Prospect Hill was William Macon, born 1693, likewise a vestryman in the same parish and colonel of the New Kent militia about the middle of the next century. Martha, a sister of this Colonel Macon, married Orlando Jones, and a granddaughter of this union, Miss Martha Dandridge, became the wife of John Parke Custis. Mrs. Custis was early left a widow, and a wealthy widow, who, as all the world knows, became Martha Washington.[2] There were many Macons in Virginia about the middle of the eighteenth century, and many of them were connected with the most prominent families in the colony. Henry Macon, of Goochland, was one of these; and Thomas Macon, a brother-in-law of James Madison, of Orange, was another.

Gideon Macon, brother to William of Prospect Hill,[3] emigrated to upper North Carolina in the early thirties of the eighteenth century, and "took up lands" on Shocco Creek within the domains of the Earl of Granville. About the same time Philemon Hawkins and Edward Jones, of Gloucester County, Virginia adjoining New Kent settled in the Shocco neighborhood.[4] This was the beginning of a veritable "trek" of the East Virginians to North Carolina. The whole scope of country lying between the Roanoke and Neuse Rivers, west of the Tarboro neighborhood, known in that day as "the Southside of Roanoke," was settled by Virginians, who found the lands of the older

---

1 Meade: *Old Churches and Parishes*, I., 387
2 William and Mary College Quarterly, July, 1897.
3 This is not shown by the records, but the author is quite satisfied as to the correctness of the statement.
4 Wheeler's *History of North Carolina*, II., 426.

colony already worn out! The Southside of Roanoke became Edgecombe county in 1741, and again the upper part of this section was made Bute county in 1760. The new courthouse was located near the Macon manor, that being the center of the most influential part of the county.

"Macon Manor," as the place is called today, was built by this first North Carolina Macon. In a short time, thanks to exemption from all disturbance, to fertile soil and industrious hands, Gideon Macon became a prosperous tobacco grower. Hawkins and Jones and many another followed the same occupation; they opened a road to Petersburg, Virginia, where they journeyed once a year to sell their tobacco. The Macon manor was the first house in the new country which boasted the superior advantage of glass windows, though Hawkins, just five miles away, was the wealthier man. None of the settlers, however, were possessed of very great wealth, as was to be expected, even as late as 1760. Most of them owned some five hundred to a thousand acres of land and a half dozen to twenty negro slaves. They were good, loyal subjects of King George, rather disposed to follow his Majesty's governors than the Eastern oligarchy, then so potent in North Carolina affairs. Hawkins actually rose to some rank as an official under Tryon, the best-hated of all our English governors.

Gideon Macon's will,[5] probated in 1763, disposed, however, of three thousand acres of land and some twenty-five to thirty negroes. Priscilla Macon,[6] widow of Gideon Macon, was made sole executrix of the estate and guardian of the Macon children. No complaint seems ever to have been made by any of the heirs concerning the administration of the property — proof enough of Mrs. Macon's ability, and of the relations which had prevailed between husband and wife.

Nathaniel Macon, the sixth child of Gideon and Priscilla Macon, was born at Macon manor, December 17, 1758. He was only five years of age when his father died. Item three of the father's will reads as follows: "I give and bequeath to my son, Nathaniel Macon, all the remainder part of the above (Shocco tract), said tract of land lying and being on both sides of Shocco Creek, and above the said court house road. I likewise give to my said son five hundred acres of land lying and being on both sides of Hubquarter Creek (on Roanoke). I likewise give my said son my blacksmith's tools at the decease of my

---

[5] Warren County Records.
[6] Priscilla Macon afterwards married James Ransom, the ancestor of Matthew W. Ransom, United States Senator and Minister to Mexico.

loving wife, Priscilla Macon, to him and his heirs forever. * * * I give and bequeath to my son, Nathaniel Macon, two negro boys, named George and Robb, and one negro girl, named Lucy, to him and his heirs forever."[7] It was not a great legacy, not so much as Thomas Jefferson's £500 a year — but a nucleus which, with his mother's careful management during the sixteen years of his minority, became no inconsiderable estate.

In 1766, Mr. Charles Pettigrew, afterwards bishop of the Protestant Episcopal Church in North Carolina — ancestor, too, of our great Confederate general of the same name — was engaged by Mrs. Macon and Philemon Hawkins to open a school near the courthouse, i.e., about half-way between the two estates. Pettigrew's school continued from 1766 to 1773, and had for pupils John and Nathaniel Macon and Joseph and Benjamin Hawkins, three of whom showed the value of the school and the success of the teacher by becoming students at the "College of New Jersey" at Princeton. In 1773, Pettigrew was called to Edenton to become Principal of the Academy recently established there by the Legislature on the active and persistent recommendation of Samuel Johnston.

It would be interesting to know what was taught in that pioneer school in the Shocco neighborhood, but no record remains except what is seen in the lives of the pupils, of which we shall see more as our subject grows. Pettigrew, though he was called to a broader and more promising field, never lost sight of the boys whom he had trained in his first school. He wrote in 1802 to Benjamin Hawkins, of Alabama: "Believe me, sir, the prosperity and respectability of any of my old pupils gives me the sincerest pleasure, and I am peculiarly happy to find that your old schoolmate, Macon, makes so respectable a figure in Congress."[8]

Whether Macon was regularly in school, whether he was a proficient, or whether he showed early signs of future distinction, neither Pettigrew nor Cotten, Macon's professed biographer, tells us. The one proof that the boy was ambitious, and therefore industrious, to some extent, at least, is shown in his early resolution to go to college, even under disadvantages. Cotten, whose business it was primarily to tell about this, fills his pages with general and impossible compliments to the paragon of a youth who "manifested at an early period of life a

---

7 Warren County Records.
8 Charles Pettigrew to Benjamin Hawkins.

curiosity incessantly engaged in pursuing enquiries and accumulating a knowledge which, to common observers, might have frequently appeared to be an obstinate, self-willed principle of mind, wasting itself in unprofitable speculations and refusing to bring its energies to bear upon a pursuit pointed out by another." Again, Macon "compressed more experience in a given time, when a youth, than any of his ordinary associates — he contemned the absurdities of youth," but was "diffident, self-suspicious, modest." This last named we are assured may "rightly be classed as an early and certain trait of Macon's character;" and, in truth, he was never over-conscious of his own importance, not even when he was undisputed leader in North Carolina and Speaker of the House of Representatives in Congress. He seems to have been, if Cotten's statements may be accepted at all, frank, high-toned, self-possessed, even in early life — a sort of man-boy, the youngster who sat with grown-up people on long Sunday evenings and talked of crops and negroes and politics, instead of swimming in some forbidden mill pond or stealing watermelons, as occasion offered; not just the boy we should admire, no matter how much his soberness and premature judgment promised as to the future. He never yielded to temptation, though he early learned to drink great gourdfuls of whiskey; never knew vice, though his "brother John" was the greatest scape-grace in the county; and never, like Jefferson, wrote sickly love epistles to country lasses. An analytical turn of mind he certainly must have manifested, a disposition to subject everything to logical inquiry, to indulge, too, in paradox and unexpected questioning. Though his mind was well balanced and capable of giving good judgments, even when a boy, he was often prone to substitute the smaller for the greater aspects of life.

CHAPTER II. AT COLLEGE.

A great deal has been said about Macon's difficulty in procuring means for the completion of his education, about the contributions of neighbors to his support, the indifference of his parents to his ambition, and, as is usual in such cases, most of it entirely without foundation. In 1774 he was only fifteen years old, and just out of Pettigrew's school, which had been closed for want of a teacher; he was heir to a very respectable estate, and was the most promising son in a well-to-do family. Now a boy of fifteen is not apt to be conducting a campaign against poverty and adverse circumstances in order to enter college, and certainly not a favorite in the second wealthiest family in his community. Macon's home was the best in the county, as it appears, and his parents were too proud, even had they been poor, to relish the idea of asking assistance in the education of their son by public or neighborhood charity. Besides, such assistance is entirely at variance with the character of Macon even as a boy. The whole story, invented by Cotten and Weldon N. Edwards, without further investigation seems to resolve itself into a myth, manufactured to suit their particular fancies. The situation was simply this: Macon's mother saw great promise in her boy, she believed in education, she had been instrumental in establishing the Pettgrew school; two of Nathaniel's young friends, Benjamin and Joseph Hawkins, were doing well at Princeton, as the college has later come to be designated. What could have been more natural than Macon's desire to join his former schoolmates, and what more reasonable than for the mother to share her son's ambition and lend all the assistance necessary? That some little difficulty arose about getting together the means for such a course, and that the "going away to college" was a matter of some notoriety among the neighbors in that simple country-side is but natural. As Cotten has told us, there may have been a farewell gathering and well-wishing, for a journey to New Jersey was almost equal to a trip to Europe.

And the College of New Jersey, not William and Mary, was chosen. All the boys who went to college from Bute County in those days, and most of those from North Carolina, went to Princeton as did many of the Virginians — Martin, the later poet-governor of North Carolina, and Madison and Monroe being examples. During the years immediately preceding the Revolution, and for many years after, there were three courses open to a young Southerner who desired a higher education. First and most desirable of all, it was to "go home" to England and spend four years at Oxford or Cambridge, finally completing the professional part of his training at one of the great law schools in London, or at the medical school of the University of Edinburgh. And this was not uncommon even with people of modest fortunes. The colonies were closer to England than "the States" ever have been, and any merchant's ship that laid in its cargo of tobacco on the James, or the Potomac, or of lumber and naval stores on the Neuse or Cape Fear, was only too glad to take on board a sprightly young man to make good cheer on the long meandering voyage across the Atlantic. It was nothing strange in the Northern Neck of Virginia, nor on the streets of colonial Edenton, to meet people who had spent years abroad — men lived in America then in order to return home to enjoy their new-won fortunes. These young men, ordinarily sons of the wealthier families, returned after a stay of four to six years as thoroughly English as had been their fathers when first they set foot on American shores. They were gentlemen in all that an Englishman considered necessary to such a character, and destined to take a lead by natural right, almost, in the affairs of the colonies. Second, the less wealthy, and Episcopalians generally, patronized William and Mary, and afterwards took law under Wythe or one of the Randolphs — Jefferson and Marshall are notable examples of these. Third, the Dissenters — "the sects," as they were persistently called — sent their sons to the College of New Jersey to enjoy the direction and instruction of Doctor Witherspoon, whose name and work were well known from Boston to Savannah. The Presbyterians were, however, pioneers in education in the South; and the service they rendered the country in sending out young school teachers can not be over-estimated.

Young Macon's career as a student at Princeton is a blank to us, the records of the college previous to 1787 having been destroyed, and none of Macon's letters referring to that period of his life having been preserved. What the institution was, we may judge from Philip Fithian's most interesting diary, and the letters of Burr, Monroe and others. It was a good Presbyterian seminary, chiefly theological — the hot-bed of strictly Calvinistic tenets. Its academic curriculum was about equivalent to a first rate academy of our time. Latin and Greek and Mathematics constituted the trinity of liberal culture everywhere in the latter years of the eighteenth century. French was taught, of course, somewhat for the same reasons that all our colleges are teaching Spanish now. Macon's friend and college mate, Benjamin

Hawkins, became such a proficient in that language that good Doctor Witherspoon recommended him to Washington for a position on his staff as interpreter of French, and that, too, before Hawkins had completed the course.[9] In fact, the tongue of the Parisians was much more commonly understood in America then than it has ever been since. Burr and Hamilton, without ever having crossed the seas, spoke French as fluently as they did their own language. But Macon did not learn French, nor Latin to any great degree of proficiency, though he was able afterwards to take up the study of law. Something of Latin he did know, as is evidenced occasionally in his correspondence of later years. His education, contrary to the general opinion, was good — not broad, but substantial, sufficient for entrance upon the study of any of the professions. It has been repeatedly asserted that he was illiterate, that he could not write English correctly. This is not true, though it can not be claimed that he wrote with ease and fluency. His letters are generally short and pithy, and sometimes the sentences are carelessly constructed; but the reading of some two hundred of them, covering the whole period of his life, will confirm one in the belief that his training at the country school of Bute and at Princeton was thorough and extensive, considering the short duration of those terms of academic drill. Fewer orthographical errors occur in his writings than in a similar amount of Jefferson's, and on such comparisons is based the argument that Macon was almost illiterate.

In the summer of 1776, Macon joined a company of New Jersey militia — a sort of local guard, it appears — and served "a tour," he tells us on the margin of a letter he wrote the North Carolina Assembly in 1828. What he did, and where those college volunteers were sent, has not been ascertained. The war soon absorbed all interest and attention, and the college was closed, its students either returning home or joining the feeble forces of Washington. It was in that sad summer and autumn, when the American army was more formidable to its commander than to Clinton and the British, when militia companies were flying hither and thither to suit their own fickle fancies, that our hero, now seventeen years old, took up his journey southward. Hawkins, his friend, had joined the army, and was beginning to make a career for himself. There was utmost need for Macon in the North; many of his fellow Carolinians were in the Continental army, and surely there was no immediate danger threatening his native

---

9 Life of Hawkins in *Wheeler's History of North Carolina*, II., 427.

State. He returned, notwithstanding, to the quiet country court house to take up the study of law, like many another of our Revolutionary leaders. His college days were over — closed perforce; what he had received has been discussed and estimated. It had not made an *American* of him, as is shown by his return to his home when *America* was most in need of his services. He was primarily a citizen of his State, as was everyone else in this country in 1776, and many years after.

Under whom Macon studied law, and with what success, like many other points in his biography, we are unable to determine. His own statements in later life, and the testimony of tradition, show that he spent the years 1777-1780 in reading law and English history under the direction of someone living at Bute Court House. But Macon never practiced law, nor even acquired the lawyer's point of view in politics or personal affairs. He was unquestionably as much a tobacco planter as a student, even in his years of study.

CHAPTER III.
NORTH CAROLINA DURING THE REVOLUTION.

Whatever may be said of North Carolina's devotion to the cause of the Confederacy in 1860-1865 — and no people ever sacrificed more — it can not be said that it gave general and heroic support to the cause of Independence. No state acted other than a selfish role in that, our first war. It was not a nation's struggle, but that of a large faction of a nascent nation — a war waged by fits and starts, and won by the greatness and heroism of one man. Foreign students of American history are not far wrong when they say that Washington was the only great, heroic figure in all that seven years drama of Liberty. No comparison can be made between the behavior of our fathers in 1776 and the people of Holland in the sixteenth century, where a whole people rose in arms and continued in arms during the lifetime of three generations, paying half of their total incomes into the coffers of the state. In America it was the self-sacrifice and cooperation of a few far-seeing individuals that gained the struggle. The people remained at home, and systematic taxation was almost unknown. Macon was one of these people, and the motives which kept him quietly studying law at Bute Court House during the years 1777-1780, were the same which kept most other North Carolinians at home, the same which prompted the Connecticut militia to go trooping back to their farms when Washington's army crossed the Hudson in 1776.

At the outbreak of the Revolution, however, North Carolina, like most of the other states, was aroused to an extraordinary degree of enthusiasm. The Royal Governor, Josiah Martin, was supplanted at once, as many another had been in the history of the colony; a new government was speedily set up, and within twelve months ten thousand troops were enlisted and actually in service, some in Virginia, others in South Carolina, and several regiments in the Continental army at the North. Great zeal for the popular cause was manifested; elections were held every six months, and when the Provincial Congress assembled at Halifax in 1776, not a member was absent. There were then in North Carolina three hundred thousand inhabitants, which would give a fighting population of sixty thousand, reckoned on the basis of one to five, the ratio of Prussia in the wars of Frederick the Great. Ten thousand volunteers was a creditable contribution to the general cause; but it did not represent, by any means, the military strength of the new government, and this was when the country was ablaze with patriotic enthusiasm.[10] The following year the ardor of the people was cooling, and in 1778 the total number of privates in Washington's army from North Carolina was nine hundred; of officers, there were five hundred and fifty, all unwilling to serve regularly except in their full rank! At home, James Iredell gave up, this year, a Superior Court Judgeship because the emoluments were insufficient; Samuel Johnston, his brother-in-law, refused to serve as State Treasurer, though he admitted the emoluments were ample enough. William Hooper, too, resigned his seat in the Continental Congress. Wise and wealthy men thought it too dangerous to be over-zealous on either side.

In order to fill the vacancies in the ranks of the North Carolina regiments the Continental Congress offered bounties of one hundred dollars each for volunteers, but without success; then the State was called on to fill up her quota, and twenty-six hundred and forty men were ordered to be drafted from the militia for terms of nine months, with the promise of exemption from further service during a period of three years, and, in addition, a bounty of fifty dollars from the State was guaranteed each man. All these rewards were designed to make the drafting less odious, and to encourage faithful service at least for the short term. The increase in the number of North Carolinians in the national service as a result of these recruiting measures was, by the end of the year, four hundred men and officers! Several additional companies were, however, finally raised, and were, during the autumn of 1778, encamped at Salisbury, Hillsboro and one or two other points; but, when Congress failed to send its promised bounties promptly, most of the troops returned to their homes *on furlough* — a semblance of discipline this last. In 1779, after the news of Saratoga and of the French alliance had permeated the State, this same indifference continued. During the spring and summer of that year an effort was made to send a strong force into South Carolina for the relief of Savannah. General Sumner, of Warren, the ranking general in North Carolina, was put in command. Seven hundred and fifty-seven men joined him, of whom four hundred and twenty-one were on hand when it came to an actual engagement!

---

10 It is worth noting here that during the War Between the States Eastern and Central North Carolina furnished one soldier to every six inhabitants.

On April 10, the nine-months term of the men expired, and, notwithstanding the great needs of the situation and the urgent entreaties of their commanders to re-enlist, every man, we are told, set out for his home. This kind of service continued unimproved until 1780.[11] But it was not worse in North Carolina than in New York and New Jersey during the same years. The Pennsylvania farmers fought in the same way. These healthy and wealthy Germans, with their neighbors, listened carefully for news from Washington's army, and when it appeared that the Americans were about to win a speedy success, they set out in troops for the front; but if bad news met them on the way, they disappeared, like prairie dogs, among their native hills.[12] But the principal cause of this supine support of the great national movement on the part of North Carolina was the neutralization of the forces of the patriots : (1) By the effects of the War of Regulation in 1769-1771; (2) by the presence of large numbers of Scotch Royalists in the middle and upper Cape Fear regions; (3) by the opponents of democratic government, *i.e.,* by the influence of the determined minority in the assemblies, led by Hooper, Johnston, Iredell and others.

1. The War of Regulation was the result of unjust taxation and oppressive methods of collecting the same. The East, wealthy and populous, was divided into plantations which were cultivated by negro slaves; the West, poor, and also populous, was composed of small farms whose owners did all their own work, receiving for their produce very small incomes after the great expense of carrying it to distant markets was deducted. The East was an oligarchy; the West a democracy. The two sections could not easily have been brought to live peaceably together under the most beneficent laws; so much the worse when the East persisted in domineering and exploiting the West. The ancient method for raising the revenue for the expenses of the province had been by levying a uniform poll tax. As the difference between the two sections of the province became greater, the more unjust did this method of taxation appear. The West, after years of petition and complaint, raised the standard of revolt in 1769. This first opposition to the East was compromised and apparently settled by the shrewd and able Governor Tryon. But when conditions grew steadily worse, and to injustice was added systematic extortion, the

---

11 N.C. State Records, XIII, and XIV, prefatory notes. The statements made above are borne out by numberless documents all through these volumes.
12 Letters of David Griffith to Leven Powell, Randolph- Macon Historical Papers, 1901.

revolt broke out afresh in 1771, with three thousand men in arms. Tryon called on the Eastern counties for sufficient quotas of troops, which were cheerfully granted. June 16, 1771, the Governor, with most of the great plantation owners as his lieutenants, completely defeated and routed the Regulators. Speedy and bloody execution was administered to the more important leaders who could be apprehended. An iron-clad oath was forced upon the people of the disaffected district, which included Orange, Guilford and parts of Rowan and Granville counties — a population of at least twenty thousand souls. The East triumphed over the West. When the Revolution broke out, these people, bound by most solemn oaths and smarting under the injustice of recent proceedings, remained, most of them, neutral; and some actually enlisted under the Royal standard. This neutralized a large section of the state; and it is not difficult to understand when it is remembered that the same men who commanded in Tryon's army in 1771 were commanding divisions in the patriot army in 1776.[13]

2. The defeat of the Scots in 1715 began the migration of that sturdy race to North Carolina; but the final overthrow of their armies at Culloden in 1746 broke forever the spirit of revolt and sent thousands in quest of new homes in the West. Large numbers of these settled in the Cape Fear regions of North Carolina. They had all taken a specially stringent oath of allegiance to the House of Hanover, either before they set out for America or before they were granted lands in North Carolina. The Scotch were royalists, and had suffered untold miseries in the defence of the rights of the Stuarts. Their cause was hopelessly lost, and they accepted the Hanovers, it seems, in good faith on condition of oblivion of the past and the possession of lands in their adopted country. They occupied Cumberland (significant name for the Scotch) and neighboring counties, embracing most of the lands lying between Bladen and Rowan counties, and extending southward to the borders of South Carolina. When Governor Martin was expelled from the state and proclaimed, like King James II in 1688, "abdicated" the Scotch made Martin's cause their own, as their ancestors had done for the House of Stuart. Wheeler tries to prove them good patriots by producing an intensely revolutionary document signed by leading citizens of Cumberland; but a glance at the signatures discovers not

---

13 Best short account of the Regulators War yet published is that by Colonel Saunders in his *Prefatory Notes to the North Carolina Colonial Records*, vol. VIII. Mr. Marshall DeLancey Haywood has just published a fuller account of this movement in his excellent life of Governor Tryon.

a single "Mac," nor a Campbell, which disproves the proof. February 27, 1776, it came to a pitched battle at Moore's Creek bridge, some miles below Fayetteville, or Campbelltown, between the Whigs and the Scotch. Two thousand Highlanders, as they were still termed, were overwhelmed by an inferior force of Whigs. The victory was so complete, and the tide of Whig enthusiasm throughout the East and North so strong, that no more attempts were made by the Scotch to assist the Royal cause for a long time to come. There were, too, in their midst so many older settlers who sided with the Revolutionists that any general movement was very difficult. Nevertheless, the presence of so many staunch friends of the House of Hanover neutralized a large amount of the state's strength, and this the more completely since the disaffected region was contiguous to that of the humiliated Regulators and to the Tory counties of South Carolina.

3. A very respectable party of the Whigs, who had assisted the American national movement in its beginning, when petitioning for redress of grievances was the avowed object of organized opposition, was alienated when men began to speak of independence and a democratic republic, or a number of republics. Many of the most prominent and best educated people of upper Eastern North Carolina, with Samuel Johnston as their leader, either secretly advocated continued obedience to England, or openly demanded the enactment of the most conservative measures. A similar party existed in and about Wilmington, with William Hooper as leader, which was the ground for Jefferson's later declaration that Hooper was a great Tory, and of course it was known that all Hooper's family publicly supported the Royal cause. These conservatives were strong enough to name the representatives to the Continental Congress during the earlier years of the War — Hooper being the leader of the delegation; rather, the Patriots made this concession in the hope of winning their support and influence. Johnston's defeat in his plan of controlling the Hillsboro Convention, and his more open defeat in Chowan for a seat in the Halifax Convention, so disappointed him that he became from that time on what would be called in modern slang a "disgruntled politician," and was continually growling and complaining in his retirement at every step taken by the dominant party. He refused to meet concessions made to him in the form of the most lucrative office in the gift of the government.[14] What Johnston thought, thought

---
14 See page 10.

also a numerous party of family and political connections living in all parts of the state. Now, as has been said, the Revolutionary War was pre-eminently a war of leaders, the popular enthusiasm seldom extending beyond state lines, and with several wealthy, educated and able men leading a positive opposition to the main measures of the new government, or even a passive opposition, which no one will dispute, at that critical juncture of our political development, it was well-nigh impossible to enforce energetic plans.

These influences — a half-spiteful neutrality or an open opposition on the part of the Regulators, positive and organized support of the British cause by the Scotch, and the paralyzing influence of lukewarm leaders — combined with intensely local patriotism, were the causes of the almost shameful lethargy of North Carolina during the long period of 1777 to 1780.

Geographically considered, the Patriots had actual control of but a small portion of North Carolina — the Southside of Roanoke, *i.e.*, a section of country containing a population of some seventy to eighty thousand people. Bute, its central county, boasted that it had not a Tory within its borders. The upper Cape Fear and the Regulator country to the neighborhood of Guilford Court House was the scene of almost constant civil strife during most of the Revolutionary War. This cut off from actual cooperation with the northern part of the state the bold Mecklenburgers and the Catawba backwoodsmen. South Carolina, too, was the home of disaffection, and being contiguous to the Royalist counties of North Carolina, the strength of the Tories was much increased.

It was to such a state that Nathaniel Macon returned in the autumn of 1776 to prepare himself further for a public career. In December following, his brother John became a captain of a company of Regulars, and marched away to join Washington. General Sumner, next-door neighbor to the Macons, was a commander in the Continental service. Macon's native county, we have seen, was the stronghold of the Whigs. In 1778, when such urgent appeals were being made for more troops to fill up the depleted ranks of North Carolina's Continental regiments, when bounties were offered for enlisting, when numbers of his fellow-countrymen were drafted into the service, when, early in 1779, South Carolina was being threatened and General Sumner marched away to Savannah with a meagre seven hundred and fifty troops, Macon kept his resolution and remained quiet at home, pursuing his studies.[15] An explanation of his not volunteering into the service of the cause, to which he was uncompromisingly attached, might be offered in that he did not care to serve as a private soldier, and that there was already a superabundance of officers, as the example of John's return in 1778 from Valley Forge shows; but his future service as a private soldier contradicts this. Those who claim Macon to have been a demagogue his whole life long would say he, like many others during those years, was waiting to see how things were going to turn, and then join the winning side. But here again future developments contradict. In 1780, when he did take active part in political and military affairs, he was chosen, without his previous knowledge, and before he was twenty-one years old, a member of the General Assembly, and of the Senate at that. Thus it is seen that the foundation of his popularity was laid during those years of study at home, and certainly a time-server, or one of doubtful loyalty, could not have been elected to any position of honor or trust in Warren county. (The name had been changed in 1779.) To the author, his intense local patriotism, his incomplete education, his youth, and the absence of any really threatening *danger to North Carolina*, is explanation enough. And, moreover, many others were following a similar course notably, James Monroe, who had retired from the position of captain in the regular army to take up the study of law under Thomas Jefferson.

Benjamin Hawkins, too, was living quietly at home since March or April, 1778 — more than likely he had returned with John Macon and for similar reasons.

---

15 Letter to Joseph H. Nicholson, August 6, 1803; Cotten's *Life of Macon*, 37.

CHAPTER IV.
IN THE ARMY AGAIN.

The disastrous attempt of D'Estiang and Lincoln on Savannah, October 9, 1777; the siege of Charleston and the rising of the Royalists in large numbers in Cumberland, Anson, Moore and Tryon counties, turned the earnest attention of all to the South. Seven hundred Virginians under Buford, three hundred under Porterfield, and seven hundred North Carolina militia under William Caswell were hurrying on to Charleston. Buford and Caswell united their forces in upper South Carolina, but on hearing of the fall of Charleston, May 12, 1780, they divided their commands. Caswell set out for Cross Creek, there to overawe the eight hundred Tories collecting in the neighborhood; Buford marched toward Charlotte, but was surprised by a strong force of British under Tarleton and utterly ruined. Porterfield went into camp at Salisbury, awaiting orders after the sad news of Charleston. These reverses heartened the loyalists in all sections; in the vicinity of Campbelltown, where Caswell's seven hundred men had dwindled down to less than four hundred, the enlisting of Royalists could not be prevented; Col. John Moore, a bold Tory of the extreme West, was collecting a force of some thirteen hundred men in Tryon county; in Moore, Guilford and Anson counties, the Whigs were driven from their homes and kept in the forests by bands of marauders, and, in the face of all this, the militia of Chowan and neighboring counties, refusing to march until their bounties were paid, took to the swamps and defied the power of the state. On the borders of Johnston, Edgecombe and Nash counties, robbers and deserters formed associations to prevent the drafting of men for the regular army, and inaugurated such a reign of lawlessness that it became necessary to send troops for their subjugation. In the far West, the Indians, too, were assuming a threatening attitude.[16]

To meet the invasion of Cornwallis from the south; to check the rising tide of anarchy at home; to guard the western frontiers against the Indians, the Assembly passed measures sweeping enough, as usual, but there was poor means of enforcing them. Richard Caswell was made Commander-in-Chief of the North Carolina militia, with instructions to begin again the raising of the four thousand troops "ordered" forward to the assistance of Lincoln at Charleston. Porter-

---

16 N.C. State Records, XIV., prefatory notes by Judge Clark.

field was still at Salisbury; Stevens was coming on from Richmond with seven hundred additional Virginians; Baron von Kalbe had two thousand Maryland and Delaware Regulars at Hillsboro; and Rutherford, a bold western commander, was strengthening himself in the neighborhood of Charlotte. This formidable array had its influence in bringing the militia into service, and in counteracting the schemes of the loyalists. During this second season of enthusiasm, and before the fall of Charleston, a company was made up in Warren County, which Nathaniel Macon joined as a volunteer without accepting the proffered bounty of one hundred and fifty dollars. He was elected lieutenant, but this he also declined, preferring to serve as a private in the ranks. John Macon, then a prominent member of the General Assembly for Warren county[17] was made Captain, a suitable choice, for he had served two years at the beginning of the war as a captain in the Regular army, and had been with Washington in the New Jersey campaigns and at Valley Forge.[18] This new company became a part of a regiment made up of similar companies from Nash, Northampton, Halifax and Edgecombe counties, and was put under the command of Benjamin Seawell. Each company marched to the plantation of a certain William Betts, in Wake County, as a place of rendezvous. At this place the soldiers were to receive their bounties and the regiment was to be organized; but the government did not meet its obligations, and the men were about to return to their homes. Seawell wrote the Governor that his soldiers were good as could be found, but that they would never cross the borders of the State unless they were paid.[19] Seawell was to have joined Summer, who was returning from South Carolina with a small command of North Carolina troops, somewhere to the south of Hillsboro. This mutiny of the whole Halifax regiment was threatening to affect seriously the plans of attack, and Cornwallis was approaching. It was now late in July. How the difficulties were settled we are not told, but some satisfactory plan was arranged, so that Seawell's regiment marched on toward the South.

General Horatio Gates, whose star had been shining so brightly since the victory at Saratoga, was appointed to the chief command of the Southern department, to succeed Lincoln. He arrived at the camp of von Kalbe, on Deep River, July 19, where the latter was drilling his regiments of Continentals, where de Armond's legion had just

---

17 N.C. State Records, XIII., Journals of the Assembly.
18 N.C. State Records, XIII., 42.
19 N.C. State Records, XV., 8.

arrived; and where three companies of artillery had been sent by the government. Against the advice of von Kalbe, who had been in the neighborhood some months, and who knew well the field of operations, Gates marched directly toward Camden, where Cornwallis was collecting his detachments, waiting for the crops to be gathered in, and attracting to him what Royalists could escape the vigilance of Caswell and Rutherford. Soon after the army marched southward it was reinforced by Porterfield's three hundred Virginians, Caswell's new levies of militia, Steven's brigade of Virginians, and by Sumner's men, strengthened by the Halifax regiment under Seawell — altogether four thousand, five hundred men. Not far away, and subject to Gates command, was Davie, with three hundred as good men as could be found; Rutherford's troop of fifteen hundred, flushed with a magnificent victory over the Royalists, was at Ramsour's Mill; Davidson, with some hundred and fifty men at least, and Sumpter, with eight hundred followers, were not far southward. Marion and Harrington were guarding the Tories toward the east and along Cape Fear, while Smallwood and Butler were doing the same on the Yadkin. Without taking into account these last-named forces, which were keeping the peace in the above-named disaffected regions, Gates could have brought into close cooperation six thousand, five hundred soldiers, most of whom had seen active service, and who were led by men of experience, acquainted with the country, and who enjoyed the absolute confidence of their followers. It was an opportunity not unlike that of Saratoga two years before: the militia were confident, their homes were about to be invaded, and there was a large population ready to resist to the last extremity the encroachment of the enemy. On the side of the enemy, everything was unfavorable, almost as much so as with Burgoyne, when the farmers of the New Hampshire and Vermont hills fell upon him with such disastrous effect. Cornwallis' whole army amounted to two thousand, five hundred men, five hundred of whom were Tory militia; the country was unknown to its leaders; the climate was extremely oppressive; large numbers of the soldiers had to be sent each day to the hospital in the rear, and the Royalist uprising, which had been calculated upon so confidently, was not succeeding. The one real difficulty with which Gates contended was scarcity of supplies, the difficulty which seems to have caused him to hasten on to Camden through the almost barren pine forests in order to gain time and to attack the enemy before his provisions were exhausted. He overrated the danger of scarcity of provisions, and seems never once to have thought of the difficulties with which his adversary was contending. Gates hastened towards the enemy's camp in the hope of taking Cornwallis by surprise, and instead of making sure of the position of his reinforcements, he left them uninformed of the whereabouts of the American army. On August 16, at early dawn, the two armies met, and the Americans, who outnumbered the English two to one, were scattered like chaff before a gust of wind. Half of the men never so much as fired their guns. Gates was soon riding in all haste toward Hillsboro, as much frightened as any of his men. Sumner alone appears to have kept his head, and maintained something like order among his troops after the day was lost: he collected what remnants could be found of the scattered commands, and attempted to bring off some of the supplies.[20]

Not a word has been found anywhere to show what share Macon had in the battle of Camden. He was, however, in Seawall's regiment which had united with Sumner before the catastrophe, and so he was present during the fight and did not run away precipitately, as did most others. Benton in his *Thirty Years View* [21] says Macon was at Camden; but he also says he was at the fall of Charleston, when Macon's own statement declares that he first enlisted May 10, 1780, only two days before the fall. Cotten says Macon was never in an active engagement during the war but at the same time adds[22] "that we are informed." The truth appears to be that he was at Camden with his company and retreated with Sumner on the following day towards Salisbury.[23] A report of September 3 shows that Colonel Seawell's Warren and Halifax companies were present. September 29th Sumner's army was in good spirits again and in camp on the Yadkin. Two thousand British occupied Charlotte, while forage and recruiting expeditions were scouring the country in all directions. Hardly a day passed without some skirmish or sharp fight between such commands as those of Davie, Cleveland, and McDowell, which, more often than otherwise, resulted in favor of the Americans.[24] These small successes aided materially in rallying the scattered forces and in

---

20 N.C. State Records. XV., 49-55; John W. Moore: *History of North Carolina*, I., 277-281; Washington Irving: *Life of Washington*, IV., 80-84.
21 Thomas H. Benton: *Thirty Years View*, I., 114.
22 See above, page 25.
23 N.C. State Records, XV., 73.
24 N.C. State Records, XV., 89.

restoring discipline and confidence among the few remaining companies.

The news of King's Mountain, October 10, restored completely the *esprit de corps* and prepared the way for General Greene, the new Commander-in-Chief of the Southern Army.

While these untoward events had been happening, a new General Assembly had been elected; Nathaniel Macon had been chosen to represent Warren County in the Senate for the year 1781. The summons of the Governor to attend the first session, which was to be held at Halifax in January, came and was read to the soldiers according to custom along with the orders of the commanding general; but Macon gave the subject no attention, preferring to remain in the ranks.[25] Finally, being called to the tent of the Commander-in-Chief to explain his action, Macon modestly announced that he had felt it a more pressing duty to remain in his present position. And well could this have appeared thus to him at a time when so many were discouraged, when the militia all over the State were refusing to serve on any terms, and when those already in the army were returning to their homes as fast as their terms expired. He was very popular as a soldier and it seems that he commanded an influence greater than most of the officers themselves, which made it the more imperative from his point of view for him to remain. Much has been said of this apparently eccentric behavior of Macon on the assumption that it was prompted by a mean motive for gaining popularity. He had volunteered without accepting the usual bounty, had refused an officer's rank when his company was organized; and if we may believe reports, he had refused promotion again when Seawell's regiment was mutinying in the neighborhood of Raleigh. Whether he had particular designs all along could hardly be ascertained. There is no way to determine the motives of any public character but by his public acts, which in Macon's case, if taken from the beginning to the end of his career, seem as thoroughly consistent with unselfish patriotism as those of any of his contemporaries and as utterly without design so far as he himself was concerned. This behavior then in the camp on the Yadkin may and does appear eccentric as in many another instance of his later life; but it was the result of the conviction that duty demanded his remaining in the army in preference to attending the legislature.

---

25 Thomas H. Benton: *Thirty Years View*, I., 114.

Richard Caswell
First and Fifth Governor of North Carolina

CHAPTER V.
IN THE GENERAL ASSEMBLY, 1781-1785.

Wheeler claims[26] in one place that Macon was first elected, while a private soldier in the army, to a seat in the Senate for the year 1781 and that without his knowledge or consent, and, in another,[27] he states that Macon was a member of the Senate from Warren County in 1780. Moore, too, claims that "he was first seen in a deliberative body in Newbern in April, 1780;"[28] and Cotton confidently declares[29] that "at the age of twenty-four years, whilst he was yet in the army his countrymen elected Mr. Macon a member of the legislature of his State without his solicitation or even his knowledge." Unfortunately the records of the Assembly for the year 1780 have been lost and we are left to decide the subject for ourselves. Wheeler in the first place asserts that the first election of Macon to the Assembly took place while he was in the army and we have Macon's own written statement[30] that he enlisted in the Southern Army May 12, 1780. This shows that if he was first elected while in the army he could not have been a member for 1780, since the elections were held in the summer and for the sessions of the Assembly for the succeeding year. But to illustrate how inaccurate and untrustworthy North Carolina history has been written, let us note the inconsistencies of statements on this subject: Wheeler has him "elected first while in the army," and further on makes him a member a year before that time; Moore says, "he first appeared in a deliberative body in Newbern in April, 1780," adding, at the same time, that he was a private in one of the Continental regiments and cites Wheeler as his authority, which citation proves Macon not to have been in Newbern at all; Cotton says Macon was twenty-four years old at his first election, which took place in the proverbial manner, namely, without his knowledge or consent and while he was in the army. The truth is Macon was not in Newbern, not a member of the Senate in 1780, and not twenty-four years old; but that he was first chosen, perhaps without his knowledge, to represent his county in the State Senate in the summer of

---

26 *History of North Carolina*, II., 432.
27 *History of North Carolina*, II., 441.
28 *History of North Carolina*, I., 259.
29 *History of North Carolina*, I., 48.
30 Letter to General Assembly, Nov. 14, 1828.

1780 for the session of 1781 when he was away on that fateful Camden campaign, and when he was just twenty-one years old.

Macon did not leave the camp on the Yadkin in time to attend the first session of the Assembly for 1781, which met at Halifax January 18th; but he was present at the Wake Court House session in the following June, and from that time on till his retirement he and John Macon were prominent members of the legislature. June 26th, three days after the meeting of the Assembly, Nathaniel Macon of the Senate and John Macon of the House, with several others, were appointed a joint committee of both houses "to settle up the depreciation of money, etc." John Macon was made chairman of this important committee.[31] This was the beginning of a reform movement, which was slow in being realized on account of the infatuation of our ancestors for large emissions of paper money.

June 28th Nathaniel Macon was named a member of a committee to prepare and bring in a bill for establishing courts of oyer and terminer. The merchants of Edenton petitioned this Assembly for relief from illegal impressment of produce for the Commissary Department of the army. Macon, as chairman of the committee to which the subject was referred, reported as follows: "The joint Committee of both houses appointed to take under Consideration a Memorial from the merchants of Edenton, setting forth that large quantities of Goods were impressed from them, do report that it is Your Committees opinion that the impressment of Goods by General Warrants is unconstitutional, oppressive and destructive to Trade; and that it also appears to Your Committee that no demand or requisition has been made to the Owners of such Goods previous to the Impressment or Seizure thereof, which is illegal. And are further of the opinion that all Goods so impressed that can be *conveniently spared*[32] from the use of the Army, be immediately returned to the Owners from which such Goods have been impressed or seized."[33] Another joint committee was appointed June 28th, to investigate the conduct of public officials, especially those who had been entrusted with public monies and to bring in a bill requiring them to render regular accounts to and make settlement with the State. On this committee were associated with Macon Colonel Jesse Benton, of Hillsboro, father of Senator Benton, Thomas Person, of Granville, Charles Johnston, of Chowan,

---
31 N.C. State Records, XVII., 812.
32 The italics are the authors.
33 N.C. State Records, XVII., 826.

and others, most of whom were prominent in the politics of the State. This committee reported a bill which met the requirements. From these records and from numberless others, which might be cited, it will be seen that Macon, though one of the youngest members, played a conspicuous part in the Assembly from the beginning; and what is more significant, he was constantly associated with reform men and measures. The chief object of his attention was the debased currency which he insisted should be remedied by a return to specie payments.

The Assembly of 1781 was still controlled by the more democratic Whigs who had directed the affairs of the State since the struggle with Johnston and the Conservatives for supremacy in the Hillsboro Constitutional Convention of 1776; but the reverses of the past year, the increasing power of the Tories in the south central portion of the State and the almost universal lawlessness then prevailing had given the Conservatives a great increase of strength. The contest between parties came up every year in the election of Governor. Nash, who had been chosen in 1779, was not considered successful chiefly because misfortune had come while he was in office. The rule in North Carolina, as in Virginia, was to re-elect a Chief Magistrate giving him the limit of the Constitution as to duration of his term of service, *i.e.*, three years. Nash was not re-elected by the Assembly of 1781 at its January meeting, but he was authorized to remain in office temporarily. Yet, according to English and American fashion, he was complimented for his great ability and devoted patriotism as a public servant. In the balloting for Governor at the end of Nash's first year Samuel Johnston was a candidate. Johnston was not chosen, but was elected a delegate to the Continental Congress, which latter office he accepted, contrary to his and his friend Hooper's previous practice. Benjamin Hawkins, who was leaning more and more toward the Conservatives, was also chosen a delegate to Congress[34]. This indicates the change of sentiment which began about this time.

From a military point of view, the State was in a deplorable condition. Nash's message to the Assembly at its second session in June, which every one seeking to understand the policies and measures of the legislature of 1781 must read, reviews in a forcible manner the condition of affairs. He said in part: "Nothing could have induced me to call you together at so inconvenient and disagreeable a season of the year, but the most pressing necessity. * * * You will no doubt pay a

---

34 N.C. State Records, XVII., 858, 872.

proper attention to the present disordered condition of this unhappy State." He then reviews the loss at Camden and its result, adding: "We had drained the Treasury, which had never since been replenished sufficiently even for the ordinary expenses of Government, and what is still worse, Terror and Consternation, which on this unhappy occasion was spread through the Country, by the multitudes who fled from the Field of Battle, discouraged the friends of Government in proportion as it gave new life and spirits to the disaffected" * * *. Then follows a recital of the withdrawal of power from the Governor and the vesting it first in a Board of War and later in General Richard Caswell, his rival, and the miserable drafting practice. The message concluded: "In short, this kind of service, carried to the disgrace we have seen it of late years, is productive of every kind of evil Consequence. Public and Private Arms and Accoutrements are lost; Household and Husbandry Utensils, Horses and other things useful to the farmer are wrested from the owner and never returned,* * *; the cultivation of land, so particularly necessary in time of War, is interrupted and neglected."[35] Such a state of affairs had been enough to alarm the strongest, and it was not surprising that the Royalists were rising in all parts of the State, that the Revolutionary party was discouraged and that the Conservatives who had all along occupied the position of public critics, men accustomed to say "we told you so," but who, nevertheless, with a few exceptions, had held the first civil offices in the gift of the Assembly, who had drawn good salaries and never smelt the smoke of gunpowder, were now gaining in influence and about to get control of the government. From 1776 until after the battle of Camden, Willie Jones and his party of Democratic republicans, the northern section of the State, with counties here and there in the eastern and western sections cooperating, had controlled affairs in North Carolina and directed its policy in all things. But by way of conciliation, this dominant, positive party had kept continually in office most of the dissatisfied Conservatives — the price that had to be paid for the loyalty of many of the wealthy Easterners.

At the Wake Court House session the Democratic Republicans, or Whigs, maintained their position, but they felt the reins of power slipping from their hands more rapidly, as the military affairs grew more hopeless; for the battle of Guilford Court House, which had taken place two months before, was not a source of encouragement

---

35 N.C. State Records, XVII, 881-882.

to North Carolinians in that day as it has since become. It was not regarded as a victory, neither did the Governor nor Assembly thank Greene for his part in it. They did not expect Cornwallis to leave the State never to return, nor had any one the remotest idea that the victory at Yorktown was to be the result of Guilford Court House.

The principal measures of the Assembly of 1781 looked to the reform of the military organization, the suppression of disaffection, confiscation of the property of those who had committed themselves to the Royalist cause, reform of the currency, and correction of the abuse of power in office and even the improvements of the courts of common law. The military reforms were soon rendered unnecessary by the news of Cornwallis' overthrow; the financial situation had not improved, as may be seen from the following quotation from the journals of the House: "This House can not agree that any larger Sum be allowed the members of Assembly, more than Five Hundred Dollars per day for going to, continuing at and in returning" from the session which was to have been held at Newbern in April last; Five Hundred Dollars per day for coming to and returning from the present session and Two Hundred and Fifty Dollars per day for attending thereon.[36] And this financial demoralization grew steadily worse until it became a disease in spite of the efforts of the best men in the State. The abuse of power by State officials did not cease until the coming of peace destroyed the opportunity for it; the habit of confiscating the property of Tories also became a disease, a disease which was constantly spreading, since so many people, toward the latter part of the war, had joined the British or grown lukewarm in their support of the American cause. The courts were not finally reorganized till the Supreme Court was established in 1818. In all these movements the Macons were prominent, generally following the lead of Willie Jones.

No man has ever wielded more power in the management of the State's affairs than Willie Jones, of Halifax, yet not two dozen lines about his life and work have ever been published. He kept the State true to the policy outlined by Virginia in the beginning of the Revolution and prevailed on the Halifax Constitutional Convention to adopt a constitution to his liking, *i. e.*, a constitution essentially similar to that of Virginia. Jones was a Virginian reformer after the pattern of Jefferson, whom he came to admire as he did no other living man.

---

36 NC. State Records, XVII., 862

In this school of politics Nathaniel Macon served his apprenticeship; and his later career shows how faithfully he listened and learned; while his own course, during the first year of his experience in the legislature, shows how thoroughly he agreed with the policy of his teacher and endorsed the Virginia reforms so generally approved in his section of North Carolina — the old "Southside of Roanoke."

The journals of the Assembly for the years 1782, '83 and '84 have been destroyed, with the exception of those of the House for 1782, which show that three Macons, John, Harrison, and Nathaniel, all brothers, were members: Nathaniel in the Senate and John and Harrison in the House.[37] John was by far the most active, serving on the most important committees and presenting lengthy reports. He also took active part as a partisan of Timothy Bloodworth in an election case which was brought up by Alexander MacLaine of Wilmington. Bloodworth was supposed to be in favor of violent measures against the Tories; he had been Treasurer of the State at the time of his election, which, MacLaine claimed, made his choice unconstitutional. MacLaine was a member of the Conservative party and his correspondence shows he was making a strenuous effort as an attorney for some wealthy refugees, especially for George Hooper of Charleston, brother of William Hooper, to have the Tories restored to their former political status. Bloodworth won, and with him the extremists on the Tory question. Nathaniel Macon belonged to the same party and, as it appears from his correspondence with Jefferson in 1801, he favored harsh treatment of those who supported the British during the war.[38]

The principal measures before the legislature in '82 were the fixing of relations between the State and the so-called National Government; the treatment of the Tories was referred to; the reestablishment of trade and the improvement of the currency. Nathaniel Macon was appointed a member of the committee to take into consideration the recommendations of the Governor on the resolves of Congress.[39]

Since there was no compulsory power vested in the Continental Congress, and now that war no longer made vigorous cooperation necessary, the recommendations of the Governor "died in committee." Macon was not the man to urge National measures. On the

---

37 N.C. State Records, XVI., 3, 23, and 34.
38 Letter of May 24, 1801
39 N.C. State Records, XVI., 23.

subject of a National trade, he was likewise an indifferent member, not so much for lack of sympathy with the efforts then making for its reestablishment, but because of his ardent local patriotism. He favored State control of commerce and industry. Thus protection, of one sort or another, was being proposed by his party as a policy for North Carolina, though it was some years later before a protective and bounty-giving system was evolved. Macon was a protectionist in North Carolina always. But his attitude toward the currency question was more characteristic, and on that subject his views were in advance of those of most of his fellows; his opinions remaining the same throughout his political life, whether applied to National or State issues, namely, that only a metallic currency was safe and just.

From 1782 to 1786 nothing is known of his career in politics save that he was an active member of the Senate and an opponent of the rising influence of the Conservatives, chief amongst whom were Samuel Johnston, James Iredell, William Hooper, and Alexander MacLaine. This party, as has been observed, had begun to steer its course in 1776 after the establishment of the State constitution. During the war it had exerted considerable influence, and at its close it championed the cause of the Tories, and as things tended to extremes, it became stronger. Washington was claimed as its leader outside of the State as early as 1782. Alexander Martin, Timothy Bloodworth and General Griffith Rutherford, with others of the Jones party, were designated by epithets which would scarcely be admissible now in the most violent political campaigns. Rutherford was "that bloodthirsty old scoundrel" and Martin an "arrant coward without the sense of a woodcock." The Conservatives advocated Johnston for Governor during these years; but by way of compromise between the two parties Richard Caswell was several times elected. The question of National Union was scarcely mentioned during this war period, and the debt of more than a million to the General Government was not troublesome, to say the least.[40]

---

40 N. C. State Records, XVI., 930 on: Hooper MacLaine correspondence.

Nathaniel Macon's home at Buck Spring.

CHAPTER VI.
FOUNDING A HOME, 1782-1791.

In 1782 Nathaniel Macon fell a victim to the charms of a very handsome lady of Warren, who bore the somewhat homely name of Hannah; she was a Miss Plummer, and her parents, like Macon's, were Virginians, and, what meant much in those days, well connected. Cotten says Macon was handsome, too; six feet tall, perfectly proportioned, of a fine presence, urbane of manner and an extravagant admirer of womankind also the admired, he occasionally hints.[41] Nevertheless, he did not have things all his own way, if we may accept, as truth, stories which still circulate in the old town of Warrenton. According to one of which, when matters had come to a crisis, so far as Macon was concerned, Miss Hannah Plummer was still receiving attentions from some other suitor, whose name, happily, has not been preserved to us. The two competitors met on one occasion at the Plummer home, and Macon, who was a dexterous card-player suggested that Miss Hannah be the prize. The offer was accepted, with the result that Macon lost. "He immediately arose, raised high both hands and, with his eyes fixed on Hannah, and sparkling with beams of affection, exclaimed: 'notwithstanding I have lost you fairly — love is superior to honesty — I can not give you up.'"[42] It is needless to add that he won the lady.

Macon and Miss Plummer were married October 9, 1783, and they made their home on Hubquarter Creek, twelve miles north of Warrenton, near the Roanoke. It was the place which had been given him by his father's will. Some five or six hundred acres of land surrounding the house constituted his estate; it was the nucleus of the plantation of later years. There was hardly a settlement within five miles, and he had preferred this to the far more valuable lands which had been given him on Shocco and in the midst of the best community in that section of the State. It shows another of those eccentric tendencies of the man, this preference for the wild forests, far removed from his relatives and associates. It is an oft-quoted saying of his in North Carolina, that "a man should not live near enough his neighbors to hear his dogs bark." There, not far from the Roanoke River, and on a small hilltop, with the help of a carpenter and his negro

---
41 Cotten's *Life of Macon*, 51-52.
42 *Ibid*, 55-56.

slaves he had cleared away the forest trees and built a new house; it is still standing and in a perfect state of preservation — the most remarkable in America. The house, which the negroes no doubt called the "great house," is sixteen feet square, one story and a half high, with a well-arranged wine cellar underneath. Two doors, directly opposite each other, and two small windows, almost six feet above the floor, furnished sufficient ventilation. It need not be said that there are only two rooms in the house, one down, the other upstairs. A very narrow, winding stairway leads up from one corner of the lower room. In each room there is an ample, well-finished open fireplace, and in every part of the house the very best workmanship is manifested; the whole is built of "heart poplar" lumber and finished in the best style. The ceiling is of the same material as the outside work and finished in the same way, except that for some unknown reason, the finished planks were turned upside down — that is, just the reverse from what we ordinarily term weatherboarding. In front of the building just described is another — an exact counterpart, except the chimney is larger and the fireplaces are twice as wide. By the side of the fireplace in the lower room is the great crane, used in former days for swinging on and off pots and kettles of no small dimensions. This second house was the kitchen, but it served also as the family sitting-room. Up stairs in it is a neatly finished room, which, it is said, was the sleeping apartment of his daughters. Between these houses was the carriage and wagon road connecting different parts of the plantation and also leading out between barns and through horse lots into a winding country pathway that led finally into the Warrenton and Virginia road. Around the "great house" — Mr. Macon's own apartments — at a distance of some fifty yards, are the remains on the one side of dozens of Negro cabins, and on the other of barns for horses, cattle, hay and tobacco. This gives, at least in part, a picture of the once well known "Buck Spring," home of Nathaniel Macon of North Carolina.

During the following years Macon was increasing his fortune steadily though not rapidly. Tobacco growing was his occupation and farming was not then, as it is not now, a means of great wealth. A tax list which has been preserved[43] indicates that he owned in 1792 seven hundred and fifty acres of land and "14 black poles," which shows that some additions to his plantation had been made, and that the number

---

43 In possession of Thomas M. Pittman, Esq., of Henderson, N.C., an indefatigable collector of North Caroliniana.

of negroes had been increased considerably, taking his early patrimony as a beginning. Negro men were at that time rated at two hundred pounds in specie,[44] that is, about four hundred dollars each. A fair estimate would make his estate worth between three and four thousand dollars in the money of that day, which was equivalent to twice that amount in our own time.

Macon's position in North Carolina during this period of retirement is shown by his election to the Continental Congress in 1786 for the eventful year of 1787 and by his appointment a year later to the office of Lieutenant Colonel of the Warren county militia. The first position he declined to accept on the ground of insufficient or unsatisfactory remuneration[45] which was inconsistent with his former practice. The real reason, no doubt, was his dislike for the Continental service. It was the year of the Philadelphia Convention, to which he was opposed in toto. His friend and neighbor, Willie Jones, refused about the same time to represent North Carolina in this Convention. His excuse was no better than Macon's. The second honor conferred by the General Assembly was more to his liking; he accepted and met regularly with the county militia to train them in the arts of war.[46]

There is an old leather-bound Bible now in the possession of Miss Laura Alston, of Warrenton, which speaks much for this period of Macon's life. The following entries in Macon's handwriting appear: "Betsey Kemp Macon, born September 12, 1784; Plummer Macon, born April 14th, 1786; Seignora Macon, born November 15th, 1787; Hannah Macon died January 11th, 1790; Plummer Macon died July 26th, 1792." The death of his wife, which is here recorded, was a blow, from which Macon never recovered. He never married again, though he was only thirty-two years old at the time of her death. It is said that he was devotedly attached to her, and his long unmarried life afterwards is a testimony to the faithfulness of the man. It was not unlike Jefferson's life of devotion and romantic obedience to a wife, who left him a widower at a comparatively early age. The remains of Mrs. Macon were buried not many yards from the husband's house on the borders of the yard. Plummer Macon, his only son, was little more than six years old, when he, too, was taken away, about a year and a half after the mother's death. It was the breaking up of a happy home,

---

44 N.C. State Records, XVI., 77.
45 N.C. State Records, vol. XX., 605.
46 N.C. State Records, vol. XX., 293, 461.

these two afflictions, and, from that time on, the father was constantly in politics, and consequently away from home. What arrangements were made for the two girls, Betsey and Seignora, for their training and education, the author has been unable to learn. Apparently they remained at Buck Spring in the care of some relative.

CHAPTER VII.
THE ADOPTION OF THE NATIONAL CONSTITUTION BY NORTH CAROLINA.

Something has been said of the Conservatives in North Carolina during the Revolution, their dissatisfaction with the Constitution of 1776, their disposition to remain neutral, their friendliness at the close of the war toward the Tories and their growing influence during the early years of peace. There is no need here of designating by name these leaders, the most important of whom have been mentioned.[47] They represented the wealthier class of Eastern slave holders, some of whom had openly sided with England; others had joined the Revolutionists, but had not approved of the ultra Democratic measures of 1776, and became lukewarm in their allegiance. They represented, too, the mercantile interests of Wilmington, Newbern and Edenton; many of them had been English or New England merchants and were not, of course, disposed to sacrifice their occupation for the service of ideals in advance of anything Europe had seen. They were the most respectable men in their neighbor hoods. When the war was ended and independence was an assured thing, they began to reckon with the new order of things. The extremists of 1776 had found it a more difficult thing than had been anticipated to control a State or direct the affairs of a people and were disposed all along to admit to office the men whose administrative experience was greater than their zeal for the cause of popular rights. When the strain was relieved and patriotic fervor again had a free course, those who had openly opposed the war were severely enough handled. The Royalists were banished and their property confiscated; no nice distinctions were made as to degrees of disaffection — to have been neutral at such a time as 1780 was especially reprehensible, and the more so if the suspected man owned considerable property.[48]

The wealthier classes felt that the rights of property were in danger, that passion and prejudice were going to be the controlling elements in the new State organization. They began at once to urge their leaders to make decided efforts in favor of property rights and "men of connections." Organized effort followed, and the old East sought

---

47 See above, pages 31, 33.
48 N.C. State Records, XVI,. 978-979.

again to wrest from the North and the West the reins of power.[49] Johnston and Iredell were the leaders. The mistake they made was the too vigorous support both in the courts and in the Assembly of the Loyalists — the wealthier of them. Extreme measures of persecution on the part of the Radicals begot in the Conservatives a spirit of extreme favoritism, which, for the time, defeated their plan of regaining control of affairs. But according to the old conciliatory policy of the "Whigs of 76," as they now began to call themselves, their opponents were sent to the Congress[50] of the Confederation, where they soon became Nationalists — "Great American" as against "Small American," as the Germans would express it. For England, the King and a general government, which could protect the interests of trade and reward the services of men of talent and means, they would substitute United America. They became Americans, not North Carolinians. And what added to this sentiment was the indifference of State Supremacy men to the claims of property; most men in North Carolina refused, to pay debts contracted with the British prior to 1776, claiming that the war annulled them; Jefferson himself and Henry apologized for this disposition and sometimes openly encouraged it; and, in fact, until now, in the history of the world, this had been the customary treatment of the vanquished party in all great struggles.

The debts of the United States, contracted during the War for Independence, were likewise ignored by the dominant party in North Carolina. In vain did Charles Thompson, the Secretary of the Congress, and Joseph Nourse, Registrar, send to the Assembly their accounts against the State. The millions of debt, which these bills called to the minds of our forefathers, did not cause them any uneasiness. A few empty resolutions were passed by the Houses, but nobody attempted to enforce them. North Carolina owed the Union in 1785 more than a million dollars in interest alone on the debt contracted during the war, but she did not pay a cent of it;[51] it really could not be paid, in specie, as was demanded, when there was so little money in the State. Whether the Assembly meant to pay these debts to the former Union, for there was none in 1785, can not be determined. A few years later regular installments of tobacco were bought by the State and sent to Philadelphia, so that slowly the debt began to be provided for, though this was so feebly done by all the States that American

---

49 *Ibid*, 992.
50 See above, page 35.
51 N.C. State Records, XVII., 534-535.

credit abroad was not sufficiently good to prevent our Minister in Holland from being dunned for his hotel bills.

Something else which added to the strength of the Nationalists was the increasing jealousy of the States toward each other, and the continuous war of trade which was going on. Virginia and Maryland were laying duties on each other's products; in New York spring chickens from New Jersey were taxed fifty per cent in favor of the farmers up the Hudson; and a cord of wood from Connecticut could not be delivered at one's back door without paying its tax to the custom's officer.[52] Jealousy, retaliation and State pride were giving rise to a state of affairs like that which overthrew the mediaeval empire of the Germans at the time of Luther. North Carolina and Virginia, even, were quarrelling about the subject of tariff in 1786, and Governor Henry and the legislature of Virginia appointed a committee to meet with a committee from North Carolina to settle these trade difficulties.[53]

Before the treaty of peace was signed, and before it was know what would be the status of America as guaranteed by the States of Europe, MacLaine, Johnston and others began to designate Washington as the leader of the conservative forces in America.[54] And there was no wiser counsel given to the leaders of the different States during all these anarchic years of 1783 to 1789 than that in Washington's famous letter to the Governors. It was at once made the platform of all those who desired a closer union of all the States; and, connecting together all the ills to which the past few years had shown the country liable in 1787, these conservative men, whose number had been increasing as the States' Rights party became consolidated, as the ills of State independence became more patent, succeeded in getting a convention of all the States together — the Philadelphia Convention. A contract of compromises was arranged and the different States were called on to ratify this contract and to become members, each of a central government, which should at least control the commercial interests of all foreign relations, and remedy the intolerable ills of a rag money system.

Samuel Johnston, an advocate of this Nationalist policy, became Governor of North Carolina in 1788. He had been the perennial candidate of his party since 1780 and consequently there was a great

---

52 John Fiske: *Critical Period of American History*, 146-147.
53 N.C. State Records., XVII., 542, 658.
54 MacLaine to Hooper, State Records, XVI., 974.

jubilee at his inauguration.[55] The elevation of Johnston to the Chief Magistracy of the State meant much for the adoption of the National Constitution. A call for a convention to consider the new constitution was issued and the election set for April. As great a fight between the advocates and opponents of adoption followed as has ever taken place in the State, with the result that a great majority of members opposing adoption was chosen. The convention met and rejected the plan of National union by a vote of one hundred and eighty-four against eighty-four, and Willie Jones, Thomas Person, Timothy Bloodworth and John Macon returned home rejoicing. The struggle which had just closed had been waged in a spirit of bitter animosity. Washington was unmercifully abused, and others, who favored a National government of practical powers, were termed Tories, conspirators against the common good.

This shows that, during the years 1782 to 1788, the spirit of particularism, the party of State independence as against National union, had been growing stronger instead of weaker. This party was still led by the redoubtable politician, Willie Jones of Halifax, a man of extraordinary mould, an aristocrat in all that pertained to his personal and every day life, a representative of one of the oldest families in the State; yet a Democrat of the most pronounced views in public policy, a man whom more men feared and loved, who was the object of more hatred and more adoration than has ever since lived in North Carolina. Thomas Person, from Granville, John Macon, a man of similar character in every respect to Jones, Thomas Benbury of Chowan, the Bloodworth brothers of New Hanover, Matthew Locke and General Rutherford of the west, were acknowledged followers of Jones. Their policy demanded (1) a free and absolutely independent State, (2) a genuinely democratic administration, (3) a general improvement in educational advantages for the people.

To secure the first of these, they advocated a rejection of all plans of union with other States, the building up of an industry which would not only supply our own demands, but which should enter into competition with the other States in their markets. Flour packers were required to observe strict regulations, both as to the grade of their products and as to the manner of shipment.[56] When crops were short in certain sections, the Assembly passed remedial laws; when a gener-

---

55 William R. Davie to James Iredell, Jan. 11, 1788.
56 N.C. Laws, 1791. I., 13.

al shortage was anticipated, exports were forbidden. It was the governor's business to enquire into the condition of crops and report to the Assembly; he recommended improvement in agriculture and suggested bounties on manufacturers. The State began now regularly to give bounties to all beginners of new manufacturing establishments, and entered into co-partnership with individuals and with companies for the building of canals and the deepening of harbors, the improvement of public highways and the advancement of public intercourse — a policy almost identical with that of Henry Clay fifty years later.[57]

For securing the second primal feature of their policy, they adhered to the letter of the Constitution of 1776 and its Bill of Rights, both of which they succeeded in so canonizing that they remained unaltered and in full force until a still more Democratic wave from the West came over the State in 1835. They advocated, for the same purpose, the cruel measures against the former Royalists, so much complained of by their opponents in the State and country at large. They demanded yearly assemblies and yearly tenure of office, constant vigilance of committees of the Legislature over public affairs, and strict accountability of members of the Continental Congress to their constituents, who, as was repeatedly declared after the adoption of the general constitution, were to be guided in their votes by the wishes of the Assembly, and not by their own opinions of public policy. The members of the Congress which sat in Philadelphia and New York had their hands sufficiently tied during these years of State supremacy.

But a remarkable feature of their era of control, and that which made out the third, part of their programme, was their attention to education. A general revival of learning seems to have set in during the earlier portion of their control. In the midst of the turmoil of war and imminent danger to the State at the beginning of the year 1780, we find the Assembly organizing a seminary of learning in Granville county, and incorporating a board for its control and government. Immediately after the war closed, their educational policy became general and effective. Nearly every Assembly insisted that "one or more universities ought to be established by law." The men who insisted on this increase in the facilities for education were the graduates of the good old Presbyterian College of New Jersey, already mentioned. The popular ex-Governor Martin, General Davie, and the Hawkins

---

57 N.C. State Records, XVIII., 418.

brothers, were making their Presbyterian training tell, though they were not all Presbyterians themselves. A dozen schools and academies, some of which received aid from the State, were established by the General Assembly in the year 1786 alone.[58] The Davidson Academy was given the benefit of the Salt Springs in the neighborhood, which had been the property of the government; and Hillsboro Academy, on the recommendation of William Hooper, was to receive aid from the State. All parties joined in this educational revival; the day had not come for rivalries and jealousies concerning the greatest duty the human race has to perform — the education of the young. The advanced views of the Virginian reformers on the subject of slavery did not, however, find a hearty welcome in North Carolina. Notwithstanding the extreme tendency for that day of the liberal reform party, in so far as the rights and privileges of white men were concerned, there was not that sympathy and solicitude for the ultimate happiness of the negro race which characterized Washington, Jefferson, Mason, and others in Virginia. The principal influence which was made, felt in North Carolina for the amelioration of the condition of the Negro had its source in the Quaker settlements and their homely meetinghouses. A law was passed in 1786 declaring the importation of negroes to be "of evil consequences and highly impolitic," and placing a tax of five pounds on each negro imported after that date, which it need scarcely be said was in advance of the time.[59]

These were the primal measures of the party which opposed any form of confederation with the other States, and their object was clearly what Jones himself desired — an independent republic administering its affairs in a fatherly manner. It was after all a sort of paternalism so much in vogue in Europe at the time. Jones and his followers outlined a plan of procedure for the State, which provided for a separate existence from the Union, for a period of five years, in which time, it was thought, such a spirit of independence and particularism would be developed as would prevent forever the adoption of the General Constitution. These men had, however, carried their plan too far; Virginia's influence in North Carolina was great; the friends of the new Constitution were powerful, and they soon gathered to them all the more conservative political forces of the State; the Federal Government guaranteed, too, the peace of the State, protection from inva-

---

58 N.C. State Records, XVIIL, 256-316.
59 See Journals of Assembly.

sion by the Indians. And it was but a short while before men began to change their opinions, and to wish that some arrangement might be made with the United States. A second convention was called to meet at Fayetteville, and the National Constitution was adopted, the convention being guaranteed, though not officially, that certain amendments should be made, which should include a Bill of Rights not unlike that appended to the North Carolina Constitution. This was done in November, 1789, only a year after the Hillsboro Convention had so peremptorily rejected all plans of union, and six months after Washington had been inaugurated. It has been generally believed that North Carolina remained out of the Union in accordance with a general understanding with the Virginia Anti-Federalists, in order to secure the above-named amendments. Whether this is true can not be definitely shown; but from the policy of the opponents of adoption one is convinced that they intended to remain out of the Union until Patrick Henry's proposed plan of forming a confederacy of Southern States could be matured.

Nathaniel Macon was not a member of either of the constitutional conventions; but John Macon was a member of the first, and presumably of the second. In the first, he staunchly opposed adoption, and assisted Jones and Person materially in defeating the plans of the Federalists. All three of the Macons who were in political life belonged to the Jones party. When, however, the northern section of the State came to favor adoption; when Jones' programme proved unpopular, even in his own county of Halifax, Nathaniel Macon acquiesced and became the first representative from the Hillsboro district in the National House of Representatives.

President George Washington

CHAPTER VIII.
FIRST YEARS IN CONGRESS, 1791-1795.

Nathaniel Macon, then almost thirty-three years old, took his seat in the House of Representatives as a member for the Hillsboro District of North Carolina on Oct. 26, 1791 (Warren, Franklin, Granville, Wake and Orange counties constituted this district). On the same day, and sworn in at the same time at the bar of the House, came Theodore Sedgwick, of Massachusetts, a man as different from Macon in political ideals, in personal demeanor, as the North is different from the South; the political antipode of Macon, was this Sedgwick, for many years to come, the man who was twice to compete with him for the Speakership of the House.[60] Macon was just entering on a career which was to continue without interruption for a period of thirty-seven years, on a career which kept him in the arena of National politics at a time when the bands of National union were being forged. The experience he brought into his new field of labor was not the most extensive. Reared on a tobacco plantation, educated in a Puritan college; a student of law and English history for three years; tried in the stress of 1780-1781 of the Revolutionary struggle in the South; a member of the North Carolina Assemblies from 1780-1786, at a time when political parties were not unevenly balanced; member-elect of the Continental Congress in 1787, and an active opponent of the adoption of the Federal Constitution, his experience could not have been inferior to that of many another, yet it had been almost entirely of a provincial nature. International affairs were then and for a long time to come beyond his political horizon. On the other hand, States' Rights, local patriotism of the Virginian type, and close affiliation with the intensest opponents of Nationalism, had tended to prejudice his mind against all matters of national concern. He was a planter of mediocre means, a gentleman whose closest companions, after the members of his family, were his thoroughbreds and his dogs. He remained a planter and isolated from the world of commerce, and his life in fields and forests tended to increase his contempt for the narrow limits of town and city.

Macon entered National politics when the first pass of arms between Jefferson and Hamilton, the representatives of the antagonistic forces of the new nation, had just taken place; and Southern mem-

---

60 Annals of Congress, 2nd Cong., 1st Sess., 143.

bers were beginning to feel sore over the defeat which it had brought them. Virginia was complaining that New England and the Dutch city on the Hudson were carrying things their own way and for selfish, commercial ends. Pennsylvania was agitated by the long and acrimonious quarrel with Connecticut about the Wyoming Valley, and the western settlers of the same state were transferring their opposition, so long directed at their own State government to that of the Nation. Foreign affairs were becoming more and more complicated and unfriendly toward the young republic, which was promising to become an everlasting monument to European jealousy. All Europe was divided into two camps — camps commanded by Frenchmen on the one side, and Englishmen on the other. The leaven of the American Revolution was working mightily in every country in the civilized world, and Americans themselves began to stand awe-stricken at the havoc they had done and were doing still; the more conservative of them in the United States, as we have seen in the State of North Carolina, became exceedingly fearful of the results, drew back and formulated a creed of reaction, while the more radical still held to the Declaration of Independence, as the chart by which not only ours, but all the ships of state should be guided. The conservatives espoused extreme Nationalist views; — the radical Republicans, as they now began to designate themselves — took up the cause of the States, and the cause of individual rights and equality. "The people," what they are, what their place in the American commonwealth was to be, were the questions which exercised every mind. Madison was becoming distasteful to the East, because he listened to "arguments ad populum;" and Jay declared, what many believe now, that "the majority of every people are deficient both in virtue and in knowledge." Madison's friend, Jefferson, was saying that instead of one honest man in fifteen among the common people, he found fourteen; and that instead of fourteen honest men in fifteen among the so-called better classes, he found only one.[61] Hamilton, Jay's friend and political patron of a later day, thought the people a "great beast," which must be securely bound if one would live at peace and under a good government. Furthermore, people were still reading and discussing two exceedingly interesting and important books : Burke's *Reflections on the French Revolution* and Tom Paine's *Rights of Man*. Besides, and old Princeton student, Philip Freneau, was publishing his most partisan and saucy *Gazette*, a

---

61 *Writings of Jefferson* (Ford), VII , 24-25.

Democratic journal, which was opposed by Fenno's *Gazette*, another paper which existed solely for partisan purposes. Members of the Cabinet and leaders of Congress wrote, under Latin *nom de plumes*, the dryest political essays, which, however, were read enough to set people guessing who the authors were, and to put the politicians at one another's ears.[62] What Macon was to become amidst these surroundings, and which side would gain his support, would not have been difficult to determine even then by those who knew him.

Macon was not present when the House was exchanging its rather Republican Speaker, Muhlenberg, for Jonathan Trumbull, of Connecticut a man of the required political complexion; but he was there to witness the two days of hair-splitting courtesy between the representatives of the sovereign people in the President's chair, and the representatives of the same sovereign people in the seventy-five chairs of the House, and all about the etiquette in the House's reply to the President's address. The first debates that Macon heard in this new arena were on the prosy subject of the apportionment of representatives; and he was made a member of the committee appointed to prepare and bring in a bill suitable to a resolution, that *thirty thousand* should be the number of voters requisite to each representative. The committee reported its bill November 31, and the first words of Macon in the House were delivered in favor of increasing the number from *thirty to thirty-five thousand*, and when Bourne, of Rhode Island, rather uselessly opposed his amendment, Macon arose and made a very pointed and sensible remark of a single sentence,[63] to the effect that Rhode Island's demand for a constitutional amendment touching the subject was not likely to be granted. Macon's amendment was lost, as was also the one for thirty-four thousand offered by Bourne, and a bill favoring one representative for every thirty thousand voters passed, but was rejected by the Senate, which, since the arrangement would leave a greater number of large fractions in the New England states, was to that body highly objectionable. It proposed thirty-three thousand, which the House in turn rejected. A second bill passed both Houses, but was vetoed by the President, because he considered it unconstitutional — first veto in our national history. The Senate plan of thirty-three thousand as a basis was then accepted by the House, and became a law April 14, 1792.[64] During these interminable debates, a

---

62 Schouler: *History of the United States*, I., 150-200.
63 Annals of Congress, 2nd Cong, 200.
64 Annals of Congress, 2nd Cong, 1st Sess., 200 on; Schouler, I , 206.

great deal of acrimony and partisanship was manifested; *vox populi* was likened to *vox diaboli* on one occasion; at other times, the aristocratic tendency of the Senate, the Slave and the Bank questions, gave opportunity for sweeping charges and general denunciations. Macon voted with his colleagues steadily, and soon after the beginning of the session ceased to make any remarks, apparently leaving Dr. Hugh Williamson to represent himself and his State. The bill as finally passed increased North Carolina's representation from five to ten.

The next subject on which Macon took decided ground, and on which he made some pointed remarks, was the granting to the widow of General Greene a sum of sixty thousand dollars to indemnify the Greene estate for losses the General had suffered as a result of his becoming surety for some Americo-British merchants of Charleston in 1783. Macon has been uniformly censured for his opposition to the petition of Mrs. Greene. The case seems to have been as follows: in November, 1782, when the American army, commanded by General Greene, was mutinying, because of lack of food and clothing, General Greene entered into a contract with Hunter, Banks & Co., of Charleston, to furnish the necessary supplies, although it was generally admitted that the price demanded was much too high. But no competitor could be found, and after due efforts were made to find the supplies elsewhere, the contract had been closed. In April of the following year the creditors of Hunter, Banks & Co. refused to cooperate further in the delivery of army supplies without security, and General Greene himself executed a bond in behalf of Banks, one of his contractors, for eight thousand pounds sterling. Hunter, Banks & Co. failed to meet their obligations, and Greene's estate became liable. The authority to enter into arrangements with contractors for supplying the army had been given Greene by Congress, and so he reported all of his actions to that body except the surety matter of April, 1783, which was not made public until it was known that a large sum would have to be paid by General Greene. When this part of the transaction came before the old Congress, there was some demur, and in the general weakness of that body, no reparation was made. In 1786, Greene died, and the executions against his property were partially carried into effect, and Mrs. Greene was about to lose altogether sixty thousand dollars in a matter which concerned chiefly the United States, for which her husband had acted. March 4, 1790, Mrs. Greene presented her claim to Hamilton, in New York, who made out a lengthy petition embodying all the facts in the case and sent it to Congress, with a recommendation for its favorable consideration. The matter did not come up for final settlement until January, 1792, when strenuous opposition to reimbursement, based on numerous conditions, developed: (1) Greene had made himself very unpopular in South Carolina, in the fall of 1782, by advocating the cause of some extreme Royalists, who were then asking favors of the State government, by his general criticisms of the behavior of the Southern states and their troops relative to the war and to his campaign in particular, and also by his disputing the authority of Governor Guerard in certain matters, which the latter claimed fell within the civil jurisdiction; (2) some letters of the Banks Company were opened by General Scott in Virginia, in the fall of 1782, which showed two of Greene's staff officers, Forsyth and Burnet, to be silent partners in the Banks concern, though apparently without Greene's knowledge; (3) Greene had not informed Congress of an important part of his transactions, until it was found that he would have to pay the surety. Naturally the Southern Congressmen, who had nearly all heard of the reports, following the opening of the Banks letters in Virginia, that Greene himself was speculating in the Banks contracts, were disposed to oppose the petition. Besides the high price which was collected for the supplies, the fact that most of these supplies came through the Banks firm from English merchants whose stocks were forced upon the market by the evacuation of Charleston, which should have lowered prices, and the entire absence of other offers in so large a town, had convinced many at the time that Greene was interested in the contracts; and in 1792 this conviction was general in the South.

It is not the author's purpose to do more than state the conditions which influenced Macon in his policy of opposing Mrs. Greene's petition. Macon, it will be recalled, entered the army without accepting the usual bounty, and it may be added here that he served during the fall and winter of 1780-1781 absolutely at his own expense. He did not, as it appears from his later actions, expect others to serve their country *gratis*; but he was always uncompromisingly opposed to any man's accepting anything as a gratuity from the government. To him Greene had become unpopular when he made reflections on North Carolina troops, whether there was ground for such reflections or not. In regard to the alleged connections of Greene with Banks, it may be said that most Southern Congressmen appear to have credited the report. Every one of the North Carolina delegation in Congress voted against granting the indemnity claimed by Mrs. Greene.[65] And what ever may be said of General Greene's integrity, which scarce any one doubts, he was indiscreet in his behavior in these transactions, and naturally questions arose in the minds of others when half his army, also, had believed him to be interested.[66] Most commanders of exceptional ability have been unfortunate in their financial affairs, either from lack of foresight or from indifference, and such seems to have been the case with General Greene. It was not because Macon opposed the allowance of the indemnity to the Greene estate; nor because he was unwilling to reimburse an officer who had "gone surety" for his country. John Steele, of Salisbury, son of the woman who had given all the money she had to Greene in 1781, and a man most likely to view the case in a favorable light, opposed the petition, and he seems to have believed that Greene had not been altogether clear of the charge which had been brought against him. Steele was a Federalist, and the Federalists almost unanimously supported Mrs. Greene's claim.[67] What still further prejudiced the case with Macon was the fact that Hamilton was a sort of attorney for Mrs. Greene before the House. Anything which Hamilton did or proposed was subject to serious question with Macon at that time.

From the beginning the Southern members of Congress had distrusted Hamilton's financial scheme and as his system further developed this distrust became open opposition. The funding of the National debt, assumption of State debts and the organization of the National Bank had been bitterly opposed by the South. Hamilton's doctrine that "a National debt will be a National blessing, a powerful cement of union, a necessity for keeping up taxation," was not an orthodox political creed south of Philadelphia. The consolidation of financial agencies; the strong and open attachment of the wealthy classes to the Treasury; the bestowal of douceurs, subsidies and commissions on those who were to be gained; the positive assurance on the part of Hamilton to the banks, that nothing should be lost to them by their support of his measures, aroused the ire of plain Republicans like Macon and challenged open attack. It was known that the Treasurer was, as Schouler says, "Feathering the nests of his favorites," and these favorites did not conceal their dislike of Democratic

---

65 Annals of Congress, 2nd Cong, 1st Sess. 531.
66 Johnson's *Life of Nathaniel Greene*, I., 383.
67 Annals of Congress, 2nd Cong., st Sess., 455.

institutions.[68] Everybody in Philadelphia, except Washington, was apparently committed to one or the other of the two parties, and most people understood in what direction Hamilton was steering and with what means. It was thought that many were corruptly connected with the Treasurer and that an investigation would bring to light transactions which would essentially check the rising influence of the Secretary.

On February 23rd Macon proposed the following resolution:

"*Resolved*, That the Secretary of the Treasury cause to be laid before this House a statement of the balances remaining unpaid, if any, which may have been due by individuals to the United States previous to the fourth day of March, one thousand, seven hundred and eighty-nine, and whether any, and what, steps have been taken to recover the same; and also a statement of the sundry sums of public money which may have been intrusted to individuals, previous to said fourth day of March, one thousand, seven hundred and eighty-nine, and have not been accounted for."

The purpose of this resolution was plain enough and it at once brought all the friends of the Treasurer into their seats; they claimed it was irregular, "out of form," and calculated to embarrass the *Comptroller* besides carrying an imputation on that officer when no charge had been made. If any thing had been going wrong, said they, let us call him to account and institute an impeachment, but let us not take a step which would bring an investigation. A storm of opposition was excited, but the supporters of Macon's resolution claimed that no imputation was meant nor could be read into it, that the House had an undoubted right to call for such statements from the Treasurer, that an opinion had gone abroad that large sums of money were due from individuals, and that the public has a right to know if settlement is being made and that, far from any reflection being intended upon the *Comptroller*, it was, on the contrary, to his interest to satisfy the public of the falsity of public opinion against him and that the disclosure of names, which the opponents of the resolution had made so much of, would only relieve good men from being suspected of illicit connection with the treasury. "No honest man need fear an investigation" was the claim of Macon and his supporters.[69]

---

68 Schouler, I., 217-218.
69 Annals of Congress, 2nd Cong., 1st Sess., 425.

Macon served on several other committees, and offered one or two other resolutions during the first session of the Second Congress. It is interesting to note, in view of his later political life, that he moved to strike out a clause of a bill which would have removed the duty on foreign cotton. The House was in Committee of the Whole, considering this bill. It had been proposed to enhance the duty on hemp and strike out that on cotton. Doctor Williamson, from Edenton, North Carolina, was so interested in a pet scheme of his for improving American navigation, which he thought would be aided by the measure, that he favored the clause against cotton. Macon, apparently better acquainted with the conditions of that infant industry, insisted that the duty on cotton should remain, that great quantities were being raised in the South for which there was not a sufficient demand. John Steele of North Carolina and John Page of Virginia made speeches in favor of Macon's protection for his "infant industry." Steele declared that "the farmers of North Carolina had gone largely into the cultivation of that article" and Page maintained further that the first varieties of cotton, which New Englanders claimed could be had only from Europe, were being grown in the South and that successful experiments had been recently made with West India cotton. Kittera of Pennsylvania opposed the encouragement of cotton-growing because it would impoverish the soil and work injury to the farmer himself. The Eastern men carried their measure and Macon's protective tariff policy was defeated; but it had required the vote of the Speaker. Two South Carolinians, William Smith and Daniel Huger voted with the Easterners.[70]

The debates on this subject occupied only a short time in the House and excited no comment in the country; but the little pass at arms was very significant, could any one have foreseen that the "infant industry" of cotton growing was to become the greatest in America and was to be the indirect cause of our greatest war. Cotton lost; and manufacturers gained; but the beginning in this sort of dispute had scarce been made. Macon was the advocate of protection and Doctor Williamson, Macon's colleague, finally voted for the measure simply because it might build up a carrying trade and give employment to "his sailors." Macon foresaw the importance of cotton, its advantage to the South, his section, and he at once took his stand. His heart was with the South primarily and afterwards with the Union,

---

70 Annals of Congress, 2nd Cong., 1st Sess., 560.

and such motives actuated most men who voted in the early is not all subsequent Congresses.

Before the second session of the Second Congress opened, the second presidential election took place. North Carolina was glad to cast its entire vote for Washington for President; but not so with Adams for Vice-President. George Clinton received the twelve electoral votes of the State for that office. The election of a successor to Samuel Johnston, who had been chosen in 1790 for a term of two years in the United States Senate, occasioned a deadlock of twelve days in the Assembly of 1792-'93. The outcome was Johnston's defeat. He was the recognized leader of the extreme Federalists and his defeat was the prime object of Macon's party. Alexander Martin, a Virginian school teacher, who had been Governor of North Carolina, a man who began his career by voting against the Federalists and ended it by voting with them, was made his successor. In the House only two members of the Second Congress from North Carolina were returned the following year, 1793, one of whom was William Barry Grove, a good Federalist from Cumberland county, who had once been the protégé of MacLaine, and the Hoopers, the other Nathaniel Macon. The cause of the sweeping change was the general dissatisfaction with the support some members had given Hamilton's Treasury measures and the excise; and, more than all, the disposition of Johnston was to ignore the people and the legislature. It had been the custom of the delegates to the old Congress to appear each year before the Assembly and, like the ambassadors of ancient Venice, give accounts of their stewardship. Johnston and Hawkins, the other Senator, had made no attempt to meet this custom but had rather shown contempt for the poffered instructions of the legislature. North Carolinians were displeased, evidently, with the first "Republican court," as Griswold has called it, and the elections of 1792 and 1793 "cleansed the seats" of those who were suspected of being tainted with Federalism. As was said, Grove alone was able by virtue of the staunch Federalism which grew out of the Moore's Creek battle to retain his place. He remained a member of Congress from his district, Cumberland and neighboring counties, for twenty years to come.[71]

The short session of this Congress was not fruitful of beneficial legislation. The opposition under the leadership of Madison, Macon and Giles directed all their blows against Hamilton with the view of

---

71 *Journals of the North Carolina Assembly,* 1792, 21-23; Moore, I., 412.

forcing him from the cabinet, as Hamilton himself had, through the papers, attempted to force Jefferson to retire. After some weeks spent in measuring fine speeches with the President, the opposition began their determined attack. The recent elections in the Southern states had shown how general was the dislike for the ways of the Secretary of Treasury. Virginia had passed scathing resolutions against the Assumption bill; the people of western Pennsylvania and North Carolina had refused to pay the excise tax on whiskey; George Clinton, with the aid of Aaron Burr, the adroitest politician in America, had gained control of New York and had finally secured the whole vote of the Republican party in that State for the Vice-Presidency despite Hamilton's greatest endeavors.[72] The opposition began their fight in some resolutions in reply to Washington's address and they managed to turn every debate in the direction of Hamilton until finally Giles, the nominal leader of the Virginia delegation in the House, brought in the series of resolutions demanding a sharp inquest in the management of the Treasury, the same plan, but differently and more elaborately outlined, which Macon had proposed at the preceding session. Madison made a long and effective speech in favor of it, while Smith of the Charleston district, South Carolina, and Sedgwick of Massachusetts, took up the defence of Hamilton. Macon's attitude was the same, judging by his vote, in this instance as it had been when he himself directed the attack. But the hour had been ill chosen, and before the final vote was taken, Giles overshot his mark by attempting to pass a vote severely censuring Hamilton; this weakened very decidedly the whole opposition scheme. Still the Secretary was only partially exonerated and rather plainly criticized for repeatedly transcending his authority in the matter of loans.[73]

The third Congress met in Philadelphia in November, 1793, with a delegation of ten members from North Carolina in the House instead of the former five. The increase in the number of delegates was due to the census of 1790 and the following reapportionment. Not a little has been said about the unfair treatment of North Carolina by the First and Second Congresses in allowing the State only five delegates. But the blame lies wholly with North Carolina. A census had been taken by order of the State government in 1786, and it was so poorly done that not half the population was enumerated.[74] This

---

72 Schouler, I., 231.
73 Annals of Congress, 2nd Cong., 2nd Sess., 899 on.
74 N.C. State Records, XVIII., 433-434.

count had been the basis of the first apportionment, which explains why the State sent only five members to Congress when it was entitled to send at least eight. The new and larger delegation was almost entirely Republican, "Antis," or "Mobocrats," as the Federalists called them.

Macon was as much their leader as any — no Republican leader among North Carolinians having developed especial strength in National politics. The democratic spirit was so prevalent in North Carolina that a sort of dead-level was kept up in its delegation; no men of great ability belonged to it, also no untrustworthy ones. Experience in legislative matters was likely to give precedence and on that ground Macon seems to have assumed a certain kind of leadership.

Macon's first work in the new Congress was to recommend, as a member of a special committee, an appropriation for increasing our naval force in order to bring the Barbary States of Africa to reason. The Federalists voted against the bill because they deemed the appropriation entirely inadequate.[75] During the months following, he was always present and served on several small committees. The debate on the Militia bill of that session was long and tedious and turned many a time against Macon's pet notions respecting the importance of militia service.

May 6th Macon introduced a series of resolutions looking to a change of the excise laws which were working so much dissatisfaction in Pennsylvania and most of the other States to the South. These resolutions provided (1) for a tax on malt beer and porter made in the United States; (2) on all imported beers; (3) on all cider made in the country, and (4) if the third resolution taxing cider passed, no tax was to be collected on brandy since that would be double taxation. The real object of these resolutions was to bring all parts of the country under the operation of the odious excise laws, which was soon to bring on insurrection in several sections of the country. As at that time enforced the excise was extremely oppressive to the distillers of Western Pennsylvania and the mountain sections of the South — men whose only means of raising a "money crop" was by transforming their abundant fruits into brandy, or their corn into whiskey, both of which were easily marketable. "Hamilton's excise," as Jefferson was fond of calling it, was pressing from the poorest classes of people a million a year, while the wealthier consumers of beer and wine

---

75 Annals of Congress, 3nd Cong., 1st Sess., 154-155.

in the East and in the cities were not taxed at all. Macon's proposed plan would have made the tax general, with advantages in favor of the South, where most cider was made and consumed on the plantation, and therefore impossible to be taxed. Madison opposed Macon's scheme along with the whole excise system; Nicholas of Virginia favored it because it would become so exasperating to the whole people that the tax would have to be removed. Macon's claim was that the present system was not just and so he offered this to equalize taxation; though he too modestly deferred to the "sentiments of the majority" at the close of his few remarks. The resolutions, after some rather ungenerous charges of inconsistency on the part of advocates of them,[75] failed of passing. At the time the Macon resolutions were before the House, Hamilton's carriage tax was being advocated. This tax would apply particularly in Virginia and the South, where the great distances between plantations made vehicles a necessity, even to the small landholders; this Macon opposed uniformly, but it could not be prevented from becoming a law.[76]

Macon became again the cause of a lively dispute about the policy of the Treasury on May 12. A resolution had just passed calling on the Treasurer to submit to the executives of the several States reports on the condition of accounts between the States and the general government. Macon had been appointed chairman of the committee to confer with Hamilton on the subject. He now made a motion that copies of another report be furnished giving clear information on other subjects, one of which was the disposition made of certain public funds about which the Federalists were reluctant to speak. Sedgwick was at once on the floor declaring that Macon desired to "raise discord and jealousy in the United States and to feed them." Some warm words followed and Macon's resolution was finally referred to a committee which never reported, which was expected.[77] Hamilton was not an object of cordial love with the North Carolina delegation and Macon, as we have seen, was particularly averse to his methods, taking every occasion to criticise them. This motion was a kind of parting shot from Macon at the close of the session.

On Macon's return to Congress after the summer and autumn vacation, he was made a member of the first standing committee on elections and, though he was not chairman, he seems to have shown

---

76 Annals of Congress, 3rd Cong., 1st Sess., 648-651.
77 Annals of Congress, 3rd Cong., 1st Sess., 672.

his judicial and upright turn of mind so clearly that by common consent he became the moving spirit of the committee and made its reports.[78] The report of the committee in the first contest was an interesting one in view of some recent disputes about resignations of members of Congress. It was between Mercer and Duvall of Maryland. Mercer had given in his resignation to the Governor and it had been accepted. A new election was called and Duvall was chosen for the unexpired term. Mercer changed his mind and claimed, it seems, that his resignation was not valid and returned to Congress, claiming his seat. The committee held that the Governor's action in accepting the resignation and ordering a new election was constitutional, and that Duvall was entitled to the seat.

The President's speech at the opening called forth an angry debate, which was kept up for weeks, and which finally resulted in the first dissent of the House from Washington's opinion. Macon voted with the dissenters, though there is no evidence of a more active opposition on his part to the President's recommendation, notwithstanding their whole tenor was against his decided convictions.[79] In the other important measures, the public debt, naturalization bill, defense of the frontiers, which excited so much acrimonious and useless debate, Macon took no part openly; but when the question of indemnity to the University of North Carolina and to many citizens of the State for losses sustained, when the United States restored to the Indians large tracts of Tennessee lands, to which these parties had claims, came up, he made a short speech in favor of indemnity and labored industriously for the petitioners until at least a measure of relief was guaranteed.[80] In this matter, as in most others, Sedgwick opposed him particularly, maintaining that the allowance of the so-called Thomas Person claims would open the way for thousands of others.

The last, public utterance of Macon during this session was against the bill granting a purse of four thousand dollars to the daughters of Count de Grasse, then living in Boston. So much has been said about the niggardliness of this sort of opposition on the part of Macon that the quoting of his speech is hardly out of place, since it sets forth his reasons for opposing the measure in the fewest possible words: "that though the claims of the petitioners were strong,

---

78 Annals of Congress, 3rd Cong., 1st Sess., 674-75.
79 Annals of Congress, 3rd Cong , 2nd Sess., 874.
80 Annals of Congress, 3rd Cong , 2nd Sess., 894-946.

yet they were not more so than those of multitudes of others. On the very day when we have come to a resolution, to receive no more petitions from our fellow citizens, we are going to give at once so large a sum to foreigners. I am aware that the Count de Grasse has done eminent services to America, and I feel them as much as any person, but still I see no reason for preferring these petitioners when there are likely an hundred of the officers of de Grasse, or of Rochambeau's army, that are in this country and in want."[81] There were many others in the country who felt as did Macon on this subject, though not many in Congress, for nearly all of his party voted for the gift to the de Grasse daughters, Madison its leader, being a member of the committee which drew the bill. Macon stood so nearly alone in this that no record was made of the votes.

Soon after the meeting of Congress in November preceding Macon had received a letter from General John Steele, who had been defeated two years before for Congress because of his supposed Federalist tendencies. This letter, as will be seen, contained a request for Macon's endorsement for some office to which he aspired, apparently Hawkin's seat in the United States Senate. Macon's reply is characteristic. He very politely declined to sign with Grove, a strong Federalist, the certificate which had been sent him. Macon could not thus commit himself to a candidate who was, to say the least, not in agreement with his party. His reply is more carefully worded than usual and the expression of his opinion of Steele's candidacy is well enough covered up under the phrase "proper reflection and time will convince any one that you deserve well of the State."

This letter deserves full quotation in view of the opinions expressed concerning his views and the state of parties at the time: "I am really sorry that it is not in my power to say a word on that subject or sign the certificate agreeable to your desire. Although I was not present when you made the speech, I remember perfectly well that you, Grove and myself agreed that the motion, which occasioned it, was a very important one and that we agreed in sentiment on the subject, and as well as I recollect the speech contains the substance of our conversation on the subject of the motion except that I thought the constitution would not warrant the giving such power to the President though I would not have made the objection in the House for a reason before mentioned. On a bill of a similar nature last session

---

81 Annals of Congress, 3rd Cong , 2nd Sess., 1155 on.

I made objection of the same kind. Indeed I am certain that I never shall consent to give such a power to any President (the privilege to lay an embargo in 1793). Grove and myself have examined the journals for the message of the President, which you want, but have not been fortunate enough to find such a one, the other papers he will send you.

"*It appears to me that proper reflection and time will convince every one that you have deserved well of the State.* It is said there are two parties in Congress, but that fact I do not positively know, if there are I know that I do not belong to either, but what is strange to tell, and at the same time must be a convincing proof that you acted independently, is, that there is good reason to believe that neither of these parties are desirous to see you here again."[82]

The State elections of 1794 were influenced chiefly by the stand the government had taken in 1793 on the question of neutrality and more especially in North Carolina, where Timothy Bloodworth of New Hanover had resigned an office in the State government, because Governor Spaight had endorsed Washington's policy. Bloodworth had become the leader of an almost violent opposition to the neutrality proclamation in the Wilmington district. He "stood for the legislature," and was elected by a large majority. The people had supported him against Washington! In the Assembly, which met in the autumn, Bloodworth was at once made Speaker, and one year later, at the time of the Congressional elections, he was chosen to succeed Benjamin Hawkins, a special friend of Washington, in the United States Senate.[83] This, with the result of the general elections, showed the growing strength of the Republican party and caused Samuel Johnston to exclaim when he heard the reports: "O tempora, tempora!" And Washington, to help the cause of Federalism in the South, at once named Hawkins Indian Commissioner for the Southwest. John Macon was the leader, after Bloodworth, of the new forces in North Carolina politics. The leaders of the old regime lost power entirely and entrenched themselves, whenever it was possible, in Federal offices from one end of the State to the other.

The new Congress which met in Philadelphia in November, 1795, was not of a temper altogether pleasing to the ardent Federalists who had controlled things in the last and who had become accustomed

---

82 Macon to General John Steele, Dec. 11, 1794.
83 Samuel Johnston to James Iredell, Feb. 14, 1795.

to carry their measures by fair means or foul. The Federal party had identified the Democratic societies with the Republicans, and with the assistance of the President these had been brought into complete disrepute.[84]

The West Pennsylvanians had been suppressed in a manner not likely to conciliate the opponents of the government, and most of the men, who now took their seats in the House, were determined to check the extravagance, as they thought, of the administration, notwithstanding the popularity of Washington. The Republicans were in a majority, quite a safe one at first. What had taken place at the polls in North Carolina had taken place in most of the States south of Connecticut. In Boston, New York, Philadelphia, Baltimore and Charleston, public meetings were held and every act of the President's foreign policy severely criticized. Add to this the effect of the extra session of the Senate, its defiant attitude toward public opinion, its ratification of the Jay treaty June, 1795, by a strictly party vote, the riots in Philadelphia, which threatened, as honest John Adams said, to break down the authority of the Government, and we have a notion of the excitement in the country and the determination of the new Congress to remedy things. It was not a tardy coming together that December as it had been when the previous Congress met, when two long weeks were lost in getting a quorum. Not a day was now lost, and what was more significant, a man whom most people took for an ardent Republican was chosen Speaker — Jonathan Dayton of New Jersey.

---

84 Washington's Correspondence, Sept.-Oct., 1764.

CHAPTER IX.
LEADER OF THE NORTH CAROLINA DELEGATION, 1795-1799.

Thomas Blount, Nathan Bryan, Jesse Franklin, "old Matthew Locke" and Absalom Tatom, with Nathaniel Macon as leader, constituted the chief men of North Carolina's delegation in the Congress of giants, which met in the old courthouse on the corner of Sixth and Chestnut streets in Philadelphia in December of 1795. It was to be the most notable congress in our history so far, as one of the most important of all. The delegation of which our hero was becoming the acknowledged leader was not composed of brilliant men, but plain, middle-class representatives, Southern Puritans, just such men as would have been good Abolitionists fifty years later, if they had lived in another section of the country. Jesse, Matthew, Absalom and Nathaniel were names which told the story of their birth and family; and they were men who believed in Bible doctrines and drew their illustrations from Hebrew history and were not apt to forget their belief or yield an inch to the "Powers of Evil." The regaining of control in North Carolina by those who had opposed the adoption of the National Constitution in 1788, which was completed during the years 1794-'95, brought the common people, Democrats of the country squire type, into places of public trust; men whose education had not been good, and who knew nothing at all of international politics, but who had, all of them, been staunch Whigs in 1776, and who had seen actual service in the war, or who had certainly never been suspected of giving comfort to the Tories. They were just such as the old politicians, statesmen even, could not bear to see in high places, and the mention of whose names brought visions of anarchy and the "rule of the many" to their cultured minds — "mobocrats," "red Republicans," and "Jacobins," were the names they bore with Johnston, Iredell and Hooper. They did not pretend to know so much about statecraft, they could not have obtained entree to Lady Washington's parlors, but they knew the difference between the demands of popular institutions and special interests. And according to the testimony of many a student of American history, our generation has just cause to be thankful to those simple-minded, plain-looking country squires whom North Carolina sent to Congress in 1794-'95.

To lead such a delegation was Macon's high calling during the stormy years just ahead. Macon's experience and seniority of service in the National legislature (though he was only thirty-seven years old), and not his forensic ability or powers of manipulation, gave him the first place among his colleagues. The first attack on the strongholds of the party in power was made by Parker of Virginia and Macon of North Carolina, when the response to the President's speech assumed its customary tone of fulsome flattery.[85] The response ran: "contemplating that probably unequalled spectacle of National happiness, which our country exhibits, to the interesting summary which you, sir, have been pleased to make, in justice to our own feelings, permit us to add the benefits which are derived from your presiding in our councils, resulting as well from the undiminished confidence of your fellow citizens as from your zealous and successful labors in their service." Macon objected to this language, and, with Parker, insisted that, not only should it be made less laudatory, but that the whole ceremony of the House proceeding in a body to present their reply, as had formerly been the custom, should be modified or abolished altogether. He proposed that a committee of three be delegated to express to the President, in simple English, the good will of the House and the readiness of its members to cooperate with him in all measures looking to the good of their common country. The plan gained ample support at once, and the reply to the President's address was chastened very considerably, though not entirely displaced by a committee as suggested. This proposition today would appear to be a very reasonable one; but not so then. It caused a somewhat angry debate, and those who favored it were looked upon by its opponents very much as the German nobles regard the advocates of a proposition to abolish the standing army. But those days, though only a single century has passed, were very different from ours; the festive twenty-fifth of December came on and the members of Congress all remained at their posts until the twenty-fourth, which was on Thursday, when they adjourned until the following Monday — two days were all the holiday they gave themselves. The simple hearts of that day loved ceremony far more than a big holiday and bodily ease.

The presentation to Congress by Adet, the French envoy, of a most handsomely wrought and fantastic flag of the French Convention occupied Congress some hours on the 4th January. This pledge

---

85 Annals of Congress, 4th Cong., 1st Sess., 131.

of "everlasting friendship" was first sent to Washington, who detailed an American army officer to present it, with numerous messages from the Committee of Safety, to the Representatives of the American people. The message is in part as follows: "Citizens Representatives, the connections which nature, reciprocal events and a happy concurrence of circumstances have formed between two free nations, can not but be indissoluble. You have strengthened those sacred ties by declarations, which the Minister Plenipotentiary of the United States has made in your name to the National Convention and to the French people.[86] They have been received with rapture by a nation who know how to appreciate every testimony which the United States have given to them of their affection. The colors of both nations, united in the centre of the National Convention, will be an everlasting evidence of the part which the United States have taken in the success of the French Republic." (We had refused to take any part, as was known and talked everywhere.)

"You were the first defenders of the rights of man in another hemisphere. Strengthened by your example, and endowed with an invincible energy, the French people have vanquished Tyranny, which, during so many centuries of ignorance, superstition and baseness, had enchained a generous nation." After much more of this kind, the message concludes: "Doubt it not, Citizens, we shall finally destroy the combinations of tyrants. You, by the picture of prosperity, which, in your vast countries, has succeeded to a bloody struggle of eight years; we, by the enthusiasm which glows in the breast of every Frenchman. Astonished nations, too long the dupes of perfidious Kings, Nobles, and Priests will eventually recover their rights and the human race will owe to the American and French nations their regeneration and a lasting peace." The reading of all this and much more took place in the hall of the Representatives and it pleased Macon heartily, though more because of the grimaces it produced on the faces of the Federalists than because of any response on his own part to so many happy French phrases. Macon had lost his French nature too completely to enjoy this declamation of his former countrymen. He was, however, a staunch advocate of the continued binding force of the French treaty of 1778 as North Carolinians generally were. On that issue the Radicals had gained the victory at the polls in 1794 and

---

86 Monroe had presented the American flag to the Convention, had made a fine speech on the occasion and had received therefor "a warm, fraternal embrace" from the president of that body.

'95; and later when a bill was about to be passed by Congress, prohibiting the sale of French prizes in American ports, he opposed it, recommending a continuance of the privilege, notwithstanding the complications that might arise.[87]

In the very beginning of the session, Giles presented to the House several resolutions and petitions from the citizens of Virginia protesting against the British treaty which was expected soon to come before that body for final settlement. The question agitating the country and occupying the minds of politicians was: Can the Representatives veto the action of the President and Senate in the exercise of their constitutional functions, because the completion of those acts require an appropriation the granting of which is exclusively the right of the Representatives? The Federalists claimed they could not, and that it was presumption on the part of the House to interfere with the treaty by refusing to make the necessary appropriation; the Republicans, with Jefferson as their counsellor, believed to the contrary, and were determined to defeat the enforcement of a treaty which they claimed sold us out to England.

It would hardly be in place here to review the merits and demerits of the Jay treaty, more than to say that it was a partisan measure, and it was so regarded by all who took any part in politics. Washington had sent Chief Justice Jay to England as Special Envoy. Jay was strictly English in sentiment, and so looked upon by Congress, a man whose brother was an officer in the English army, and who had himself given proof enough of his own admiration for the politics of that country. When he appeared at Court, George III received him graciously, remarking at the same time: "I am sure you can succeed in your mission." After the treaty was finally agreed upon Washington determined to have it become law by proclamation according to the custom, and so he was more than impatient at the threatened opposition of the House. But the Republicans came fresh from the people; they believed it their duty to annul the proceedings of the Government and a partisan Senate, and they were decidedly in the majority, which, for the first time in our history, presented the spectacle of a government divided into opposite camps and thus rendered almost helpless.

The long and bitter fight was begun by Livingston of New York, when he introduced on March 2, 1796, a resolution calling on the President to submit to the House, before the appropriation could be

---

87 Annals of Congress, 4th Cong., 1st Sess., 1342.

voted, the secret papers and instructions relative to Jay's mission.[88] From that time until March 31st a fierce war of words was kept up, and it seemed to some that the Government would go to pieces; but the resolution finally passed and Washington was called on for the papers. He refused peremptorily, which was the cause of no little glee among the opponents of the resolution. Until that time the President had maintained an absolute silence on the subject. This had annoyed and puzzled both parties. This refusal appeared to be a victory for the Federalists, since, as they were convinced, the influence of Washington given decidedly in their favor would so dishearten many of the Republicans as to cause them to give up their plan. The subject was opened again April 13th, when Sedgwick introduced a resolution providing for the appropriations necessary to the execution of the Jay treaty; and for several others which were now all thrown together, according to ancient Roman log-rolling maneuvers, in order to secure the money necessary for the one which was expected to be defeated. These extra treaties settled our relations (1) with the Indians on the Ohio, (2) with Algiers, (3) with Spain, all of which the Southern and Western members were desirous of carrying into effect at once. The *en bloc* method was soon defeated by the Republican majority and each treaty was made to stand or fall according to its own merits. All were passed favorably in a single day except the one with Great Britain, and then came the test of party strength on the final and great measure of the session. The debate lasted more than two weeks and there had never been a dispute in Congress which brought forward such an array of able disputants, or one in which more intense partisanship was manifested. The Republicans had begun the session with presenting petitions from their constituents; the Federalist petitions were introduced in ever increasing volume as the debate went on; Boston held town meetings against those Virginia leaders who disputed the right of the East to rule; New York had a riotous meeting and Philadelphia threatened to fall upon the members of the House and chase them from the city unless they made the necessary appropriation; the English *Charge des Affairs* sent a message to the Federalists that post horses were held in readiness to carry an order for the evacuation of the posts which England held, contrary to former treaty stipulations within the bounds of the United States, if only the appropriations were granted. When all these influences were bearing down

---

88 Annals of Congress, 4th Cong., 1st Sess., 426.

upon the Republicans and when several of their weak-kneed members were getting sick or receiving urgent messages to come home to see their wives, Fisher Ames of Massachusetts arose to make that famous and impassioned speech in favor of the treaty — the address which so excited Judge Iredell, then on the Supreme Court bench, as to cause him to exclaim from the gallery of the House: "Great God, he's great!" and which brought from his companion, John Adams, an oath or two of praise. At the close of Ames' address the Federalists pressed the question for a vote, thinking the day had been won, but without success. The pressure had become so strong that still another Republican, Patton from New Jersey, became ill; Varnum, too, was absent; Freeman, a member from New Hampshire, who had voted with the Republicans in the beginning of the session, was away on leave, and Duvall's newly elected successor — a Maryland Republican — postponed taking his seat until a day or two after the vote. All this was thinning the ranks of the opposition while the Federalists were present in full strength. But Macon and every member of his delegation were present and moved a postponement of the final vote until the faint-hearted could be comforted. Macon's motion for delay and the discussion of the ninth article of the treaty, which touched the interests of all North Carolinians living on the original Granville lands, postponed matters for only one day when the yeas and nays on the Jay treaty showed fifty-one for the appropriation and forty-eight against. William Barry Grove of Cumberland was the only representative from North Carolina who voted for the treaty.[89]

It was not because of Macon's public and conspicuous activity in this long debate that the subject has been gone over somewhat in detail; but because he remained firm at his post and kept his friends in their position and on their guard. It is not a question of right or wrong, good policy or bad, that has been considered here, but the faithfulness of Macon to the creed he professed that of a strict constructionist and States' Rights man. By nature he would have been disposed to scrutinize very closely any call for an appropriation, but the question which he asked himself in this measure was: "Is it to the interests of North Carolinians?" just as most others were asking the same question whether they lived south or north of the line of Pennsylvania and Maryland. The only letter of his bearing on the events of that important session now extant was written from the Hall of the

---

[89] Annals of Congress, 4th Cong., 1st Sess., 1280-1292.

Representatives, April 15, 1796. After some remarks about the different treaties he says: "The British treaty is to be acted on today, and will, *I suppose*, produce some debating. It is very doubtful what the vote of the House will be on it. My opinion is that no vote in favor of it can be obtained. I have enclosed Col. Ashe[90] the debates on Mr. Livingston's motion to request certain papers from the President."[91]

The other matters in which Macon took active part during the closing days of the session were the admission of Tennessee as a State and the bill for increasing the salaries of public officers. He favored the admission of Tennessee with two Senators and two Representatives, which latter would have been unusual and strictly speaking unlawful. The census of Tennessee showed a voting population of sixty-seven thousand. The ratio of representation was thirty-four thousand, which, if the census of the State was to be accepted, gave, with only one representative, an unrepresented fraction of thirty-three thousand. Macon claimed that two representatives ought to be allowed in view of this, and of course it was against his political creed to discredit, as some were doing, a census taken by order of a State, or even a prospective State.[92] The House disagreed and allowed the new State one representative until the next general census. On the subject of increased salaries, he favored a reduction rather than an increase. The argument that respectability of government official living and the need of entertaining distinguished foreigners had no influence with him. His claim was that the officers should live beneath their incomes and set the pace for a plain, simple life which might be an object lesson to those foreigners on account of whose visits so much was claimed.

The defeat of the Republicans on the Jay treaty was a sore disappointment to their leaders, but it was the cause of Jefferson's return to political life from which he had retired nearly three years before. He had watched closely the movements of the Federalists and counseled regularly the leaders of the opposition; his advice at the beginning of the session had been to set aside the treaty by refusing the appropriation, which was *"their right to do."* Madison wrote him almost daily how matters stood, and still further, Madison had been suggesting to Jefferson, as early as December preceding, "unpleasant truths" about the latter becoming the Republican candidate for the Presidency. In

---
90 John Baptiste Ashe of Halifax.
91 Macon to John R. Eaton, April 15, 1796.
92 Annals of Congress, 4th Cong., 1st Sess., 1818, 1474

fact a poll of Pennsylvania had been taken at the order of the Republicans in Congress for the purpose of determining the party's strength with Jefferson as its leader, which had shown the chances strongly in their favor. When the question of defeating the British treaty was decided adversely, Madison wrote at once to Jefferson representing that he alone could bring success to their cause. Monroe, who was still in Paris, was informed of this plan. In June Jefferson decided to enter the race and in July he wrote most hopefully to Monroe about the hasty coming of the day of relief.[93]

Macon remained in Philadelphia through all the closing days of the session, when only a bare quorum of members were in their seats, paying attention to the long, dry reports of the Finance Committee on the condition of the Treasury. It was a part of his creed to be present every day in the session. June 1st, after the adjournment of Congress, he set out for Buck Spring, where he was accustomed to take the place of a regular field hand during the summer. And it is significant that his letters are at all times as much given up to comments on the state of the crops, work on the plantation and the condition of the markets as were those of Washington himself.

It is not probable that Macon returned to North Carolina that June without knowing the plans of Madison, Giles and Gallatin, another rising star in the Republican firmament, as to the Presidential election which was coming on, and such good politicians as Jefferson's followers were not likely to leave him in the dark or to leave room for any misunderstandings. North Carolina was, during the decade following 1789, an uncertain State in a presidential election, and for the reason that the ablest men, with the exception of Willie Jones, were contesting with the popular leaders the control of affairs. Johnston and his friends, with the mighty leverage of Washington's name, were not easily relegated to a back seat. During the summer and early autumn months, the party of Jefferson was at work throughout the country; in North Carolina, its leaders were the same as of old, for Willie Jones was again a candidate for a seat in the Assembly. John Macon was a leader in the State Senate; Timothy and Thomas Bloodworth, in the Wilmington district, were directing things according to Jefferson's plans. In the election of 1792, North Carolina's vote, as has been seen, had been given unanimously to Washington for President, and to Clinton, of New York, for Vice-President; in 1796 it was

---

93 See author's thesis: Jefferson's Rueckkehr zur Politik in 1796. Leipzig, 1899.

thought the Federalists could secure four of the electoral votes to Adams, and every effort was made to do this, but without avail. Six votes in all were now asked of the South for Adams, but as it turned out only two were given: one from Virginia and one from North Carolina, all the others being cast for Thomas Jefferson. The Radicals won, and very much to the chagrin of some of the best men in the country. John Marshall deplored, in a letter to Iredell, this disposition of North Carolinians to follow the erratic course of his own State.[94] In producing this result, there can be no doubt that the leader of the State's delegation in the House had a share, though, there appears nowhere any record of his activity in that first trial of strength between Adams and Jefferson.

Washington's address delivered to the Houses at the beginning of the next session, reminding men as it did of his final withdrawal from public life, occasioned a good deal of debate. The Federalists, making use for the last time, as they thought, of his great popularity, were anxious to carry the reply to the greatest extreme of adulation, mixing in, at the same time, as much as possible of their politics. The Republicans would not risk, as was thought, the semblance of opposition, lest their actions should excite violent criticism. But Macon and eleven others had the hardihood to brave public opinion and vote against the address on the ground of its being too laudatory.[95] Among those who voted with Macon was a tall, thin, dark-visaged man, some years before a country school teacher in the neighborhood of Salisbury, North Carolina, but now Andrew Jackson, of Tennessee. Macon had helped bring that cadaverous-looking backwoodsman into the House by vigorously advocating the admission of Tennessee at a former session. The two men were much alike in character, though they were not to discover this until forty years later, when the Tennesseean declared from the President's chair ever lasting war on the United States Bank. For the present the man with his hair tied up in an eel-skin was content to express himself in a sarcastic remark about Washington and by a negative vote which was to Macon, perhaps, a recommendation for independence. To the great majority of the Representatives it was an exceedingly bad beginning. Macon's opposition to the address was in keeping with his past policy; he respected and honored Washington, eulogized him to the highest degree as long as he lived,

---

94 *Iredell's Life and Correspondence,* by McKee, II., 482.
95 Annals of Congress, 4th Cong., 2d Sess., 1668.

though he never claimed him as a kinsman, as he might have done. The address really expressed a declaration in the first paragraph, and others in the last, which reflected on Macon's whole political career, and he was too honest to vote for a measure, with a Jesuitical reservation in mind, to avoid criticism. The resolutions contained in the address expressed what the Republicans could not admit, and if blame attaches to any one on this point, it is not to the twelve negative voters.

The first object of Macon's special displeasure in the short session of Congress was Washington's plan of a National university. Madison reported from the committee appointed to take into consideration the part of Washington's address recommending the establishment of such an institution, the following resolution: "That it is at present expedient that authority should be given to enroll proper persons to receive in trust pecuniary donations in aid of the donations already given, toward the establishment of a university within the District of Columbia." Madison argued in favor of the resolution, claiming that Congress was in no way called on to obligate itself to its support; that it was only to enable gifts of private individuals to be accepted and applied. He stated that the State of Virginia had given Washington fifty shares in the Potomac Canal Company, which he refused to accept for his own use, but which he did accept to be used in the cause of education, and that Washington now offered these shares to such an institution as the resolution contemplated. Madison added that others were offering lands for the same purpose. Livingston, of New York, changed his attitude after hearing this statement, and others were in favor of appointing trustees for "an university in the District of Columbia," so that the plan seemed about to be agreed to; but a motion to postpone the subject prevailed by a vote of thirty-seven to thirty-six, and Washington's gift was refused. It was turned in another direction, and became the nucleus of the endowment of Washington College, now Washington and Lee University, in Virginia. Macon opposed the University, not because of indifference to higher education, but from repugnance to increasing the national establishment, and from a fear that it would somehow or other necessitate an appropriation.[96] Giles and Venable, of Virginia, opposed the plan from similarly overstrained notions of States' rights.

---

96 Annals of Congress, 4th Cong., 2d Sess., 1698-1711.

At this session the Connecticut members made a vigorous effort, in the form of a resolution, to compel the numerous debtor states (states which, in the assumption of State debts by the Union, were left with balances due the old confederacy now due the United States) to pay their arrears into the treasury. North Carolina's debt to the Union was $501,000, with interest for three years; New York owed more than two million.[97] There was a strong sentiment in North Carolina that this debt was not fairly estimated which, in fact, was not without foundation. Macon made several short speeches against the proposed plan of compelling payment, and he was joined by Dempsey Burges, his colleague, in an enthusiastic, if not very wise, plea for North Carolina and in favor of the sentiment prevailing there against payment. He closed as follows: "North Carolina, far removed from the seat of public information, and with little advantage of frequent commercial intercourse, had not the opportunity of equal benefit from the pittance of the rigid economy which her agents had left her citizens. With honest indignation, she now reflects that her public securities are swept away by foreigners and citizens who, with more prompt information, perverted her every village and almost every farm as the enemy in time of war, and with little less fatality and almost without money and without price. * * *

"North Carolina, sir, claims, her representatives conceive, she may with modest decency, that the claims contained in the resolution on your table, if not relinquished, should be suspended.[98] * * *

Burges expressed the views of the North Carolina delegation when he declared that the claims against the State should be relinquished, though not all had such confused notions about the foundation on which those claims were based. These lines quoted from Burges, as they were directed to his constituents, show also how the people of his State felt, and that they were prejudiced against any claim of the United States on account of the sharp maneuvers of Northern financiers in getting possession of the State securities just prior to the passage of the Assumption Bill in 1790. New York joined North Carolina in the protest against the above-named resolution, and these, with the general support of the Southerners, postponed indefinitely a measure threatening at that time so much commotion, particularly in New York, where the debt was so great.

---

97 Annals of Congress, 4th Cong., 2nd Sess., 1813-1816.
98 Annals of Congress, 4th Cong , 2nd Sess., 1800-1801.

Nicholas J. Roosevelt, the present President's great uncle, and Jacob Mark had presented a petition to Congress nearly a year before this, asking for protection in the mining and manufacture of iron. They had engaged miners and workers in Europe, and had brought them to America with a view to establishing the proposed industry on a firm basis. A committee of Congress considered their application, and reported a resolution in their favor, recommending the giving to them of any mines they might discover and open on the public lands of the United States, and further guaranteeing them undisturbed possession for ... years, "the said applicants to render an equitable proportion of the gross products to the government as a co-partner." Henderson, of New Jersey, and Gallatin were willing to grant the protection asked; but Macon, altogether at variance from the policy of his party in North Carolina, opposed the resolution, saying "such a resolution would give a monopoly of all the mines of the United States. The best policy, I believe, in all such cases is to leave the business to the industry of our citizens. They will work the mines if it is to their interest to do so; if not, I do not want to offer them any inducement to do it."[99] This was outlining in the fewest possible words the policy of his later political life, as well as the policy of one of our great political parties for many years. The Republican party was, however, at that time, as has been noted, advocating a protective tariff policy for infant industry, and at home, Macon himself would have voted for bounties to such beginners in any promising undertaking.

In the long debates of this session on direct and indirect taxation, Macon took no part, though he was in principle favorable to direct taxes — the same that Jefferson constantly advocated but never attempted to put into practice, but when those most pathetic petitions of some emancipated negroes from North Carolina, praying relief from persecution under a recent statute of the State against their freedom were presented, he rather reluctantly spoke against their reception by the House. The Nicholson negroes, for such were their names, with two others from Eastern North Carolina, had been given their freedom by their masters; but when a stricter policy regarding the manumission of slaves was adopted, and a law passed allowing any one to take up negroes to whose freedom the State had not consented, and sell them into slavery again, they had been compelled to flee the State or go back into bondage. They were then in Philadelphia, and

---

99 Annals of Congress, 4th Cong., 2nd Sess., 1819-1820.

asking the interference of Congress. Macon said: "No man wishes to encourage petitions more than I, and no man has considered the subject more. These men can not receive any aid from the general government; but by application to the State, justice will be done them. Trials of this kind have very frequently been brought on in all the different Courts of that State, and very often they have ended in the freedom of the slaves. I think it a very delicate subject for the general government to act on: and I shall not be sorry if the petition is sent back." This somewhat heartless view was Macon's life-long policy on this subject.

Macon was again active when the proposition for increasing the salaries of the President and members of Congress came up. Salaries were large enough, he thought; the principle of increasing them did not suit him, and he was fond of saying, "I oppose the plan in toto." In order to defeat it, he moved for postponement till March 4, when the session would close by limitation; but Gallatin came to his aid, and a speedy vote was secured against the bill, the yeas and nays being requested by its opponents.[100] But this was not to be the end of Macon's opposition to the increasing of salaries; for on the day following the counting of the votes for President and Vice-President, a resolution was introduced and passed requiring a committee to be appointed to inquire into the state of the President's household furniture and report any needs. And Macon's friend, Sedgwick, was appointed chairman of the committee. Everybody knew at once what kind of report would be made. On February 25 a bill was introduced recommending fourteen thousand dollars for repairing and improving the furniture for the President-elect as soon as Washington retired. Honest farmer Macon began to see how desirous some people were for money. He had never charged a cent more than his actual mileage, when he had the privilege of collecting double mileage. His six dollars a day was amply sufficient for meeting his expenses while attending the sessions of Congress, and so he could not understand how others could not get along on their allowances. As was to be expected, he spoke out against the bill, and more than once. He reviewed the whole practice of furnishing apartments for the Presidents of the old Congress, declaring that, that officer received no salary, and that furnishing him apartments was but natural. Sitgreaves wished to correct him by pointing out the fact that the President of Congress

---

100 Annals of Congress, 4th Cong., 2d Sess., 2104-2105.

had received eighty-three thousand dollars in two years to supply his household; but Macon immediately replied with the question, "What sort of money?" Which was enough to call to mind the picture of the worthless Continental paper which went begging everywhere at that time, and in which the officer in question had been paid. He added a little later, when Smith, of New Hampshire was trying to convince the members how small a sum had been asked, "I do not know how it can require fourteen thousand dollars to repair furniture which at first cost only thirteen thousand." The bill passed, though, by a vote of sixty-three to twenty-seven, all the North Carolina delegates, good farmers that they were, voting with the minority.[101]

The opposition of Macon to almost all appropriation bills had given him something of a name already, and it drew to him all those simple-lived men like himself who represented the small farmer districts in the South and West. His opposition was such that most of those who disagreed with him took pains in their speeches to refer respectfully to his arguments. There was a tendency from the very beginning of the new government to extravagance; the members of Congress managed their mileage so adroitly that it amounted to more than a third of their pay for a whole session's attendance. Twenty-six thousand for mileage and seventy-six thousand for attendance on the session showed how men could manage to increase their bills against the government when there was a fair excuse. No man scrutinized these items of expense more closely than the plain gentleman from Buck Spring, who never in his life presented an account to the government for a dollar more than he would have expected from an individual.[102]

The extra session of Congress convened by a proclamation of President Adams in May, 1797, for the purpose of putting the country in a state of defence, was disappointing in the extreme to the Federalists, who desired to organize an artillery corps, to strengthen fortifications and call out more men to man them, to build nine ships of war, and to provide for a provisional army, subject to the President's call. In short, a strong Federalist program was offered, calling for a general system of taxation. This system was to take the form of duties on imported wines and liquors, on salt and paper, parchment, etc.[103]

---

101 Annals of Congress, 4th Cong., 2nd Sess., 2307-2319.
102 Letter of Macon to the North Carolina Assembly, Nov. 14, 1828.
103 Annals of Congress, 5th Cong., Extra Sess., 390; Schouler, I., 366.

Macon opposed the fortifications as unnecessary, recommending the removal of men in the well-equipped forts to the weaker and endangered ones. But contrary to what might have been expected of such a staunch States' rights man, he favored the unqualified granting by the States to the United States of the lands on which forts were built. At the time this extreme friend of State sovereignty was acting rather liberally, the representatives of the extremely national State of Massachusetts refused to grant to the general government the possession of her fortifications, refusing also to accept supplies from any outside source.[104] Macon furthermore opposed the equipment of additional artillery corps, and would not think of supporting the measure for a provincial army, but favored as a substitute, a bill calling on the States for a national militia. A bill looking towards this end was proposed by Blount and McDowell, members from North Carolina, and heartily approved by their colleagues.[105] This measure was meant as a means of defence which should at the same time not be subject entirely to the orders of the President, or, in other words, its advocates would avoid the establishment of an odious standing army, which it was claimed the Federalists desired. On the subject of increasing the navy, Macon was not to be moved, no matter how threatening the attitude of foreign powers; and, when the bill for calling into service some large frigates seemed about to pass, he offered a substitute for a clause of the bill which directed the President to use the proposed ships of war wherever his judgment directed. The Macon substitute, which was first ruled out of order but finally accepted, prescribed the use to which the vessels should be put, i.e., the President was not to send them outside of American waters except as convoys to trading vessels in threatened seas. In a short time he changed his opinion about the convoying of fleets of trading vessels, opposing the plan altogether, lest that be used as an excuse for sending the warships abroad; as it finally appeared, then, the new frigates, the number of which was reduced to three instead of nine, as formerly called for, were not under any conditions to leave the American coasts. This was tying the President's hands with a vengeance, and when the bill came before the Senate it was almost immediately returned with this clause rejected. The Senate also objected to the other Republican features of the measure. A compromise on the amended parts of the bill was fi-

---

104 Annals of Congress, 5th Cong., Extra Sess., 302.
105 Annals of Congress, 5th Cong., Extra Sess., 322 on.

nally agreed upon, and the three ships, "*United States,*" "*Constitution*" and "*Constellation,*" were allowed to be built and placed at Adams' disposal in a restricted sense. These ships became the nucleus of our navy,[106] and did fine service against England in the war of 1812-1815.

Considerable sectional feeling was manifested in the debates on these amendments. The Republicans opposed the Federalist program, because it granted protection to trade which, as they said, was chiefly a private interest, and therefore not a subject for national legislation. The Eastern members of the House were enraged at the determined resistance of Republicans south and west, claiming that it was a narrow agrarian policy which actuated their opponents. Samuel Sewall, of Massachusetts, declared: "Gentlemen who depend upon agriculture for everything, need not put themselves to the expense of protecting the commerce of the country; commerce is able to protect itself if they will only suffer it to do so. Let those States which live by commerce be separated from the confederacy. I have in mind those people who live by commerce, and I can not concede that they live by the mere good-will of the Union. Let them be abandoned, but let it be done before they are reduced to poverty and wretchedness. Their collected industry and property are equal to their own protection, and let other parts of the confederacy take care of themselves." To which Macon replied that was such language as he had never before heard in the House.[107]

Sewall was ruled out of order, but he was the only man who was strictly in order. The two parties had been at daggers drawn for weeks, but no one confessed the real cause of their dispute until Sewall could contain himself no longer and spoke out his thoughts. From the very day the government went into operation, even long before, the line of cleavage between parties had been drawn by agriculture and commerce, the two conflicting interests of the country. The establishment of an agricultural aristocracy, if the word must be used in describing men of affairs in those days, or the establishment of a commercial aristocracy, were the questions at issue. The Constitution itself represented a drawn battle between these forces, and as soon as it became the highest law of the land, binding alike on both parties, each began seeking allies to strengthen itself in order to gain control of the government and interpret in its own interest the instru-

---

106 Annals of Congress, 5th Cong., Extra Sess., 364-366; Schouler I., 366.
107 Annals of Congress, 5th Cong., Extra Sess., 385.

ment of their compromise; commerce sought, through Hamilton, the aid of capitalized wealth; agriculture opposed, and rallied to itself the powerful influences of democratic ideas which were at that time epidemic throughout the western world. England, the commercial country of Europe, naturally came to the help of her elder daughter, New England, and with this came necessarily the revival of the essentially English political institutions in America, and the building up of an English party; France, the hereditary foe of England, attempted a similar alliance with the South, and so men formed Jacobin clubs and wore the red cockade — Federalist vs. Republican parties. These two forces met together in Pennsylvania — the recruiting field for both — and the final outcome of the election of 1796 had depended on the turn the struggle took there amongst a motley population of Connecticutt Yankees, Virginia backwoodsmen, English Quakers and South German Protestants.[108] When Washington, the great neutral character in National politics, retired in 1797, the way was cleared, and both parties began the race for a victory in 1800. Macon was one who had wished Washington well in his retirement, and was evidently not unwilling to see him out of the way. This extra session of the Fifth Congress was one stage on the way toward 1800, and all the debating and hot words about ships, armies and tariff duties were not so much directed for and against Adams as for and against the creed he stood for — commercialism. Sewall named the real subject in dispute, the control of the government, which was to come out again and again in Macon's political life and under the most different names: War with England, National Banks and Protective Tariff, Slavery, Nullification, and finally, twenty-five years after his death, Civil War and Reconstruction — victory of an economic principle and not of idealism and agitation.

---

108 Annual Register, 1796, p. 90.

President John Adams

CHAPTER X.
MACON AND THE FEDERALIST SUPREMACY, 1797-1801.

The Federalists came together at the beginning of the regular session of Congress, in November, 1797, determined to have things their own way, and they had been partially united by the trend of events during the summer: France had been seizing New England ships on the high seas, and the Directory had refused to recognize Pinckney, the new American envoy, because he was "an aristocrat;" England, too, was still complicating the situation by the most ill-advised disregard of the rights of neutrals; Hamilton, the Federalist's beau ideal, had been forced into a confession of an adulterous connection with the wife of a worthless wretch employed at one time in the Treasury Department, in order to prove himself innocent of what he regarded as a worse crime, that of misappropriating public funds; Monroe had returned from France in disgrace, but was given a public dinner in Philadelphia, with the Governor and Chief Justice of Pennsylvania and other high officials attending; the violently partisan papers, the *Monitor* and the *Minerva*, the *Aurora* and the *National Gazette*, were keeping alive all the quarrels, scandals and animosities of angry politicians, and in the midst of all this and somewhat in triumphant dignity, sat Jefferson, the most hated opponent of the administration, secure in the Vice-President's chair, there to watch and profit by all the blunders of a majority none too well agreed among themselves. Still further, the Federalists felt the chagrin of failure at the last session — a failure caused also by the lack of unity and harmony in their own councils.[109]

And the Republicans were not better satisfied; one of their number, William Blount, of Tennessee, had been proven guilty of treason; the meddling of the French Minister Adet in political affairs, the indefensible behavior of France toward American seamen, and, besides, the shifting, vacillating policy of some of their own members in Congress, who, as Jefferson himself said, "governed by the panic or prowess of the moment, flapped as the breeze blew, now to the one side, now to the other."[110] And the disappointment and bitterness of parties increased when these disappointed men came together; for at

---
109 Schouler, I., 369-381.
110 Jefferson's Writings, June 1797; Schouler, I., 369-381.

that time the foreign dangers of the immediate future seemed suddenly to increase, while the failure of great business houses and the utter ruin of credit darkened the prospects of individuals and government alike. Robert Morris, the financial wizard of the Revolution, succumbed and was compelled to lie in the jails of Philadelphia for many long months because of inability to pay his debts. And to make matters worse in the eyes of decent people, these representatives of the people, at the very beginning of the session, fell to wrangling over the miserable and disgraceful personal encounter between two members: Griswold, Federalist, of Connecticut and Lyon, Republican, from Vermont. This encounter began with Lyon spitting in Griswold's face, in the presence of the whole House, was kept up by cuffs and blows, with canes and fire tongs, off and on for two days, and ended, after weeks of debate and vain attempts at expulsion, in the House finally binding both under oath to keep peace during the remainder of the session.

This was not an encouraging spectacle to the people who looked forward every day to dangers of the gravest kind; and the members themselves must have been heartily ashamed of coming together a month earlier than usual for the purpose of attending to the pressing affairs of the nation only to join in angry disputes and wranglings over a matter which would have excited only ridicule on the meanest street of the meanest town in the country. One month of time and thousands of dollars were spent in settling a dispute which any country magistrate could have settled in thirty minutes. It looked, indeed, to many as if partisanship were going to wreck the National Government; yet every man from the philosophic Gallatin down to the latest comer had a voice in this small business.

Macon took a lively interest in this Lyon affair, because, like the others, he saw that the opponents of Lyon were demanding his expulsion in order to get rid of a disagreeable Republican. Lyon had begun his career in Congress at the previous session by asking to be excused from joining the procession of the House to the President's house on the occasion of the reply to the annual message. At this session he asked rather impertinently to be excused again from waiting on the President, which brought on some sarcastic debate because, as some one remarked, this exception declared that the others were "making fools of themselves." Macon favored the granting of Lyon's request, because, as he said, the House waited on the President out of respect for that officer, and respect must always be voluntary, besides the

House had no power to compel a member to parade himself on the streets of Philadelphia. Later, when the vote for the expulsion of Lyon for his insult to Griswold, which certainly was provoked, was about to be taken, Macon declared the punishment too great for the offense, that he would as soon be hanged as expelled in that way from a seat in the House,[111] but after the second encounter between Lyon and Griswold, brought on by the latter, he favored the expulsion of both members, which, however, could not be done, since a two-thirds vote is required to expel, which neither party had; and besides the Federalists were not willing to pair Griswold with Lyon, who, to be sure, made a sorry figure among his aristocratic friends from Virginia.

The first speech of considerable length Macon made in Congress was on the Nicholas resolution for curtailing the expense of foreign intercourse. Adams had called for a larger sum than usual for that item of the budget; he had secured a recommendation from Washington to the Senate that his son, John Quincy, a briefless attorney, only twenty-four years old, should be appointed Minister to Prussia, and the Senate had approved, but the country was not convinced that merit alone actuated the President. Nicholas, of Virginia, moved a resolution for retrenchment by abolishing the post at Berlin and reducing the allowances for other diplomatic establishments. Macon declared, what was no doubt true to him, that all the foreign ministers who had been in this country from July 4, 1776, to his day had done more harm than ours abroad had done good; that he was almost ready to abolish the foreign establishments altogether; he had heard it declared that Jefferson's disappointment in the recent election had inspired Nicholas motion, and that the Southerners were supporting that sentiment of the Vice-President, that these Southern Republicans were even attempting to overthrow the Government. "I will not," he continued, "boast of what the Southern States have done, but certainly I may say what they have not done: they have not been promoters of banks, funding and excise systems, Stamp Acts, and so forth." He closed by asserting that the House had a right to regulate the salaries of foreign ministers, though it could not be denied the President had the sole prerogative of saying to what courts they should be sent. It was the authority to *originate and lay taxes* by the House which he cited in this case, as he had done in the Jay treaty controversy a year before. The larger portion of the speech, however, dealt with the

---

111 Annals of Congress, 5th Cong., 2nd Sess., 962, 1008.

charges of partisanship on the one side or the other, which he thought a disgrace to the House. Adams' disposition to appoint only Federalists to office, Macon criticized as a flagrant abuse of power. He opposed the appointing of men to office except on the grounds of merit and capacity to serve the public.[112] Later on we shall see that he modified, though very modestly indeed, this policy. Nicholas' resolution was finally defeated by a majority of four votes, one member only of the North Carolina delegation voting with the majority.[113]

While the two parties were measuring arms in the House, and the measures of Government were dragging heavily along under the great burden of political animosity, a new issue was preparing. March 5, 1798, Adams, thoroughly disappointed at the treatment his representatives had received at the hands of Talleyrand, and convinced that his olive branch of the preceding spring was about to be returned unaccepted, sent a message to Congress which let it clearly be seen that war was not only probable in the near future, but the fixed policy of the administration.[114] Fourteen days later he warned the House that a bold, united front should be shown to France; "zeal, vigor and concert in defence of the national rights, proportioned to the danger with which we are threatened."

The Cabinet decided on a declaration of war, published the President's message with the correspondence of the envoys, which caused intense excitement throughout the land. The Federalists, with Hamilton's assistance, began to press measures calling for ten more ships of war, an increase of the army to fifty thousand besides the militia; efficient fortifications, a new revenue system, and the abrogation of the treaty of 1778 with France. The Senate readily assented to all the plans of the Executive. Outside influence which should overcome all opposition was again, as in 1796, to be brought to bear on the House. The Republican's following Jefferson's advice, recommended an adjournment, in order that they might learn the will of the people; but the Senate scouted the idea. The opponents of war with France held a caucus, and outlined a policy, which Spriggs, of Maryland, offered in the House on the 23rd of March: (1) It was inexpedient to bring on war with France; (2) arming merchant vessels ought to be restricted; (3) protection of sea coasts and internal defence should be adequately provided for — small concessions indeed to the majority. In order the

---

112 Annals of Congress, 5th Cong., 2nd Sess., 1111-1113,
113 Annals of Congress, 5th Cong., 2nd Sess., 1234.
114 Annals of Congress, 5th Cong., 2nd Sess., 1201.

more completely to overwhelm the Republicans and set them in the wrong before the people, the Federalists in the House called on the President for the secret correspondence bearing on the treatment of the American ministers in Paris. The Cabinet readily responded, and the X Y Z papers were given to the world.[115] These papers proved conclusively that France had attempted to bribe the American government into supporting that country against England. The administration at once became popular and received the heartiest assurances of support from all parts of the country. The President became enthusiastic as a boy, and enjoyed to heart's content the returning popularity, which was not undeserved, and which he so much coveted.

Macon's share in the lively debates which followed was comparatively small. Before the excitement was full grown, and when the question of building and equipping a navy was being discussed under the head of protection to trade, he made a second set speech on the subject, in which he said if the Federalists desired war, let a declaration of war be proposed, and men would know how to vote; "for a fighting peace our measures are too strong, and for war too weak. Some strange charges have been made against men who are desirous of preserving the peace as long as possible, such as being under the French influence. These charges are not made to have an influence here, but out of doors, where the characters of persons charged are not known. Gentlemen talk about compelling Congress to act. If one were to be compelled to act, of what use was it for his constituents to send him here. I assure that gentleman (Dana, of Connecticut) that I will not be compelled to act (referring to outside influence)."[116] He thus resented again and again the charges that members of his party were under the influence of French diplomats — as for himself he had "never known a half dozen Frenchmen." When the bill for a provisional army was before the House, he spoke once more, recurring to his favorite militia plan, which he declared to be amply sufficient in any crisis. He was highly indignant at the plan of sending troops into the Southern States where, it was charged, there were neither troops nor disposition to raise them.[117]

Gallatin, one of the noblest men on the floor of the House, and perhaps the ablest, had now become leader of the Republicans. He had outshone Madison as a speaker, and as a logical thinker he was

---

115 Schouler, I., 398-399.
116 Annals of Congress, 5th Cong., 2nd Sess., 1506-1507.
117 Annals of Congress, 5th Cong., 2nd Sess., 1537.

equal to all the intricate financiering schemes of Hamilton, and of Wolcott, his agent and protege. When Madison, on Jefferson's elevation to the Vice-President's chair, had retired to the Virginia Legislature, there to keep that State true to "Republicanism," as Jefferson insisted on saying, "until the people could be aroused to a sense of their danger," he had taken up officially the leadership of the opposition. Gallatin was a Genevese who had emigrated to this country before the Revolution, fought for the Americans, was afterwards elected to the United States Senate, where he was refused admittance because he was not a Federalist; elected in 1795 to the House, he soon became influential, and was now the powerful champion of the opinions which the Vice-President could not, by the nature of his office, advocate in the Senate. Macon seems to have acquired a respect and admiration for this Republican friend from Pennsylvania which he never lost, and which, as will be seen further on, ripened into a life-long intimacy. But the opposition was unable to stem the tide which was setting in against it, no matter how able and determined its leaders. The war spirit was abroad in the land, and those who remember the foolish doings and sayings of the people just prior to the Spanish-American war, will not fail to appreciate its influence: "Towns and private societies, grand juries, militia companies, merchant organizations and the Cincinnati" held boisterous meetings, made out long petitions to Congress and sent congratulatory addresses to the President. It became dangerous for a Frenchman to appear on the streets in the large cities, and any man suspected of holding Jacobin opinions was an object of aversion. An address of the young men of Philadelphia, with five thousand signatures, was borne to Adams at the head of a procession of twelve hundred enthusiasts for war; *Hail Columbia* was composed at this time, and became as popular as *After the Ball* in our day, which so many of us remember with regret; Boston went beside itself over the song of "Adams and Liberty," and the students of Harvard college toasted General Suwarrow, as the Russian messenger of freedom! Jefferson said it was impossible for a Republican to appear on the streets of Philadelphia without danger of personal insult, and that in private social circles leading members of Congress were ostracized because they voted "against the government." The "rogue's march" was played under the Vice-President's window at night. It is not surprising that these influences told on the votes of the opposition; some yielded, others absented themselves from the sessions. By the middle of May all the main measures of the Administration were carried.

Macon's speeches against these measures were in general defensive; at times he was rather personal, though never offensive, even when he was an object of constant attack on the part of the New England members; he was always politic and apparently always cool-headed, while those around him were ofttimes beside themselves with anger and excitement.

While the Federalist majority was carrying every thing its own way, and holding indignation meetings over their opponents, whom they regarded as completely overthrown, some resolutions of another nature were presented by Josiah Parker, of Virginia. They were from a company of grenadiers of Portsmouth. After a preamble, in which the Virginia Declaration of Rights and one's duty to posterity were duly touched upon, it said "we view with extreme concern the attempts that are evidently making by men high in authority to widen the breach between the United States and the French Republic, by holding up to the good people of these States the late unworthy propositions of certain unauthorized persons at Paris, as the act of the French Government, when in reality the face of the despatches can not warrant any such conclusions.

"That we can not but view the man, or any set of men, as inimical to the rights of the people, and the sound principle of self-government, who shall endeavor, by any false coloring, to give the stamp of authenticity to that which in itself is extremely doubtful and problematical; and who shall, by such means, strive to involve us all in the calamities of war with the most powerful republic on earth." Then follow resolutions against an alliance with England, which the war would necessarily bring; against lavish expenditure in a free government; in favor of a well-regulated militia "composed of the body of the people, which is the proper, natural and safe defence of a free state;" another endorsing all "wise and patriotic measures of defence" passed by the last Congress, and still another declaring what would seem strange at any other stage in our history, that "in case of actual invasion we hold it to be the duty of all good citizens and militiamen to rally round the standard of government, and to defend our rights against all encroachments whatever." The resolutions close with an order that "copy of these proceedings be forwarded to our Representative in Congress, with positive instructions for it to be laid by him before that body as the sense of their meeting."[118]

---

118 Annals of Congress, 6th Cong., 2nd Sess., 1707-1708.

These resolves embrace the policy of the Southern Republicans, and were more than likely inspired from Philadelphia. In addition, however, to denouncing the party in power and its leaders, toward the close, we see the refutation of the charges so commonly made on the floor of Congress that the Republicans were such good friends of France that in case of war they would not defend their country. The resolutions declare, in answer to these charges, that only in case of actual *invasion* does it become the duty of all good citizens to take up arms, which is no other than saying that the sea warfare of the Government, or any expedition against French possessions on this continent would not be supported. The last words of the resolutions are characteristic of the fierce Republicanism of that day: that "their Representative be *ordered* to lay these proceedings before Congress — a theory which was so universally accepted in North Carolina in 1792 and 1795 as to have caused the recall of the State's first and ablest Senators — Johnston and Hawkins — chiefly because they ignored the right of the people to instruct.

When these Portsmouth resolves were read in the House, the Federalists desired to burn them publicly. Sitgreaves, the extreme advocate of warlike measures, was in favor of rejecting them as a libel on the Government; while Brooks, of New York, said "why do they (the Republican supporters of such resolutions) not come forward and impeach the President. I can scarcely believe that such illiberal and scandalous abuse could proceed from any other than vicious dispositions." And Dana but expressed the views of his party when he declared that to refer these libellous statements to a committee and to allow them to become the basis of a resolution would be charging the President and Senate with almost treasonable behavior. The Republicans admitted the improper language of the resolutions, but insisted on their being received and referred. Gallatin made a speech insisting on the reference of all petitions without debate, and Macon claimed that this was the first instance where even a *reference of petitions* was opposed. "In the case of the British treaty, addresses had been received on both sides of the question, couched in very strong terms indeed. It would be imprudent at a time like the present when all believe this country is in danger, to reject addresses from persons well attached to the Government, merely on the ground of etiquette. And furthermore, our Constitution guarantees the people the right of petition, without defining the manner in which they shall do it, and this right we can not abridge. Again, the refusal to give fair consideration to the Portsmouth petitioners would be tantamount to acknowledging that the House was afraid of investigation" — a rather plain hit at its opponents. The resolutions were finally received and referred to a committee which consigned them to oblivion successfully enough.

Toward the end of May, as the war spirit continued to rise, the Federalists became more and more aggressive: they were anxious to lay hands on those liberal, perhaps extreme, advocates of democratic government, who were of foreign descent; and they began by directing legislation toward a series of naturalization laws, which should require a foreigner to live in the country five years before he might ask for papers looking toward citizenship, and fourteen years before he should finally acquire the rights of a citizen; that all foreigners not already citizens are "liable to be arrested as suspected persons." Gallatin began his customary roll of shrewd amendment and obstruction, but he was voted down regularly by majorities of one or two votes. Macon assisted the Pennsylvanian, and offered a plea for "the great body of persons who live remote from centres of information, and who, entirely ignorant of all this excitement against them, are innocently pursuing their callings, expecting to become citizens at the expiration of the old term of five years. The new measure would press hardly on such people, and without their having been in any way deserving of ill treatment." But no speeches could check the onward course of the supporters of the Administration. Gallatin himself had been refused his seat in a Federalist Senate; why not so construct a bill now as to drive him out of the House, which had also fallen into their hands? Harper, of South Carolina, had found the able Genevan democrat a most objectionable opponent, and in the honesty of his American soul he declared "it is high time for us to recover from the mistake with which we set out under the Constitution of admitting foreigners to citizenship; for nothing but *birth* should entitle a man to citizenship, and we ought so to declare it." And Otis, a kinsman of the greater Otis of 1769, offered a resolution which was a source of only partial satisfaction to the South Carolinian, requiring that no alien-born should hereafter hold office under the United States. The zeal of Gallatin's enemies happily was cooled by a reminder that the Constitution itself spoke out on the subject, and so they had to accustom themselves to looking without becoming nauseated upon quiet, genteel-looking Mr. Gallatin, occupying his post of leadership on the opposite side of the House.[119]

---

119 Annals of Congress, 5th Cong., 2nd Sess., 1776 on.

As the bill finally became a law by a vote of forty-six to forty-four, on May 23, it gave the president absolute powers over the large class of people in the country designated by Congress (1) as Alien friends, and (2) as Alien enemies. Alien friends he could banish without assigning cause, and failing to observe the Presidential order to leave the country, the Executive could consign them to jail for three years, while the right of citizenship was thereby forfeited forever. And this, the Federalist vengeance still insisted, might be followed by forcible deportation. If a Frenchman or a Dutchman who had been ordered away returned without permission, he was subject to imprisonment and hard labor for life. So much for alien friends. Alien enemies were to be apprehended whenever and wherever the president chose, and to be treated as he thought best. Let us hope it was not much worse than the treatment accorded to alien friends. Those who gave shelter or comfort to alien enemies, according to medieval precedent, might likewise be seized and imprisoned. Well might Gallatin and his friends begin to look to their own cases, lest by associating with Doctor Cooper or the eminent French scientist, Volney, both friends of theirs, they themselves wake up some morning in a Philadelphia jail.

Two days after the alien law was enacted, a new bill for the "more effectual protection of commerce" came up — the same that had given occasion to Sewall's threat to secede from the Union at the extra session a year before. Macon claimed that these "Resolutions for the further Protection of Trade" brought in by Sitgreaves were equivalent to a declaration of war against France, and he moved an amendment declaring war on all nations whose treatment of our trading vessels was the same as that complained of from France. Provocation sufficient for a formal declaration of war had been repeatedly given by "more than one nation during the past two years. If it must come, let us be just to all alike." He added that peace even under the insolent treatment from foreign ships of war was preferable to war: "our trade and our revenue are continually increasing." Which was true. The American carrying trade, thanks to the bold New England ship builders and sailors, was then second only to that of England. New England towns were becoming rich in times of war, like those of Holland in 1580-1600, when all the greater states of Europe were at war; their traders were to be seen on every shore driving hard bargains with the natives. Macon insisted on peace for the benefit then of the South, which did not desire war, and which found its best market for its enormous tobacco crop in France. He asked at that stage of affairs a postponement of action until a further report from the Paris commissioners could be received. Harper replied by accusing Macon of inconsistency, and others censured him severely for desiring so to amend the resolution of Mr. Sitgreaves as to make them a declaration of war against both France and England. Macon answered these criticisms when the House took up the report of the Committee of the Whole, saying that "instead of blaming him, the gentleman ought to be obliged to him for giving them opportunity of making studied speeches, which they otherwise could not have done," a remark, to be sure, too trivial for the occasion. To the statement of Harper that Macon's amendment gave the lie to his former sentiments, he returned a rather sharp but courteous rebuke: "It is the gentleman's custom to speak thus." The Speaker called him to order for the first time since he had been a member of Congress, when he went so far as to state that in the Revolutionary war no man east of the Delaware had ever been seen fighting in the Southern States, and that now the South was willing to be left alone. He declared that the country was divided in political sentiment geographically, and would always remain so; that there were sections which always opposed each other, but that this, like every State and county in the Union, did not signify a lack of patriotism, and that statements to that effect made in the House were directed only to the galleries. After rehearsing the ills suffered under the British policy of impressment, he renewed his demand that war should be made on all foreign countries alike, if at all; and he knew only too well if there were any danger of England's being threatened by the bill as amended, it would never pass. Bayard, of New Jersey, followed with the final speech on the Macon amendment, in which the latter was again the object of considerable animus. Bayard entered into a lengthy justification of Great Britain's policy toward America since the signing of the Treaty of Paris, and eulogized the country which, he said, out of pure love for us! convoyed our trading vessels from their ports all the way across the Atlantic to keep them from falling into the hands of the French. Macon's motion was lost, seventy to twenty, the twenty supporters being those extreme anti-English Republicans like himself and Matthew Locke, of North Carolina, old General Sumpter, of South Carolina, and the good Dutchman, Van Cortlandt, of New York.[120] This resolution of Macon's and its rejection show him even at that time one of those independents who so often disconcert party plans and measures.

---

120 Annals of Congress, 5th Cong., 2nd Sess., 1815-1827.

A letter of his,[121] dated May 24, shows his private opinion of the bill he had just been opposing: "An act passed both Houses of the legislature yesterday, which, in my opinion, amounts to a declaration of war against the French Republic, and I have no doubt but the president will approve it early tomorrow, so that it will be a law as soon as possible." On May 30 he laid before the House a resolution for adjournment on June 14 — his plan being, of course, to escape Federalist legislation and at the same time get back to his plantation. In the letter above referred to, he said: "You ask when I expect to be at home; it is not possible to form at this day any correct opinion as to the time, though I hope to be there in all the next month" — hopes consistent enough with his motion, but not with the wishes of the majority of the House. At the time of this writing the Direct Taxation plan, often suggested before this time by the leaders of the opposition themselves, was before the House. Macon neither favored nor opposed it in this letter to his friend: "No new tax law has yet passed, though the large appropriations that have been made will render one necessary, it is expected, and a bill is before the House of R. laying a direct tax on land, houses and slaves, to be apportioned among the States according to the rule prescribed in the Constitution of the United States."

When this bill came up, Macon proposed to change it so that all improvements aside from dwelling-houses — the specific object of taxation after land contemplated in the bill — should be taxed. This change he based on the claims of common justice that every species of property should bear its proportion of the burdens of government. Gallatin took the same view, and the motion to strike out the clause to which Macon objected passed. Instead of the adjournment which Macon pressed to a vote and lost, thirty-four to thirty-two, Congress remained in session through the month of June and far into July. On the 5th of July, the Senate bill for the "Punishment of Crime" was brought in by the Federalists. It provided that "if any person shall unlawfully combine or conspire together with intent to oppose any measure of the Government of the United States, or to impede the operation of any law, or to intimidate or prevent any person holding office under the Government from exercising his trust;[122] if any person shall, by writing, printing or speaking, threaten such officer,

---

121 Macon to Roger Bigelow of Warren County, N.C., May 24, 1798.
122 One is reminded here of the experience of the English in the attempt to enforce the Stamp Act.

* * * he shall be deemed guilty of a high misdemeanor, and punished by a fine, on conviction, not exceeding five thousand dollars, and by imprisonment not less than six months nor exceeding five years. If any person shall, by any libelous or scandalous writing, printing, publishing or speaking, traduce or defame the legislature of the United States, * * * with intent to create a belief in the citizens thereof that the said legislature, in enacting any law, was induced thereto by motives hostile to the Constitution or liberties and happiness of the people thereof; or shall in any manner aforesaid traduce or defame the President of the United States, or any Court, or Judge thereof, the person so offending, being convicted, shall be punished by a fine not exceeding two thousand dollars and by imprisonment not exceeding two years."

The best comment from both points of view on the introduction of this bill into the House appears in the first motions made: Otis, Federalist, that it be read a second time; Harrison, Republican, that the amendments to the Constitution be read. When a determined opposition was at once manifested, the Federalists betrayed a chief cause of this legislation: their animosity toward the leading Republican journals. Allen, of Connecticut, said: "Let gentlemen look at certain papers printed in this city and elsewhere, and ask themselves whether an unwarrantable and dangerous combination does not exist to overturn and ruin the Government by publishing the most shameless falsehoods against the representatives of the people of all denominations, that they are hostile to free government and genuine liberty, and of course to the welfare of the country; that they ought, therefore, to be displaced, and that the people ought to raise an *insurrection* against the Government." He then read paragraphs from the *Aurora*, organ of the Republicans; charged the Republicans in and out of the House with being in a conspiracy with Gerry, the supposed *Republican* member of the French commission, their agent in Paris, to treat with France in spite of the Government; and coming back to the newspapers again, he quotes the *Aurora* as saying: "The period is now at hand when it will be a question difficult to determine whether there is more safety and liberty to be enjoyed at Constantinople or Philadelphia." Livingston was charged with making war on the Government through the same paper, and "this infamous printer follows him with the tocsin of insurrection. Can gentlemen hear these things and lie quietly on their pillows? Are these approaches to revolution and Jacobinic domination to be observed with the eye of meek submission? No, sir, they are indeed terrible; they are calculated to freeze the blood in our veins. Such liberty of the press and of opinion is calculated to destroy all confidence between man and man; it cuts asunder every ligament that unites man to his fellows, man to his neighbor, man to society, man to government. God deliver us from such liberty!"[123] Harper, in a moderate manner, went over the same ground, asserting that libelous speeches had been made in the House, and libelous letters were being written from it to many parts of the country. He favored the measure, and with him was the cooler-headed portion of the Federalist party.

Macon spoke somewhat at length in opposition to the Senate's Sedition bill: It was in direct opposition to the Constitution and if Congress could pass a law to abridge the liberty of the press, it could pass a law establishing a state religion; if the Constitution be violated in one respect, it may as well be violated in others. "Laws of restraint, like this, always operate in a contrary direction from that which they are intended to take. The people suspect something is not right when free discussion is feared by government, They know that truth is not afraid of investigation." Calling to mind the methods of 1776 he said, "if people are so dissatisfied as men claim, this law will force them to combine; they will establish corresponding societies throughout the Union, and communications will be made in secret instead of publicly. I believe the people may be as safely trusted with free discussion as they whom they have chosen to do their business." In reply to Otis' statement that the proposed bill was not different from the common law of the land, he went to the heart of the thing, for Otis had said the States had prosecuted the people for libel in just such cases: "let the States continue to punish, when necessary, licentiousness of the press." But that was a power which the National Government desired to usurp in order to punish those whom the States ignored and in many cases encouraged. Allen of New York had said that Republican papers claimed the Federalists were seeking to destroy the liberty of the press. "The passage of this bill," said Macon, "will cause a hundred such charges to be made where there is now one." As to Bache's paper, the *Aurora*, he asserted, and rightly, that *Cobbott's*, the Federalist organ, was equally licentious, and that he, Macon, depended on the "lies in the one paper to be counteracted by the lies in another of the opposing party." This very practical speech was concluded by a warning

---

123 Annals of Congress, 5th Cong., 2nd Sess., 2092-2101.

to his opponents not to seek their precedents beyond the water, referring, of course, to Pitt's recent measures against the Liberalist press in England; that "conditions in America are so different as to make all imitations failures; the people in our country understand their State and Federal governments, are jealous of any encroachments of the one upon the other; they are extremely jealous of their liberty as freemen ought to be."[124]

After the original bill had been modified by allowing the truth as evidence in the courts in favor of the defendant, and the operation of the proposed measure limited to two years, which improvements passed in the one instance by the vote of the Speaker and in the other by a very small majority, the report of the Committee of the Whole came before the House for a final decision and Macon again spoke against it: (1) by citing the first amendment to the Constitution, and asking, "How can so plain language be misunderstood or interpreted into consistency with the bill before us; (2) this very subject had come up in the conventions which adopted the Constitution and every advocate of the General Government had denied that, even without the amendments, prosecutions for libel could be made under its authority, or that the full and complete freedom of the press could be abridged, except through State interference." Quoting from the debates in the North Carolina Convention, and from Judge Iredell's argument, he made a strong point against his opponents. Iredell was then a violent Federalist and a Judge of the Supreme Court; he had said at Hillsboro, in the North Carolina Convention: "Where is the power given them to do this? They (Congress) have power to define and punish piracies and felonies committed on the high seas and offenses against the law of nations; but they have no power to define any other crime whatever * * *. They can claim no other but such as are so enumerated." (3) Then he cited the opinions of members of Congress when the amendments were passed and they were unanimously against any such measures as were then before the House; and, "how is it come to pass, notwithstanding all the positive opinions which I have quoted to the contrary, that Congress should now conceive that they have power to pass laws on this subject?" (4) As to the policy of such action, he believed it bad, that the States had heretofore exercised jurisdiction in this matter and that any lack of confidence expressed in the State governments was dangerous. *"This Government*

---

124 Annals of Congress, 5th Cong., 2nd Sess., 2105-2106.

depends upon the State Legislatures for existence. They have only to refuse to elect Senators to Congress and all is gone." It was a vain hope he expressed as he took his seat: "but if there be a majority determined to pass it, I can only hope that the judges (the Supreme Court) will exercise the power placed in them of determining the law an unconstitutional law, if, upon scrutiny, they find it to be so."[125]

This speech of Macon's contains his political creed, so far as the relation of the States to the National Constitution and vice versa is concerned. It is all a very simple matter; the nation is an emanation, of the State governments and entirely dependent on them. His opinion, both as to the constitutionality and the expediency of the Sedition laws as expressed above, have been shown to be entirely correct; within four years but few of the Federalists would have disputed this with him.

It is not necessary here to discuss a policy which has been admitted by all students of our history to have been an egregious blunder on the part of the party which took it up. The object of the Federalists was to muzzle public opinion, and since the State governments were not to be counted on to cooperate, they usurped powers which had not been granted.

When Macon suggested that the States alone had the punishment of libel and of the so-called sedition in their control, he touched upon the "heart of the matter;" the persons aimed at in the law lived in States which were not likely to interfere with an occasional or even daily castigation of the Federalists in the public prints. From Pennsylvania south, including South Carolina even, there was neither a court nor a grand jury which could be depended on to punish these offenders against Eastern ideas of political propriety. The National Government, on the contrary, was then in the hands of the party which had erected it, and this party was looking for an opportunity to teach the people the wholesome lesson of respectful authority and dutiful silence in matters which little concerned them: the management of a nation, its finance, its laws, its wars. "The people," to the leading Federalists, were "a great beast," whose business it was to pay taxes, fight in the wars, be obedient to the laws and forever hold their peace; they existed for the benefit of "friends of government," for the "intelligent and educated classes." And as to the bounds set by the Constitution, especially those obnoxious amendments, which were the product of

---

125 Annals of Congress, 5th Cong., 2nd Sess., 2151-2152.

those very "people" who now disputed with the Federalists the path to national glory, they were not over scrupulous. All that Macon said was to them but an echo of that violent opposition which burst forth in 1788 in the Southern States against the Constitution in its original form; his arguments convinced some perhaps of the unconstitutionality of their bill, judged by the amendments; but the amendments themselves were unconstitutional.[126] What gave the dominant party the assurance to go to such extremes as the acts of this session of Congress committed them was the constantly rising of the tide of excitement against France, rather in favor of a Jingoistic nationalism, with commercialism in the saddle. Adams could not understand popular sentiment, nor keep his head in the midst of popular applause. One single remonstrance against the administration came from the people during that long session, while thousands of addresses poured into the President's office endorsing his spirited action. This excitement increased as the summer of 1798 came on: May 8th was appointed by the President as day of National fasting and prayer, though he himself did not believe particularly in prayer, and the people gathered in the churches, as they had done in 1776, to listen to political harangues from the pulpit. On July 4th the American spirit reached its climax, "the revolutionary watch-fires were kindled at the old altar; the native-born of the North sported the black cockade, and Tallyrand, the apostate Bishop of Autun, was burned in effigy."[127] And all this came just at the time when then Naturalization, the Alien and Sedition laws were passing. How could it be other than overwhelming public approval? It was on the 5th of July that Allen made his long speech of indictment against the public press, that Harper demanded the passage of the last great Federalist measure of repression and Otis grew hot with anger as he contemplated the villainy of these "Jacobin leaders" in the House of Representatives itself. What availed the speeches and protests of Livingston, notwithstanding "his respectable connections," of Gallatin and Macon! The bill passed on July 10th and the majority adjourned in songs of jubilee, anticipating sweeping elections in their favor; while the Republicans resting on their oars, "repaired to their respective Legislatures," as Jefferson said, leaving a few of the faithful on the watch in Philadelphia, while they, the retiring members, were to bring up the sober opinions of the people when they came again to Congress.

---

126 Compare Schouler, I., 409-410.
127 Schouler, I., 400.

Macon had enough to contemplate as he returned on horseback to his plantation on the Roanoke about the middle of July. While war was imminent, and the President, in obedience to the acts of Congress, was organizing a large army with Washington as Commander-in-Chief, North Carolina supported vigorously the measures of the administration. Davie, a leading Federalist, of Halifax, was appointed a Brigadier General and was given the power to name all the new army officers from his State, provided he selected "only good Federalists," as Washington instructed him.[128] The elections came on soon after the adjournment of Congress and the Federalists gained control of the Legislature by a small majority. Davie was sent to the House again after years of absence, and Samuel Johnston to the Senate. John Macon was defeated in Warren for the first time in his life and Willie Jones, too, had failed to represent and satisfy public opinion in Halifax; Timothy Bloodworth, the wizard of Wilmington politics, was scarce heard of, so completely had the storm of enthusiasm turned in favor of his opponents. The defeat of the Republicans was general, but the dissatisfaction with their actions was not great enough, however, to return to the United States Senate Alexander Martin, because of having voted in favor of the Alien and Sedition laws. Martin had been elected to the Senate as a successor to Samuel Johnston in 1792 because of his Republican principles. When everything seemed to be going to suit the wishes of the Federalists he had changed his policy and had voted for the Alien and Sedition laws. Martin was defeated in 1798 in the Legislature by Jesse Franklin, a second Macon in politics. Bloodworth, his colleague in the Senate, remained firm in his Republican policy and received the endorsement of the Legislature. Notwithstanding the decidedly anti-Republican turn of the North Carolina elections, its delegation in Congress was expressly instructed by the Legislature to labor for the repeal of the principal Federalist measures of the past session — the Alien and Sedition laws. The North Carolina Federalists drew a distinction between Adams' foreign and domestic policies; the former they heartily approved, while the latter was as heartily opposed.[129] These actions show the mild character of the policy of the conservatives and the ultra-conservatives in North Carolina. To reward the Federalists, Adams nominated Governor Davie as envoy to France in September, 1799, and Benjamin Smith, a

---

128 Washington to Davie, *Washington's Works*, (Sparks), XI., 336.
129 House Journals N.C. Assembly, 1798, 76-77.

Federalist and the Speaker of the Senate, succeeded him. But Smith was soon followed in office by Benjamin Williams, of Moore, an unassuming Democrat, and from this time the Senate steadily turned again to a hearty support of the Jeffersonian leaders. Nothing did more to weaken the party in that State than the appointment of Davie.

While the elections all over the country were going against the Republicans and the rank and file of the Federalists were still jubilant over their victory, the two leaders of these opposing parties in the nation were laying significant plans for the future:

(1) Jefferson gave letters of introduction to good Doctor Logan, who was going abroad on a personal mission, for the reestablishment of friendly relations between France and the United States. These letters gave Logan a semi-official character in Paris, and most of the influential leaders there regarded him as a representative of the Republican influence in Philadelphia. Gerry's departure from Paris a few days before Logan's arrival was such as to leave the way well paved for the beginning of better diplomatic relations. Merlin and Talleyrand received the benevolent Philadelphia Quaker with abundant affection; he was feted as an envoy from the "States favorable to the French interests," *i.e.* from the South. In a short time he returned to America with assurances of peace and knocked at the door of the Department of State, naively thinking his message would be joyfully received; but stern Mr. Pickering kept it barred against him. Logan then payed a visit to Washington, who was then in the city on a mission of war, only to meet a more "icy reception." On the President his story made a more favorable impression. Adams had been spending the summer at Quincy and his old friend Gerry had been talking to him about French affairs, and with the result that the president had returned to Philadelphia just before the meeting of Congress firmly resolved to send another envoy to France. This olive branch the Quaker had brought came to him in good time; it was the result of Jefferson's influence brought to bear in a most extraordinary way, viewed in the light of present diplomatic practice.[130]

(2) Hamilton's plan was of a different nature: the South American colonies of Spain were in a mood for revolt, which has been a constant quantity with them ever since; France and Spain had mutually guaranteed each other's possessions in that quarter of the globe, and

---

130 *Washington's Works*, XI., 384-385; Schouler, I., 426-429.

the two powers were, moreover, otherwise too amicable to please the English cabinet. What better stroke could be made than to strike Spain at her most vulnerable point. Hence when John Miranda, an able South American Revolutionist, asked assistance about this time in London, a grand scheme of conquest began to take shape. Rufus King, the American ambassador at the Court of St. James, was at once approached, and he in turn approached Hamilton. Hamilton, Pickering's political mentor, opened secret correspondence with the Department of State in Philadelphia. Adams was not to know anything of the plan, which was to lend assistance to Miranda, until it was fully developed and prevented in such a way that he could be coerced into compliance. This was all begun at the same time the warlike measures toward France were first being pressed in Congress. The plan was this: war was to be declared against France, Pickering was to pick a quarrel with Spain, Washington was to be given nominal command of our army while Hamilton was to be its actual head. Our navy, which was having such a struggle to get itself born into the world, should guard our coasts, while England, coming to the assistance of America, was to send a great fleet against South America with which our army should cooperate. In case the expedition prove successful the United States were to receive the Floridas and all of Spanish Louisiana *east* of the Mississippi; England was to have undisputed possession of the West Indies and exclusive rights across the isthmus of Panama and both Anglo-Saxon nations were to be perpetual allies. Pitt, King, Hamilton, Pickering and perhaps Harper of South Carolina were the promoters of the plan, and all the leading Federalists were cooperating with Hamilton without knowing just what was to be undertaken. The organization of the army during the summer, and the inflammable disposition of France gave promise that the opportunity for active operations would soon come. Miranda wrote Hamilton late in October: "All is ready for your president to give the word."[131]

When Congress assembled in December, and when it was ready to hear the President's address, Washington, Hamilton and Pinckney, the ranking generals in the new army, appeared and took their seats on the right of the Speaker's chair; to the left sat the British and Portuguese ministers with their secretaries — an array of dignity and authority imposing enough to make obstinate Republicans think more than once before opposing the measures of administration.[132] The

---

131 See Rufus King's Correspondance, 1797-1798; Schouler, I., 422-424.
132 Annals of Congress, 5th Cong., 3rd Sess., 2420.

schemes of the two astute political leaders above described were bearing heavily from both directions on the president, but as yet he had yielded to neither and in his message he was still bellicose, though decidedly in favor of the navy as opposed to the army, which was not only natural but which showed that some inkling of the schemes of his faithless Cabinet and political rival in the army had come to his knowledge. Preparations for war went on and the intrigues of the Federalist leaders continued to complicate our foreign relations; yet none but the initiated suspected what an explosion was to come in Congress on February 18th following.

If Macon experienced any joy in seeing his opponents in straights he had ample opportunity from the very beginning of that short session to indulge himself. Harper's first move in the House was for getting twenty thousand copies of the Alien and Sedition laws printed for distribution among the people, who he declared were being worked upon and woefully deceived by designing people interested in the humiliation of the Government. He had heard some of the complaints which were beginning to come in from all parts of the country and he was very desirous of giving the people opportunity for a "correct understanding of the laws" to which objection was being made. Macon's friend, Claiborne of Tennessee, replied by moving a resolution for publishing forty thousand copies of the Constitution to be sent out at the same time as the copies of the Alien laws. Macon spoke favorably to Claiborne's motion, referring in a tantalizing way to the prevailing *ignorance* concerning the Constitution in the most *populous* sections of the country. Claiborne's resolution blocked the way to Harper's so completely that neither passed.

Doctor Logan was to escape but narrowly a much more serious result of his activity in Paris than the coldness of Washington and the closed doors of the State Department. A resolution was brought into Congress, which would have had him hanged as a traitor for going to Paris and bringing back a peace message, and would have brought Jefferson, the Vice-President, before the bar of the Senate on the charge of conspiring with traitors. Griswold, having seen what a successful case his friend Sitgreaves had made out against Blount in getting him expelled from the Senate, which to be sure was richly deserved, was ready to try what could be done with the arch-enemy of Federalism for having given countenance to and been in correspondence with

Logan.[133] Macon made his first speech in favor of Jefferson during the angry debate on this resolution. He said in part: "I have heard a great hue and cry against a French party in this country. If such a party exists, why can they not be pointed out? It might as well be said that there is a British party in this country. I believe there exists full as much reason for saying the one as the Other. * * * British subjects and British capital are seen from one end of the continent to the other. And will not this capital and these persons produce a British interest? The diplomatic skill of France is continually preached up. It has been clearly shown that they have never discovered any of this skill in sending ministers here. But to speak out my opinion I believe the British have discovered more diplomatic skill in this country than any other nation, and that the present British minister has shown more of it than any other. * * *

"It has been said that certain gentlemen high in authority in this country are privy to the departure of the gentleman who was lately in France. For aught I know, these gentlemen may have named him. But it is a little extraordinary that in our discussion on this floor, we should be talking of an officer in our government (Jefferson) being a traitor. Such kind of language can have no other effect but to create suspicions in the minds of people that this man is an enemy to this country. This does not look much like a wish to conciliate differences of opinion, but the contrary. If gentlemen possess proof of any malconduct in the person particularly alluded to, it is their duty to bring it for ward and put him from the situation in which he was placed; and if any such should be brought, no man would be more desirous of seeing him displaced than I should. But if no such proof exists, it is a strange way of supporting the constituted authorities thus to calumniate a man whom the people have thought proper to place in so high a position.

"* * * I see no good to be answered by this law; I can not see how an individual can usurp the authority of the Executive (which was the charge against Logan) * * *. If we were even in a state of war, and an individual could prevail upon our enemy to offer such terms of peace as our Government would be willing to accept, it would be a good thing. I can not conceive of a situation in which such a law as is proposed can operate; and I believe our Government is as firmly fixed as the land we live on."

---

133 Annals of Congress, 5th Cong., 3rd Sess., 2493 on.

The resolution against which Macon was contending passed and Griswold was named chairman of a special committee to bring in a suitable bill, which was reported in the Committee of the Whole a few days later. The proposed law was aimed directly to fit the case of Logan and Jefferson and to go into effect immediately. The penalty was to be a heavy fine and imprisonment. Gallatin and Macon attempted so to amend the bill that Logan might escape but to no effect.[134] Logan became the object of most virulent abuse in the papers and of weeks of debate in Congress. January 14th it was so threatening that he published a letter in the papers explaining his situation in Paris and declaring that he never usurped or supported any official character while in the French capital. So far as his motives were concerned no one had reason to complain. He had undertaken an independent mission to Paris with the aim of bringing about peace between the two countries, hardly suspecting that it would be other than welcome news he should bring back, if his enterprise should prove successful. Jefferson's motives were equally honorable, though his countenancing such a scheme as Logan's can not be understood other than as an attempt to frustrate what he regarded as a positive policy of the administration. Macon saw nothing wrong in anyone's going abroad on a mission of peace and did not deny that the leaders of his party had countenanced Logan. Had Logan been sent as an avowed representative of leading Republicans, so long as the aim was honorable and clearly for the benefit of the people, Macon could not see in it anything reprehensible. The measure became a law,[135] but no prosecution was undertaken because the Federalists soon had so much trouble in their own camp that there was little time left for the punishment of such a powerful opponent as the vice-president.

From the beginning of this session of Congress petitions against the Alien and Sedition laws were pouring in. On January 31st petitions from New York and Pennsylvania, signed by more than four thousand persons, were presented. This continued through the month of February, but with the result of making the Federalists only the more dogged in their support of the questionable legislation. Such petitions were to them proofs of the perverseness of the people. Debate after debate followed as these expressions of universal dissatisfaction piled up on the table of the House. It will be remembered that the North Carolina delegation was expressly instructed to work for the

---

134 Annals of Congress, 5th Cong., 3rd Sess., 2725.
135 Annals of Congress, 5th Cong., 3rd Sess., 2721, also 3795.

repeal of the unpopular laws. Macon spoke often, and sometimes with intense partisan spirit, for the referring of the petitions and for a repeal of the laws.

Jefferson had proposed a still more effective way of bringing outside influence to bear. The legislatures of the States were to pass formal resolutions against the Alien and Sedition acts. He wrote a series of reserves which were sent to Kentucky in November and which were soon carried through the Assembly of that State and sent to the other States for endorsement. These resolutions contained the gist of the Republican platform of that time and they became a sort of final word in the arguments of States' Rights men from that time until 1860. They simply declared the Constitution to be a *compact* between sovereign States which are individually the judges of the infraction of the same, that a State may legally withdraw from the Union or refuse to observe a law of Congress which it believes unconstitutional. These resolutions were presented to the North Carolina Assembly during the next year and "voted under the table," as Madison said.[136] They were during the present session of Congress giving the New England legislatures opportunity for endless abuse of the men who favored them. They influenced Hamilton, too, to make his extraordinary proposition for dividing the States. Hamilton's ideas were promptly brought to bear on Congress by his friends in the debates of this session.

On the subject of the French relations progress was singularly slow. The Republicans had been calling for the reports of our envoys since the opening of the session, and especially for the later despatches of Gerry, which were known to be of a more friendly nature than the preceding ones.

These documents had been in Pickering's hands since October, but since they were not likely to fan the embers of war into flames, the Secretary of State was preparing a report on them to suit his and, Hamilton's ends. Hamilton had made known his plans to Dayton, Speaker of the House, to Gunn and Otis: (1) that war with France was to be brought on as soon as possible, to which end Congress was to go on increasing the army and navy; (2) that a division of the great States in such a way as to weaken the force of their opposition was necessary; (3) that the Alien laws should be more strictly enforced. "Why," he asked, "are not these renegade Aliens connected with some

---

136 Madison's Works, II., 152.

of these (Republican) presses sent away? These laws should not be a dead letter."[137] Hamilton was becoming impatient with the delay of the war and was helping Pickering "touch up" his message on the French question so that Congress and the country would be excited into an immediate declaration of hostilities. A despatch which came from France about the beginning of the session informing the State Department that the most obnoxious of their laws concerning us had been repealed was not suffered to be made public. This dispatch announced that the French Government had repealed its law authorizing the seizure as pirates of all Americans who were found on the enemy's ships.[138] Pickering did all he could to get Hamilton's ideas expressed officially to the House, but Adams had grown unmanageable, and he gave the Secretary's message, a chaste pruning down, remarking at the time, "I am not going to send to Congress a phillipic against Mr. Gerry." Still the administration kept up a show of war, and apparently endorsed Otis' resolution of January 18th, which demanded a suspension of all diplomatic relations with France. While Otis was speaking the long looked-for documents were brought into the House, and after three hours of reading, a motion was made for publishing them and especially Pickering's opinions. This paper of Pickering's was meant chiefly as a campaign document. Macon staunchly opposed the suspension of formal relations with France because the outlook for peace was more promising than ever before; and the resolution ordering all the State Department documents, with Pickering's commentary, printed, he opposed in his characteristic way: "I object because it is not founded in custom; let the official papers in this instance as formerly go out to the people as heretofore. They went without comment and so should these. I do not think there is any occasion to direct the people how to think. *I believe the great body of them will always think right if left to themselves.* Was it because former communications (on this subject) looked more like war than these, that they were given to the people without commentary; and, that because these have the appearance of peace, it is necessary to twist them to look a contrary way?"[139]

---

137 Schouler, I., 438-439.
138 This and other practices of both France and England of that day show only too clearly that American Independence was not acknowledged by the European powers.
139 Annals of Congress, 5th Cong., 3rd Sess., 2736.

The wrangling in the House and the intriguing in the Cabinet were still going on when Adams, casting all but the real interest of the country to the winds, threw a bomb into the Senate by nominating, on February 18th, William Vans Murray, then Minister in Holland, Minister Plenipotentiary to the French republic. On the same day Sedgwick, then a member of the Senate, having some fears, it seems, that Adams was about to break bounds, had gone to the President asking his opinion of Hamilton's army measures. The President said: "If you must have an army, I will give it to you; but remember it will make the government more unpopular than all *their* other acts. The people have submitted with more patience than any people ever did, to the burden of taxes, which have been liberally laid on, but their patience will not last always." And a moment later Adams asked what additional authority the Senate meant to give Washington. Sedgwick somewhat demurely replied: "None, all that has been proposed is to give him a new title — that of General" (Hamilton desired to be Lieutenant-General). Adams: "What! Are you going to appoint him general over the President? I have not been so blind but I have seen a combined effort among those who call themselves friends of government, to annihilate the essential powers given to the President." Hamilton was in Philadelphia at the time and Sedgwick went at once to report to him Adams' ill humor. The Federalists were expecting some difficulty with their President, but that he would destroy at one blow all their schemes by sending another representative to Paris was a bolder step than they thought his love of office would allow him to take. In order to conciliate the Senate Adams finally added Patrick Henry and Chief Justice Ellsworth to the nomination. Henry declined to serve and Governor Davie of North Carolina, as has been noted, was sent in his stead.

This independent move of Adams deserved for him a better reward than he ever received. It kept the nation from entering into an alliance with England against Revolutionary France, from entering into those very entangling alliances against which Washington had so earnestly warned Congress two years before. It dismayed and disconcerted the Federalists for a while; still the President did not allow preparations for war to relax and so the large appropriations were all voted. And in defiance of public opinion the salaries of public officials were liberally increased. Adams hastened away to Quincy at the close of Congress, leaving his disgruntled Cabinet at Hamilton's beck and call. An army of officers without companies and ensigns of a navy on paper drew their salaries regularly and having nothing to do they were very much in evidence about Philadelphia. Hamilton and King still urged the President to allow the Miranda expedition to be entered upon, and the sharp encounter between the French and the American naval vessels, *L'Insurgente* and *Constellation*, gave ample opportunity for beginning war in earnest.

On the dissolution of the Merlin Directory Pickering and Hamilton made a last attempt to undo what the President had done toward bringing about more peaceable relations, by delaying the departure of our Commissioners. Message after message was hastened off to Quincy to get the order for a suspension; Cabot, Senator from Massachusetts, was sent to see Adams in person. Pickering, Wolcott and McHenry, of the Cabinet, threatened to take matters into their own hands. Stoddard, true to Adams as he was, suggested to him a speedy return to Philadelphia. The President came at once and met the Cabinet in Trenton, its temporary headquarters. Hamilton and Ellsworth were there, which still further excited the jealousy of Adams and determined him on sending off the Commissioners at once. Next morning at daybreak, *i. e.*, October 15, 1799, he sent Pickering peremptory orders for the Commissioners to depart for France. Hamilton hastened to see the President in order to dissuade him from this final step, but to no avail.

During this summer and autumn the State elections in Pennsylvania, the Fries riots in the same State, and the tumult of the Sedition lawsuits, all tended to discourage the dominant party. Adams alone had reason for satisfaction in the staunch personal support of New England in the autumn elections. Lyon was prosecuted for sedition and cast into prison; the editor of a Republican paper, the *New London Bee*, in Connecticut, was also imprisoned; Duane, of the *Aurora*, was arrested on a warrant issued for him before the Sedition act became law, so anxious were the Federalists to punish him. Judge Chase rode the southern circuit and sought out the enemies of his party to administer them a wholesome chastisement so that Virginia and North Carolina were beginning to tire of the men they had so enthusiastically endorsed a year before.

It was not then a discouraging outlook for the Republicans when they met in Congress December 2, 1799. Their opponents were divided into Eastern and Southern wings. John Marshall of Virginia was dubious of the constitutionality of the Alien and Sedition laws, as were Ames and Sedgwick of the true Federalism of any man who opposed them. The majority of the party in power was overwhelmingly nominally, but when test votes were taken in matters that affected seriously the interest of the South the Federalists found it a greater difficulty than ever to keep their new members in line.

In the organization of the Sixth Congress, Macon developed unexpected strength for the Speakership; it was only by a majority of six that his old competitor, Sedgwick, now returned to the House, was chosen over him.[140] Since he became the leader of the North Carolina delegation in 1795, Macon had been steadily gaining in popularity; during the extra session of 1797 he was constantly referred to on matters of unfinished business of the previous session. The previous practice of the House in almost all important cases he remembered and stated on occasion; for the saving of time and the expedition of measures his suggestions had become more and more apt.[141] He had developed, too, as keen a sense of precedent as if he had been an English parliamentarian. Speakers were chosen then for their ability as moderators, for their judicious trend of mind and their knowledge of parliamentary practice, all of which Macon possessed in so eminent a degree as to be the undisputed choice of his party. This session was important in Macon's career because he then for the first time met that extraordinary young man from "up the Roanoke," who was to exert more influence over Macon's future life than any other person ever did, and who was in turn to be more influenced by him than by any other. This was John Randolph, not yet "of Roanoke." Macon had made a short speech against a proposed change in the census law and soon afterward that youthful figure arose and in a strangely fascinating voice addressed some remarks to the House in agreement with what Macon had said. Randolph was only twenty-six years old and looked still younger; he had attained notoriety a year before this time by making a three hours harangue at Charlotte Court House in Virginia against the aged Henry; he had been defeated for the Assembly by his distinguished opponent, but had won such distinction in the campaign of 1798 that he was sent the next year to Congress. John Randolph was a man who could not pass through a street without attracting all eyes to himself. One who knew him has left us the following description: "His long thin legs, about as thick as a stout walking cane, and of much the same shape, were encased in a pair of tight, small clothes, so tight that they seemed part and parcel of the limbs

---

140 Annals of Congress, 6th Cong., 1st Sess., 186.
141 Annals of Congress, 5th Cong., 1st Sess., 238.

of the wearer. Handsome white stockings were fastened with great tidiness at the knees by a small gold buckle, and over them, coming about halfway up the calf, were a pair of what I believe are called hose, coarse and country-knit * * *. He trod like an Indian, without turning his toes out, but planking them down straight ahead. It was the fashion of those days to wear a fan-tailed coat with a small collar, and buttons far apart behind, and few on the breast. Mr. Randolph's were the reverse of all this, and instead of his coat being fan-tailed, it was what Knights of the Needle call swallow-tailed * * *. His waist was remarkably slender, so slender that, as he stood with his arms akimbo, he could easily, as I thought, with his long bony fingers have spanned it * * *. About his neck he wore a large white cravat, in which his chin was occasionally buried as he moved his head in conversation; no shirt collar was perceptible; every other person seemed to pride himself on the size of his, as they wore them large. Mr. Randolph's complexion was precisely that of a mummy; withered, saffron, dry, and bloodless; you could not have placed a pin's point on his face where you would not have touched a wrinkle. His lips were thin and compressed and colorless; the chin, beardless as a boy's, was broad for the size of his face, which was small; his nose was straight, with nothing remarkable in it, except, perhaps, it was too short. He wore a fur cap, which he took off, standing a few moments uncovered. I observed that his head was quite small, a characteristic which is said to have marked many men of talent * * *. Mr. Randolph's hair was remarkably fine — fine as an infant's and thin; it was very long, and was parted with great care on the top of the head, and was tied behind with a bit of black ribbon, about three inches from his neck; the whole of it formed a queue no thicker than the little finger of a delicate girl. His forehead was low with no bumpology about it; but his eye, though sunken, was startling in its glance. It was not an eye of profound, but of impulsive and passionate thought, with an expression at times such as physicians describe to be that of insanity; but an insanity which seemed to quicken, not to destroy intellectual acuteness. I never beheld an eye that struck me more. He lifted his long, bony finger impressively as he conversed, and jesticulated with it in a peculiar manner."[142]

Whether Macon had ever met Randolph before the opening of Congress, there is no means of telling. It is not improbable, however,

---

142 F. W. Thomas: *Character Sketches: Randolph*, 14-16.

that he had heard of the impertinent youth and kinsman of Jefferson, who had met Patrick Henry in debate and had not come off worsted, for all these remarkable men lived in adjoining districts and were almost neighbors in that day of hard riding. But if Macon had never heard of the man, the second speech he made, of only one short paragraph, was sufficient to invite his friendship. A petition of "free blacks" — the very words were objectionable to Macon — had been presented to the House by Mr. Wain of Pennsylvania. After some debate, the new member from Virginia began to rise from his seat, gradually unfolding his long-jointed limbs until it appeared there was no end to his length. When he was fully erect he declared that no encouragement whatever should be given to such petitions, and he hoped that this would be "the last time the business of the House would be entered upon, and the interests and feelings of the Southern States be put in jeopardy, by similar applications." It was beyond the power of the House and he thought it might be so declared once for all. Such a speech as this went straight to Macon's heart. This was surely no compromising Virginia Federalist who had come into Congress by the political eruptions of the past year. The yeas and nays on this "embarrassing question" were taken once and then only on the part of the petition calling for legislative relief from Congress. It was decided by a vote of eighty-five to one that Congress had no constitutional powers whatever to deal with the subject. The one dissenter was George Thatcher of Massachusetts.

The third time Randolph took any part in the debates completed, as it appears, the probationary state of their almost life-long friendship. With all hopes of the war gone the Federalists, it appears, would have ceased calling for appropriations. On the contrary additional expenditure was asked, and, when Nicholas introduced a resolution for a reduction of the army, it met with determined opposition. Macon made his usual speech along the line of "Retrenchment and reform." "Some people think borrowing five or six millions a trifling thing," he said. "We may leave it for our children to pay. This is unjust. If we contract a debt we ought to pay it, and not leave it to your children. What should we think of a father who would run in debt and leave it for his children to pay? But the want of money is not regarded. To be sure it is much easier to vote money than to lay taxes, because people do not directly feel the vote, but if taxed they must instantly know it; therefore loaning is the way most practiced. Notwithstanding the great increase of capital which the gentleman (Henry Lee) told us of, from eighteen to fifty millions, yet we have been obliged with all this increase to borrow money, and now are told we want somewhere about five millions more this year. We are told the people are fond of economy, this is true, and I think they will willingly pay all the taxes that we can convince them are necessary; but ought we not to save all the expenses which are not absolutely necessary ? * * * Another loan? We can not make money here by any means but work; labor is our only resource, therefore our money concerns ought to be well husbanded." And a little further, "If we get ourselves poor while the enemy is at a distance we shall be obliged to resort to enormous taxes if he should really come to our doors." The army was to him entirely useless. "Whenever an army is really wanted the patriotism of the people will always supply the emergency" — a militia, a good militia was everything "a free country" required. A little later Randolph arose to defend the resolution for the reduction of the army by ridiculing in his inimitable manner this *hireling* army, in a way which every Southern Republican must have enjoyed, and which Macon seems to have liked, though his own even-tempered nature would never have permitted him to say the same: "The military parade which meets the eye in almost every direction excites the gall of our citizens; they feel a just indignation at the sight of loungers, who live upon the public, who consume the fruits of their honest industry under the pretext of protecting them from a foreign yoke. They put no confidence, sir, in the protection of a handful of ragamuffins; they know that when danger comes they must meet it, and they only ask arms at your hands." After a rather long, but telling address, which seems to have made the Federalists wince, to which they were compelled, however, to listen, by his fascinating manner and startling wit, Randolph took his seat. He had said too much, perhaps, for some of his party, but all recognized in him a leader whose tongue was equal to the proverbial two-edged sword.[143]

That night Macon and Randolph went to the theater together and some young officers of the navy took occasion to resent in a personal way the epithet, *ragamuffin*, which had been so successfully applied in the speech of the afternoon. The officers came repeatedly into the box where Macon and Randolph were sitting, repeating at every opportunity the word "ragamuffin" until it was quite clear that some difficulty might be expected. Macon called the attention of Van Rensa-

---

143 Annals of Congress, 6th Cong., 1st Sess. 298.

laer, who sat near him, to the matter, and when the theater was over, Macon and his friends formed a sort of guard to see Randolph safely home. On descending the steps an attempt at personal violence was made, but Macon's stalwart form and big walking cane were sufficient to convince the young navy officers that a safe distance in the rear would be better for them. Randolph was escorted to his apartments. Next day he very unwisely laid the matter before the President and that, too, in a half-insulting manner. Adams humiliated Randolph by sending the letter at once to the House, where it was read publicly and not a little merriment was had at the expense of its author. A committee was appointed to investigate the subject and Macon was named a member of it, but he was, by special request, excused from serving. Nothing was done by the committee; but the ridiculous attitude into which this episode, especially the latter part of it, brought Randolph, did not lessen Macon's admiration for him. From this time on they were inseparable friends, though as different as two human beings could well be: Macon plain, ten years older, experienced in parliamentary practice, gifted with no powers of eloquence whatever, a staid judge in the halls of Congress; Randolph young, inexperienced, a brilliant wit and more brilliant orator and "proud as forty kings." On one point they were entirely agreed: *The State is everything in this American Union*. And this it was, that brought them to agree in most other things, and which caused them to call each other Davids and Jonathans and to spend weeks on each other's plantation during the intervals of Congress like school boys on their vacation trips.

Macon, faithful to the instructions from the North Carolina Assembly, introduced a resolution in Congress on January 23rd demanding the repeal of the Sedition law. It was as follows:

"Resolved, That the second section of the act, passed 14th of July, one thousand, seven hundred and ninety-eight, entitled an act in addition to an act, etc., * * * ought to be repealed; and the offences therein specified shall remain punishable as at common law."

Though the Federalists purposely interrupted him by laughing and talking, he proceeded at length to defend the resolution: (1) beyond a doubt this was not a subject over which the National Government had any authority, which, he claimed, was shown by the debates of the several State conventions, 1787-'88. To convince the House of this he quoted somewhat at length from the debates of these conventions. (2) It was good policy that any citizen be allowed absolute freedom to discuss every act of government, and that there was no other effective means for this but the press. "If elections are to be free, the people ought to have the liberty of freely investigating the character, conduct and ability of each candidate for any place of public trust." (3) The press is amongst the best gifts bestowed on man, its benefits are incalculable and if we had the power to touch it, prudence would dictate to us to do it with great caution. Bayard of Delaware made an amendment with intent to destroy the repealing resolution of Macon and supported his amendment with a long speech. The amendment was passed and Macon voted against his own motion in that emasculated form, so that the Sedition laws were left standing until they expired by limitation a year later.

At the opening of the second session of the Sixth Congress, Macon, in recognition of his ten years' opposition to almost all claims, was made Chairman of the Committee on Claims, and, as it used to be said of that honest German "Watchdog of the Treasury," Peter Hagner, the Second Auditor, it was indeed a deserving claim which ran the gauntlet of Macon's committee. Such a Chairman of the Committee on Claims in Washington at the beginning of the twentieth century would be a holy terror, would hardly escape lynching at the hands of hungry soldiers who never shot a gun. One of the first resolutions which came before the House at this session was that "a mausoleum of American granite and marble, in pyramid form, one hundred feet square at the base, and of a proportionate height, shall be erected in testimony of the love and gratitude of the citizens of the United States to George Washington." Macon distinguished himself unenviably by making a speech against the resolution, which, since it gave rise to much criticism of an adverse nature, deserves some special attention here. He opposed it (1) because the cost ($70,000, estimated) was too great: "I well know how hardly earned is the money from which this enormous (!) sum must proceed. But this is only a beginning; the final cost might be many times more. (2) I saw no good purpose likely to be answered by it under the sun. Can stones show gratitude? If the nation wished to show gratitude, let them do it by making an history of the life of Washington a school-book. Our children then will learn and imitate his virtues. This will be rendering the highest tribute to his fame, by making it the instrument of enlightening the mind and improving the heart." (3) This expending of millions, which he predicted would be the result, was "useless and pernicious ostentation." He then referred naively to Aristides and Hampden, saying no monuments had ever been erected to them, yet every man knew of their service. "Washington is admired and beloved by all. No one can be charged with a desire to diminish his fame by opposing a useless expenditure of money. The *precedent we now establish* will be auspicious to our future measures. If we decline raising a mausoleum to Washington, no man who succeeds him can ever expect one reared to his memory."

These are the principal grounds of Macon's opposition. Whether they were founded in generous and reasonable gratitude, the reader may determine for himself. They were principles of life with him, both in public and private things. His coterie of followers, rather the followers of Jefferson in the strictest sense, held the same views. It will be remembered that the Sage of Monticello made provision in his will directing that only a plain granite stone some six feet tall should mark his grave. And later it will be seen how extremely eccentric were Macon's own directions in this particular. He surely believed what he said in this opposition to Washington's monument; and most of his Republican colleagues agreed with him, as did the majority of his party at home. Randolph, too, opposed the Washington monument; but he spoke more in defence of his beloved Virginia than to the question under consideration. Virginians had been called vandals in the debates on this subject, and Williamsburg was pointed out as a place where they had torn down monuments erected to the dead. The bill making the necessary appropriations finally passed by a vote of forty-five to thirty-seven. Among the negatives appeared six North Carolinians, one an ex-Governor of the State who had done most to get the crowning work of Washington, the Constitution, adopted by his State.[144]

Instead of allowing the sedition law to die an easy death, the Federalists brought in a resolution this session to renew it. This was more than Macon could endure, and once more we find him contending with his superiors in debate for the liberty of the press. He went over the usual arguments, and preferred the customary charges against his opponents. Answering the taunt that he always found a measure unconstitutional when it did not agree with his policy, he said: "The answer to this question is very easy. There is another part of the House that never questions the constitutionality of anything; and if one part questions the constitutionality of everything, the other does not of anything; one side believes it has limits, the other believes it

---

144 Richard Dobbs Spaight.

has no limits." The Committee of the Whole, to which Macon spoke, reported favorably on the resolution, but only by the deciding vote of the Speaker. When the bill came up for a final reading, and after Jefferson's election had sealed the fate of the Federalists, it failed only by the opposing vote of some new members who had come in to take places accidentally made vacant.

This last speech of Macon on the sedition acts, shows more of partisanship than any of the previous ones, as it also shows him to be more conversant with the plans of his party and those of his opponents. During the ten years of constant service in the House, Macon had been steadily gaining in experience; he remembered perfectly its important precedents, and was recognized at this time as being the best informed member on the rules of every Congress since he had been attending. He was, by sheer force of character and by ten years of unflinching consistency, the leader, after Gallatin, of his party in the House. I have already pointed out that the bent of his mind was toward the judicial, which, as the House was then organized, and with its show of non-partisanship in the proceedings, had won him so nearly a majority of votes for the Speakership in 1799. When Macon made his first speech in Congress, he was scarcely listened to; now the leaders of the Federalists thought it necessary to oppose his arguments and to counteract his influence.[145]

---

145 Annals of Congress, 5th Cong., 2nd Sess., 966; note Dennis' reply to Macon; Schouler, I., 465.

John Randolph of Roanoke

CHAPTER XI THE REVOLUTION OF 1800.

The struggles of the two great parties described in the last chapters had aroused the country by the autumn of 1800 as it had never been before since 1776. Each party was doing its utmost to win in the coming contest. Jefferson directed the campaign of the Republicans from his seat at the head of the Senate, and in every State his lieutenants carried out these directions; copies of the Virginia and Kentucky Resolutions, as they were designated after the debates of Virginia on the subject in 1799, were sent out in great numbers; trials under the sedition laws were being used as object lessons, protests against the carrying of State law cases into the Federal Courts were drawn by Jefferson himself and after being assigned by the most prominent men in Virginia, they were published broadcast. Aaron Burr began the National campaign by carrying the city of New York for the Republicans. Gerry exerted a powerful influence for the rising party in Massachusetts. McKean and Mifflin, having gained the legislature of Pennsylvania for their party in the fall of 1799, were fanning the popular prejudice against the Federalists in that State by sending out handbills, which represented that Adams, if re-elected, would help Connecticut win in the great lawsuit then pending against Pennsylvania — claims for large indemnity arising out of the old Connecticut land patents. When Jefferson took his seat as Vice-President, in 1796, Madison had resigned from Congress in order to re-enter the Virginia Assembly for the purpose of keeping that great State true to the tenets of the Jefferson party. From 1796 to 1800 Madison managed Virginia as adroitly as Burr was managing New York, but without adopting such questionable means as have been charged against the latter. Monroe's sudden recall from Paris, in 1796, had been the means of greatly increasing the popularity of his party. Monroe was Jefferson's candidate for governor of Virginia in 1800, and he was elected. The Breckenridge and Nicholson families led in the Kentucky campaign for Jefferson; and Henry Clay, then a young man just entering politics, made speeches advocating Jefferson's election. South Carolina, still nominally under the control of the Federalists had been wrought upon by the maltreatment of John Rutledge because of his opposition to the Jay treaty; Washington had nominated him, in 1795, for a seat on the Supreme Court bench; but the Senate rejected the nomination because of a speech made in Charleston against the adoption of the celebrated treaty. Rutledge had been a friend of both

Washington and Jefferson. This affair carried him and all his connections over the Republicans. Edward Rutledge and Charles Pinckney were both taken into Jefferson's political correspondence. All of these, with others such as Gideon Granger of the hopelessly Federalist state of Connecticut, and brave old Sam Adams, of Massachusetts were constantly receiving Jefferson's winsome letters.

In the year 1796 there came to Philadelphia a man who had an influential role in the Revolution of 1800, a political refugee from Pitt's Alien and Sedition laws in England, young Joseph Gales, editor of the Sheffield *Register*. Gales was a sensible, well-educated man, whose newspaper had brought him more persecution than wealth. Finding it impossible for one of his political faith to edit a paper in peace under George III, he migrated to America, where he began again in Philadelphia; but to his surprise the City of Brotherly Love was a no safer place for him than Sheffieid had been. It would have been next to impossible for him to steer safely between the Scylla and Charybdis of Federalist and Republican politics in that chaldron of commotion. One day he met Nathaniel Macon, who apparently recognized the worth of the man and the difficulties of his situation, and at once recommended to him the establishment of a newspaper in the new North Carolina capital — Raleigh. Gales was pleased with the prospect, and in due time the old Sheffield *Register* became the Raleigh *Register*.[146] All the liberal ideas, which had brought confiscation of type and worse in old England, were brought along and soon became the permanent stock of the new Raleigh paper. Its editor at once took decided stand for good schools, good morals and *Republican* politics. Not a year had passed before good Mr. Gales had mortally offended Mr. Boylan, editor of the Federalist paper in the town, and the two met one day on Hillsboro street, and without let or hindrance from the police, fought out their differences to their own satisfaction. The source of the trouble was that Gales had espoused the cause of Jefferson and Macon in the state, and his paper had turned out to be a better one than the Republicans were supposed to be capable of establishing or supporting. The *Register* was arousing public opinion in North Carolina against the Adams administration. It published each week the accounts of prosecutions under the Sedition laws and gave full space to denunciations of a standing army, citing an example close at home in the shape of the Sixth U.S. Regiment, then encamped

---

146 Hudson: *Journalism in the United States*, 229.

in Raleigh two years after all danger of war was passed, which the Republicans thought was a sort of garrison to keep the Carolinians in subjection.[147] Besides, the editor of the *Register* managed to send his paper free to prospective converts to his party in all parts of the State.[148] Such was the work of Macon's young friend.

The operation of the Federal land tax was having its effect also on the voters of North Carolina country gentlemen. The *Register* claimed that it took directly from the people $200,000 a year for the purposes of the general government which amounted to more than one-third of the total annual exports of the State.[149] This no doubt is an exaggerated statement, for it is doubtful if more than sixty thousand a year was collected in North Carolina from the land tax. The Tories, who had been pardoned for their behavior in the Revolution and larger numbers still who had been open sympathizers with the British, but who had not become amenable to the law, all supported the Federalist party.[150] Judge Chase rode the Southern Circuit of the Supreme Court again in 1800, and gave such round abuse or partizan advice to the grand juries wherever he went, and consigned to jail or punishment with such heavy fines so many who were considered Republicans, that his party could not escape the charge of using the National judiciary for political purposes. The appointment of Davie in 1799 in place of Patrick Henry as envoy to France had been a graceful recognition of the enthusiastic support the North Carolina Federalists had given the president; but in the then so evenly balanced state of parties it was an unwise step. Davie, more than any other man, could have controlled the politics of the State in the interest of Adams. It will be remembered Davie had been chosen governor in 1798. The general practice of both parties was to retain a governor three years, which would certainly have been continued with so popular and able a man as Davie. This would have given the state a Federalist governor in 1800. The State Senate was still in their hands and the House was Republican by only a small majority. With Davie removed from the state, the balance of power fell to the party of Jefferson, a Republican governor — Benjamin Williams — having succeeded him. Jefferson would never have made such a blunder in his appointments.

---

147 Raleigh *Register*, July 29, 1800: Sept., 5, 1801.
148 Letter of Duncan Cameron to John Moore of Lincolnton, Sept. 1802.
149 Raleigh *Register*, July 29, 1800.
150 Judge Schenck: North Carolina, 1780-81: case of Duncan McFarland; See also Legislative Journals for 1802.

What share Macon had in the exciting campaign of 1800 can not be determined exactly, since so few records exist to show it. That he was the leader of the Republicans is shown by his correspondence with Jefferson during the following spring.[151] The president gave Macon the control of Federal patronage and called on him for nominations of men suitable for Federal appointments whether there were vacancies or not. And many years later Jefferson refers to Macon as one of those "old Republicans" who helped him save the country in 1800. Macon's assistance in the establishment of a strong Republican newspaper shows, too, how great an interest he had in the issues at stake.

The presidential electors were then regularly chosen in North Carolina by popular vote in the districts very much as at present. In view of the popularity of Jefferson the Federalist Senate and Governor in 1798 attempted to change the method of choosing electors so that they should be appointed by the Houses of the Assembly in joint session. This would probably have given Adams all of the electors, since the House was Republican by so small a majority; or if not all, certainly some of the body. The plan was clearly to prevent the will of the majority from being expressed. The Federalists had the example of Pennsylvania before them. There the Republicans carried the state by five thousand majority in the fall of 1799, but they failed to gain control of the Senate. The Senate refused to go into joint session with the Republican House for the purpose of choosing presidential electors, having determined to prevent the vote of the state from being cast at all. The House insisting that the people were with them clamored for a joint session until it became evident to the Senate that persistency in their policy would call down upon their party everlasting infamy. It yielded at last, but only by a compromise which gave Adams seven votes to Jefferson's eight, which was a neutralization of Pennsylvania's strength with the exception of one vote — this, too, when the governor and the House and a decided majority of the people were Republican. The same state of affairs existed in Raleigh after Davie's departure for France, except the law changing the manner of selecting electors had not passed and in Davie's stead there was a Republican governor. The slight Republican majority in the House defeated the new election law and so prevented the state from being neutralized at least to the same extent Pennsylvania had been.[152]

---

151 Macon to Jefferson, April 20 and 27, 1801, and Jefferson to Macon, May 4, 1801.
152 Compare Schouler, I., 492-493.

North Carolina, the plan of "capturing the legislature" failing, became the scene of a most lively popular excitement. In 1796 there had been but a single electoral vote cast for Adams, that of the Fayetteville district; but since that time a great Federalist rally had taken place; in 1797 Archibald Henderson "carried" the Salisbury district for the Federalists; in 1799 New Hanover and adjoining counties sent an Adams man to Congress and at the same time Joseph Dickson, of Duplin, prevailed in a similar way over the Republican candidate. So that there were four Federalists in the National House of Representatives at the time Macon was trying, with the help of his lively editor, Gales, to "carry" North Carolina for the Republicans. His undertaking was not an easy one. Madison wrote concerning North Carolina on December 29th, 1799: "But it is impossible to calculate the progress of delusion, especially in a state where it is said to be under systematic management, and where there is so little, either of system or of exertion to oppose it;"[153] and Jefferson's opinion of North Carolina politics, August 11, 1800, was: "The state of the public mind in North Carolina appears mysterious to us."[154] And it is interesting to note that the above named districts were for years to come faithful to the principles of Federalism; Fayetteville and Salisbury districts sent Federalists to Congress as long as there was a Federalist party and in the latter district Archibald Henderson acquired a kind of hereditary claim to a seat in Congress. When the election came off, the Republicans won six and the Federalists four of the electoral votes.[155]

The same practice of "capturing the legislature" prevailed in all parts of the Union. In Massachusetts, where there were two or three Republican districts, the legislature selected all sixteen of her electors from the Federalists; in New York a worse than Pennsylvania scheme would have succeeded but for Jay's patriotism and Burr's powers of manipulation; the vote of New Jersey, another close state, was given entire to Adams. South Carolina was divided also, and Hamilton, seeking by a shrewd maneuver to get Pinckney, candidate for vice-presidency, into the president's chair over Adams, the regular candidate, advised the Federalists to agree to a swapping of candidates, *i.e.*, to cast their eight votes *for Jefferson* and Pinckney. But Pinckney, true to Adams as he was, refused to cooperate in the dishonorable plan. The outcome was that the state voted for Jefferson and Burr, the regu-

---
153 Works, II., 152.
154 Writings, VII., 449.
155 Annals of Congress, 6th Cong., 2nd Sess., 1024.

lar Republican candidates. Virginia, North Carolina, and Maryland were the only states whose electors were chosen by popular vote in districts. And Maryland being evenly divided cast six votes for Adams and six for Jefferson. Virginia, under the control of Madison, Monroe, and Jefferson himself, cast all her votes for the Republican candidates.[156]

But with so many contingencies in the choice of electors in the state legislatures, there was no certainty as to the final outcome of the momentous campaign until late in December, when the returns all came in, and so the politicians were busy until the very last legislature had cast its vote. The announcement of a tie between Jefferson and Burr to both Houses on February 11, 1801, was the signal for the beginning of a second campaign of Federalist intrigue against the will of the majority plainly expressed. They meant to use Burr as an entering wedge; and he was too ambitious not to accept the presidency at the hands of his political opponents, could they but bring about a combination which would secure them the necessary majority. Burr had been vilified almost as much as Jefferson himself, and what was worse, he was believed to be dishonorable. The Federalists were ready to accept him in the hope that, owing his election to them, he would give them control of Federal patronage. The best commentary on the motives of the Federalists at this juncture is a letter from their leader, James A. Bayard, of Delaware, to Allen McLane, a Federal office holder in Wilmington, Delaware: "Mr. Jefferson is our President. Our opposition was continued till it was demonstrated that Burr would not be brought in, and even if he could, he meant to come in as a Democrat. In such case to evidence his sincerity *he must have swept every office* in the United States. I have direct information that Jefferson will not pursue this plan. The New England gentlemen came out and declared *they meant to go without a constitution* and take the risk of civil war. They agreed that those who would not agree to incur such an extremity ought to *secede without loss of time*. We pressed them to go with us and preserve unity in our measures. After great agitation and much heat they all agreed but one. But in consequence of his standing: out the others refused to abandon their old friend. Mr. Jay did not get a Federal vote. Vermont gave a vote by means of Morris' withdrawing. The same thing happened with Maryland and the votes of South Carolina and Delaware were blank. *I have taken good*

---

156 Annals of Congress, 6th Cong., 2nd Sess., 1024.

care of you and think if prudent you are safe."[157] A Virginia Federalist wrote some of his constituents for advice whom to vote for, as follows: "With respect to the two men who stand before us for the presidency, from the best information that I am able to get, in point of character and moral principles they are pretty equal; in point of talents, with a mind fearless of the boldest undertaking, Burr has greatly the superiority, and therefore abundantly the most dangerous * * *. Not being able to make up my mind as to which would be best I shall write to my friends and be governed by their opinions."[158]

One of his constituents wrote in reply: "Since I have seen the dangerous doctrine said to be advanced by Jefferson, I am induced decidedly to give the preference to Mr. Burr. Jefferson is less probable to be governed by *generous* principles than Mr. Burr." Colonel Francis Peyton, one of his most influential constituents, advised him to support Jefferson, since the election of the latter would have the effect of quieting things in Virginia. Thomas J. Page, of the same district, deplored the "dreadful alternative" of being compelled to choose between two such bad characters: "Burr's character is suspicious and Jefferson will destroy the support of our commerce. If Jefferson be chosen, not the smallest vestige of our navy will remain. Yet the people of our section all prefer him to Burr."[159]

From February 11 to February 17 this last and most serious struggle between the opposing sections of the country continued. Every means of defeating the popular will was resorted to, and at one stage of the conflict it was agreed among the Federalists to maintain the deadlock in the House until March 4th, when the Adams' administration would expire. This would have brought the government to an end and they counted on one of their own party to take the reins of government in hand; a bill passing Congress for that purpose, which would not have been improbable, since both houses were controlled by Federalist majorities. In case such a program had been adopted, Jefferson's counter-plan was a call of a new convention of States to be issued by the new Congress, called together by himself and Burr, the two candidates nearest the Presidency by the late election.

---

157 Bayard to MacLane, February 17, 1801. A copy of this letter may be found in the Macon MSS. in possession of Mrs. W. K. Martin of Richmond, Va.
158 Leven Powell, London County, Va., to Burr Powell, Jan. 12, 1801. The Leven Powell MSS. are in possession of Miss Rebecca Powell, Alexandria, Va.
159 Branch Historical Papers, I., 57-62, Randolph-Macon College, Va.

The intensest excitement prevailed throughout the country; special couriers were placed along the great road to the South via Alexandria, Richmond, and Weldon to carry the news from Washington. Caucuses of either party were held daily; wild reports were constantly circulating to the effect that Virginia and Pennsylvania militia were about to march on Washington or that now one, now another, of the leading Federalists was about to make a *coup d'etat*. In Virginia "the violent Dems," said Colonel Peyton "are determined to shoulder their muskets in case Jefferson or Burr is not elected." In North Carolina the excitement was not so great and no threats to rise in arms for Jefferson, so far as can be ascertained, were made.

Macon voted steadily for Jefferson on every ballot while four of his colleagues, Henderson, Hill, Dickson, and Grove, generally voted for Burr.[160] At the end of the thirty-sixth ballot, Macon wrote his friend Bigelow on the Roanoke:

"The House of Representatives this day made the 36 ballot for President, when Jefferson was elected by ten states.
"I am, Sir, yr most obt svt
                                        NATHL MACON."

Jefferson accordingly became President and Burr Vice-President, and they were peaceably inaugurated on the 4th of March following in the little city of Washington, whence the government had been transferred during the preceding summer. The few remaining days of the session after the Presidential election brought forward nothing new. Macon was present to the last to witness what he had so long wished and worked for — the inauguration of his friend Jefferson, from whom he expected everything possible in the way of good government. And after witnessing that extremely informal event and hearing the inaugural address with some dissatisfaction, he returned to his beloved Buck Spring.

---

160 Annals of Congress, 6th Cong., 2nd Sess., 1032.

CHAPTER XII.
REPUBLICAN SUPREMACY, 1801-1805.

Mention has already been made of the semi-dissatisfaction with which Macon heard some of the statements of Jefferson's short inaugural address. Scarce a month had passed before we find him inquiring of Jefferson directly what the country might expect. April 20, 23, and again May 1, Macon wrote concerning this subject. From Jefferson's reply[161] we learn in the main what had been Macon's inquiries. They were: What about the levees, a subject of some concern to the Southern republicans generally; How will communications from the President to Congress be made, Will the diplomatic corps be reduced? Can't the salaries of Custom House officers be cut down? And last, what changes do you propose to make in the army and navy establishments? Macon took the policy of his party seriously and meant that every promise of the past few years should now be fulfilled, and he was not quite sure about Jefferson's purpose now that he was elected. Another subject seems also to have been discussed in Macon's letters: What rules were to be observed in the appointments of the executive? And here the author shows himself a partisan, though a mild one. He does not think men who had assisted the British in the Revolution should be permitted to hold office under the government of the United States. The Federalists had been indifferent to this subject and, as will appear later, they had appointed men to office who had actually borne arms against America.

On May 14, Jefferson answered all Macon's inquiries: "Levees are done away; communications to Congress will be by message; the diplomatic corps will be reduced to three ministers; the army and navy will undergo a chaste reform; the salaries of Revenue officers depend on you the Representatives. We shall push you to the utmost in economy." Nothing more could have been desired, and we have no further record of Macon's fears for some time to come.

As to appointments, no foreigner, no Revolutionary Tory was to be given employment. And in response to a recommendation Macon had made in favor of the appointment of Henry Potter as district Judge in North Carolina, the President forwarded to Macon the commission,[162] asking him to insist upon Potter's acceptance: "Should it

---

161 Jefferson's Writings (Ford), VII: Letters of April and May, passim.
162 Macon to Jefferson, May 24, 1801.

be otherwise," he continued, "you must recommend some other good person. I had rather be guided by your opinion than that of the persons you referred me to …; let me receive a recommendation from you as quickly as possible, and in all cases when an office becomes vacant in your state, as the distance would occasion a great delay were you to wait to be consulted. I shall be much obliged to you to recommend the best characters. There is nothing I am so anxious about as making the best appointments." The policy then of the administration was in full accord with Macon's with regard to patronage, and what must have been flattering to himself, he was to name the Federal officers for North Carolina. And no man in the state would have been more likely to name the very best men. That this was no empty compliment of the President to one of his party lieutenants is shown by a second request of the same nature eighteen months later.[163] Macon succeeded in getting Potter to become United States Judge and wrote Jefferson, May 24, following : "In every recommendation I shall carefully endeavor to select such as can discharge the duty of the office, and *have been uniformly democratic, although I do not wish any person turned out of office,* who was a Whig in the Revolutionary war, for any opinions he may now hold, yet I would not recommend one for office who had not always been Republican." To illustrate how careful he was on the question of loyalty during the Revolution, he added in the same letter: "I have been informed that the collector at Edenton was, during the war, a New York-Long Island-Tory, but of the fact I have not sufficient information to speak positively. If it be so, ought he to be continued? The fact, I suppose, can be ascertained next winter in Washington." He was then in earnest about this part of his policy, and who among his opponents even could have censured him for this?

The letter concludes with the following information concerning North Carolina politics in the spring of 1801: "I am pretty well assured, that a systematic opposition may be expected. It was probably organized at Washington last winter. I have been a good deal about since my return, and find the feds, everywhere trying to impress their principles on the people, but without effect. General Davie is not returned. I shall endeavor to see him as soon as possible. I sincerely hope that he may be willing to undertake the negotiation with the Indians. Your acquaintance, Mr. Willie Jones, is, I fear not long for this world. He is unable to walk, and there is no probability that he

---

163 October 18, 1802.

ever will again." These few lines hint clearly at the policy of Jefferson as respects North Carolina. Davie, on his return from Paris, was to be offered an important commission. This was for the purpose of arranging treaties with the Indians of the Southwest and incidentally to weaken the opposition by gaining its most powerful leader. Macon was in formed of the plan and was delegated to visit Davie and urge him to accept. About the same time Jefferson wrote Benjamin Hawkins, an ardent Federalist who had lost caste in North Carolina in 1796, asking him to recommend fit persons for appointment to vacancies in North Carolina. The same request which had been made of Macon on May 14. This of course was an attempt to conciliate another powerful opposing influence in the South. Hawkins was won and he was continued many years in the lucrative office of Indian Commissioner to the Creek nation. Davie, too, accepted office under the new administration, but he did not give it his support. A year later[164] Macon saw Davie in Raleigh and had some conversation with him; but Davie was noncommittal. Macon was active during the summer of 1801 in finding out the political status of his State; he "went much among the people" and reported the prevailing sentiment. It was a touching reference he makes to the condition of his old captain of years gone by, Willie Jones: "I fear he is not long for this world." This is the only recorded reference I have been able to find bearing on the final end of that extraordinary man, except that he died about this time in Raleigh, where he had gone to live, and was buried in a field near the present site of the St. Augustine school for negroes, about a mile northeast of the Capitol. No stone, no inscription marks his resting place.

Congress assembled promptly that December, and on the first day of their session and on the first ballot Nathaniel Macon was elected Speaker. Schouler, in his history of the United States, says Macon "was a man of independent views and upright character, of frugal tendencies in public and private, not always in full sympathy with his party, but differing dispassionately when he differed at all; and so constantly re-elected, as in later years to be called the Father of the House."[165] These characteristics were in the main the cause of his election to the speakership. He had developed in Congress more of the character of a judge than of a party leader and a wise judge, too, and as has been noted in a former chapter, he knew the history of the

---

164 Macon to Jefferson, June 17, 1802.
165 Schouler, II., 20.

House, its precedents in all important measures; he had served ten years, had seldom been absent from his seat and had taken a decided stand in every debate which had come up during those years; he had done good work on various committees and had but once in his ten years in Congress been called to order by the Speaker; besides, he had the confidence of the President and consequently the support of the great Virginia delegation, especially that of the tall, sallow youth from up the Roanoke John Randolph. On the following day the new Speaker appointed young Randolph chairman of the Committee on Ways and Means. With Jefferson as President, Macon as Speaker of the House and Randolph at the head of the most important committee in Congress, genuine Republican measures and manners were sure to have the right of way in Washington; and the Republican political machine was in fine order, well oiled and ready for the fierce onslaughts, which every one expected. One head, one mind dominated that Congress and several succeeding ones, and for the time being there was smooth sailing for the ship of state.

Jefferson recommended in his message just what he had promised Macon on May 14, preceding — cutting down of expenditure and, what was not promised and what no President has since done, he greatly reduced the patronage of his own office; he dispersed all those miserable hangers-on for secret service money, and soon, with the help of his able Secretary of the Treasury, Albert Gallatin, he reduced the accounts of a great government to the simplicity of a merchant's account books. The first Republican president set the fashionable world, what there was in Washington, to guessing what would happen next — no levees, no restraint, no fashionable hours, every one being admitted at any time to the President's presence; foreign ambassadors having no special claim over an ordinary American citizen! First one party, then another took offense at the unceremonious treatment accorded them, but no attention was given them, no amends made, until finally men came to realize that it was indeed a Republican government, planted there in the woods on the banks of the Potomac and no hybrid monarchy with a court of country snobs. Macon enjoyed such an atmosphere and he talked of his "mess" with as much self-satisfaction as if it had been the most fashionable twentieth century hotel. He lived with Randolph and Joseph H. Nicholson in a small house near the present Treasury department in about such style as a college boy with small means now lives, and when a friend or constituent visited him, he never thought it inconvenient to share his bed with the visitor. He came to congress on horseback, kept the horse close by his "mess," and during the intervals of the sessions of Congress he was often in the saddle going about the "City of magnificent distances," or riding far out the old Georgetown turnpike. His friend Randolph, however, came to Washington in a "coach and four" bringing his fox hounds, and it was not unusual, we are told, to see him enter the House of Representatives with a pair of dogs at his heels. It was a part of the plantation life of the Roanoke valley that these two men brought into the little Capital when they came, and carried away with them when they went. The two were often seen together, Macon, now forty-three years old, a tall, well-proportioned, healthy physique; Randolph, only twenty-eight, slender, delicate-looking, sallow-complexioned, with the promise of scarce another decade of life. But both were gentlemen, gentle-born, and Virginian in sentiment. They seldom disagreed, never during these brighter years of their lives. They were determined to give this country such a government as had never been seen any where, a government as simply conducted as a country debating society.

The Federalists were making sport among themselves of this rustic regime from the South, the more than Roman virtue in public places. But it was all too serious a business to be laughed down. When Jefferson's retrenchment measures reducing the running expenses of the government from 7,500,000 to 3,500,000 dollars a year came up, they declared it "impossible," made a strong fight against it, but were quieted by sheer numbers in the voting. It was on the repeal of the Judiciary bill that they made their last determined stand. The Republicans had opposed from the beginning the extension of the Judiciary, but to no avail. A cumbrous system had been devised by Hamilton in 1799, submitted to Congress in the latter part of the session of 1801, and became a law a short time before Adams' term of office expired. The Federalists had made themselves berths against the day of defeat, and Adams was accommodating enough to help them all into these berths during his last days in Washington. The Republicans began early in the next session, in an unmerciful way, not to molest their opponents in their ease merely, but to break up the very foundations of it by abolishing all the new courts. John Breckenridge, of Kentucky, brought the dire resolution into the Senate January 6, 1802, and in a few days it passed; then the House took it up and passed it by a vote of 59 to 32! The lawyers of the large cities made a blustering opposition and a meeting of the New York bar resolved solemnly that if the bill before Congress should pass "this Union will at once crumble to pieces." Bayard did all that eloquence could do against a determined majority, *i.e.*, he predicted that all the direful calamities known to ancient Egypt would befall the country if the Republicans persisted in their perverse legislation. Randolph replied: "It is not on account of the paltry expense that I wish to see it (the new judiciary) put down, but to give the death-blow to the pretension of rendering the judiciary a hospital for decayed politicians." After the bill had passed, the House re-arranged the United States courts, greatly reducing the number of office holders, on a plan which served the purposes of judicial administration until after the close of the War Between the States.

While these measures were taking place in Congress the apportionment of Representatives was made the subject of a short debate. In this debate Randolph advanced a theory which was henceforth to become the text of his and Macon's political lives, and which was ultimately to end with William Lowndes Yancey and War. It was this: "The members of this House are not the representatives of the people over the United States," (not people of the United States; Randolph believed there were none such) "but the representatives of the *people of the individual States in their sovereign State capacities.*" Bayard took Randolph to task and expressed the opinion that he was as much a representative of Virginia as Randolph himself. This was Federalism's extreme claim. As to the subject of the ratio of members the positions taken by both political parties was exactly the reverse of their positions in 1791: the Federalists had then favored a small House of Representatives, now they advocated a large one; the Republicans had said in 1791 that the salvation of the country depended on a large House, now they were equally sure of a disaster from a large one. Macon's first service in Congress had been connected with this subject, and he then held opinions contrary to his party; likewise in 1802 he differed from its leaders, even with his friend Randolph, except in the matter of State's individuality. As to the representation, he declared he would like a ratio so small that every man might know personally his representative in Congress.[166] (After the passing of the retrenchment and reform measures both Republican and Federalist members of Congress began to sound public opinion. The work of undoing Federalist legislation of which the new Administration disapproved

---

166 Annals of Congress, 7th Cong., 1st Sess., 365-373.

was begun and completed in one session and by May 3, the members of Congress were returning to their constituents. The Administration and the general politics of Thomas Jefferson have been said to have been merely destructive — his life was successful only as that of an obstructionist and his politics were beneficial only in the sense of correcting abuses. In a single session he cleared the way for progressive, positive measures, fulfilled all the promises his party had made to the people and was ready to put into effect the first of his own plans of expansion — the most important step in our history after the adoption of the Federal Constitution. But before we take up the study of Jefferson's politics, let us see how North Carolina was viewing the new regime, how it regarded the new President and his reforms.

Macon wrote Jefferson within a month[167] after his return to Buck Spring: "Believing that it will not be disagreeable to you to hear the sentiments of the people in different parts of the Union, and having since my return been in three of the adjoining counties I with real pleasure inform you that all (except those who were not expected to be pleased) seem to be perfectly satisfied with the conduct of those, to whom they have entrusted the management of their public affairs. Some who before the electoral elections appeared to be almost indifferent as to the elector have declared their sincere approbation of the choice and their joy that the late election gave birth to an administration which deserves the support of every American." In Raleigh things were going well, he thought; and let us hope he called to see his friend Gales, the editor. Davie was not ready to join the ranks of the Jefferson party as it seems from Macon's account of an interview. Davie was in reality preparing "to stand for Congress" against Willis Alston of Halifax, and rumors to that effect were already rife about Washington. Macon closes his letter by saying: "The only hope of the dissatisfied is to produce a division among the Republicans, of which I hope there is no danger. I also hope none of them want offices, office hunters are never to be satisfied."

The plan of producing "a division among the Republicans" was soon a principal part of the Federalist program. In September, 1802, Duncan Cameron, Federalist of Hillsboro, wrote John Moore, Revolutionary Tory of Lincoln county, a long letter outlining the scheme of rehabilitating the party in the State. He says in the beginning, "The political opinions of a great portion of our citizens[168] seem to me to

---
167 Macon to Jefferson, June 17, 1802.
168 The Nathaniel Macon MSS.

grow out of hatred and party principles. They are in the habit of reading — Duane's and Gales' papers" and Gales was, like Duane, sending out papers free, or nearly so, to all parts of the State. "It was proposed at this place some weeks ago that a subscription should be set on foot in each district to raise money sufficient to furnish about ten newspapers for each county, which should be sent to men of democratic principles of a moderate kind by the printer. Mr. Boylan has said that he will furnish 600 papers weekly at $1.25 each for a year (the subscription rate was then $3.00 a year), which is as low as the price of labor and paper would enable him to print them. This scheme it was further agreed shall be communicated to the following persons: William Boylan for Newbern, W. B. Grove for Fayetteville, Col. Ashe for Wilmington, John Moore for Morgan, Archibald Henderson for Salisbury, D. Cameron for Hillsboro, W. R. Davie for Halifax, who was also to select some person for Edenton. Col. Ashe has already procured subscriptions for the Wilmington district. From what I have already understood to be your political character with perfect confidence in your zealous cooperation with us in executing a plan which has for its end the noble objects of suppressing falsehood and disseminating truth, of subverting the wild and visionary projects and opinions of Democracy and advocating in their place sound, substantial, practical principles of Federalism." In Hillsboro seventy-five dollars was at once subscribed and Cameron was sure that there would be no difficulty in finding men in every town and county to come forward with subscriptions. Five dollars each was the assessment. This plan was a result of a conference of leading Federalists held at Hillsboro, but it had been first suggested and outlined in Raleigh during the June session of the United States Circuit Court, the same that Macon had attended in order to find out what was the public opinion of Jefferson and the Republican administration. Boylan, the editor of the Raleigh *Minerva*, was its originator. But the idea and practice, too, had been started already in North Carolina by Joseph Gales. The Raleigh *Register* had come to be feared and the maneuvers of its editor were now to be imitated by the opposing party.

Macon knew in a vague way that something was being proposed; rumors of it reached him at Raleigh. But he seems not to have been disturbed. He wrote at this very time (September 15, 1802) to one of the Federalists — John Steele of Salisbury — asking him to bring his whole family to Buck Spring and remain a week. Macon sustained a peculiar relation to the leading Federalists during all these years. He wrote to them, appeared to be on the friendliest terms with them and never manifested any party animosity. Steele was, however, a mild Federalist and one whom both Jefferson and Macon were anxious to win for their party. After his defeat for Congress in 1795, he had been appointed by Washington as Comptroller of the Treasury, which office he held under Adams and Jefferson until late in the fall of 1802. Steele's feeling at this time may be best illustrated by a quotation from a note on one of Macon's letters dated September 15, 1802: "It is my ambition to be useful, but I am aware that a man can not be really so without possessing a share of political power and patronage which I have no reason to expect" — a remark sad enough for a politician of that time, yet one which showed its author to have understood well the trend of political thought in North Carolina in 1802. Steele was wealthy, had distinguished himself in war and, feeling as he did about the outlook of his party, he informed the President that he should resign his position and retire to private life on his farm. Macon heard of the proposed step and wrote Steele, October 10, urging him, though not successfully, to remain at his post. In this letter Macon's confidence in and friendship for Steele are clearly shown — different now from what he was when Steele desired Macon's endorsement as a candidate for Congress in 1794. Jefferson also insisted on Steele's remaining in office at Washington, but to no avail. He entered the North Carolina Assembly and was made commissioner for the settling of the long-disputed boundary line between North and South Carolina, but never again figured in national affairs.

General Davie, the other object of Jefferson's friendly offices, was not detached from the Federalist party and, contrary to Macon's hopes for his finally yielding his support or remaining in quiet retirement, he joined the active opponents of the President, even while holding a commission under the Administration, and "stood for Congress" in the summer of 1803 against Willis Alston, a staunch Democrat of Halifax. Concerning the partisanship of that campaign Macon wrote: "I am informed that Jaycocks has ceased being a candidate, so that Alston and Davie seem to be alone. I have also been informed that great exertions have been made, and will be continued till the election, which is next Thursday and Friday. In other districts conditions remain as in my last."[169] It was a notorious contest, and it is still talked about in Halifax; but Davie was defeated. Chagrined at his de-

---

169 Macon to Nicholson, August 6, 1803.

feat, and being separated from the powerful Jones family by the death of his wife, he retired not only from politics, but from the State, never to return again. He spent the remaining years of his life at Tivoli on the Catawba river in South Carolina, near the scenes of his valiant fighting during the Revolution.

The newspaper plans of Duncan Cameron and others; the "hue and cry" as Macon says, raised in defense of the Constitution, which was so endangered; the retirement from tacit support of Jefferson of Gen. John Steele, and the violent campaign in favor of so prominent a man as General Davie, all came to naught in 1803. Every man in Congress from North Carolina who voted against the repeal of the Judiciary act in 1802 was defeated in the election of 1803. Henderson, Stanly, Hill, and even Grove of Fayetteville, were all superseded.

As Macon said so many times on the floor of the House and elsewhere, the people were behind the Republicans. Jefferson was endorsed almost unanimously and Macon with him. From this time until his voluntary retirement in 1828, Macon was easily the foremost figure in North Carolina politics. He wrote Jefferson nearly a month after the August elections concerning the political situation in his State as follows:[170] "It is with real pleasure, that I inform you, that the Republican cause is daily gaining ground with us. Not only the late elections, but the candid acknowledgment of many that they have been deceived, fully confirm the fact. And this gaining is clearly the effect of observation on the difference between the present and past times by the people, and it is worthy of notice that the district (Fayetteville) which sends only Federalists from the State to Congress, gave a majority of votes to Republican candidates, and I must add what is also worthy of notice, that during the present administration, not a single person has been dismissed from office in this State, although with one exception I believe they were all Federal, though not I hope of the same sort which abound in some other places." Meanwhile Jefferson had been pursuing steadily his policy of annexing Louisiana, a country toward which he had been looking with jealous eyes ever since 1790. The story of Monroe's second mission to Paris and Napoleon's final policy in the Louisiana purchase has been too often told to require any very extended review here. This positive policy of the President was first intimated in the House of Representatives by Randolph's call for information from the Executive on December

---

170 Macon to Jefferson, September 3, 1803.

17, 1802. All the information at the disposal of the Administration was gladly furnished. The Federalists at once returned to their old cry of war against France, and Hamilton declared that a sensible President would recommend at once the annexation of all the land east of the Mississippi without negotiation either with France or Spain. The opposition failed to force a rupture while the Republicans authorized the Administration to call out good militia and equip fifteen vessels of war. Jefferson, however, turned to his old friend Monroe, the popular Governor of Virginia, a favorite of the Kentuckians, and insisted on his undertaking the negotiation of the purchase of the disputed territory. Monroe accepted the mission, and Louisiana was secured for the comparatively inconsiderable sum of fifteen million dollars. But the end had not come — Congress had not been consulted, and it would rest with it whether or not the action of the Executive would be sustained.

While Monroe was working out his mission in Paris, with the assistance of Livingston, the regular representative — rather while he was assisting Livingston at the court of the First Consul, a most interesting and important constitutional question was agitating the minds of Congress and of thoughtful men everywhere. The Marbury vs. Madison decision of Chief Justice Marshall was the cause, and it was the beginning of a new tendency of the Supreme Court. Marbury was one of Adams' "midnight" appointees; and Madison refused to give him the commission which the appointment required. Marbury was to have been a Justice of the Peace for the District of Columbia. He instituted suit against Madison as Secretary of State and obtained Marshall's judgment that "to withhold his commission is an act deemed by the court not warranted by law, but violative of a legal vested right."[171] The sessions of the Supreme Court had been suspended some time by act of Congress. This decision was a retort which did not please the majority. It was the first manifestation of that spirit of Marshall which was soon to dominate the Supreme Court and finally to become the directing element in the whole American Judiciary. Men now for the first time began seriously to inquire whether the Constitution gave to the Supreme Court the authority to declare void the acts of Congress, not because no provision was made for such rulings on the part of the Court, but because men had not accustomed themselves to submitting to an all-powerful Court. The Federalists

---

171 Foundation stone for the decision of Judge Ruffin, so famous in North Carolina, in the case of Hoke vs. Henderson.

rejoiced that such a man as Marshall had been placed on the Supreme Bench. The Republicans prepared to silence them by impeaching John Pickering for maladministration of his office. Pickering was Federalist Judge of the United States District Court of New Hampshire. Articles of impeachment were brought before the Senate on the last day of the session, March 3, 1803 — beginning of a bad business for the party in power.

During the spring and summer of 1803, Macon corresponded with his friends on the subject of the jurisdiction of the United States judges, their duties and their relations to the other branches of the National government. Steele wrote Macon denying the right of Marshall to issue the mandamus in favor of Marbury, and attacking the "fashionable doctrine that the courts have power to pronounce acts of Congress unconstitutional and void." He then insinuates that Henry Lee, of Virginia, was the author of Marshall's decision. "By the theory of our Government, the Legislative, the Executive and Judicial departments are in a certain degree and for certain purposes distinct. The officers who compose the President's council are his constitutional advisers, and with him form what is denominated the Executive. Should the Secretary of State, a constituent part of this great department, do wrong in his official capacity to an individual or the public, with or without the sanction of the President, the intimate relation which the Constitution supposes to exist between him and the President may be dissolved by removal or impeachment, after which he is amenable to the judicial authority in the form of an indictment, and perhaps by civil process. Until that connection be dissolved, the official acts of a Secretary of State are to be regarded as the acts of the President. With respect to them he stands on the Executive ground not examinable by the Judiciary." And further, "I doubt the right of the Supreme Court to step on Executive ground in the case of a patent on a pension; (if so) you will subject at once the country to Judicial discipline and all the vast concerns of the treasury to the revision of a department which, in theory, is the third, but in practice aims at becoming the first power of the State." In this way a staunch Federalist argues that the Supreme Court had no right to give a decision in the Marbury vs. Madison case. After citing precedents in English judicial practice, which Macon did not relish, to be sure, and again in the Pennsylvania controversy between Governor McKean and the Adjutant-General, he comes to the conclusion that the Supreme Court was quietly usurping powers not given it. He does not agree that it may annul a law of Congress constitutionally, but asserts that Congress is supreme and is not to be dominated by the Court. Macon, as we have seen, repeatedly referred to the Court as supreme, and in the case of the Sedition laws, he called upon the Judges to declare the act of Congress unconstitutional. It was not thus so much the Court itself to which men were objecting, but its evidently partisan attitude towards the Administration. In the case of Marbury vs. Madison, Marshall finally decided that the ruling of the Court could not apply, and that the mandamus which he himself had granted could not be enforced. Macon declared this behavior reminded him of a certain member of Congress, who always spoke on one side of a question and voted on the other. Macon was willing to grant the supremacy of the Court over Congress, but he said the Judges would always decide a constitutional question at their peril, because of their accountability to Congress. Marshall's early constructive rulings were not approved by Macon; they were to him partisan, and viewed in the light of unbiased history, he was correct. Their aim was to carry into effect political opinions held and maintained by a small minority of the people. John Marshall had not then been canonized, and so his decisions were not received as dicta of heaven-born justice.

The position of the Court encouraged the Republicans in their determination to administer a whole some chastisement. The Administration, in accordance with public sentiment, recommended the impeachment of Judge Chase, the most violently partisan of the Justices of the Supreme Court. Chase deserved impeachment, it was thought, especially on the grounds of his behavior on the Bench in Richmond in the Callender trial in 1800. And adding to the exasperation of the Republicans, Chase, in a charge to a grand jury, declared: "The independence of the National judiciary is already shaken to its foundations, and the virtue of the people alone can restore it. * * * Our republican Constitution will sink into a mobocracy, * * * the worst of all possible government."[172] This was "pouring oil into the flames" indeed. The leaders of the House, on Jefferson's advice, determined long before Congress met on impeaching Chase at the next session. Those leaders were Macon, Randolph and Jos. H. Nicholson, of Maryland. But Macon wrote; to Nicholson, August 6, 1803: "I have thought a little on Judge Chase's charge, and submit for your consideration the following queries:

---

172 Hart: *Formation of the Union*, 180.

"1. Ought a Judge to be impeached for a charge to a grand jury because it contains matters of which the grand jury have not cognizance?

"2. Ought a Judge to be impeached for a charge to a grand jury, not legal but political?

"3. Ought a Judge to be impeached for delivering in his charge to the grand jury, political opinions which every man may fully enjoy arid freely express?

"4. Ought a Judge to be impeached for delivering his political opinions in a charge to the grand jury, and which any member of Congress might deliver to the House of which he is a member?

"5. Ought a Judge to be impeached because he avows monarchical opinions in his charge to a grand jury?

"Is error of opinion to be dreaded when inquiry is free? Is the liberty of the press of any real value when the political charges of a Judge are dreaded? What effect have they (judicio-political charges) in the United States? If a Judge ought to be impeached for avowing monarchical principles to the grand jury in his charge, what ought to be done with those who appoint them, who actually supported them in the field. Change the scene, and suppose Chase had stretched as far on the other side, and had praised where no praise was deserving, would it be proper to impeach, because by such conduct he might lull the people to sleep while their interest was destroyed? I have said this much to hear your opinions on some of the points, nor can I quite withhold expressing to you my firm conviction that you, if any attempt be made to impeach, ought not to be the leader." Nicholson desired the appointment on the bench in case Chase was convicted and removed, which explains Macon's last sentence. The plan was preparing and the leaders already thinking about the division of the spoils. From the tenor of Macon's letter, he opposed the impeachment of Chase, and this course would have been a much wiser policy for his party. Randolph, it appears, was bent on impeachment, and favored Nicholson's being named Chase's successor. But ere this unfortunate scheme comes before Congress, let us view the better and nobler work of the party in power.

Macon's letter of August 6, shows his ignorance of the favorable turn of the negotiations at Paris on June 24, but in September he informs Jefferson that "the acquisition of Louisiana has given general satisfaction, though the terms are not correctly known. But if it is within the compass of the present revenue, the purchase, when the terms are known, will be more admired than even now." And then adding what must have given his correspondent genuine satisfaction, and which indicates Macon's own statesman-like vision, "if the Floridas can be obtained on tolerable terms, we [shall] have nothing to make us uneasy, unless it be the party madness of some of our dissatisfied citizens." This, then, is the policy of him who had opposed every warlike measure the Federalists had formerly followed and would have carried out in order to gain the Floridas. He would obtain all that they coveted; and, with his beau ideal in the President's chair, he actually hoped and expected to acquire all the country needed for its own expansion and safety. Randolph, Nicholson, Giles and Macon all united in supporting the President's plans, even when these plans were only imperfectly known to them. And how gladly did Macon inform Jefferson that the people of North Carolina were rallying to him almost unanimously! The constitutionality of the purchase was not so much as mentioned.

Congress was called together on the 17th of October, to consider the Louisiana purchase; it was a glad meeting. The whole country was rejoicing at its good fortune, and nine men in every ten found in Thomas Jefferson the personification of his own political ideals. Nothing to which he turned his attention failed to realize; and now the President submits his action, touching the long-disputed territory, to the legislature, saying he had transcended his constitutional bounds, but that he had done it in the interest of the people who made the Constitution, he had done it as their agent; they could examine for themselves and repudiate if they wished, but his recommendation, based on long political experience, was that they should accept his action, pay the expense and amend the Constitution to cover the case. The Senate ratified the treaty within two days by a vote of 24 to 7; the House passed a bill providing for the extra appropriations on November 10, by a majority of 89 to 23. There was no difficulty now in carrying government measures. If ever a President had reason for self-gratulation, it was Jefferson in the fall and winter of 1803 and 1804. All the unbending opposition of the Seventh Congress was gone. In Massachusetts and Connecticutt a change was slowly working, and on the Louisiana purchase, John Quincy Adams, son of his father in every fibre, yielding to reason, gave the Administration his vote, though not his influence otherwise. Virginia was so well pleased with her distinguished son that she sent both his sons-in-law to Congress, and another relative of his was undisputed leader on the floor of the

House.[173]

Jefferson continued his retrenchment and reform, first in removing from the statute books an unpopular and expensive Bankrupt law, then in still further reducing the patronage of his own office. Jefferson was not friendly to office-seekers, and he was especially unfriendly to any of his relatives who ventured to apply. A remark he was accustomed to make during these years was, that no connection of his, no matter how deserving, need expect appointment under his administration, for the people could never be brought to see the merit, but only the favoritism of the case, and thus the very design of the appointment would be defeated. If any of his relatives desired to enter the public service, it must be, said he, by means of election on the part of the people. How great a pity some less important men do not under stand the subject thus!

Congress chose again, on the first day of its assembling, Nathaniel Macon as its Speaker; and Macon immediately appointed his friend Randolph chairman of the Ways and Means committee. Randolph was truly the spokesman of the Administration. The only important measure, after the passing of the Louisiana Purchase bill, in which Macon figured conspicuously, was the amendment to the Constitution. The long dead-lock on the election of the President in 1801, caused solely by the practice of taking the candidates in order of the number of votes cast, was a lesson sufficiently impressive to demand a remedy before the recurrence of a second similar crisis. When the reform measure — the present electoral plan — came before the House, strong opposition, more for opposition's sake than for any other reason, was developed. When the vote was taken, Macon insisted on voting, and it was his vote which decided the matter, a two-thirds failing without it. This occasioned some criticism, but he was strong enough to ignore it. It had not, and has not since, been the custom of the Speaker to vote, except in case of a tie. So when we cast our votes for President and Vice-President, separate and distinct, we may recall that an unprecedented act of Nathaniel Macon gave us the constitutional amendment which prescribes such a course.

Toward the end of the session the slavery question was brought again, after some years of silence on the subject, to the attention of Congress in the form of a resolution placing a tax of ten dollars a head on each slave imported into the United States.[174] Obedient to

---

173 Schouler, vol. I,, p. 59-60; Annals of Congress, 7th Cong., passim.
174 Annals of Congress, 8th Cong., I., 991.

the anti-slavery movement of the time, all the States had passed laws against the further importation of slaves. But South Carolina now removed all restriction on the importation of slaves, a step which practically annulled the slavery laws of all other States, since any man could carry his slave any where, either to sell or to use himself.[175] Lowndes, a younger member from South Carolina, made a long speech in defence of the action of his State Legislature, on the ground that the non-importation laws could not be enforced, and that Congress itself had been chiefly responsible for that state of affairs. Macon opposed the resolution because it "looks like an attempt in the General Government to correct a State for the undisputed exercise of its constitutional powers. It appears to me to be something like putting a State to the ban of the empire. It will operate as a censure thrown on the State. To this I can never consent." His additional argument was that a tax would legalize the trade, to which he was also very much opposed.[176] The principal cause of Macon's opposition was that a sovereign State would be interfered with. Here again he foreshadows his later political course. The resolution was passed, but when Randolph, as chairman of the Ways and Means committee presented a bill in conformity to the resolution, it was postponed indefinitely.[177]

Before the adjournment in the spring of 1804, a caucus of the Republican members of Congress was held for the purpose of deciding on the candidates for the Presidency and Vice-Presidency. Jefferson had often said that the President should serve only one term, but the great desire of his party was so strong in favor of his nomination for a second term that he yielded and became a third time an open candidate for the highest office in the land. No doubt but his personal objections were easily waived. Burr did not possess the confidence of his party, and Jefferson himself did not favor his re-nomination. Only the evening before the caucus was to meet, the Vice-President had called on Jefferson with a view to winning his support. It was refused, and George Clinton, an extreme States' Rights man from New York, received his support, and was nominated. There was scarce a doubt that the nominee of the Republican caucus would be elected. Macon attended this caucus,[178] it seems, and was so much displeased with its

---

175 Schouler, II., 62.
176 Annals of Congress, 8th Cong., I., 998.
177 Annals of Congress, 8th Cong., I., 1020-1036.
178 Macon to Bartlett Yancey, Dec. 12, 1823.

proceedings that he resolved never to attend another. He was in no doubt, however, about supporting its candidates, and he was all interest during the summer elections in North Carolina. September 2, he wrote to Jefferson: "Our elections are over, and at the next Congress North Carolina will be unanimous on the Republican side." There was actually only one Federalist candidate in the field — Purviance, from Fayetteville. "American politics are scarcely ever mentioned, nearly all seem to be satisfied." And in reference to the National election which was soon to follow, he said in a letter to Nicholson, September 7, 1804: "The Federalists in this part of the State have not yet mentioned a name for elector, nor is it probable they will, unless they do it a few days before the election." No other reference to the election was made in any of his letters which have been preserved.

Congress was called together earlier than usual, in the autumn of 1804, the President anticipating trouble in steering the ship of state in safety between Great Britain on the one hand and warlike France on the other. Macon was perplexed what to do, and said so in a letter to Nicholson before the opening of Congress.[179] Jefferson was not fond of deciding difficult foreign questions. As he had recommended often enough before, Congress should decide these matters. It was the irony of fate that the troubles which wrecked Adams' administration were now to wreck Jefferson's, and to be in part the cause of the almost universal criticism and abuse which hounded him back to Monticello at the end of his term, sick and tired of the world and its turbulent politics. But other elements contributed to his misfortunes during his second term, and other subjects arose which well-nigh wrecked his party. These will be given in the following chapter.

The last act of the Republicans, united and militant, was the attempt to impeach Judge Samuel Chase, of the Supreme Court. Chase had been a mill-stone about the neck of the Federalist party; now he becomes a stumbling block in the path of the Republicans, more particularly in that of John Randolph.

From the beginning of our government, impeachments have been very difficult to accomplish. The ablest lawyers in North Carolina, supported by all the weight of wealth and rank in the State, had been enlisted in the impeachment of Judges Ashe, Williams, and Spencer, of the Superior Court, in 1786. William Hooper and Alexander MacLaine exerted themselves to the utmost to have the Judges found

---

179 Nathaniel Macon to Jos. H. Nicholson, September 7, 1804.

guilty of maladministration and dismissed, but to no effect. The notorious case of Blount, of the United States Senate, was of such a nature as to make it exceptionable. There were few precedents, and the early legislatures were not fond of transcending precedent. The Republicans had success fully impeached Judge Pickering, and since that had been so well carried out, and their exasperation at the defiant attitude of the Federal Courts was in no way appeased, it was finally resolved to call the Judges of the Supreme Court to account.

On the second day of the session, John Randolph reminded the Speaker of the House of the Chase impeachment proposition, and he was made chairman of a special committee to review the work of the former impeachment committee and report to the House.[180] In accordance with his instructions, Randolph reported articles of impeachment to the Representatives on November 20, 1804. This report was taken up December 3, and, after a debate of three days, Randolph, Nicholson and Rodney, of Delaware, were appointed to prosecute Chase "for high crimes and misdemeanors before the Senate."[181] On February 4, the trial was opened in the Senate. Judge Chase had retained Henry Lee, of Virginia, former Attorney-General of the United States, Luther Martin of Baltimore, the "Federal Bulldog," as Jefferson termed him, and the distinguished Federalist leader, Harper, of South Carolina, as counsel. Nicholson and Rodney were, perhaps, able to cope with Chase's counsel, but Randolph was not, and especially not in such an arena as the United States Senate. He was entirely unfitted for the prosecution, and he blundered even worse than was to have been expected, claimed extension of time to get his final address ready, and when ready it was more harmful to his own than to Chase's party. After a month of harangue and dispute in a cause which would have been sustained if ably and properly presented, the impeachment failed and the Administration was humiliated as no other had ever been.[182] Why so shrewd a man as Jefferson allowed such blundering it is difficult to say. He had been misled, perhaps, by Randolph's success in the House, or he was too sure the strength of the case was sufficient *per se* to compel a verdict of impeachment. It was all a sad business: Chase remained on the bench, Randolph returned to the Roanoke, not quite so "proud as forty kings," his political influence had passed

---

180 See page 134.
181 Annals of Congress, 8th Cong., 2nd Sess., 726-763.
182 Schouler, II., 86-88.

its zenith; Nicholson never sat on the Supreme Court bench; and Jefferson was compelled to accommodate himself to the decisions of Judge Marshall and his powerful associates. Macon, the wisest of the Republican leaders, had opposed impeachment all along; he returned home feeling keenly enough the humiliation of his party, regretting, as well he might, that his own advice had not been taken.

The first four years of Republican administration was, on the whole, satisfactory to Macon. He had seen government stripped of all its formality; the levees, which had called forth from him an occasional sarcasm, were abolished, and two great pell-mell receptions took their places. These were on New Year's day and the Fourth of July. The President, though he owned "a coach and four," we are told, rode horseback like a country congressman about the little capital, or even to and from Monticello. Members of Congress called at the White House at will, and were received without ceremony or formality. Macon[183] tells with apparent satisfaction in one of his letters that The British Minister has kicked up a little dust about his and his wife's rank, such as going first out of the sitting into the dining-room! having number one given to his wife at the dancing assembly; and this prank of the Briton has acted as a spur to the Spaniard, and the Marquis de Hrujo has also taken it into his head to show a trick or two about this new-fangled doctrine of rank, where neither the people nor their new form of government acknowledges any. However, I suspect both their claims, although not for money, will meet the same fate, which claims so often meet from the Committee on Claims, that is, leave to withdraw." It was with a supreme contempt that Macon viewed the small practices of the diplomatic corps, whose members were then, as they have continued till this day, trying to give *tone* to Washington society, despite the plain, practical President.

Jefferson's reputed atheism proved itself simply a figment in the minds of New England clergymen, and when he took charge of the government neither were the churches demolished nor all the Bibles burned. Things went on as before, with the exception that religious liberty received a new impetus. The President attended church, as other good Americans did then and do now, and encouraged the building of new ones, studied the Bible closely, and practised its teachings in numerous ways; all of which pleased Macon since he

---

183 Macon to John Steele, February 12, 1804.

himself was a Christian, "of the Baptist persuasion," and a life-long student of the Scriptures.

The government expense, as has been noted, had fallen off four millions a year, and the National debt was slowly disappearing. All the affairs of State had been simplified, all its workings were being brought as nearly as possible within the comprehension of the plainest farmer. The foreign establishments, though not appreciably changed, had become far less expensive. The civil service, too, had undergone a "chaste reformation." No "old Tories" were given employment under the "Whig" regime, and the United States Courts were stopped from encroaching on those of the States. Comfortable thoughts, all these, to Macon and his constituents.

But there were other thoughts in Macon's mind that spring as he turned his steps southward; he was beginning, like Randolph, to drift away from the Administration. The day of the "Old Republicans," as he and Jefferson termed them twenty years later, was passing its zenith; its sun was taking its downward course.

President Thomas Jefferson

CHAPTER XIII.
MACON AND THE "QUIDS," 1805-1808.

The first intimation of Macon's dissatisfaction with the Administration appears in a letter to Monroe, November 15, 1803.[184] His language is unusually guarded, yet it shows clearly enough that he was displeased with the State department, that is, with its head, Madison, Jefferson's most intimate friend. Beginning with the "purchasing" policy of Jefferson, he said, "the whole transaction is generally well received and popular; though it is due to truth to say that some of your friends would rather the two millions of dollars appropriated at the last session of Congress should have been otherwise applied; it is feared that the application has some thing local in it, though not towards Virginia. You will pardon my saying this much, and be assured that it has proceeded from a sincere desire to communicate that which I think you ought to know. More would have been said, but it is believed some of your many friends must have written to you on the subject." Just what Macon wished to tell Monroe would be difficult to determine positively; but he was an intimate friend of Randolph's, and Randolph had already conceived a jealousy for Madison, and was soon attempting to detach Monroe from the Administration — at least so far as its foreign policy was concerned. Monroe had won a great deal of popularity in the West before he went to Paris to assist in the Louisiana Purchase; the successful issue of that undertaking made him a rival of Madison's for the Presidency. That Macon and Randolph were advocating the preference of Monroe over Madison as early as November, 1803, is contrary to the accepted opinion, yet this letter points clearly to that conclusion. How Macon came to dislike Madison does not appear, except that he, on Randolph's advices, began to believe Madison improperly connected with the famous Yazoo frauds in Georgia.

Other tendencies toward alienation from the Administration have already appeared in his tardy acquiescence in the impeachment movements of 1803-1805. He was not a violent opponent of the Supreme Court, and had he been he would have preferred to let it cut off its own head by partisan decisions rather than to have undertaken this difficult task as a part of his party program. Macon was a decided advocate of the corrective power of public opinion, and preferred

---

184 Monroe Papers, State Department.

always to let it have its free course, and at that particular time he had not thought public sentiment demanded the impeachment of Chase.

Some reference has been made to the Yazoo land frauds. During the last session it had been shown that speculators had corruptly procured from the Georgia Legislature, in 1795, grants for large areas of Western lands. The next Legislature annulled the grants, and now the speculators were claiming relief from Congress. A commission of the Cabinet, composed of Madison, Gallatin and Lincoln, proposed to compromise the difficulty by allowing five million acres of land to the petitioners. To Macon and Randolph this was proposing a compromise with the devil, more especially since the chief claimants were New Englanders. Randolph had made violent speeches against the proposed compromise, and Macon agreed with him, which was, of course, the same thing as charging the Administration with winking at a fraud.[185] And again, towards the end of the session, when the claim was presented to the House asking fourteen thousand dollars for repairs on the furniture of the President's house hold,[186] Macon's sense of consistency and notions of economy were violated. It was the same claim Adams' friends had made, and which he himself had strenuously opposed as extravagant and useless. Should his own favorite leader and candidate, now that he was in power, practice the same wasteful policy? These were the causes of Macon's partial disaffection to his party, and the beginning, even at the close of the Eighth Congress, of the storms of the Ninth.

As a result of the disaffection of Macon and Randolph, there was sufficient reason for the friends of Macon to fear he would not be re-elected Speaker at the opening of the Ninth Congress. Not a word on the subject seems ever to have been uttered by Macon. But Randolph was anxious about his friend's election, and more than a month before Congress was to meet he wrote Nicholson:[187] "I am now seriously apprehensive for his election; and more on his account than from public considerations, although there is not a man in the House, himself and one other excepted, who is in any respect qualified for the office. I can not deny that the insult offered to the man would move me more than the injury done the public by his rejection. Indeed, I am not sure that such a step, although productive of temporary inconve-

---

185 Schouler, II., 83.
186 Annals of Congress, 8th Cong. 2nd Sess., 1211
187 *Life of John Randolph*, by Henry Adams, 158.

nience, would not be followed by permanent good effects. It would open the eyes of many well-meaning persons, who, in avoiding the scylla of innovation, have plunged into the charybdis of federalism. * * * Do not fail to be in Washington time enough to counteract the plot against the Speaker, and pray apprise such of his friends as are within your reach of its existence." That there was a plan on foot to defeat Macon can hardly be doubted, and because of the events of the last session of Congress, not because of unfitness. Randolph said he was the only man, with one exception, fitted for the Speaker's chair. From the letter just quoted it may be inferred that the Administration was trying to secure Macon's defeat. But this was not true. Jefferson could, indeed, have defeated Macon by a single word; but that word was not given. In fact, the President was trying to conciliate all but Randolph, and so if he had any share in the election of the Speaker at all, it was in the interest of Macon. Still it was by a bare majority, after three ballots, that Macon was elected. He was thought to be too friendly to Randolph, and Randolph had lost his prestige during the last session of Congress so completely that the ever-increasing Northern wing of the party demanded an other leader. It was not the Speaker so much to whom objection was made, as the former chairman of the committee on Ways and Means. But both these men had come to stand for a policy which was much to the disliking of the Eastern Republicans. It was the policy of Southern supremacy and States' Rights, begun with the Louisiana Purchase, and which was to end a half a century later at the beginning of the War Between the States. Macon, as we know, advised Jefferson during the summer of 1802 to secure Florida at any reasonable cost, and assured him of the hearty support of the South in such event. Randolph stood for the same along with his State-supremacy creed. These men, with their aristocratic manners and their democratic policy, were dominating the Union — the chief cause of complaint in New England. The narrow margin of party support, and the almost general discontent of the Republicans, did not prevent Macon's promptly placing Randolph at the head of the Committee on Ways and Means.[188]

Macon's appointment of his friend proved at once to be a great blunder. Jefferson asked Congress for the sum of two million dollars, with which to purchase Florida; but because this request was not made quite to the liking of Randolph, the latter refused to bring

---

188 Annals of Congress, 9th Cong., 1st sess.,254; Schouler, II., III.

in a favorable bill. The President was annoyed, but soon turned to Varnum, Macon's competitor for the Speakership, and asked him and Bidwell, a very influential member from Massachusetts, .to bring a proper resolution before the House. The House at once passed the resolution and granted the appropriation accordingly — the breach was there; the Speaker and the committee on Ways and Means were out of accord with the President, and the latter still had control of the House. This was the beginning of a stormy session, and Macon, Randolph and Nicholson became the first members of the little group of independents called "the Quids."

Before Congress met, we find Macon lamenting the action of Great Britain in returning again to her former policy of domineering the trade of the powers which refused to take part in the fierce war then waging between England and the French Empire. He was at a loss what to do or recommend, and went to Washington with ominous forebodings as to the immediate future of the country. When the President recommended, by secret message, that some thing be done to bring England to terms, Randolph feigned sickness, and ran off to Baltimore for a month, thus baffling the Executive in its most important measure. No report, no recommendation of any kind, had been made by the end of January, and the House agreed to discharge Randolph's committee and take up the subject itself in Committee of the Whole. Accordingly, Gregg of Pennsylvania offered resolutions suspending all commercial relations with Great Britain.[189] Macon opposed the resolution in a lengthy speech. His opposition was based on the ground that the proposed measure would provoke war, to which he was opposed under almost all circumstances. It was to no great advantage that he appeared in this address, and he was at some difficulty to prove his course not inconsistent with his past conduct. It was Randolph's influence over him which seems to have dictated much of his argument. His agrarian policy now became narrow, indeed, and rather merited the ungainly name it won about this time — the "mud-turtle policy of Southern Republicans."[190]

Macon, Randolph and Nicholson, alienated from the Administration, began actively to scheme against Madison's succession for the Presidency, which was thought to be Jefferson's wish. Macon's rather enigmatical letter to Monroe had perhaps been the beginning

---

[189] Annals of Congress, 9th Cong., 1st Sess., 411-414.
[190] Annals of Congress, 9th Cong., 1st Sess., 686.

of overtures to Monroe. Before the close of the present session, Randolph wrote Monroe[191] to hurry home to defeat the plan "for bringing Madison in," and assured him of the support of "the old Republicans." April 22, he wrote again, "A decided division has taken place in the Republican party, which has been followed by a proscription of the anti-ministerialists. Among the number of the proscribed are Mr. Nicholson, who has retired in strong disgust (sic?), the Speaker, who will soon follow him from like sentiment, and many others of minor consequence, such as the writer of this letter, *cum multis aliis*."[192] And June 10, William Wirt wrote Monroe that "Randolph told the President in company he was for no more milk-and-water Presidents."[193] June 1, Macon wrote Nicholson from Buck Spring: "The Madisonians will not lose any thing by neglect or indolence; they may overact their part, and in their zeal to keep Randolph down, may make some lukewarm about Madison. If Randolph had have stuck to the embargo, he would have been up in spite of them. * * * Madison will, I think, get the votes of North Carolina for President, and a part of them merely because there is not a serious opposition to him."[194]

What does all this mean but, what the Annals of Congress point to, that these three men began their plan of "President-making" — what Macon so much deprecated in others a little later as soon as Randolph's break with the Administration took place, and kept it up all through the session. Randolph was conscious that his loss of influence was due to his failure in impeaching Chase, as is shown in his resolutions for amending the Constitution, giving Congress the power to remove at will any judge of the United States Courts.[195] He was seeking someone on whom to put the blame of his own errors, and he found the Administration. Randolph had aimed at the Presidency; and Macon had not discouraged him. And going a step further, he then declared himself a party by himself, set up to oppose all men and measures when he believed any incorrect methods used. He was "the man who spoke out his thoughts" on all occasions, and knowing that the Constitution had been violated, at least in the letter, by both political parties, he constituted himself the champion of that instrument, and invited to him all who favored strict construction. Randolph and

---

191 March 20, 1806, in Nathaniel Macon Papers.
192 Nathaniel Macon Papers.
193 Nathaniel Macon Papers.
194 J. H. Nicholson Papers.
195 Annals of Congress, 9th Cong., 1st Sess., 500.

the Constitution, the Constitution and Randolph, were his texts on all occasions when *Virginia* was not. Macon's political creed was similar, and so it was not difficult for him to desert Jefferson for Randolph, to become a stricter champion of the Constitution than ever before.

When the Yazoo dispute came again before the House in the form of a Senate bill, Randolph made most violent opposition, and charged the Administration with smothering all opposition, insinuating further that the great Administration paper, the *National Intelligencer*, whose editors were the reporters for Congress, had suppressed his speech at the suggestion of the Government.[196] "The Man of the Mountain (Jefferson)," he continued, "is the truest prophet that ever lived. He has only to prophesy to insure the perdition of any man." To him the whole cause of the division of the Republican party was the Yazoo fraud, and since the Administration had "sold the country," he was ready to speak his mind against any man, and in the most sarcastic and drastic manner. And still sore about the impeachment, he said, "At the last session I had the honor to carry up and conduct an impeachment before the other House. It proved unsuccessful, and one of the principal causes was this Yazoo sin. I overheard a conversation between a worthy friend of mine from Georgia, who has gone home, and a great officer of the Government, when they were filling the green boxes for the magnates of the land. I heard the great officer of the Government tampering with that man to get his vote. * * * Why, sir, this is nothing; it is done everyday, and every hour of the day. It is there at the fireside and — not on the floor — that the affairs of the country are discussed. * * * What have we seen as late as yesterday? A vote of fifty-six in favor of a resolution dwindled down by conversation in the lobby to twenty-five." These were just such charges, supported by a certain appearance of evidence as they were, which won Macon to the little group of politicians who followed Randolph and undertook to avenge his wrong. Macon's whole life was a protest against caucusing, against underhanded scheming; and now that Jefferson seemed guilty of such practices, he was ready to fall away from him, and almost ready to exclaim with the Federalists, "O tempora, temporal!"

That this split in the ranks of the dominant party was due in the first instance to the disagreement about the successorship, as Schouler suggests, is quite probable; yet the impeachment disaster seems, at

---

[196] Annals of Congress, 9th Cong., 1st Sess., 908.

least so far as Randolph was concerned, to have been its immediate cause. Randolph claimed that Jefferson had caused the defeat of his own plan. Macon, though he wrote a very compromising letter to Monroe in 1804, was not an ardent advocate of Monroe's candidacy. In this Randolph did not command him. "I have been at a public dinner," wrote Macon, June 1, 1806 (quoted above), "where there were a considerable number of people present. I gave my opinion freely as to the next President, and the character talked of for it, and the man whom I would prefer. Some stared, and after awhile objected to the man in the usual cant, that he came from Geneva (Gallatin, of course), but the number that objected was not large, nor did the objection (foreign birth) seem to have weight with many. Having named him, I defended him with true democratic zeal." Macon's advocacy of Gallatin for Jefferson's successor was not meant as a check to Madison, and ultimately to help Monroe. Notwithstanding Randolph's influence, Macon never, except in the letter above referred to, expressed any preference for Monroe, and what proves till more conclusively the sincerity of his advocacy of the Pennsylvanian appears later in his life when he again turns to him for President.

Jefferson regretted very much the "family quarrel," and sought by all reasonable means to conciliate those who found fault with his administration. Before Congress adjourned he wrote Macon[197] that someone was "sowing tares" among the Republican leaders; that this, however, could not prove effective in Macon's case. A full and mutual confidence in each other, he said, would prevent this. He closed the letter by inviting Macon to dine with him. Whether the latter accepted we do not know, but it is doubtful in view of the influence Randolph and Nicholson were exerting over him at that time. To William Duane[198] he wrote similarly explaining Randolph's attitude, and declaring that the reputed coolness between the President and the Southern members did not exist, except possibly on the part of a few men who followed Randolph. Jefferson answers the charges against him, and with regard to the Quids, he says, "That I have avowed or entertain any predilection for those called Quids is in every tittle false." To Monroe, who, as we have seen, was the object of Randolph's caresses, the President had the following to say of Randolph and his followers: "Our old friend, Mercer, broke off from us some time ago;

---

197 Macon Papers.
198 Jeflerson's Writings, VII, 431.

at first disdaining to join the Federalists, yet, from the habit of voting together, becoming soon identified with them. * * * Mr. J. Randolph is in the same track, and will end in the same way. * * * Upon all trying questions, exclusive of the Federalists, the minority of Republicans voting with him has been from 4 to 6 or 8." And after further particulars regarding the split in their party, he says, "But it is unfortunate for you to be embarrassed with a soi-disant friend. You must not commit yourself to him."[199] This was at the very time when Randolph was attempting to get Monroe to come home and enter the race for the Presidency against Madison. What Jefferson accomplished by his adroit letter writing was to win to himself the less violent of the disaffected, and leave Randolph alone in his greatness. Macon maintained his independence towards all but Randolph, and towards him in the presidential successorship.

Just how many of the North Carolina delegates in the House joined Randolph's little group can not be determined accurately. On the first test vote, on the Non-importation bill, not a vote of North Carolina was given against the Administration, and Randolph, in order not to be alone, absented himself from the House. But on other occasions, Richard Stanford of Hillsborough, an able man and determined Republican, Thomas Wynne of Hertford, and Joseph Winston of Surry, affiliated with the Quids. There were never more than a dozen Republicans in the whole country who joined the ranks of the Macon-Randolph-Nicholson group.[200]

The Ninth Congress assembled for its last session on December 1, 1806, and the Northern Republicans, fearing Randolph's re-appointment at the head of the committee on Ways and Means, proposed to take from the Speaker the right of naming the standing committees. Alston, of North Carolina, and a friend of Macon's, favored the new plan, thus showing that the fear of Randolph's re-appointment was prevalent in the South, and on the Roanoke even. By an amendment to the resolution, it was finally passed in favor of the Speaker's appointing power as heretofore, but by a majority of only two. Macon understood the opposition to himself, and recognized the bad policy of placing the President's bitterest opponent at the head of the most important committee of the House, and so he appointed Joseph Clay of Pennsylvania as Randolph's successor. Clay had defeated the resolution to *elect* standing committees, by bringing up the amendment

---

199 Jefferson's Writings, VIII, 447-48.
200 Annals of Congress, 9th Cong., 2nd Sess., 127.

just referred to. But Macon regretted much the circumstances, and wrote his friend Nicholson the next day,[201] "In the disagreeable seat of Speaker I write. I have been obliged to hear the journal read in which the name of J. R. was not on the Committee of Ways and Means. Many may no doubt think my feelings were too nice on this occasion; but such was my sense of duty that I could not act otherwise. My mind was so agitated last night after writing to you, that I spent a sleepless night — write me your opinion on this to me delicate subject." What a simple, honest, straightforward mind is here portrayed! Randolph was his friend, he had been chairman of the committee by Macon's appointment since December, 1801. How trying it was to the Speaker to decide between devotion to his friend and loyalty to his country! But duty won, and Randolph was not appointed.[202] A few days after Congress began its work, it was *ordered* by the House "that Mr. Garnett be excused from serving on the Committee on Ways and Means and that Mr. John Randolph be appointed of the said committee in his stead" — a sort of "sop to Cerberus." But Cerberus did not accept.

Opposition to the navy was a characteristic feature of Macon's policy. In the struggle between the Federalists and Republicans in 1798 on the subject of Protection of Trade, he had refused to vote any protection whatever, and had opposed allowing war vessels to convoy trading fleets across the Atlantic, even incase a large navy was built. When Jefferson's Non-importation measure came before Congress, the clause for authorizing additional war vessels and coast fortifications met Macon's positive opposition: "I cannot but consider the present resolution as the commencement of a system of fortifications from one end of the continent to the other. I can see neither the necessity nor the policy of this second trial of the credit of this Government; it was once found that money could not be procured on the credit of the United States for less than eight per cent per annum. * * * Gentlemen tell us of an American spirit. I hope I have as much of it as any gentleman; but it is as much the character of the American spirit to conclude coolly, and act accordingly, as to talk loudly. Members of this House are not the only persons to judge of this spirit; *our constituents are the proper judges.* * * * On the subject of gun-boats, I believe them better adapted to the defence of our harbors than any other. If we were now at war with any nation, however gentlemen may be sur-

---

201 Nicholson Papers, December 2, 1806.
202 Annals of Congress, 9th Cong., 2nd Sess., 110-112.

prised at the declaration, I think we should do well to lend our navy to another nation also at war with that with which we might be at war; for I think such nations would manage it more to our advantage than ourselves."[203] A curious policy, to be sure, was this; but it was in accord with Macon's general attitude toward naval armaments.

The Southern agriculturists had from the beginning opposed all such outlay, claiming that it was useless, and believing, without saying so, however, that every ship built to protect trade was putting arms in the hands of New England with which to fight them ultimately. In view of this, Macon was not so unwise, nor his political foresight so short as some have claimed. During the quarrel between his erratic Virginian friend and the Administration, when the subject of foreign intercourse was constantly before the House, Macon held this policy firmly in view, and opposed on every occasion any appropriation looking to the building of a navy. He even opposed the fortifying of harbors, claiming the gun-boat method sufficient for purposes of defense. In this policy Randolph joined him, though as much from motives of enmity to the President as from set conviction. But both Macon and Randolph were advocates of the so-called "mud-turtle" plan of Southern expansionists. Randolph spoke out distinctly this Southern view of things when he said in the debate on the Non-importation Act: "What is the question in dispute? The carrying trade. What part of it? The fair, the honest and useful trade, that is engaged in carrying our own productions to foreign markets and bringing back their productions in exchange? No, sir; it is that carrying trade which covers enemy's property, and carries the coffee, the sugar, and other West Indian products to the mother country. No sir; if this great agricultural nation is to be governed by Salem and Boston, New York and Philadelphia, Baltimore and Norfolk, and Charleston, let gentlemen come out and say so. * * * I, for one, will not mortgage my property and my liberty to carry on this trade."[204] When Randolph declared he would never vote a shilling for a navy, and Macon said "lend your navy to a foreign enemy of our enemy, they can use it to better advantage than we," they were opposing New England and speaking for the South, not speaking out their "American spirit." Since the navy was commanded by Easterners and trade controlled the Eastern cities, Macon's advice was meant more as a reflection on that section than as an admission of America's inferiority.

---

203 Annals of Congress, 9th Cong., 1st Sess., 524.
204 Garland's Randolph, I., 233.

Judged in the light of future events, the most important act of this session of Congress[205] was that which settled for a long time to come the status of the slave trade. Importation of foreign slaves into the United States had been prohibited by the Constitution after January 1, 1808. This bill was drawn in accordance with the compromise of the Constitution, which had won for the Constitution the support of South Carolina in 1788. It had been conceded then that the slave trade might continue until 1808, and in consideration of this concession South Carolina voted in the Constitutional Convention for the right of "regulating foreign commerce" to be given to the proposed Union. The period of twenty years had now passed; South Carolina, having broken with her former ally, New England, had been favoring its extension, and now boldly claimed that Congress could not constitutionally prevent the trade being carried on if the State persisted in favoring it. And here began a new application of the doctrine of State sovereignty, which Jefferson himself could not have opposed consistently, and which Macon and Randolph incorporated into their political creed. This, like their opposition to the navy, was based upon agrarian principles. As yet the prosperity of the East depended on commerce, that of the South on agriculture based on slave labor. The East nominally in the name of humanity, but really in the interest of its own supremacy was striking a blow at slavery; the South, in the name of agricultural America, but really in support of its own supremacy, attempted to ward off this blow by resorting to the popular doctrine of States' Rights. As has been remarked before, it was an economic struggle, a war for *dollars*, and both parties recognized this without admitting it.

Macon said in Committee of the Whole on this subject: "I still consider this a *commercial* question. The laws of nations have nothing more to do with it than the laws of the Turks or the Hindoos. * * * If this is not a commercial question, I would thank the gentleman to show what part of the Constitution gives any right to legislate on this subject. It is in vain to talk of turning these creatures loose to cut our throats." According to one clause of the bill, any attempt to import a slave was to be followed by forfeiture. An amendment was offered by Bidwell of Massachusetts which provided that no person should be sold as a slave as a result of this forfeiture, *i. e.*, the negro was to be set free. The vote on this clause was a tie, and Macon promptly vetoed

---

205 Annals of Congress, 9th Cong., 2nd Sess., 506-507.

it.[206] The only North Carolina member who voted against Macon on this question was Joseph Winston of Surry, a hint that the West was not at one with the East on slavery. A bill was finally drawn up and passed by the Senate, which included the clause Macon had opposed, but which passed the House by a majority of 113 to 5, and which abolished forever the foreign slave trade. Macon made no opposition, and Randolph did not vote;[207] it was an Administration measure in its final form.

Congress was about to close with a duel between the two Randolphs, Thomas M. and John, about an imagined insult to the former in one of the speeches of the latter. The matter was patched up somewhat to the disadvantage of the former, he evidently not desiring it to appear that the Administration (Thomas M. Randolph was a son-in-law of the President) was taking this means to get rid of a powerful opponent. Three or four days before the adjournment, Macon and Randolph had an amusing encounter. The latter, speaking against a proposed salt tax, said, "It appears to me that the motion before the House is nothing more or less than a prologue to the same miserable farce of tergiversation relative to the salt tax and the Mediterranean fund played over the last session. Their high mightinesses, the Senate —" Macon called the speaker to order, who continued, however, without any change in his thought, to speak out his opinion of the Senate, culminating in: "If the Senate will descend from their supercilious elevation." Macon again called Randolph to order, and the speech was closed after a few remarks more.

Before the end of this session Macon broke with Randolph politically; he gradually turned again to the Administration, but without offending his friend, and, as we shall see, without yielding his independence. June 1, 1807, he wrote Nicholson, "Since my return, I have been mostly at home and scarcely ever heard the next presidential election mentioned, though I am inclined to think at this time Clinton would unite more votes in this State than any other man. Madison probably more than Monroe. * * * As to myself, I would prefer Gallatin to any man in the nation, and were the Republicans to make such an effort as they made to get Jefferson elected the first time, I am sure he would be elected by a great majority. * * * The sending back the treaty (the work of Monroe in London) will, I think, injure

---

206 Annals of Congress, 9th Cong. 2nd Sess., 266; also Boyd's Nathaniel Macon in National Legislation, Trinity Archive, XIII, 156.
207 Annals of Congress, 9th Cong., 2nd Sess., 486.

(Monroe; it will be taken as a proof that Jefferson did not approve his conduct, and certainly his signing it without making provision for the sailors (who were still being impressed), will injure him in all the Commercial towns."[208] This is not the letter of a partisan. His opinion that North Carolina would vote for Clinton was based on the growth of States' Rights ideas. It was notorious that Clinton was an extremist on this subject and he was building up the individual interests of New York in a way which has caused his impress to be stamped indelibly on the history of that young empire. Sentiment in North Carolina and the South was as strongly particularist as ever. Macon's continued preference for Gallatin was proof of his independence and his remarks on Monroe's political status show that he appreciated Monroe's position, but at the same time could do justice to Jefferson, which Randolph certainly could not. Before the assembling of the tenth Congress, Macon was ready for a final separation from "the Quids" and prepared to cooperate with the Republican party even if Madison should become President. The Quids, with Randolph as their chief and political idol, continued their course and were to embarrass the main body of republicans on many an important occasion.

Macon's speakership was ended. No one thought of his being elected again in the following December. He had been made Speaker without any exertions on his part; he had been elected three times in succession without any scheming of his own; he had supported the faction headed by Randolph and had given it up at his own discretion, and was now again in full accord with his party in the Nation. In North Carolina his supremacy was unquestioned, and there, too, without any of that organizing industry and practice so common and usually so necessary to political leaders. He stood plainly, in 1808 as in 1791, on the platform of the people's Sovereignty, never wavering, never faltering even at the risk sometimes of being charged with inconsistency. The people recognized his platform and believed in his sincerity to a degree approximating knowledge. This it was which gave him primacy, and this it was, with his special gifts as a moderator, which had given him the Speakership in 1801, and continued to give it to him as long as the South remained dominant in the councils of the Republicans. His Speakership marks the period of American politics ruled by Virginia and North Carolina, and a singularly interesting rule it was.

---
208 Macon Papers.

Twice during Jefferson's administration Macon was offered a place in the cabinet as postmaster-general, but he declined. Just when these overtures were made has not been determined, no record of it appearing either in Jefferson's writings or among the collection of fragmentary papers which Macon's family have preserved. It is probable that one of these offers was made in 1806, when the President was exerting himself to detach Macon from Randolph's group of faultfinders.[209]

NOTE — March 22 of that year Jefferson wrote Macon as follows: "Some enemy, whom we know not, is sowing tares among us; between you and myself nothing but opportunities of explanation can be necessary to defeat these endeavors, at least on my part. My confidence in you is so unqualified that nothing further is necessary for my satisfaction. I must therefore ask a conversation with you this evening my company may perhaps stay late; but to-morrow evening or the next I can be alone. I mention the evening because it is the time at which when we can be free from interruption. However, take the day and hour most convenient to yourself. Accept my affectionate salutations."

---

209 The Macon Papers. See page 207.

CHAPTER XIV.
OF THE EMBARGO, 1807-1809.

During the summer of 1807 the tension between Great Britain and the Administration became so great that two war vessels, the *Leopard*, of the British navy, and the *Chesapeake* of the American, came to blows off the Coast of Virginia. The *Chesapeake* was ordered by the *Leopard* to surrender four deserters from the English service, which order was not obeyed, and in a few moments the American ship was under a heavy fire and Commodore Barron, taken by surprise, was at a loss how to defend himself. After the loss of three men killed and eighteen wounded he sent up the white flag, ordered all his men on deck for inspection and gave up all whom the enemy claimed. Three negroes and one white man were taken; the negroes were put to work on British ships, the white man was shot. The *Chesapeake* hastened to Norfolk where its wounded could get medical relief; the English went away rejoicing in the belief that an American war vessel was a useless old tub and that American officers were struck dumb with terror at the sight of an English man of war.[210]

Macon wrote his friend Nicholson: "Indeed the attack on the *Chesapeake* was war on the part of Great Britain. We must either repeal the law which authorized the President to issue the proclamation (the Non-importation) or take some steps to enforce it." New Englanders hailed the event with secret delight hoping to see their *bête noire*, Jefferson, forced to give up his measure of coercing England incidentally impoverishing New England traders, especially in contraband of war. The Federalists, so insignificant in Washington, were fast becoming as potent as ever in the East; they had retired to their respective States, there "to die in the last ditches," as Jefferson's own followers had done in 1798-99. And they were doing Jefferson almost as much mischief in 1807 as his followers had done Adams in 1799; their rise meant the undoing of his favorite measure for bringing Europe to terms by trade restrictions.

The Non-importation bill of the last session had been a subject of angry debate, a subject which Randolph pretended to make the cause of his opposition to the President. Non-importation was an imitation of the Revolutionary policy of coercing England. Jefferson thought, that, by ceasing to buy European manufactures altogether the war-

---
210 Schouler, vol. II., 166-67.

ring powers would find it to their interest to adopt a reasonable policy toward America, that impressment of American seamen and unlawful seizure of American trading vessels would be stopped. And had the whole nation acted in good faith at the President's suggestion and observed strictly the proclamation which he had been authorized to issue, there is little doubt that the desired result would have been attained. But the East was closest to England geographically, it was also bound by family ties among the most influential people, and the daily occupation of the people was trade and seafaring. Massachusetts people drove a trade nine times as great as that of Virginia; wherever there was a sea there was a New England skipper driving hard bargains, capturing African negroes to be sold on the sly in Virginia or in the Carolinas, delivering goods to the belligerent powers of Europe without regard for the rules of neutrals in war, winning for Americans the epithet, "Yankees." Men went out from Boston or Newport or New London poor and returned a year or two hence wealthy. How could they be expected to take seriously Jefferson's policy looking to the good of the whole Union and not to that of New England alone? The answer they made to the proclamation was secret overtures to the English Premier, Canning, and open beckonings to Canadian governors to come over the borders and have talks with their great men, the members of the Essex Junto. They did not mean to be bound by a Congress which sat in a Southern city and was controlled by Southern men.

Jefferson called Congress together more than a month earlier than usual in order to get the much needed help of that body in settling the trying questions which were crowding upon his administration. The Tenth Congress had been elected when Jefferson's ship of state was sailing most smoothly and when the Administration was universally popular. It was a Jefferson Congress, Randolph excepted, ready to do the President's bidding. It organized at once, putting Macon's former rival and competitor, Joseph B. Varnum of Massachusetts, in the Speaker's Chair and George Washington Campbell of Tennessee at the head of the Committee on Ways and Means. The North was then getting back into the saddle and the new Southwest, which Jefferson always loved next to Virginia, was second in line of promotion. Virginia and Carolina, the lords of the Roanoke, Macon and Randolph, were left out altogether. This change Macon had expected, and in order not to witness his own and Randolph's humiliation he remained at Buck Spring well nigh a month after Congress met — what he had never done before and never did again in his remaining twenty years of service in Washington. Macon did not appear until November 16, and then it was sometime before he took part in the debates. He refused to vote December 5 on an appeal from the ruling of Speaker Varnum, thus showing his sensitiveness. Yet Macon was not super-sensitive like Randolph nor did he allow the change of leaders in the House to set him blindly against the Administration.

One of the first measures of the new Congress was one for arming the militia, a sort of reply to England's warlike attitude. The whole plan of the Government embraced the effective organization and equipment of the State troops, the fortification of harbors and the building of a fleet of gun boats. Macon at once gave hearty and enthusiastic support to the part of the program which aimed to improve the militia. This was his favorite means of defense and in this way alone was he willing to grant large sums of money. "This is one of the most important questions that ever came before this House," and then to show his pride in always speaking *extempore* he added, "It is one on which I have not reflected before coming into the House this morning. As to the probability of war, I may stand alone in the opinion which I entertain; but I have considered that the nation has been actually at war from the moment of the affair of the *Chesapeake*. * * * The late attack on the *Chesapeake* was as much war as the attack on Copenhagen. And what are we now doing? Are we not disputing about details? * * * I think the public money should be applied to the best purposes; no doubt there will be a diversity of opinion as to what is best. We should immediately purchase ten or twenty thousand stand of arms or any other number and put them into the hands of the States most exposed to attack from sea, which is particularly necessary at present, as the people on the seacoast are most exposed to danger." His friend Alston more nearly representing the Administration tried to convince Macon and those who agreed with him that war was not already begun and that wholesale measures ought not to be taken. Macon repeated his former arguments the more earnestly, urging the immediate purchase of arms and equipments for the States which were to have them properly distributed amongst a well-organized militia. This plan was the more acceptable to him because of his belief in the independent sovereignty of the States, and because it would counterbalance the growing power, of the Union.

The second part of the program providing for the fortification of harbors and for the building of gun boats, he opposed with as much vehemence as he had favored the first part. During the preceding summer we find him ready to support the Administration in the building of gun boats and ready even to make terms with Madison should the latter be elected President. Such was Macon's real intention but he did not one time think of supporting measures of which he disapproved simply because they were Administration measures. So the bill for gun boats and harbor fortifications which the President was now urging met his positive opposition. Jefferson had asked first for the building of the gun boats, then he meant to ask for the equipments and finally for the men to man them. Macon opposed that kind of legislation by piece-meal and he asked for estimates of the cost of the total establishment. Blount of North Carolina, an ardent supporter of the Administration, undertook to explain the bill by saying the committee had another bill almost ready which would empower the President to equip and man the gun boats. This shows Jefferson's easy way of leading his party into measures which if presented complete would have been opposed. It is needless to say Macon voted against the bill.[211] He wrote a little later: "By the public prints you have discovered that Congress have made very liberal appropriations for fortifications and gun boats; to this liberality I have no claim. The first seems now to be almost useless in Europe, and as to the second, we ought to have a little more experience before we adopt it as a measure of defence."[212] How our ports were to be defended he did not attempt to say, and his opposition does him little credit since he suggests no remedy whatever. When the bill to which Blount referred came up for discussion, Macon maintained his opposition first on the ground of his life-long opposition to all naval armaments, and second, because the measure proposed to give the President discretionary powers for raising a marine corps: "I am opposed to giving to the President the power of raising an army of marine, or of any description whatever. This discretion is what I have always thought wrong; and no argument ever convinced my mind to the contrary."[213] The bill finally passed, Macon voting with a minority of ten against one hundred and eight. Richard Stanford of North Carolina and John Randolph also voted with the little group of opponents.

---

211 Annals of Congress, 10th Cong., 1st Sess., 1171.
212 Letter to John Steele, January 10, 1808.
213 Annals of Congress, 10th Cong., 1st Sess., 1498.

North Carolina's delegation in this Congress was scarcely more brilliant than that of 1795-'97, when Macon first began to lead. Willis Alston was its ablest member after Macon. Thomas Blount, Thomas Kenan and erratic Lemuel Sawyer were the Eastern representatives. Evan Alexander from Mecklenburg was there, and Richard Stanford, Randolph's friend, and Meshack Franklin, brother of the Governor, both of whom our historian, Wheeler, did not know, represented the middle West. Duncan MacFarland, the perpetual candidate in North Carolina of that day, was knocking at the door of the House in the form of a contest for John Culpeper's seat. Culpeper had gone in by a close vote in the Fayetteville district, and MacFarland, Federalist, was ready to contest the election. The House committee on elections declared the seat vacant and called on the Governor to issue writs for a new election, which was done, and Culpeper was returned by a safe majority, though he seems never to have done anything except in a religious way. Culpeper was a Baptist preacher in a Presbyterian section, was elected to the State legislature and was declared ineligible because of his being a minister of the Gospel. He was returned to Congress several times in later years, thus gaining in the Nation what was not allowed him in the State. This was MacFarland's last fiasco in the House of Representatives. There was no leader of the delegation, most of its members, however, were strict adherents to the Administration and left Macon and Stanford alone in their independence.

After the passage of the militia and gun-boat bill Congress took up seriously the President's plan of trade retaliation against England. Ten years before Jefferson had formulated a plan which he thought, if it could only be put into effect, would render war obsolete in America. It was at the time when he was wishing that an ocean of fire separated America from Europe that he first came to believe in an embargo as a substitute for war. Now he was President and an overwhelming majority in both Houses of Congress did his bidding and England still persisted in insulting American naval officers by searching their ships for deserters, or impressing their sailors because they could not at all times furnish written proof of their citizenship, or, simply because they spoke English. Was it not the best time imaginable to try the virtues of such a beneficial policy? The provocation was there, English war vessels were actually chasing American seamen from their ships in our very harbors. The plan was resolved upon; embargo should follow Non-importation and England was to feel the effect of famine prices, to see her factories closed for the want of raw material, while at the same time her storehouses were filled to overflowing with unsalable manufactures. Our ships were to keep close in the harbors or high up the rivers, no foreign trader was to depart without special orders from the President on pain of confiscation; the coast traders were to dart in and out from harbor to harbor like spring chickens dodging a hawk. Ship-owners and traders were to be fined twice the value of each ship if found violating the provisions of the proposed law and all the forces of the army and navy were to be placed at the disposal of the Executive for its effective enforcement.[214] In a few days the embargo was before Congress and within four days it became a law with all the clauses necessary for the enforcement of the ideas pointed out above. Never did a President have his wishes more speedily complied with. The embargo was an experiment and a reasonable one; there was no ground for doubting that it would bring England to terms if it were enforced strictly everywhere for one or two years. Warring Europe was in need of supplies which America chiefly furnished. But, as already said, the enforcement was the question and many doubted the ability of the government to enforce a law which required large numbers of wealthy men to close up their business.[215] The law went into effect at once and complaints and petitions began to pour in upon the President and Congress.

Macon approved of the embargo especially since it would render increase of the navy unnecessary; Randolph at first favored but finally opposed it. But the plan was in full accord with the political principles of both Randolph and Macon.[216]

Evasion of the law became general at once in the maritime States and England lent her assistance. Canada was made a dumping ground for New England merchants. On Lake Champlain New England traders defied the officers of the United States and carried their goods in triumph past the custom houses. Prosecutions for violation of law proved abortive, because the juries were all against it; the President's authority was made ridiculous from the Hudson to St. Croix. Under such circumstances England not only refused to sue for peace, but became more arrogant as New England became more violent.[217] France, too, against which the embargo was also directed, refused to give any serious attention to a policy which was not enforced at

---

214 See Act of January 9, 1808 Annals of Congress, passim.
215 See Schouler II., 180-185.
216 Garland's *Life of Randolph*, I., 266- 67.
217 See Hart's *Formation of the Union*.

home and which therefore had no serious influence on the French food supply. All through the first session of the Tenth Congress, that is, in 1807-1808, the Administration was bolstering up its unpopular law in order to make it effective and thus to bring foreign powers to some kind of terms, but it was all in vain. Macon remained firm in his support of the bill even though it brought immediate loss to him as a tobacco grower. He claimed with Randolph that it only required a steady adherence to the policy to bring about the desired effect and he blamed bitterly the Eastern men for practically annulling a law of the Union — that Union which they had loved and adored so much in 1798. Toward the end of the session, the Administration, becoming more apprehensive of war, called on Congress for an increase of the army by 6,000 men. Macon recognized the need of a stronger force and decided in the beginning to give the President his support. He wrote Nicholson,[218] * * * "Our situation is every day growing worse and it seems to me that we must prepare for the last reasoning of nations or rather of governments, and in this situation we must raise a few troops for some defenceless places." Macon expected Randolph would oppose the bill and said as much in this letter, explaining at the same time his own attitude: "Randolph will, I expect, oppose the bill for raising 6,000 men, so that he and myself will split on the question. You remember that two years ago we split on the same question for raising troops, he for, and myself against." On the same day that this was written he felt constrained to explain his vote and to show why he reversed his lifetime policy with, regard to this subject. Randolph had alluded to the attitude of the Republicans in 1798 and hinted at Macon's inconsistency. "There is no analogy," said Macon, "between the present crisis and that of 1798, * * * then we seemed to try to provoke a war — in fact were the attacking party; now we have been attacked. The attack on the *Chesapeake* is not disputed. Notwithstanding this, I do not believe that we shall have any serious invasion; yet it is certainly probable after what has taken place, that attempts may be made to attack some of our towns, for the purpose of laying contributions on them. Under this impression I shall act." He continued in a rather long speech justifying his actions, though with some difficulty from his point of view. He drew the distinction between the present plan and former ones, saying: "I do not consider the troops to be raised intended for a Peace Establishment. If I did, I should not vote for the

---

218 Macon to Joseph H. Nicholson, April 4, 1808.

bill. * * * It has been said there would be great difficulty in getting the men. This will in some measure depend on the proper selection of officers; but be this as it may, notwithstanding I am in favor of the bill, I feel no reluctance in saying, that I believe it is almost as difficult to get clear of a Military Peace Establishment, as it is to enlist the privates for the establishment. * * * I have heard today, and at former times, a maxim boldly advanced, which to me never appeared correct or true; that to preserve peace you must be prepared for war. In all countries, especially those which are free, the thirst for military fame is greater than that for civil, and if it gets a complete ascendency, is extremely difficult to allay. It may be observed, that our country is not exempt from this passion which has done so much injury to the human race. We seem to admire the heroic actions of our young men, more than we do the civil virtues of Franklin, Hancock, Adams, and Dickinson; though it would be no easy question to decide whether Washington was a greater civil or a military character, yet his military character is that which I believe gives the nation the most delight."[219]

Macon was in fact inconsistent with many of his former professions but not inconsistent with his Republican creed. The army increase was necessary; Gallatin, his best friend in the Administration, was in favor of it. Ample assurance was given that these new troops would be disbanded when the danger was passed and so it was Randolph, not Macon, who was open to criticism from his party.

It was during this session that Macon and Randolph were oftenest found disagreeing, and it is not a little amusing to see how each tried to explain to the other the cause of his opposing vote. Macon speaks "with respect" when he finds himself not in accord with his friend, and Randolph with many compliments to his "worthy and much respected" friend from North Carolina. Fair examples of their references are as follows: Macon: "I should not have spoken on this subject, had not allusions been made by a gentleman from Virginia (Randolph) to what had been done in the year 1795 — a gentleman whom I much respect and who, I believe, perfectly reciprocates my respect. A sincere desire to retain this respect induces me to speak." Randolph: "My worthy friend from North Carolina, whose dissent from my opinion would have caused me to distrust it if I had not conceived that his own speech in favor of the army was one of the most masterly arguments against it:" and again, "I feel the deepest

---

[219] Annals of Congress, 10th Cong., 1st Sess., vol. II., 1934-38.

concern whenever I differ with the gentleman in question, and nothing but the impulse of honest duty, knowing as I did of the difference which existed between us on the subject, could have prevailed upon me to rise yesterday. I say, it is a matter of surprise and regret to me that he should support this bill; that he should declare the present establishment useless, and, at the same time, declare his willingness to increase it threefold. I hope the gentleman will pardon me for taking this notice of his arguments."[220] It appeared at times as if they would fall into each other's arms and weep. Congress must have been amused at the Damon and Pythias exhibitions of this session and certainly the close-trading New Englanders enjoyed seeing their enemies undo each other's speeches and votes. Whatever the other members thought, Randolph and Macon were sincere friends, neither of whom had sufficient sense of humor to appreciate the ridiculous figure they made in their declarations of love before the House.

During this session of Congress several questions arose and were determined in a way very interesting to us. The capital was about to be removed from Washington back to Philadelphia. Northern members complained at the poor conveniences for living in the little city on the Potomac. Macon responded: "It is possible you might live better in Philadelphia than here, but not cheaper. If we should move I should be opposed to going to any large city. * * * There is scarce any other place in the United States to which I had *not rather* go than to Philadelphia — I had rather go to Frederickstown, Hagerstown or Winchester. We may talk about our independence, but everyman in Congress, when at Philadelphia, knew that city had more than its proportionate weight in the representation of the Union. Go to any city and the same influence will be experienced. Do gentlemen recollect what was the state of the public mind there during the years 1797 and 1798 the time when the name of Republican and Democrat was accounted a disgrace? There are gentlemen in my hearing who were then associated with me in legislation, and who know and will attest the truth of what I say, that we were shunned as a pestilence the yellow fever could not have been more carefully avoided. I do not mention this as a reflection on the Administration, but as an evidence of what may be expected in large cities. We may do very well in peaceable times, but come to the times which try men's souls, and we shall have to desert them for Princeton or some other conve-

---

220 Annals of Congress, 10th Cong., 1st Sess., vol. II., 1952, 1965-70.

nient village."²²¹ And a little further on he gives another reason which caused him to oppose removal to Philadelphia and it was equivalent to a formal announcement of his policy: "The charter of the Bank of the United States expires in 1811. In 1809, it is proposed we shall be in Philadelphia. We shall then have two years before to talk and be talked to about this bank. If we must remove, let us go over the Alleghanies. * * * These large cities have always had too much influence in this body; go among them and it will be increased a hundred fold." Dislike of cities, a fear of their riotous behavior during national crises, hatred for their snobbish ways and positive opposition to the National Bank in Philadelphia were the controlling motives with him on this subject. As a matter of fact he could not forget the hatred of Philadelphia for himself and party, how Jefferson had been avoided there in 1798 as though he were a public enemy, how McPherson's Band of musicians played the rogue's march at the doors of himself and friends in 1798 because fashionable life in Philadelphia detested their politics.²²² He was not alone in his opinion that a great city is no place for the capital of a republic. Adams, the best of Federalists, said there was danger in a big city. Jefferson was of like opinion.

Another subject came up several times and its treatment shows the whole Democratic party had come to hold unfriendly opinions toward the Supreme Court. It was proposed now by Massachusetts men that the Judges be removed on petition of both Houses of Congress. This, as we have seen, had been Randolph's plan some three years before. There must have been general fear of the encroachments of the Court under the strong hand of John Marshall, else both wings of the great Democratic party would scarce have come over to Randolph's apparently partisan and personal policy. Senators, too, it was proposed by the Virginia legislature to Congress, should be removable by a majority vote of their respective State Assemblies.²²³ Republicanism was growing stronger and so it desired to lop off all the aristocratic features of the government. There was to be only one supreme body, Congress, and that was to be subject to biennial elections, *i. e.*, the people were the real sovereigns and they must so be recognized. Men were getting as far from Hamilton's ideals as pos-

---

221 Annals of Congress, 10th Cong., 1st Sess., vol. II., 340.
222 Annals of Congress, 10th Cong., 1st Sess., vol II., 1562.
223 Annals of Congress, 10th Cong., 1st Sess., vol. II., 1615-96.

sible; Jefferson's were in full ascendency notwithstanding the "family quarrel" and the ominous growls in the East.

The engineering and wire-pulling relative to the successorship to the presidency were so much in evidence this session that Macon thought the public interests as well as the characters of public leaders were suffering. Between Madison, Monroe, Clinton and Gallatin he was at no loss for whom to vote; but with Gallatin's name stricken from the list of availables he knew not where to place his influence. "When great men, so-called, agree in general principles, or in other words, when the men held up for the next President are of the same political party, is it worth while for little men, so-called, to take great concern which of these shall fill the office or the Great House? * * * The Clintonians evidently are on the Monroe side. In reflecting on this subject I have been inclined to an opinion, that the great, so-called, might as well take care of themselves and their characters as those who are not so-called. When a principle is involved in the election of a particular man, it is then quite a different question; where men of the same principles are candidates for the same office it looks much like a contest for the loaves and fishes. * * * But with us there may be another cause for supporting candidates with the same principles, this is State prejudice or partiality, to which may be added the general unwillingness of great States to have either P. or V.-P. from small States." Then showing his appreciation of the rising tide of opposition from New England and commercial centres generally to the embargo laws, he concluded : "I suspect we shall have a dust raised in the House before the adjournment; * * * seems to me there must be an explosion before we part. Too much heat has been collected since we have been reading and not speaking to be suffered to pass quietly away."[224] And six days later he again wrote his friend: "Yours of the 2d instant was last night received, the opinion mentioned by you as given by some federalists is the universal doctrine of that party and I fear that some [Madison] of another party are not very different in their sentiments; but our situation is every day growing worse and it seems to me that we must prepare for the last reasoning of nations or rather of governments. * * * We must either repeal the law which authorized the President to issue the proclamation or to take some steps to enforce it."[225] Thus the idea of repealing the embargo came to him

---

224 To Joseph H. Nicholson, March 29, 1808.
225 Jos. H. Nicholson, March 29, 1808; compare letter of April 4, p. 226.

within four months from its passage. In April, 1808, our choice in foreign policy was restricted either to rigid enforcement of the embargo or a declaration of war. And he made up his mind, as we shall see, for the former.

Macon's attitude toward the coming campaign was painfully uncertain. Again and again he was approached by the warring factions and again and again he refused each any assurance of his support. And his influence was important; the weight of North Carolina's vote would go according to his suggestion. That he was himself much at sea and out of touch with both parties at this time is shown by the following letter: "I am not in the secrets of any one here, no not one; all, all, except myself, are engaged in making Presidents. And you (Nicholson) know enough of public life to know that in great election contests, he that does not take an active part on one side or the other, is generally hated by both, and always suspected by both, no matter how honest his indifference or how sincerely he may believe the contest a matter of no consequence." And coming again to his old favorite, Gallatin, he adds, "or how willing he may be to support one, whom he would prefer to either of those named, and one whom he thought better qualified in every respect for the appointment, but whom neither of the parties would take, not because he is unfit."[226]

While the embargo was beginning to go into effect, Pickering, the former Secretary of State, and George Cabot announced to New England their program of opposition which called for concerted action of all the commercial States against the Administration. Cabot declared "our best citizens consider the interests of the United States interwoven with those of Great Britain, and that our safety depends on hers." Rufus King, Hamilton's friend in the Miranda scheme, joined the New England malcontents, all of whom now entered into a close league with each other and opened correspondence with the representatives of Great Britain relative to concerted action between Old and New England against Jefferson and his Southerners.[227] This opposition found public expression in all the New England papers and so impressed the Executive that Campbell as Chairman of the committee on Ways and Means recommended to Congress, April 12, a measure looking to the suspension of the embargo during the coming vacation in case the President deemed it necessary. Crowningshield of Mas-

---

[226] To Joseph H. Nicholson, April 6, 1808.
[227] Schouler, II., 202-03.

sachusetts made his last speech in favor of the new resolution hoping that pressure could be brought to bear from his section sufficient to compel Jefferson to yield. The opportunity was too tempting to Randolph for him not to chastise the Administration with his unmerciful invective and sarcasm. Macon contented himself with voting against the proposition on the ground that it would place too much power in the President's hands.[228] He had always voted against the granting of such powers even in the case of Washington in the crisis of 1793. The Administration prevailed, and the act conferring on the President the power to suspend the embargo passed April 21. But Jefferson was not desirous of using plenary powers in these trying times and so he recommended an early reassembling of Congress.

As was anticipated the first proposition brought before Congress at the next session, which began November 7, with almost every member present, was one for immediately repealing the embargo. The East, not strong in numbers, was determined in aspect and speech-making. Madison, whose election was already a certainty, had agreed to take up the President's burden but he was not as yet willing to repeal the law. Campbell made a long report but was unable to unite the House on any measure. Then Gallatin, Madison and Macon put their heads together with the result that Macon introduced a series of resolutions on November 17. These were as follows:

1. "That the committee appointed on that part of the President's message which relates to our foreign relations, be instructed to inquire into the expediency of excluding by law from the ports, harbors and waters of the United States all armed ships and vessels belonging to any of the belligerent powers having in force orders or decrees violating the lawful commerce of the United States as a nation.

2. "That the same be instructed to inquire into the expediency of prohibiting by law the admission into the ports, harbors, and waters of the United States, any ship or vessel belonging to or coming from any place in the possession of any of the above mentioned powers, and also the importation of any goods, wares and merchandise, the growth, produce and manufactures of the dominions of any of the said powers.

3. "That the same committee be instructed to inquire into the expediency of amending the act laying an embargo, and the several acts supplementary and additional thereto."

---

228 Annals of Congress, 10th Cong., 1st Sess., vol. II., 2243-44.

When introducing these resolutions Macon declared that America should enforce to the letter the whole embargo system. "Has the love of gain superseded every other motive in the breasts of Americans? Shall the majority govern, or shall a few wicked and abandoned men drive this nation from the ground it has taken? Is it come to this that a law constitutionally enacted, even after a formal decision in favor of its constitutionality, can not be enforced? Shall a nation give way to the opposition of a few, and those the most profligate part of the community? * * * Just as our measure is beginning to operate, just as provisions are becoming scarce in the West Indies and elsewhere, not withstanding the evasion of our law, we are called upon to repeal it." Then, reviewing the latest proclamation of England against neutral commerce, he said: "This proclamation then tells our citizens, Evade the laws of your country, and we will receive and protect you. If the mad Powers of Europe had entered into a compact to injure us as much as they could, they could not have taken a more direct course to it. I consider them both (France and England) alike, and the measures I would take would place them both on the same footing. I have thought proper to bring forward all these resolutions together to show my own opinion on what ought to be done. * * * I believe the embargo was right; that it was right to pass laws to enforce it. And believing this, I feel no hesitation in avowing it. Time has been when the improvement of our seamen was cried out against by a large majority of Congress. Now the cry is, that we will not let them go out and be taken, for if they go out they must be taken. Neither of the two great Powers of Europe have shown the least disposition to relax their measures; neither, I hope, shall we. I believe we have but three alternatives, *war, embargo* or *submission*. The last I discard; * * * then the only question is, whether in the present state of the world, the embargo or war is the best for us. * * * I am for the embargo yet." And in answer to the statement that the embargo was not burdensome to the South, he said, "The country in which I live feels the measure as much as any; they are agriculturists, and their crops remain unsold; and they will do without the principal, and resist imposition by withholding their produce; those who make a profit by the freight of our produce may afford to lose that profit."[229]

Josiah Quincy replied to Macon: "Is this House touched with that insanity which is the never-failing precursor of the intention

---

[229] Annals of Congress, 10th Cong., 2nd Sess., 497-99.

of Heaven to destroy? Are the people of New England, after eleven months of deprivation of the ocean, to be commanded still longer to abandon it for an undefined period, to hold their unalienable rights, at the tenure of Britain or Bonaparte, a people, commercial in all respects, in all their relations, in all their recollections of the past, in all their prospects of the future a people, whose first love was the ocean, the choice of their childhood, the approbation of their manly years, the most precious inheritance of their fathers, "*et cetera*, * * * I am lost in astonishment, Mr. Chairman. I have not words to express the matchless absurdity of this attempt. I have no tongue to express the swift and headlong destruction which a blind perseverance in such a system must bring upon the nation. The gentleman from North Carolina exclaimed the other day, in a strain of patriotic ardor, What, shall not our laws be executed? Shall their authority be defied? I am for enforcing them at every hazard. I honor that gentleman's zeal; and I mean no deviation from that true respect I entertain for him when I tell him that in this in stance his zeal is not in accordance with his knowledge. I ask this House, is there no control to its authority, is there no limit to the power of this National Legislature? I hope I shall offend no man when I intimate that two limits exist: Nature and the Constitution. * * * Suppose some one, in 1788, in the Convention of Massachusetts, while debating upon the adoption of this Constitution, and with an eye looking deep into futurity, with a prophet's ken, had thus addressed the Assembly: Fellow citizens of Massachusetts, to what ruin are you hastening? * * * Sir, does any man believe that, with such a prospect into futurity, the people of that State would have for one moment listened to its adoption?"[230] This was returning Macon's own argument against the Alien and Sedition laws of 1798; the situation was reversed exactly, and the representatives of Massachusetts were ready to draw their Virginia and Kentucky resolutions to make solemn protest in the name of their sovereign State. The Macon resolutions of November 17 were given the form of a bill, and he made a very long speech in its favor on December 3, and on this occasion he waxes eloquent in his advocacy of the bill. "We have not Hannibal at the gate; but Rome and Carthage have both declared against us. * * * I am now willing, and always willing, to go as far as any member of the House in the protection of the trade which fairly grew out of the agriculture and fisheries of the United States. I never will consent to risk

---

[230] Annals of Congress, 10th Cong., 2nd Sess., 537-545.

the best interests of the nation for a trade which we can carry on only when Europe is at war." New England had no just cause of complaint. "Before the war tobacco was ten dollars a hundred at Petersburg, in Virginia, and in great demand; and before the war ended it was less than three dollars at the same place, and not in demand," which, he maintained, was evidence enough that his section was suffering as much from the embargo as any other. It is well known, says Schouler, that Jefferson's final bankruptcy was set in motion by the very laws which he recommended as the best for the whole country. Macon suffered fully as much relatively. It was at this time that Macon began earnestly to exhort members of Congress that to maintain the Union as inviolable was our only means of safety. "It appears to me that there never was a time in which it was more necessary than the present, practically to observe one of the admonitions printed on the old Continental money — *United we stand, divided we fall.* Nothing but a strict attention to this can secure our rights; it will, as formerly, secure to us all that we ought in justice to expect."[231]

On the following day, *i. e.* December 4, 1808, Macon wrote Nicholson: "The war men in the House of Representatives are, I conceive, gaining strength, and I should not be surprised if we should not be at war with both Great Britain and France before the 4th March. Gallatin is most decidedly for war, and I think the Vice-President and W. C. Nicholas are of the same opinion. It is said that the President gives no opinion as to the measure that ought to be adopted; it is not known whether he be for war or for peace. It is reported that Mr. Madison is for the plan which I have submitted, with the addition of high protecting duties to encourage the manufactures of the U.S. I am as much against war as Gallatin is in favor of it; then I have continued in Congress till there is not one of my old fellow-laborers that agree with me in opinion. I do not know what plan Randolph will pursue. He is against continuing the embargo. I wish he would lay some plan before the House. (Why?) It grieves me to the heart to be compelled, from a sense of right and duty, to oppose him." And then again referring to his own isolation, he said: "I am not consulted, as you seem to suppose, about any thing, nor do I consult any one. I am about as much out of fashion as our grandmothers' ruffle cuffs, and I do not believe I shall be in fashion [again] as soon as they will." And then, in the postscript, although he was doing all he could in a contrary

---

231 Annals of Congress, 10th Cong., 2nd Sess., 669-674.

direction, he added: "It is probable that the embargo may be taken off before the adjournment. We have those who think it will, and that war will immediately follow. I suspect all the N. E. Republicans are for war and no embargo. You know it is no easy task to prevent what they want." Macon's bill was superseded by another, which provided for repealing the obnoxious embargo altogether. This last attempt at repeal was successful. New England was up in arms, and Congress was almost forced by an insignificant minority to pass a measure which the majority had made the most prominent article of its policy. It was a question of Union or dis-Union, and the South shrank from such a catastrophe at that stage of its existence. Macon wrote, February 28, 1809: "Otis, the Secretary of the Senate, has this minute informed the H. of R. that the Senate have agreed to the amendments made by the House to the bill to repeal the embargo, etc. The Lord, the Mighty God, must come to our assistance, or I fear we are undone as a nation"[232] Macon did what he could to prevent a bill for a repeal from coming before the House; failing in this, he had little to say during the last days of this Congress. He had regained his position in his party, and was from this time till the outbreak of war three years later one of the foremost figures in American politics.

As is shown in his letter, the Administration was deserting its favorite plan. Jefferson was longing for Monticello as sincerely as Washington had sighed for Mount Vernon, and feeling keenly his defeat by his ancient enemies, the Easterners, he said not a word and let things drift till a few days before the 4th of March, when he gave reluctant assent to the bill which undid his whole foreign policy and stamped the seal of failure on his favorite scheme of rendering war unnecessary in settling the disputes of nations. Jefferson retired amid the jeers of the wealthy classes in New England, but conscious that the love and admiration of the American people followed him.[233]

---

232 To Joseph H. Nicholson.
233 Compare Schouler, II., 216, 220.

CHAPTER XV.
MACON A NATIONAL CHARACTER, 1809-1812.

The Republican party lost considerable strength in North Carolina as a result of Jefferson's embargo policy, and the State's delegation in the Eleventh Congress was not altogether to Macon's liking. John Stanly, Lemuel Sawyer, Richmond Pearson and Archibald McBryde, in the main new members, were more often found voting with the Federalists than with the Republicans. And on no occasion did all the North Carolinians vote on the same side of a question. Macon was not the leader of this delegation, as he had been of the previous ones. Party lines were not drawn so closely in the South as they had been, and everybody was in a tolerant humor at the first session of Congress, May and June, 1809. The East, to be sure, was still firm, and actually regaining what had been lost in 1804 and 1805. In the Middle States, as in the South, lukewarm Republicans had been returned. So that there were practically three parties in Congress: the Federalists, the "old" Republicans of the South, and the "manufacturing" Republicans of the North. In the election of Speaker, the two sections of the Republican party found positive expression. The Northern Republicans supported Varnum, while the Southerners voted for Macon; Pitkin, of Connecticutt, received the vote of the Federalists. On the second ballot, Macon received 45 against Varnum's 65 votes; this rather unexpected popularity and special strength with Southern Republicans was the immediate cause of Macon's becoming a national character of first-rate importance in 1809-1811.[234]

The political situation of 1809 was unique. Madison, a fine old lady, occupied the President's chair. In his cabinet were two factions, or cliques. Robert Smith, of Maryland, who was "backed" by a large family influence both in his own State and in Virginia, and whose brother was not an insignificant member of the Senate, had forced his way into the position of Secretary of State, an office for which Gallatin was preeminently fitted, and which Jefferson and Madison had already agreed he should have. But Gallatin was losing caste in Pennsylvania, was none too popular elsewhere, and was too unsuspecting, Macon thought, to compete with the active influences of Smith's "friends." Madison was not the man to say "no" to these new influences, and the able Pennsylvanian did not receive the promotion

---

234 Annals of Congress, 11th Cong., vol. I., 54-56; Schouler, vol. II., 317.

he deserved. This caused discord in the Cabinet not unlike that of Adams' administration, and these factions extended their ramifications into both houses of Congress.

Before Madison was inaugurated, Gallatin told Erskine, the British Envoy, that the President-elect was not so anti-English as Jefferson had been, which led to condescending overtures from London touching a better understanding on the subject of neutral trade. Erskine promised more than his master, Canning, had authorized the Orders in Council were to be revoked, notwithstanding England had captured one hundred and eight merchant men the year before! Madison lent a willing ear to these assurances, and issued a proclamation that the strict Non-intercourse laws would, with a few exceptions, cease to be effective after June 10. Madison suddenly became the hero of the New Englanders, and Jefferson was looked at askance even in his own faithful South for having given the country so many lean years of embargo, when, as it appeared under the new régime, there had been no need for it.

Congress had come together May 22, and the back-country and Southern members learned for the first time that the war storm in which the campaign had been made had blown over; there was only good news for the mild and pacific Madison to communicate to the assembled legislature. The ships of New England had all been set a-going, tobacco and wheat from the South were in great demand already, England was the kindliest of nations. The "new broom was sweeping clean."

What was there for good Republicans to do? Reduce the army, reform the navy, and correct abuses. Jefferson had, very much against his will, as every one knew, increased the standing army in 1808. Randolph very adroitly moved on the second day of the new session that those "troops raised under the act of April 12, 1808, be immediately disbanded," and that any balance of public money intended for building gun-boats "be applied toward arming and equipping the whole body of militia of the United States." And going beyond this undoing of Jefferson's work, he introduced a second resolution calling for a committee of investigation to examine into the accounts of the last two administrations, to report irregularities and submit recommendations how to curtail expenditure. The members of the House, delighting so much in the sunshine of the new Administration, suffered Randolph to make several sarcastic speeches on the policy of the retiring President. Macon, recalling the investigations which Washington had asked in 1796, and which an irate House had forced on Adams in 1801, and favoring investigation from principle, reinforced Randolph by saying: "I would establish it as a rule never to be departed from, that whenever a man goes out of office, there should be an investigation into the money transactions conducted by him. I wish it were a part of the National Constitution."[235] Macon was Jefferson's staunchest friend, yet he wrote Nicholson, May 25: "I am for striking out the part which relates to reporting provision for the better accountability of public money, and for leaving the committee nothing to do except the examination of the expenditure and the application of public money. I wish the committee may have no excuse for not making a full investigation." But Macon was not so content with Randolph when he passed severe strictures on Jefferson's embargo. "I differ totally from the gentleman from Virginia," he said. And again, when Randolph urged a vote of approbation for Madison, Macon opposed him, seeing clearly the mean partisanship of his friend.[236] This last resolution of Randolph's was lost only by the Speaker's vote. Thus while half the members of a Republican Congress were bowing down before the throne of the new power and criticizing in the severest manner all the important measures of the man who had made Madison possible, Macon declared openly before all that he was for the embargo, that it was not the fault of the bill or of Jefferson but of the people that made it a failure; yet much as he admired Jefferson he opposed giving him the privilege of mailing his letters free of charge.[237] Macon was appointed a member of the investigating committee provided for in Randolph's first two resolutions and as appears from a letter of June 23, he served: "Everything in my power will be done; and I may tell you in confidence that although the committee are well disposed, owing to Randolph's engagements on [other] committees, [it] leaves me much of the inquiring part. Gallatin's answers to the inquiries are not received by the committee."[238]

While things were as yet going smoothly with the great warring nations of Europe, while the embargo was fast expiring and almost all the protective features of the Non-importation laws were disappearing, the "manufacturing" Republicans in cooperation with some

---

235 Annals of Congress, 11th Cong., 1., 66-67.
236 Annals of Congress, 11th Cong., 1., 107.
237 Annals of Congress, 11th Cong., 1., 148.
238 To Joseph H. Nicholson, June 23, 1809; also Annals of Congress, 11th Cong., 1., 163.

Federalists began to revive and expand Hamilton's policy of protecting manufacturers.[239] In view of Macon's uncompromising opposition to all forms of protection, and especially from this time on, it may be well to quote the main resolution: "Resolved, that for the protection of those who have commenced, and the encouragement of those who may be disposed to set on foot, manufacturers within the United States, etc., provision ought forth with to be made by law to subject to additional duties on their importation into the United States all articles of which leather, hemp, and cotton are the chief materials; woolen cloths above six shillings per yard; woolen hosiery, glass, paper, silver, nails, hats, clothing ready made, beer, ale and porter."

Macon replied to Lyon's remarks on this subject: "In the country in which I live, the people want no protecting duties to encourage domestic manufactures; the only way to encourage them is for our great people, for instance the Presidents and Heads of Departments, to make them fashionable. I have no idea of laying a tax to induce men to work in iron, leather or any other article. The people who favored the embargo, did not look upon it as does the gentleman, as an encouragement to manufacturing. Whilst the present Constitution remains to the United States it is utterly impossible for the United States to become a manufacturing nation. The Government must be materially changed before it can succeed."[240] Protection as a policy was not begun at this session but a resolution passed calling on the Secretary of the Treasury to submit plans for the adoption of such a system at the next session of Congress. Yet a majority of the members voted for the principle under the head of non-intercourse with France which had to be arranged as a result of the English friendliness. And Madison, as we have seen, had favored protective duties since 1808, when it was seen that embargo must be abandoned. Madison, true to his compromising disposition, was willing to make friends with this new element of his party. Hamilton's devoted followers in the East opposed this policy of their great leader now that it appeared in Republican garb. But a deeper reason was that the interests of commerce would apparently suffer if domestic manufacturing should become general and prosperous. The South was likewise opposed to protection as it had always been except from the individual States to their own industries. The Middle States and Kentucky were its champions

---

239 Bacon's and Lyon's resolutions, Annals of Congress, 11th Cong., 1., 182-184.
240 Annals of Congress, 11th Cong., 1., 185-186.

— the way was preparing for Henry Clay.

A letter of Macon's written near the close of the session shows how close an observer he was and manifests at the same time his aversion to secret methods: "I sincerely wish that it may never so happen that the invisibles govern the nation without a check. Last spring their power in the Treasury department [was manifest]. In conversation many declare independence of them, yet on a vote they never fail to have a majority. If they are to govern, it would be better that they governed according to the constitution, than in the way they do, another now stands between them and the people."[241] He refers here to the rising power of the bank and commercial men, as well as the Smith faction.

Congress adjourned in good spirits but anxious enough on the subject of foreign intercourse to provide for reassembling, a week earlier than usual. Already the British envoy had shown signs of the sad dilemma into which Canning was inveigling the American Cabinet. In July the whole arrangement between Erskine and Madison which had brought such a peaceful and promising state of things during the session just closing was annulled; in August Erskine was openly disgraced and Madison issued a proclamation announcing that England had not revoked the Orders in Council and that trade with Great Britain was forbidden. Jackson was the next English envoy, but he soon got himself dismissed by grossly insulting the Government and made a tour through New England where he was received with great enthusiasm and entertained as a public guest.[242] France was equally overbearing. Napoleon at the very pinnacle of power was only too desirous to reap advantage from American trade and if possible embroil us in a war with England.

It was a sad condition of things which the returning Legislature had to meet in November, 1809: American trading vessels were scattered over the whole world, their owners fearing capture or ready to accept *en masse* the protection of England; Eastern politicians were hotly demanding peace and their representatives in Congress, Quincy, Pitkin and Dana stood ready for any move their constituents demanded; the Middle States were divided in sentiment, some following Duane's *Aurora* were clamoring for immediate war, others were making love to New England politicians; the Southerners without a leader

---

241 To Joseph H. Nicholson, June 23, 1809.
242 See Hart's *Formation of the Union*, 201.

were subject to Randolph's caresses or abuse according to his whim. Helpless itself this Republican Congress was subject to a crossfire: first through the Senate by means of the Giles resolutions commending the policy of the Executive, and second through the celebrated Macon bill, No. 1, by way of the House. Giles engineered his measures through the Senate but in the House the Federalists under the guidance of Quincy and others talked them to death, which led to the establishment by the House of its celebrated "rules" system. This was not the first time a minority had "talked" down a majority measure; but iron-clad rules to prevent this had until now looked too much like despotic suppression of free speech.[243] Macon was appointed chairman of the committee to draft rules. Macon had often deprecated the speech-making tendency of most members and he now recommended the "previous question" practice which was accepted and which at present spoils the plans of so many aspiring young representatives. The main features of the "House rules" as they obtain today were put into use before the end of this session and Macon was just the man to urge them.

The Macon bill, No. 1, was the second fire. The resolutions of November 17, 1808, and the bill following were Macon's first attempts at a solution of the complicated foreign problems of the Republican era. His first efforts had not been successful but they received due attention from his party. Again in June, 1809, he had taken a leading share in the discussion of foreign complications and advocated that foreign war vessels be prohibited from entering American harbors.[244] December 1, at the very beginning of the new session, he introduced resolutions which he said embraced the ideas of Early, of Georgia, D. R. Williams, of South Carolina, Dana, of Connecticut, and himself, and which would altogether constitute a system, a regular foreign policy. These resolutions looked to the complete exclusion of foreign war vessels from the ports of the United States and to the suppression of the illicit trade which foreign merchants were conducting under our flag. "I would put them out of the nation, and have no vessels belonging to the United States which are not perfectly American. I would have our vessels wholly American, or they shall not at all partake of the character of American vessels."[245] His resolutions were referred to the committee of Commerce and Manufactures. But the

---
243 Schouler, II., 325.
244 Annals of Congress, 11th Cong., I., 1269; Schouler II., 325.
245 Annals of Congress, 11th Cong., I., 686- 87.

President's message[246] had made similar recommendations and so a select committee of the House was appointed to draw up a bill which should meet the demands of the occasion and at the same time satisfy the wishes of the Administration and of the majority in Congress.[247] The letters above cited as well as many previous ones show Macon to have been on most intimate terms with Gallatin. Adams says in his life of Gallatin that the Secretary of the Treasury suggested the outline of the bill which their committee soon presented. This I have been unable to establish, but it is quite apparent from the few letters of Macon which have been preserved that Gallatin, Madison and Macon all cooperated in drawing up the first Macon bill. The Secretary of State was scarcely equal to the undertaking and not popular enough in the House to be of much service to the President. Madison and Gallatin seem to have been the authors of the bill, yet Gallatin could not openly espouse it lest Shith's friends in the Senate defeat it. Macon was the choice of the Administration to father the bill in the House, and to further the plans of the Administration he was made Chairman of the Committee on Foreign Relations[248] as well as because of his great influence with Southern members; Varnum, his successful rival for the speakership, was of course in sympathy with any plan the Executive might offer.[249]

Macon's bill contained the following provisions: The first, second and third items embodied Macon's own resolutions of the previous year; the fourth to the eighth articles prohibited the importation of English and French products except in vessels wholly manned by citizens of the United States, except such products come direct from England or France or their respective colonies. This was the principle of the ancient Navigation laws of England and it was designed to have the same effect on the warring powers of Europe as their policies had had on America; the ninth to the twelfth clauses gave the President power to suspend these laws in favor of either England or France in case either should abandon its warlike policy towards American trade, and repealed the former Non-importation bill.[250]

The bill was read a second time and referred to the Committee of the Whole for Friday, January 5. But Giles bill had the attention of the

---

246 Annals of Congress, 11th Cong., III., 3, 13.
247 Schouler, II., 326.
248 Annals of Congress, 11th Cong., I., 753.
249 Annals of Congress, 11th Cong., I., 1269; Schouler, II., 325.
250 Annals of Congress, 11th Cong., I., 754- 55; Schouler, II., 326.

House and the Federalists were carrying out the plan of talking down the Administration. It was not until the majority threatened to adopt and enforce the "previous question" rule, that is on Monday, January 8, that the Macon bill could get a hearing.

The wrangling over the Giles bill and the standing threat of the majority to adopt measures restraining everlasting speech prepared the way for a warmly partisan debate on the Macon bill. Livermore from Massachusetts opposed it because it would have an injurious effect on American, not foreign, commerce, since it went too far in the way of restriction; and Sawyer, an erratic colleague of Macon, charged the Committee with tame submission to England, with asking no reparation for the *Chesapeake* affair, no release of our impressed seamen, no revocation of the Orders in Council. Such acquiescence on the part of America was not only debasing the people as a nation but every individual must be contemptible in his own eyes.[251] Macon responded to both: "The gentleman from Massachusetts thinks the bill so strong that it will ruin us, by drawing upon us counterveiling acts; and my colleague thinks its weakness will only warrant further aggression on us. The Committee," he continued, "was well aware of the situation in which they were placed. The Message of the 29th was pacific; it was acknowledged on all hands that non-intercourse was totally useless; it was necessary that something should be done; and the committee agreed to report this bill." The granting of letters of marque and reprisal as advocated by many he opposed as impracticable and against the sentiment of the House, citing the very small favor a measure of that kind had received a year before.

He insisted that his bill was the most elastic possible admitting of being made stronger or weaker at the discretion of the President, that it sought to remove the burdens of our commerce from our shoulders to those of the English, that it deserved the support of the members if but for the repeal of the non-intercourse law. Sawyer had said the proposed measure would not satisfy the public. Macon replied: "Whether the bill will satisfy the people or not I am totally ignorant. I can never tell what will satisfy the people I represent; all I can do is to act as I think right and depend on such conduct for their approbation. I am not for a declaration of war just now, and I take this opportunity of saying so. The nation is not as much prepared now for war as it was last winter, or as it was when the *Chesapeake* was at-

---

251 Annals of Congress, 11th Cong., I., 1161.

tacked.[252] In his advocacy of the bill, Macon was willing to give the President discretionary powers in its execution, should it become a law, which he would under any other circumstances have denied. He had voted against such powers being given Washington in 1793 and Jefferson in 1807. Macon spoke again and again in favor of the bill and was in general recognized as the mouthpiece of the Government. Ross, of Pennsylvania, dealt in some condescending remarks about its supporters and not a few were constantly striving to make a sectional measure of Macon's bill, innocent as it was of any partisan designs. Macon made apology for rising again to this question, and begged the indulgence of the House. He spoke perhaps an hour: "Without referring to Æsop or Grotius, it seems to me that common sense would in the present case decide our course. But the bill contains embargo principles, we are told — these seem to be quite as much dreaded as the fatal submission which the bill contains. Yes, sir, I am an embargo man, and hesitate not to say, that the day Congress gave up the embargo for the non-intercourse, if there be submission, that day it began; if we wish war, either against England or France, or against both, instead of the non-intercourse act, we ought then to have made a declaration of war; we had then our sailors, our property, and our vessels at home. I can not perceive the great wisdom, and undaunted courage, in these war speeches, when there is no war motion." Gold of New York had insinuated that Macon had attempted privately to win his support. Macon resented the charge: "I deny it as to myself; I call upon no man for aid. The bill must stand or fall on its own merits. It has never been, nor ever will be my practice to be running about the city by day or by night, prowling after men, to support any measure I may propose; if right they ought to be adopted, if wrong they ought to be rejected. To have solicited the aid of the men who declare the bill to be submission, and that nothing but war will save the nation, would be, in my opinion, to have insulted them. Nor have I requested or demanded of them to come out as party men to support the bill. No, sir, I have never asked any man to yield his judgment to party. The same gentleman says the present discussion at the next election will put men who are for more energetic measures in Congress from the Eastern and Southern States. As to the people from the East, personally I know but little about them, having never been among them; if, however, a judgment may be formed of them, from their members

---

252 Annals of Congress, 11th Cong., I., 1163.

here, they will be found as tenacious of their opinions as most people are. Whatever may be the decision of those of the South, which I represent, it will be perfectly agreeable to me; but I am yet to learn that the people in the East and in the South are more fickle than those of the Middle States."

He then spoke of Southern conditions interspersing a bit of shrewd sarcasm occasionally: "It is true that the people in the South do not make a practice to pass fiery resolutions, which in general mean nothing more than that the first mover of the meeting and of the resolutions wants an office. On the day of election they pass on the conduct of their representatives and then tell them whether they have done well or not." His concluding words were: "Sir, it appears to me that the bill will promote the welfare and happiness of the nation by preserving peace. It offers to Great Britain and France another proof of the sincerity of our desire to remain neutral and to settle our disputes with them in a friendly way. It justly places them on the same ground in relation to us. It is a measure which we can maintain because it promotes the interest of all and particularly the interest of those who might with the most facility evade its operation. The Orders and Decrees of Great Britain and France are certainly against their interests; it will afford them time to reconsider them and I hope to with draw them; and as no other system has been proposed, either in the Committee of the Whole or in the House, I trust it will meet the approbation of the Legislature."[253] Macon's bill finally passed the House, 73 to 52, on January 29.[254]

The bill was introduced into the Senate January 30, and next day it was read a second time and consigned to the tender mercies of Senator Smith as chairman of a select committee for its consideration. Smith was at the head of the anti-Gallatin clique and, suspecting that Madison had drawn the bill according to Gallatin's suggestions, thus ignoring his incompetent Secretary of State, Robert Smith, this intensely jealous faction first delayed, then amended, and finally passed the bill with every clause removed, except those repealing the non-intercourse.[255] This emasculated bill was then returned to the House where Macon and his friends urged entire rejection, or the passage of the original measure. A conference of both Houses took place with the result that no agreement could be obtained, and so all the efforts

---

253 Annals of Congress, 11th Cong., II., 1283-84.
254 Annals of Congress, 11th Cong., II., 1354.
255 Annals of Congress, 11th Cong., I., 550-577; Adams Gallatin, 416; Schouler, II., 328.

of the Administration came to naught.[256] This was March 31, 1810.

The policy outlined in Macon's plan was a good one, and, as Schouler says, it would very likely have solved the problems of neutral commerce as they were in 1808 instead of 1810. Macon was indignant at the action of the Senate and of many members of the House. Numerous letters, he said, were coming to him daily urging the passage of his bill, the state of the public mind was unsettled, gamblers were taking advantage of the fluctuating prices. In fact the country was becoming disgusted at this wrangling, useless Congress dominated by cliques and extravagant partisans.[257]

The sole cause of this failure of three months continuous effort on Macon's part, supported, too, by the whole weight of the Administration, was the determination on the part of the Smith family to drive Gallatin from the Cabinet. Giles, of Virginia, Leib, of Pennsylvania, and Duane, of the *Aurora*, joined the opponents of the Secretary of the Treasury; the influence of Duane's paper was given entirely to the great Maryland family. Macon was an open advocate of Gallatin for the presidency. To kill Macon's bill, they argued, was to undo the plan of Gallatin, which, if successful, would bring him again to the forefront in Washington. Giles was perhaps a little jealous, too, on his own score at the national prominence which Macon's bill obtained while his own attracted no general or extended attention. While the Macon bill was dying "between the Houses" the Senate was trying to revive the old convoy policy of 1798. Resolutions looking to sending out armed convoys with trading vessels bound for European ports were introduced on the same day Macon's bill was brought in; and again a week later these resolutions were submitted to the committee on Foreign Relations in order that a bill might be prepared.[258]

On the day when Macon's bill finally came to naught, Randolph suddenly appeared in the House and introduced a resolution calling for immediate repeal of the non-intercourse laws. He took this occasion to review again the whole policy of embargo and non-intercourse,[259] and so wrought upon the House as to make a return to the Gallatin system still revolving in Macon's methodical brain impossible. Macon was not a little annoyed at Randolph though he was not himself very hopeful of any satisfactory solution of the problems

---

256 Annals of Congress, 11th Cong., I., 1559, 1635, 1701.
257 Annals of Congress, 11th Cong., I., 1635- 36.
258 Annals of Congress, 11th Cong., I., 550, 587.
259 Annals of Congress, 11th Cong., II., 1702.

with which he had been so long wrestling. He wrote Nicholson, April 3: "By the papers you will see that we are debating a motion by Randolph to repeal the non-intercourse law. This motion is hardly worth the time that has already been consumed, and I apprehend we shall hardly decide it today. Among many members there is a desire to do something, by which is meant to pass some act, which shall operate on both the belligerents. But I have not discovered any system except that which has been lost between the two Houses, which would not also operate very strongly on us. An embargo, could it be carried, is the only measure which would bring G. Britain to terms. There is no chance for that, and that would probably have more effect on France than any other measure."[260]

On Saturday, April 7, Macon introduced bill No. 2 on the subject of foreign intercourse. This was called "Macon's bill No. 2." It abandoned the policy of retaliation on Great Britain of bill No. 1, provided for the repeal of non-intercourse at the end of the session and concluded by authorizing the President to revive non-importation against either England or France in case either of those powers should abandon its present policy, that is, he should say to the two great powers of Europe: "We have done forever with non-intercourse measures towards both of you; but if one of *you* will cease capturing and confiscating our trading vessels, we will immediately return to our non-intercourse with the other."[261] Macon reported this bill from the committee which still acted for the Administration, though it was helpless before the treacherous Smith clique in Congress. Macon was in no way enthusiastic over his second bill, and he wrote as much to his friend: "I am at a loss to guess what we shall do on the subject of foreign relations. The bill in the enclosed paper called Macon's No. 2 is not really Macon's, though he reported it as namesake. It is in truth Taylor's (of S.C.). This I only mention to you, because, when it comes to be debated I shall not act the part of a father or a stepfather. Burwell and Eppes still talk about their convoy, each professing his own convoy. The Ways and Means and the bank will make some warm talk, I expect."[262]

Macon did not "father" the bill. It passed after much angry debate and an attempt at turning the main issue to protection for domestic manufactures by Johnson of Kentucky. Bill No. 2 received the approv-

---

260 Macon to Nicholson, April 3, 1810.
261 Annals of Congress, 11th Cong., II., 1763.
262 Macon to Nicholson, April 10, 1810.

al of the House by a vote of 61 to 40. Macon wrote on April 21 concerning the part he took in its passage: "We have passed and sent to the Senate the 2nd bill reported by me, with an amendment proposed by Johnson of Kentucky to lay 50 percent on the duties now payable on French and English goods, but which new duties are to cease when the Decrees and Orders of G. B. and France are withdrawn which is to be notified by proclamation of the President when either or both shall with draw their edicts.

"This plan is said to be a Cabinet project. If so it satisfies me that the Cabinet is hard pushed for a plan, but it may have been taken to prevent a worse or to prevent the continuance of the present non-intercourse system. Some who opposed No. 1 wished it had become a law. I mean feds. I am almost apprehensive that the *invisibles* may be at the bottom of this amendment before mentioned (Johnson's) with a view to injure Gallatin. They may if they can ascertain its fate in the Senate by indirect means and before a vote is taken, take the side which may best answer their purpose. If it will not pass they may (if it be a Cabinet measure) support it to show their zeal for the Administration, and if it will pass without their aid, they may oppose it to show that G. neither understands how to get money in the Treasury by new taxes, nor how to encourage manufactures. He, G., I am afraid, is not enough on his guard as to these people. I have shown this to Randolph. I write while Love is speaking on the Bank."[263]

Johnson's amendment referred to in the letter just cited was incorporated into the Macon bill No. 2. in the House but was stricken out in the Senate in favor of a second amendment granting public convoys to private merchant ships. A conference of both Houses resulted in the loss of this second amendment and the original bill became a law late Saturday evening, the last day of the session, May 1, 1810.[264]

But Macon had not only ceased to advocate his bill, he actually voted against its final passage.[265] So far had things drifted and changed since December. In fact, the measure expressed no one's policy. It was simply a feeble assertion of authority on the part of the President who exercised no authority — a plan which forestalled Randolph's repeal of the non-intercourse law then in force, which on its very surface showed that the Senate held the reins of power if there were any reins at that chaotic time.

---

263 Macon to Nicholson, April 21, 1810.
264 Annals of Congress, 11th Cong., I., 678.
265 Annals of Congress, 11th Cong., II., 1931.

The reason Macon refused to support the measure which bore his name was that Johnson's protective clause had been tacked on. These ideas which Lyon had advocated some months before and which Macon deprecated so much had been taken up by another Kentuckian, a powerful and popular man, and nearly carried. Macon did not think the amendment of itself so dangerous. It was the political opinion which it manifested. This opinion, too, was spreading. The New England, Pennsylvania, New Jersey, Kentucky, and even some Virginia Republicans, said he, were "full of manufacturing."[266]

April 14, Eppes, from the committee on Ways and Means, presented the estimates for the expenses of the coming year. In this estimate it was shown that an increase of $3,000,000 in the annual income would be required, or that a reduction in the expenditure must be made. Gallatin recommended either a reduction in the army and navy establishments, or an increased duty of five percent on all *ad valorem*, and 33 1/3 percent on all specific imports, his preference being the latter method. Eppes submitted a clear and open statement of fiscal conditions and moved that the additional duty be laid.[267] No better showing could have been expected under the circumstances and no more reasonable demands were ever made on the representatives. Yet Randolph burst forth again in a lengthy tirade against the Jefferson regime contrasting, as he claimed, sharply with the economical administrations of Washington and Adams. Macon would not admit Randolph's claims for the Federalists to be true, yet opposed the increased tariff proposition: "I am at a loss to understand this bill. I do not know whether it is meant to encourage manufactures or for what other object we are asked to raise this money." The point on which he was most sensitive and on which his opinion was made up was that of "encouraging manufactures." "If you want money, I am ready to agree that you can not get it by internal taxes; but rather than saddle those whom I represent with a tax to encourage manufactures, if that be the object, I would vote for a direct tax. What does this system lead to? To this: that you will go on by tax on tax until you manufacture within the limits of the United States everything that can there be raised for the purpose of manufacturing. This may be a good thing to the part of the country which will be the manufacturing part. They may laugh and sing; but to that part that will never manufacture it will be death. The latter may wring their hands and cry, but in vain; for once but get

---

266 Macon to Nicholson, April 21, 1810.
267 Annals of Congress, 11th Cong., II., 1819-24.

the manufacturing mania fixed on the nation and we shall be saddled with it as long as the nation exists. I can state an opinion that I entertain, which may by many be thought not to be correct. It is this: that precisely as you encourage this manufacturing spirit, in the same ratio will you depress all the domestic manufactures of the country I live in. Sir, I voted for the embargo to avoid war, under the belief that if we adhered to it we should settle our disputes with one of the belligerents, but never meant by it to encourage manufactures. As to the non-intercourse laws, as I never voted for them, I do not know on what principle they were voted for."

His solution of the difficulty is given in the following: "As it appears to me, sir, that the question is pretty well settled that we do not mean to take any very energetic measures at the present session of Congress, what use is there in keeping up the navy and that skeleton of an army? Can any man tell me the use of them unless they are expressly for the purpose of spending money?" He then goes on to show the uselessness of both establishments, especially of the navy, concluding: "Reduce the Army and Navy and let us be told what money is wanting and I will vote a loan to that amount. But vote first to raise money and afterwards to reduce it is what I will not do. If we want money it ought to be gotten in the way most convenient to the people; and it would seem as if, when we once lay a tax, it is impossible to get it off again. I recollect when the two and a half per cent duty (commonly entitled the Mediterranean fund) was laid it was stated that we would scarcely ever get it off again; and it has been kept on so far, though the original cause of it has ceased.[268]

A proposition for the reduction of the army and navy gained the precedence over Eppes' tariff bill. Macon moved an amendment to the proposition which called for disbanding the entire army. A miserable feud which arose out of the Wilkinson controversy had actually spread through all ranks of the organization, and, because of this, Macon desired the complete demolition of that branch of the public service instead of a reduction which he assented to in the case of the navy.[269] But enmity to both was deep rooted in his mind. He had inherited from his ancestors, political and otherwise of the seventeenth century, a hatred for all standing armies and permanent navies and a special liking for defense alone in times of war. This radical disposition to disband our defensive forces in the very face of foreign com-

---

268 Annals of Congress, 11th Cong., II., 1847.
269 Annals of Congress, 11th Cong., II., 1863.

plication, coupled with the many complaints against Wilkinson, had already set in motion an investigation of the affairs of the army, and General Wilkinson was called on to submit a large number of papers bearing on the conduct of the army since the Burr conspiracy of 1805 and '06. The papers had mysteriously disappeared and unfortunately for the army and the country the business was not cleared up. The army was not disbanded as perhaps would have been best, and the navy was not reduced; Macon's attack took the form later of a resolution to sell most of the war vessels and trust to buying and arming merchantmen in case of war. In fact Macon was in bad spirits with everything toward the end of the session, as a private letter shows: "The House is engaged on the bill to reduce the naval establishment and have begun to take yeas and nays. It is quite probable that all the attempts to reduce expenditure at this session will prove abortive. It is possible it may tend to make some of the public functionaries a little more attentive to economy. The speeches on the floor may produce this effect. All agree that the expenditure in the navy department ought to be checked and yet it will not be I fear. Hamilton (Paul Hamilton of S.C.) I believe is honest and determined, but the abuses have got such strong hold that it may be questioned whether he has power to tear them up by the roots. It is also doubtful whether the army will be reduced. Difficult as it may be thought to get an expensive establishment fixed on a free nation, it is certainly more difficult to get clear of one when it is fixed. These establishments generally make convenient places for the governmental connections and their more obliging friends and cruel is the task which uprightness imposes to take these snug places from those that may be dear and necessary to the rulers.

"The times have changed; the navy is now a Republican institution and must be supported on loans. Who of those who loves one but must delight in the other. And with these the admirer must embrace executive discretion which, contrary to general laws of nature, grows more lovely and comely the more it is used and the older it grows. It is not strange when the quality of their discretion is known, that those who some years past spoke of it as being more deformed and ugly than Cyclops, should now think it more comely than Venus and more to be admired than Christian faith or pure Gold. Nay, had Solomon lived in this day he would have acknowledged that a Navy was more to be coveted than true wisdom; and if Solomon had not have been a man of peace how eloquently could he have portrayed the great advantages of a well-dressed standing army to preserve national liberty over the ragged militia of the nation itself, nay how easy could he have proved the people to be their own worst enemies."[270]

While the Macon bill No. I was in the hands of the anti-Gallatin clique, Gardenier, a Federalist of New York, read before the House an article from the Virginia *Argus*, signed Camillus, which contained charges of misappropriation of public money, of speculating in United States securities and in public lands. Gardenier was one of the most influential members of the opposition in Congress. He turned this reading of anonymous charges in an insignificant newspaper into serious resolutions, demanding that Gallatin's administration of the Treasury be investigated. This was the work of the Smiths and it was intended to force their enemy in the cabinet to resign. Ross of Pennsylvania gave voice to the disgust of many others at the mean fight the Smiths were making against the Secretary of the Treasury. He said: "While his (Gallatin's) political enemies are so careful of his reputation, why are they not equally careful of the reputation of the Secretary of State, who was equally abused by the writer under the signature of Philolaos or Mutius?" Inquiry in the one place demanded inquiry in the other, he said.[271] Macon was willing for the investigation to be ordered. "If the Secretary of the Treasury were my own brother, if he were my father, and an inquiry was asked into his conduct, I would grant it. Seventeen members out of the one hundred and twenty-three voted for the Gardenier resolutions, among them Richard Stanford and Nathaniel Macon. The Smith move in the House was a failure, as was also their attempt in the following summer to ruin Gallatin in Maryland.[272]

The effect of the second Macon bill was that France removed its Decrees in August, this to take effect November 1. According to the terms of our law this concession on the part of Napoleon compelled the President to proclaim non-importation against England. England paid no attention to the Macon law and treated with contempt all remonstrances of our representatives against the sham blockade of Europe and against the impressment of seamen. Madison revived non-importation against England in November. Still England gave no assurance that any change of policy might be expected.

---

270 Macon to Nicholson, April 28, 1810.
271 Annals of Congress, 11th Cong., 1414-1421.
272 Schouler, II., 328.

Congress reassembled for its final session December 3. The President could give no encouraging picture of foreign affairs. England's silence compelled Congress to sit still until February, the date when the revived non-importation act would go into effect. There would then remain only one month more in which to formulate a policy and enact laws accordingly. Hence there was little chance of any decisive measure on foreign intercourse being taken by the Eleventh Congress. In default of anything to do along the lines of the last session's legislation, Congress took up seriously the great bank question, the admission of Orleans territory as a State, and other domestic matters.

In the assignments to committees at the beginning of the session Macon had not been placed on the committee on Foreign Relations, but he was given a place on the committee to consider the establishment of a National University at Washington, a pet scheme, it will be remembered, both of Washington and Madison. Macon was not then so important a character as he had been, yet he was one of the foremost leaders of the Administration party in the House.[273] Nothing came of the National University, as was to be expected.

The charter of the United States bank as established in 1791 was about to expire. Gallatin, originally a strong opponent of Hamilton's bank and other policies, was now ready to advocate a new charter. The cause of his change of opinion need not interest us here except to say that perhaps the growing power of the Smith influence, which enjoyed now, in addition to the unqualified support of Duane's paper, the support of the Richmond *Enquirer*, one of the most potent powers in the Republican party, had made him look about for active adherents. Gallatin outlined a plan for the new bank and had it soon brought before Congress. A similar proposition had occupied the attention of the House during the past session, but it had been forced to yield to the sterner demands of foreign complications. It was now to become the great question not only before the National legislature but before the whole country. The new charter asked for a capital stock of three million dollars, of which the States might take half the stock; it promised to establish branch banks in each State, with the allowance of a certain number of State directors; and also agreed to give the United States government a bonus of one million two hundred and fifty thousand dollars, to pay interest on United States deposits, and to loan the nation three-fifths of its capital at six per cent interest, or

---

273 Schouler, II., 352.

under.²⁷⁴ The strict constructionists feared such a monster institution; the Southern planters were astounded that any institution could pay such an enormous bonus simply for the privilege of driving an honest business. Macon cried out constantly against the re-charter; he never ceased to declaim against the bank from this time until its final overthrow by Jackson. His admiration for Gallatin waned. But he made no set speech against the bank. A letter of January 17, 1811, shows something of his feelings: "Yesterday and today the House has been engaged on the bill to renew the charter of the U.S. bank. The bill will not, I imagine, pass. It is reported that it has fewer friends than at the last session. The present friends to a National bank may be divided into four classes: (1) For the renewal of the charter with some modification; (2) for a new bank; (3) establish a National bank at the next or some future session; (4) use the State banks and their paper. All these are considered as having no constitutional objections."²⁷⁵ Macon's objection to the bank was on constitutional as well as partisan grounds; his was not a banking state and his people were simple farmers whom he himself had trained for twenty years to distrust any and all additions to the powers of the National government.

The re-charter bill was lost on a narrower margin than he had thought. The final vote in the House stood 63 for, 64 against; and in the Senate a separate bill for the same purpose was lost by Vice-President Clinton's vote.²⁷⁶ Macon did not control the vote of his State. Willis Alston, Jr., Archibald McBryde, Joseph Pearson, Richard Stanford and John Stanly, all of North Carolina, voted favorably to the bank.

Early in the session Macon introduced a resolution for amending the United States Constitution as follows: "Resolved, that no Senator or Representative, after having taken his seat, shall, during the time for which he was elected, be eligible to any civil appointment under the authority of the United States, nor shall any person be eligible to any such appointment until the expiration of the Presidential term, during which such person shall have been a Senator or Representative."²⁷⁷ This proposed amendment of his was the outcome of long fixed opinion on the subject. Opinion in North Carolina at that time was almost a unit with him, and his letters before this time gave ex-

---

274 Schouler, II., 350.
275 Macon to Nicholson, January 17, 1811.
276 Annals of Congress, 11th Cong., III., 826.
277 Annals of Congress, 11th Cong., III., 386.

pression to much of his disgust at the nepotism growing up around the presidency and the great departmental offices. His plan was clear enough and wise enough but it never realized. It might find no easy road through Congress today, if we may judge by the appointments of a recent administration. He made several speeches in behalf of his plan; in these he does not appear to disadvantage to all those who love purity in politics and unselfish devotion to the public good.[278]

At this same session Macon became a powerful advocate of the embryo policy of Southern expansion to meet Eastern aggression. We have seen how he advised Jefferson in 1803 to purchase Florida on any reasonable terms. The purchase of Louisiana was in entire accord with his ideas of wise policy. But Louisiana had not been bought without a protest from Eastern members. Now when Orleans begins to knock at the doors of Congress for admittance as a "free and independent republic," as Macon was fond of saying, the forces of Federalism rallied a last time under the leader ship of the brilliant declaimer, Josiah Quincy. They asserted that the Constitution would not allow new States to be carved out of the purchased territory west of the Mississippi, that only states within the bounds of the old Northwest territory could ever hope to enter the Union.[279] Macon had no patience with such distinctions. He declared that "the right of creating States out of acquired territory" was one which he had always contended for; and it had been stated by at least one of those who had formed the Constitution, that this article had reference to Canada. "New states may be admitted by Congress into the Union. At the time this provision was made, Florida and Louisiana were not thought of. Canada was the territory kept in view."[280] Quincy expressed the view of his section when he vehemently declared: "If this bill passes it is my deliberate opinion that it is virtually a dissolution of this Union; that it will free the states from their moral obligation and as it will be the right of all, so it will be the duty of some definitely to prepare for a separation, amicably if they can, violently if they must."[281] The question in the angry dispute on the first attempt to create a state out of the territory beyond the Mississippi was not one of constitutionality so much as one of interest. Going beyond the great river meant an almost illimitable expansion of the South. The South was agricul-

---

278 Annals of Congress, 11th Cong., III., 454-55.
279 Annals of Congress 11th Cong., III., January; see Josiah Quincy and others.
280 Annals of Congress, 11th Cong., III., 1810-11.
281 Annals of Congress, 11th Cong., III., 526.

tural, rural; New England commercial, urban in character; the former dependent on plenteous slave labor, the latter on an active, bustling, free life and competition. By the compromises of the Constitution the South had a larger representation on account of the negroes than a similar free population of the North. So far in the history of the Union the balance of power had been held by the Middle States. These were now beginning to ally themselves with New England (protective tariff policy above referred to) which would bring the South as it then was into a helpless minority and the East would rule. Since 1803 the South had been expanding toward the Southwest. It was now about to reap permanent reward from this expansion. This was not to be allowed. To gain some voters in the Middle States the cry was raised against the monster iniquity of the South — slavery. It was, however, the old question of dollars and cents which has decided so many of the great issues recorded in human history. Macon demanded admission for his new State be cause of the advantage it would give his party in Congress. Quincy threatened to secede should the new State come into the Union because of the comparative loss his party would sustain.

The subject was postponed till the next session and Congress came to an end again without having done anything but wrangle and draw salaries. Many old members returned home on that fourth of March never again to occupy a seat in the National Legislature. The next elections fulfilled a prophecy made on the floor of the House at the previous session, that the people were going to send more aggressive, more progressive men to Congress next time. It was the yielding of the old Revolutionary statesmen and politicians to the rising influence and power of young America — the first stage of the revolution of 1828. But Macon was not superseded. He went home still sure of his place in the affections of his constituents — better constituents from his point of view than those of whom Randolph boasted so often and so loudly.

JAMES MONROE.
Fifth President of the United States

CHAPTER XVI.
REVOLUTION IN CONGRESS AND THE WAR OF 1812.

Before the assembling of Congress in 1811, Macon noted a significant change in the Administration, a change which would have made his bill No. 1 a success. It was the appointment of Monroe as Secretary of State. Macon had for a short time in 1806 favored Randolph's plan of making Monroe, instead of Madison, President. He seems to have been slightly opposed to Monroe in 1811; he wrote Nicholson in April: "Can you tell me how the change in the Department of State came about. The office of State seems to be the path to the Presidency, and the mission to Russia a sort of political deathbed, not withstanding J. Q. A. has been made a Judge. The history of the transaction I should like to know. * * * By the by, it seems to me that Monroe will be hard pressed with British negotiations on account of the treaty he made which Mr. J. would not lay before the Senate.

Madison had at last resolved to rid his cabinet of its intriguing members. He flattered Virginia and at the same time delighted the West by appointing Monroe to the Department of State. It was making an end also of the political schisms in the Republican ranks. It completed the isolation of Randolph and his little group of followers, of whom Richard Stanford, of North Carolina, was a typical member.

When Congress assembled a month earlier than usual, with the special purpose of settling the quarrel with England, it was plain to anyone that a revolution had taken place. The time had passed for Macon and Randolph and other old leaders to take the direction of affairs into their hands. Macon and the peace Republicans had been given a fair opportunity at the last session to settle the great problems before the Nation. On account of factions in their own ranks, more especially in the Cabinet, nothing had been accomplished. Congress had "made great haste," as Macon himself said, "to do nothing." Six long months had been spent in doing nothing in this way, and the country was sick and tired of speeches; and not a few saw the cause of it all in the President's lack of decision. Madison was not popular during the summer of 1811. But the revolution had now come. The new members from the West and South were the products; Clay, tired of the slow-going Senate, where he was, in deed, out of place, entered the House, and on the same day was made Speaker. Calhoun, Grundy, Lowndes and Cheves were the other young Southerners who, violating at the very beginning the customs of the House, pushed forward so strongly as to get things into their hands within a month's time. It was young America, conscious of its rising importance and ready for a conflict, even without arms, with any nation that refused to recognize its rights and privileges as "a free and independent power."

What would Macon, the conservative, cautious, experienced politician do under these new conditions? And how would North Carolina view the change? — are questions we naturally ask ourselves. Macon had already concluded to vote for war, though he more than ever dreaded its consequences. As for the North Carolinians, they were hopelessly divided. The dissatisfaction with Madison and the failure of the Macon bills at the last session had not been without effect on the party politics of that State. New Bern and the surrounding country sent Judge Gaston, a Federalist, to the House; the Salisbury district, never slow to yield to the embraces of the same party, sent Joseph Pearson back after an absence of ten years; Archibald McBryde, of Fayetteville, was another Federalist; and Willis Alston, of Halifax, voted as often with one party as the other; the dissipated and somewhat uncertain Lemuel Sawyer, from the Edenton section, went entirely over to the Federalists; and Richard Stanford had long since become the counterpart of Randolph, and with Randolph voted favorably to the interests of England, because, forsooth, the English gentleman was to him the most perfect type of the human species. Macon, Meshack Franklin, from Surry, and William R. King, a talented new member from Sampson, were almost alone in their support of Administration measures and of ancient Republican manners. North Carolina was, in fact, becoming doubtful territory again, and the Democrats were casting about to find a way to "save the State." Some were proposing the appointment of Presidential electors by the Legislature, instead of by popular vote, in order to prevent the districts of New Bern, Fayetteville and Salisbury from giving their votes to the opponents of Madison. But the plan was not yet matured.[282]

When Porter, of New York, reported for the committee on Foreign Relations that all hopes for a peaceful settlement of the quarrel with Great Britain must be given up, that the army should at once be increased to 13,000 men, that 50,000 volunteers should be called for,

---

282 Annals of Congress, 13th Cong., I., 836.

that the State militias should be put in readiness, and that the navy should be equipped for service and merchant vessels allowed to arm themselves, Macon joined heartily in these measures of the younger party leaders. Warlike speeches were made on every hand, and Macon, "peace" man that he had always been, declared that the time for war had come. Still his super-cautious nature impelled him to insist on the most open and accurate statements from the Administration as to the number of troops for the national service. Where the States commanded the troops he asked no questions. Grundy, of Tennessee, Lowndes, Calhoun, and all the new members from the South, were clamorous for the adoption of the Porter resolutions looking to war. Randolph employed all his wit and sarcasm to defeat them. Richard Stanford, of North Carolina, made a strong speech against war and the proposed invasion of Canada, to which William R. King replied: "Sir, the demon avarice, which benumbs every warm emotion of the soul, has not yet gained the ascendency in the South. * * * Our country is agricultural, but so intimately blended with commerce that one can not long exist unaided by the other. Sir, I will not yield an inch of ground when, by so doing, I destroy an essential right of my country — or sap the foundation of that independence cemented by the blood of our fathers. We were told by a gentleman from Virginia (Randolph), a few days since, that we have sufficient cause for war. I ask you, then, why do we hesitate? Shall we always yield? The adoption of this resolution is the touchstone — by it we rise or fall."[283] King concluded by denouncing the policy of his colleagues, who still advocated compromise and peace. This bold language which called on the commercial sections of the country to join the agricultural South in an aggressive war against England was new to the Republicans. It was the language of buoyant young America, which could no longer be restrained by the bonds of party.

In a second speech on the Porter resolutions, Macon appeared to no advantage, favoring war and yet opposing the Government's plan for increasing the army. His immovable confidence in militia armaments, not the fear of the unpopularity of voting a tax, explains his speech; for every member of the House seems to have entertained the greatest respect for his character. Men went out of their way to pay him deference as a man and patriot, though not so often now as a political leader.

---

283 Annals of Congress, 12th Cong., I., 517-518.

Early in the session, Gallatin made a report to Congress which encouraged the "war hawks" to assume a still more defiant attitude toward Great Britain. The Secretary had practically assured the legislature that he could meet the expense of war, even without laying an additional tax. The committee on Foreign Relations and Cheves committee on Naval Affairs, both supported by Clay's animating and fiery eloquence, reported still more aggressive plans than they had at first been willing to risk. And while Gallatin was reasoning with the House in order to prevent the overstepping of the bounds of his estimates, the Republican governors and legislatures throughout the country began to send in their resolutions of applause and assurance of hearty support; the militia of the South and Southwest was volunteering. Madison was like to lose his head, as John Adams had done in 1798. The Federalists, as a party, stood somewhat aloof until the large appropriations for the army and navy came up, when they voted consistently enough with the majority.

These institutions had always been their pets. Perchance a way of escape from war might be found, and then woe to the party which had built up these branches of the public service.

This was not to come. On March 11, when the Gallatin explanations of his former over-sanguine estimates were exasperating the House, Madison sent to Congress a batch of papers which proved to be the beginning of the end of the Federalist party. These were a series of letters to and from an English agent in New England, John Henry by name. The papers had been purchased from Henry at a cost of $50,000. Henry had been sent to Massachusetts by Sir James Craig, Governor of Canada, to promote secession from the Union by the New England States in 1809, when embargo was bearing so heavily upon that section. The mission of Henry was not without a cause. The Legislature of Massachusetts was ready to call a Congress of Eastern States to consider the subject of secession. Quincy, it will be remembered, had deliberately advocated separation of the New England States from the Union. Henry had reported to his government that Eastern politicians favored secession, but that it was doubtful whether they would take the final step except as a last resort against Jefferson's embargo. No names had been given in the Henry reports, and the closest investigations revealed no traitorous relations to have been established so far as the Federalists were concerned. At least at that time no prominent Federalist was found to be guilty of overt acts. The reception given the discredited English Minister, Jackson, in 1807, in New England, already referred to, pointed out clearly enough the road New England leaders would have taken had the way been open. John Quincy Adams in his history of New England Federalism, says that not only neutrality in the event of war, but actual support of the English, was the aim of many, chief among whom was good Timothy Pickering. That disgruntled member of the Adams' Cabinet had suggested Henry's mission.[284] And it is more than probable that Josiah Quincy, while a leader in Congress, was suggesting to the English Minister how to bring America to terms.

The papers served to let the world know what England was doing in time of peace, and what Massachusetts might do in the event of war. Congress was excited; animated debates followed, and the eyes of the whole country were turned toward Boston, this time with strong distrust.

Macon, always a staunch partisan, refrained in a short speech on referring the papers to the committee on Foreign Relations, from going further than to rebuke the Federalists who were trying to laugh down the whole proceedings, and declaring that both England and France were accustomed to maintain spies in America. He concluded: "Our affairs are in such a state that we must try what has been called the last resort of kings. I have made up my mind on the subject, and whenever we are ready to declare war, I shall vote for it."[285]

Macon was early given the opportunity of casting such a vote. After a session of preparatory measures, and the passage of a sixty days embargo, the plan of a special mission to England, with Bayard as its chief, was proposed. This was to be another *last resort* at settling our difficulties. This embargo was calculated to give support to the American envoys; but Madison, with public sentiment strongly in favor of hostilities, gave the peace proposition scant consideration. June 4, the House passed a bill declaring war, and Macon gave it his hearty support. North Carolina's delegation was divided, however, owing to the recent gains of the Federalists in that State. Joseph Pearson, Archibald McBryde and Richard Stanford, two Federalists and one Democrat, voted against war. The Senate, on June 18, concurred with the House resolutions, and open hostilities began.[286]

When Congress met again in November, Macon was promptly placed on the committee on Foreign Relations, along with Grundy

---

284 Schouler, II., 384.
285 Annals of Congress, 12th Cong., II., 1191.
286 Annals of Congress, 12th Cong., II., 1632- 34; Schouler II., 396.

and Calhoun. Before the war began, Macon had favored the invasion of Canada, as, indeed, had all the Republicans. The annexation of Canada had been looked forward to since the beginning of the Revolution. It had been contemplated by the Constitutionalists of 1789. What was more natural now than to round up our northern boundaries? At the same time, Macon declared openly that he went to war for sailors rights: "One part of the nation delights in using the sea; another in agriculture; we supply each other's wants; we ought never to dream of separation."[287] Yet it was at this time, as it had ever been, Macon's policy to extend the boundaries of the United States. He was in this quite generous, since any annexation from Canada could mean no other than increase of the influence of the Northern States. It was an imperial democracy which he would see expand in all directions. While the East and North were constantly chiding him for desiring to admit new States from the Southwest, in order to extend slavery, he without hesitation advocated the extension of our boundaries in the North, where only free states could be expected to be created.

War had been made, but Congress and the Administration were not sure as to the reality of public support, and hence the first campaign was but feebly supported by the authorities in Washington.

The re-election of Madison was a matter of greater concern to most of the politicians at the National capital than the vigorous prosecution of the war. The Democratic members of Congress met in caucus late in May to determine on their candidates. Madison and Gerry were chosen, not without much dissent, for Madison was not a Jefferson. De Witt Clinton, nephew of the deceased vice-president, calculating on the influence of the New England States and his own popularity in New York, now deserted the Republican ranks to become the standard-bearer of the Federalists. Macon wrote concerning this political move: "Mr. Adams long since wrote to his friend Pinckney that they had fallen on evil times. We certainly live in strange ones. Mr. Adams is the leading candidate on the Republican ticket for the election of P. and V.-P., and De W. Clinton, the Federal candidate. Mr. A. was always, in my opinion, an honest man, but still that does not change the strange appearance he and Mr. Clinton make in the present contest for the Presidency."[288] There was great dissatisfaction with the caucusing methods of Congress. In New York and New Jer-

---

287 Annals of Congress, 12th Cong., II., 1191.
288 Letter to Joseph H. Nicholson, November 7, 1812.

sey this dissatisfaction was so widespread as to turn the tide again in favor of the Federalists. New York, too, gave its support to its favorite son. Pennsylvania, Jefferson's second Republican pillar of the Union, remained faithful to the Administration, though there was much clamor raised against unpopular Gallatin and his Virginian friends. Virginia and the West were firm in their support of Madison and war. North Carolina was witnessing a change in its politics and public men not unlike that which had come with Clay into Congress in 1811. Strong men were entering politics, and that, too, on the side of the opposition. Judge Gaston, the Pearsons, and others were threatening, in the summer of 1812, to carry the State for Clinton. It will be remembered that the Clintons were popular in North Carolina as States' Rights men. Madison had been unpopular there in 1808. In order to make sure of the result, the Republican Legislature of 1811 changed the mode of choosing Presidential electors. It had always been done by popular vote in districts; it was now to be left to the Assembly, which, it was conceded, would be safely Republican. In this way Madison was given the full strength of the State.[289] South Carolina and Georgia had been doubtful; but the result showed that the Jefferson party still had the upper hand there. Madison was re-elected by a vote of 128 to 89, a canvass of the vote showing that the Potomac, with the exception of Pennsylvania, was the dividing line between the candidates, between agriculture favoring war and commerce opposing it. Federalist or commercial states had generally chosen their electors by the indirect method of election, by their legislatures; the Republican States had usually pursued the opposite method, on the ground that it was more democratic, but now they were making exceptions to their rule. The contest of 1812 was for a time regarded as quite doubtful, hence the change in North Carolina. But the sense of fair play and almost instinctively democratic leanings of the people compelled the next Legislature to return to its former practice.

James Madison, even under the most favorable circumstances, was the last man prominent in public affairs who would have been called a War president, He had been no soldier in the Revolution; had, like Jefferson, hated the very name of war. What would he now do in a great contest with England, and that, too, when the country was woefully ill-prepared, and when a refractory element of his own party stood ready at any time to embarrass his operations? The event

---

289 See Gaston's speech, Annals of Congress, January, 1804.

was worse than might have been expected. An American army invaded Canada, to be sure, but that was all. On the sea some creditable show was made, but England was only playing war with her erstwhile revolted colonists. Madison, in his longing for some stay, some strong hand on which to rest his administration, was seriously contemplating making Henry Clay a general, and entrusting to him the field operations, as he had done those of Congress!

Massachusetts protested against the invasion of an "innocent and friendly people," and sent her protest to Congress in November, 1813; the South rallied the more strongly to Madison's administration. A high tariff was laid, to which New England responded by wholesale smuggling. The committee on Ways and Means proposed a direct tax, a most dangerous step for any party to pursue; but this was voted down, Macon doing his utmost to prevent its passage, doubtless remembering what havoc a former direct tax had done in the Federalist ranks.

In February, 1814, Maryland remonstrated against the war, and in the debate which followed the presentation of the remonstrance, it was often charged against the party in power that embargo, non-importation, and finally the war itself, were all the measures of backwoodsmen who knew little or nothing of the affairs of a civilized government. Macon replied : "And when, in the Revolution, the back countrymen went to Boston, a different sentiment prevailed there. It was never complained of the brave Morgan, when he went there, that he was a back countryman." He repeatedly asserted that if the Government would go back to the old-fashioned war methods of the Revolution, we should win. Just what those methods were he did not explain. In fact, Macon knew little about military affairs; he was, by his intense dislike of all regular army establishments and his simple faith in citizen soldiers, unfit to pass judgment on the operations of war.

Macon was made chairman of the committee of Congress "to report on the spirit and manner in which the war had been waged by the enemy." His committee sat in Washington and examined witnesses from different parts of the country, and reported to Congress in July, 1813, that Great Britain had violated the rules of war in carrying Americans to England and placing them in close prisons without giving any reason for such conduct; that she had claimed American prisoners as subjects, and forced them into battle against America; that all American sailors in England at the outbreak of war had been seized and detained as prisoners; that flags of truce had been violated; that England had regularly employed the Indians by paying set prices for all American prisoners they would deliver into the hands of English officers; that the Indians were systematically instigated to the commission of the most heinous crimes all along the borders by English commanders. Every possible crime was found to be commonly practiced by the enemy, and there was sufficient evidence submitted, as it appears, to warrant the finding. Macon's ancient grudge against England was in no way lessened by his experience on this committee. His report was exhaustive, and his statements to Congress were eminently moderate in view of the facts which had been elicited by the investigation.[290]

At the second session of Congress, in March, 1814, the deplorable state of finances was attempted to be remedied by means of a loan. The opposition took this opportunity to oppose again the whole policy of the Government, and most prominent among the opposition at this time were Gaston and Pearson, of North Carolina. Macon was unequal to his colleagues, both in talents and education, yet he made a very successful speech in favor of the loan and against them, in which he took occasion again to defend his Westerners, "backwoodsmen," as our polished Carolinians insisted on calling them. Gaston, Pearson and Macon all spoke of disunion; Gaston and Pearson as though it would be preferable to the burden of democratic government, Macon as though democratic government throughout the world depended on the continued existence of the American Union. Gaston even charged the majority with the responsibility of the curse of slavery, which was getting such a hold on North Carolina. Macon responded: "I sincerely lament that my colleague has thought it necessary to refer to the unfortunate situation of our native State; I agree that slavery is a lamentable thing, and I should be glad if there were not an African in this country. But slave or no slave, I am determined with her (North Carolina); I will stick to her as well in adversity, if it overtake her, as in prosperity. No misfortune that can happen to her could induce me to leave her, and I religiously believe that no State in the Union is better governed."[291]

It was indeed a strange revolution in North Carolina politics when Macon voted for loans, and Pearson and his political friends

---

290 Annals of Congress, 13th Cong., I., 489-492.
291 Annals of Congress, 13th Cong., II., 1777.

opposed them. But other propositions equally inconsistent with Macon's previous career were favored by him at this time. William H. Murfree, a new member from the Edenton district of North Carolina, reported to Congress an extensive plan of public improvements, consisting of a network of canals designed to connect the larger towns of the Carolinas from Norfolk to Savannah. Macon submitted at the same time a series of petitions asking for the same thing. The plan was a magnificent one, not unlike Clay's great policy two years later, and quite similar to the plan submitted by Archibald Murphy to the Legislature of North Carolina some years later. It was the day of great schemes, and when any of them looked to the developing of North Carolina, Macon did not scruple to endorse them, though such expenditure was entirely out of harmony with his system of constitutional interpretation.[292]

Toward the end of the year 1814, when the country seemed to be passing through its darkest days, a bill was brought before Congress for drafting into the army 80,000 militia. The number of troops from each State was to be proportioned according to representation in the House of Representatives, which naturally would have borne much more heavily on the South than on the North. Macon proposed an amendment, which provided for the drafting to be done according to white population — a change which meant a reduction of some four hundred troops for North Carolina, of two thousand for Virginia.[293] It was evidently unjust to fix the drafts according to representation in Congress, for, as every one knows, the negroes counted three-fifths of their population in National politics. But figures are interesting. Massachusetts, opposing the war bitterly from the beginning, was called on for ten thousand troops; Virginia, favoring the war, and having a much larger vote in Congress, was to supply nine thousand. And in the apportionment of the proposed direct tax of the previous year, Massachusetts was to have paid $316,000, while Virginia would have paid $369,000. Macon's amendment was lost, 66 to 91, Calhoun and the younger Republicans voting against it on the ground of liberality, the South having been in favor of the war all along. The debate on the bill for drafting the militia occupied much time. The bill passed, Macon voting nay, on December 14. But the back woodsman, Andrew Jackson, was getting things in readiness for striking a blow which would render the new war measure unnecessary.

---

292 Annals of Congress, 13th Cong., II., 1767.
293 Annals of Congress, 13th Cong., III., 713, 870.

The events of the last days of 1814 and the first of 1815 no doubt made a great impression on Macon's mind, determined and uncompromising enemy of Great Britain that he was, yet not an opinion, not a written word, has been preserved. His long career in the House was drawing to a close. There remains a single speech to note and his reelection in 1815. When the war was ended, many of the leaders of the war movement in 1811 favored retaining at least ten thousand troops in the regular army. Calhoun was outspoken in his defence of a large "peace establishment," as it was called. Pickering and the Federalists, so many as remained in Congress, at once joined the young Republicans in support of a larger army and navy. Calhoun saw danger in Canada still, and Florida was also a contiguous territory in possession of a European power. A larger army than the old one (three thousand men) was absolutely necessary. Macon, true to his ancient notions, opposed the army plan: "If it (the treaty) were only a truce, then we ought not to stop at ten thousand men; instead of disbanding our forces we ought to go on recruiting them. During all the trouble with Great Britain and Spain, the standing army consisted of one brigade only. With that force we took possession of Louisiana, had maintained and had kept up our garrisons." And, falling back on his militia again, he said: "The true way to safety is the militia, and the way to make our militia efficient is to let them know that the safety of the Nation depends on them, and to take nothing more from the products of their labor to support regular soldiers than is absolutely necessary. In proportion as men live easily and comfortably, in proportion as they are free from the burdens of taxation, they will be attached to the government in which they live."[295]

This, perhaps, is the best expression of his political faith to be found in all his speeches and in the few writings of his still extant. His theory, and experience was the basis of his theory, was that to get rid of an army, to get taxes once laid repealed, was much more difficult than to get armies and taxes voted. And every one who has reviewed the acts of Congress and the steady growth of the unrepublican features of our government, will admit the truth of this statement. Macon voted again with the "old Republicans" on this measure.

Never did the legislators of a nation cease their labors and retire to their homes in more joyous mood than did the members of the old Thirteenth Congress on March 4, 1815; their last act provided for a

---
294 Annals of Congress, 13th Cong., III., 882.
295 Annals of Congress, 13th Cong., III., 1229-30.

day of thanksgiving to "Almighty God for His great goodness manifested in restoring to these United States the blessings of peace."

The end of the war marked the final dissolution of the great political party whose overthrow in North Carolina and the Union had been one of the principal objects of Macon's political life. From 1791 to 1815, he voted against nearly every measure they advocated, both in and out of Congress. In North Carolina he had succeeded admirably until the rise of the new party in 1811 and 1812, until the beginning of a new era, and not only in his State, but in the whole Union. The people of North Carolina had come to regard Macon as their own, as their truest representative, and never once had his district discarded him. His success in the Warrenton district, a highly cultured section of the State, was the strongest possible proof that he was neither a rough, uncultured man, nor an old fogy, but a man who reflected the sterner manly virtues of the people themselves. If Randolph had the right to boast of his Charlotte county constituents, certainly Macon could be proud of his fellow citizens of Warren and neighboring counties. As he came to be one of the first figures of the land, they boasted of him, and when he favored war against England, with taxes for its support, they did not desert him. In the summer of 1815, they returned him once again, but he was soon to change his constituency from a single district to the whole State.

Eleven days after his appearance in Washington, in December 1815, he was informed that the Legislature of North Carolina had elected him to a seat in the United States Senate, to fill the place of David Stone, resigned. Macon's twenty-four years in the House were closed in the following simple but appropriate words: "To the Speaker of the House of Representatives: I deem it my duty to inform you and the members of the House, that I have this day, by letter to the Governor of North Carolina, resigned my seat in the House of Representatives. I cannot withdraw from those with whom I have been associated for years without expressing the grateful sense I entertain of their uniform kindness, and assuring them that it wall be remembered with pleasure during my life."

His relations with Randolph, about which so much has been said, are well pictured in the following quotation from a letter to his old friend, Nicholson, dated February 1, 1815: "Jonathan did not love David more than I have Randolph, and I still have that same feeling towards him; but somehow or other I am constrained from saying anything about it or him; unless now and then to defend him against false accusations, or what I believe to be such. There is hardly any evil that afflicts one more than the loss of a friend, especially when not conscious of having given any cause for it. I cannot account for the coldness with which you say he treated you, or his not staying at your house while in Baltimore. Stanford now and then comes to where I sit in the House and shows me a letter from R. to him, which is all I see from him. He has not wrote me since I left Congress, nor I but once to him, which was to enclose a book of his that I found in the city when I came to the next session. I have said this much in answer to your letter, and it is more than has been said or written to any other person. God bless you and yours."

President Andrew Jackson

CHAPTER XVII.
IN THE UNITED STATES SENATE, 1815-1828.
I.

The later period of Macon's political life easily divides itself into two parts, the first beginning with his election to the Senate in 1815 and closing with the vote on the Missouri Compromise; the second embracing the years 1820 to 1828, a period taken up almost entirely with the almost shameful personal scramble for office which resulted in the election of John Quincey Adams, and with the apparently permanent establishment of the Clay doctrine of protective tariffs and internal improvements.

When Macon entered the so-called upper branch of our National legislature, it was a different body from what it had been when Jefferson presided over it in 1796-1800. The changes of the years 1800-1804 had substituted a strong Republican for the former determined Federalist majority, so that until 1812 the Senate was little better than a registering organ for the party in power. Great debates were practically unknown in the Senate, even as late as 1815. The House had been the National debating society, and not infrequently its members were twitted with the remark that their's was the turbulent, unruly, democratic branch of Congress. A member of the Senate in these earlier days felt himself immeasurably more dignified, more aristocratic, than a Representative, and the prevailing sentiment of Americans of that time indulged him in his sense of superiority.

But just after the War of 1812, when that brisk, healthy breeze from the frontier, the spirit which had in fact forced the nation into war, became the prevailing wind at Washington, a rapid change took place in the character of the Senate. It became an arena of debate, of political contest, the like of which has seldom been seen in the world's history. The greatest minds of the country met there, and, ignoring some traditional notions of decorum and silent dignity, fought out in weeks and months of able discussion the issues whose decision fixed the destiny of this western world of ours. From this time until 1860, the Senate was pre-eminently the more important branch of Congress. Among the older members of this body in 1815 were Harrison Gray Otis of Hartford Convention fame, Samuel W. Dana of Connecticutt, and Rufus King of New York, the ex-ambassador at the Court of St. James, all Federalists of the old school, and unfriendly in the extreme to the party in power, as well as to the energetic younger men who had come into almost absolute control of the House of Representatives since 1811. Jefferson's son-in-law, John W. Eppes, James Barbour of Virginia, John Gailliard of South Carolina, and George W. Campbell of Tennessee were some of the more influential Southern Republicans.[296] Macon came into the Senate at the time when the change was taking place; he brought a reputation and a long experience in National legislation, which entitled him to the greatest respect. His standing in the country is perhaps best illustrated by an article which appeared in the *Richmond Enquirer* a few years before, the spirit of which is summed up in the following words: "Nathaniel Macon, too, has been made the mark of ridicule! Sir, to what lengths is this mad career to be pushed? Though I differ from N. Macon in some measures, my heart does him homage. He may err, but his integrity soars a sightless distance above the reach of suspicion. Firm, sterling in his faith, blunt in his manners, he can never prove a recreant to his principles. Never can I forget the tears which streamed into my eyes when, during last winter, I saw him coming forward and leading the van of his country's defenders." And again, in 1812, on the occasion of the declaration of war, Macon is given very high rank in the nation by the *Enquirer*.[297]

The country was in a deplorable condition when Macon took his seat in the Senate. There was a deficit of the year 1814 of $1,000,000. There was no system of finance. Nowhere outside of New England did the banks redeem their notes in specie, the Government itself being unable to meet its obligations. A depreciated paper currency ran riot in all the Southern and Middle States; and to make matters worse, not even the individual States were responsible for their bank issues. The only remedy appeared to be a second national bank, the plans of which Gallatin had outlined in 1811. Secretary of Treasury, Dallas, good Republican that he was, made the proposition to Congress, which soon took the form of a National Bank bill, and was engineered through the House by Clay and Calhoun, while Webster opposed! The object of the bill was first to supersede the cheap paper issues of the State banks by giving the people a sound convertible national

---

296 Annals of Congress, 14th Cong., 1st Sess., 10-20; Schouler, III., 21.
297 These references apply to his service in connection with the second war with Great Britain. They are cited at this point to show Macon's standing: in Virginia at this time, and especially to show how the great Democratic editor, Thomas Richie, regarded him.

paper currency, and, second, to aid the Government in the negotiation and payment of loans. The plan of organization was strikingly similar to that of Hamilton's bank in 1791; the capital was placed at $35,000,000, $7,000,000 of which was to be taken by the Government, the remainder to be offered to the public: individuals, corporations and states. There were to be twenty-five directors, five of whom were to be appointed annually by the Government, and twenty to be elected by the stockholders. The Government was to control the establishment of branch banks, and the Secretary of the Treasury could at any time curtail its functions as a national depository; besides, Congress reserved the right of examination and rigid inspection of its affairs. After passing the House, the bill was reported to the Senate from the committee on Finance, of which George W. Campbell was chairman, on March 25, 1816; Federalists and Republicans voted together for and against it. Macon was determined in his opposition, based on the ground of unconstitutionality. When Mason, of New Hampshire, proposed to amend the bill in order that Congress might redeem its notes in specie, Macon joined him, favoring as he did what he called "hard money" currency alone. And when King, of New York, tried to modify the measure so that not more than three of the five Government directors should be appointed from any one State, Macon agreed. As a last resort to defeat the plan before it came to an issue, Macon voted with only five others for indefinite postponement. The bank law was finally passed on April the third by a vote of 22 to 12,[298] Macon, of course, being among the nays. Macon's colleague, James Turner,[299] voted for the bill and was not returned to the Senate at the next election. No other course was to have been expected of Macon; but that the ablest Southern democrats should have joined forces with the younger and less distinguished Federalists of the North and East, and carried through a national banking system which was in most essentials a copy of Hamilton's plan of 1791, must have caused no little surprise throughout the country. The men who opposed the bank were those who followed most closely the policy outlined by Jefferson while he was leader of the opposition; those who voted for it were

---

298 Annals of Congress, 14th Cong., 1st Sess., 235-281.
299 It is worth noting in this connection, and it shows the influence of the county in North Carolina, that Turner and Macon, both United States Senators at this time, Weldon N. Edwards, M.C. from that district, Judge Potter of the United States District Court, and John Hall, next year appointed a Judge of the new State Supreme Court, all lived in Warren.

the same men who incorporated into their own creed the best of the Federalist platform, taking care, however, to avoid acknowledging the source of their wisdom.

For those who love party names, it may be proper to say that the Republican-Democratic party gave the country the bank which the greatest of Democrats, Andrew Jackson, devoted the best of his official life to destroying. And most of the men who opposed the establishment of the second United States bank, Webster for example, made it the great fight of their lives to defeat Jackson's anti-bank policy of 1832-1836. The country at this time was passing through a crisis, and most of the greater leaders had not found their proper places. Parties were going asunder. It was to require eight years for their recrystalization. The South was placed by Calhoun and Clay in unnatural relations; it was made for the time the mainstay of doctrines, anti-Southern, anti-agricultural, and many years of bitter impoverishment, as we shall see, was the result. Macon stood almost alone among the greater men of his time refusing to be allured by the glowing eloquence of misdirected talent, such, for example, as Clay's. He stood as one crying in the wilderness, not eloquent, not even a master leader, yet one who by instinct scented from afar the dangers for his "South country," as he begins now to call it, against which very destiny itself seemed inevitably drifting.

Early in the next session of the same Congress, and while Monroe was quietly waiting for the next inauguration to confer on him the insignia of power, Calhoun and Clay, ever resourceful in new schemes, projected the famous Internal Improvements policy. Prosperity had already set in; the bank, too, was working beneficial ends almost as miraculously as had Hamilton's twenty-five years before. Peace, public confidence, and a buoyant young people, not any fiscal or political *agency*, brought back the years of plenty. The receipts were surpassing the expenditures. A surplus — that most extraordinary of bugbears to American politicians — was imminent. It was determined by the young Republicans "to lay aside a fund to be used for the purpose hereinafter to be stated." A bill actually passed both branches of Congress to lay aside this sum, which was to be increased from year to year. It was clearly understood that this money was to be used on internal improvements.

From the time Washington began to agitate the plan of establishing a closer connection between the Chesapeake Bay, especially Norfolk, Virginia, and the Northwest, till the appearance of Clay in

Congress, after the War of 1812, the idea of public expenditure for public improvements, in the way of canals and turnpike roads, had constantly grown on the public mind. Virginia, New York, North Carolina, and other States, had undertaken, or were about to undertake, magnificent works of one kind or another. It was long since fairly well admitted that the National government was not empowered by the Constitution to collect taxes or expend public revenue in this way. The States were left to under take such tasks. Perhaps the greatest advocate of this on the part of the States was De Witt Clinton, whose foresight has an everlasting monument in the greatness and wealth of New York City, the fruit of his Erie Canal.

But since the war was ended and a surplus was threatening, even at the very gates, Clay hit upon the happy idea of warding off the danger and, what was equally important to him, of winning popularity in the Western and Middle States.

The bill looking to this end was introduced into the Senate on February 10 under the name of "An act to set apart and pledge as a permanent fund for internal improvements the *bonus* of the National Bank, and the United States' share of its dividends."[300] The wording of the bill was enough to excite Macon's opposition, and, accordingly, when the subject was open for debate he declared "this to be a new plan of legislation in this country. It makes an appropriation of millions for roads and canals, with out directing a cent to be expended on any particular road or canal. It is as incorrect as it is new and against the invariable practice of the Government, which has been to make appropriations of money as specific as possible. Who can tell what effect this general appropriation may have in a few years?" Clay had not favored a rapid payment of the public debt. Macon now called on the Senate to use this surplus in payment of all National obligations. The bill "locks up millions uselessly, for years to come, in the Treasury, which ought to be employed in the payment of the public debt. In time of peace no exertion ought to be spared to discharge it. It is a safe and good rule to pay debts when you have the means." As to the constitutionality of building roads and canals, he was as strict a constructionist as ever, and he had himself recorded once again as opposed to all latitudinarian interpretation of what he called the National Charter. James Barbour, of Virginia, inconsistent with the best traditions of that State, maintained that precedent was suf-

---

300 Annals of Congress, 14th Cong., 2nd Sess., 165.

ficient justification of the bill. This Macon refused to recognize; else, said he, "you will admit the alien and sedition laws to be justification of other alien and sedition laws. I am in favor of improvements of every kind," so he went on to say, "but by individual enterprise, not by the United States."[301] A resolution for indefinite postponement failed by a vote of 19 to 18, and the several attempts at radical amendments failed by similarly close votes, but the final decision stood 20 to 15 in favor of its passage.[302] In the debates on this bill the same grounds were covered as in the National Bank discussion at the previous session, and in general both Representatives and members of the Senate took the same relative positions, though the party of strict construction in the Senate gained the influence of Campbell, of Tennessee, whose voice had been potent in carrying the bank scheme at the previous session. To the chagrin of Clay and the great delight of Macon, Madison vetoed the bill, which, since the necessary two-thirds vote could not be had, ended for the time this second scheme of the Republicans looking toward the establishment of the doctrine of their ancient opponents.

It was a matter of no little gratification to Macon that on the assembling of the Fifteenth Congress, in December 1817, the new President, Monroe, announced most conclusively in his first annual message that the Executive would regard any bill similar to the Internal Improvements measure of the last session as unconstitutional. Though Monroe admitted unhesitatingly that the improvement of the great public highways, especially those connecting the East with the West, was good policy, he was unwilling to read into the Constitution the powers necessary to its accomplishment by the National government. He proposed at once a constitutional amendment to that end.[303]

Before entering upon a discussion of the two great contests between rival factions of the Republican party in Congress during Monroe's first term, and the results of which cast a gloom over Macon's later political life, let us see what were the environments of a member of the Senate during Monroe's administration, and how Macon adjusted himself to these environments.

1. Although Monroe was a good Virginian of the old school, a diligent follower of Jefferson, and an exceedingly wise and able President, he was not by any means the simple, unaffected man in official

---

301 Annals of Congress, 14th Cong., 2nd Sess., 177-179.
302 Annals of Congress, 14th Cong., 2nd Sess., 101.
303 Schouler, III., 5; See Message of December, 1816, Annals of Cong.

life that our first Republican President had been. Monroe desired to direct the affairs of the Nation, as Washington had done, that is, as one who stood above party. Believing party government to be an evil in the United States, he sought first of all to ignore party lines and to break down party barriers.[304] Jefferson had believed that parties were necessary evils in a free country; but Macon, somewhat like Monroe in this, believed there should be only one party in the country, and that the most democratic imaginable. The various plans and practices of the fifth President to dissolve parties do not require to be reviewed here, except to say that he was so successful as to bring about the "Era of Good Feeling" so much spoken of during his second term, just when there was the most rancorous ill-feeling ever known at Washington, with two exceptions; he was successful enough not to meet with any opposition at his second election — a single elector voting against him to prevent his coming in the same category with Washington in popularity. But in matters of etiquette and ceremony, Monroe's imitation of Washington was much less pleasing to Macon. It had been determined in Cabinet meeting to restrict the free, easy-going manners in official circles in Washington so prevalent since 1801. The levees of Lady Washington reappeared, now that the commodious White House was complete; only on stated days of the week were Congressmen expected to visit the President, except on special business. Washington City always responds to the prevailing sentiment of the incumbents of the White House, so that balls and birthday parties multiplied thick and fast; fashion gained a greater sway, and notions of precedence were strictly observed by the ladies of the Cabinet. All this annoyed and even disgusted Macon, who believed in no social or class distinctions "among freemen." A letter of his to a friend in North Carolina[305] gives his views on the subject: "There has been some change in the etiquette among the ladies, which has furnished a subject for conversation; Mrs. Monroe returns no visits, and Mrs. Adams expects to be visited first by the wives of Congressmen." And on the same theme to another friend (Jos. H. Nicholson), a little earlier, on the occasion of an invitation to a Christmas dinner, he wrote: "But pride, vain pride multiplieth food of the plain kind into such a variety of forms and tastes, that a plain, respectable countryman who hath enough to eat and to spare hardly knows the flesh of the beef

---

304 Schouler, III., 5. — Monroe's words are quoted in 26 Niles Register, 160-167.
305 Macon to Bartlett Yancey, February 8, 1818, in the Macon-Yancey Papers in possession of the University of North Carolina.

or any other animal when by chance he happens to be at the table of the rich in a commercial city; so much has cooking changed in a few years that one scarcely knows the name of a dish; and if he scarcely knows beef, how will he find out the new-fashioned pies, puddings, etc. ? * * * There is an aristocracy in everything but downright work. The rich can not bear that the food of the poor should be cooked or dressed like theirs, nor that they should use the same words to convey the same meaning, nor that their clothes should be cut in the same fashion. Hence, the constant change in these and many other things which concern the great family of mankind. Do not judge from this that I am unwilling that those who have the means of getting good things should not have them. I only object to this universal change, which constantly tends to separate the more fortunate class of society from the less fortunate. * * * Like all other old folks, I think the politics of former days better than those of the present, and that every change of fashion which tends to separate farther the rich and the poor has a strong tendency to aristocracy, and that these changes will, if they have not already, tend to give a wide construction to the Constitution of the United States, in fact to make it unlimited by degrees and without a regular amendment in the proper and constitutional method. In no other way, it seems to me, can any one account for the great and almost universal change which has taken place in what is now called Republican politics; * * * fashion has enabled them to do it, and fashion will probably enable them to go forward till it is [completely] changed. Even religion itself is not entirely free from the influence of the tyrant, fashion."

2. Congressmen then lived in "messes" about the city, or over in ancient Georgetown; kept, as in Jefferson's time, horses in their own hired stables, and rode to the new halls of Congress, or at will out among the neighboring hills of Virginia and Maryland for a fox chase in season. Macon's horses were the very best thoroughbreds, groomed in true "Virginia style." Macon lived in Washington, not far from the government buildings, as he tells Nicholson in a letter of February 15, 1815: "I live at Mrs. Clark's, in F street, not far east of the burnt treasury office. Rhea of Tennessee, Hall[306] of Georgia, John Roane and Burwell of Virginia, and Franklin[307] of North Carolina. The house is about middling, and I can, I believe, get a bed put in my room for you

---

306 Boiling Hall, son of a Warren county family, and a member of Congress for several terms.
307 Meshack Franklin, not Jesse, a former Representative and Governor of his State.

if you should visit the city. Let me know a day beforehand, that the room may be fixed." But life at Washington was not all so simple and unaffected as that of Macon and some of his friends. Clay and Webster were both addicted to card playing and wine to such an extent as to injure them politically. Randolph, as indeed was Macon in this, was an inveterate card-player. It has been said that Calhoun was almost the only pure man in national politics at this time. Whether this is not exaggeration the author will not undertake to show. It is safe to say that public life was not more ideal than it now is, and that Macon was an equally exceptionally pure man morally and otherwise with Calhoun.

3. As has been gleaned already from this chapter, the whole trend of public opinion at the National capital among the better educated and more successful classes was towards a lavish public expenditure. Lowndes and Calhoun of South Carolina, Mercer and St. George Tucker of Virginia, Gaston of North Carolina, and a host of other semi-Federalists of the South, all following in the lead of Clay and overcome by the fact that our National income had increased from $7,000,000 in 1815 to more than $36,000,000 in 1817, and by seeing an annual surplus of $4,000,000 in the treasury, were ready to launch the Government on any sort of extravagant policy. And again, as Macon's letter to Nicholson shows, fashion and what he regarded as extravagant living, were coming more and more into evidence. Clay could not support himself on the six dollars a day from the Government, and this was true, perhaps, of more than a majority of the members of Congress, as is rather sadly shown by the vote on the increase of the pay of Congressmen. Not so with Macon, whose suit of "best navy blue, turn-over top boots" and immaculate linen cost him no more than they had cost at the close of the Revolution, when the leaders of Republican society, at least, were all plain-lived country gentlemen. His manner of living being very simple, his "mess" scarcely more expensive than a school-boy's boarding place today, there was small demand on his income. So while many another member exiled himself forever from the National legislature by voting himself the very moderate increase of $2 a day, he was altogether satisfied with his former per diem, asking no more of the people than had been given from the first.

While Macon had kept in line with his party in the main, Randolph and his devoted friend Stanford had opposed the war of 1812, had cooperated with the opponents of the Government itself, the former going so far as to write long public letters to the New Englanders praising their disloyalty and declaring that an honest and independent man could not get a hearing in Virginia; asking himself the cause of his addressing his remarks to the New England press in the form of a letter to one of her Senators in Congress, he said:[308] "It is because the avenue to the public ear is shut against me in Virginia, and I have been flattered to believe that the sound of my voice may reach New England. Nay, that it would be heard there, not without attention and respect. With us the press is under a virtual *imprimatur*, and it would be more easy, at this time, to force into circulation the treasury notes, than opinions militating against the administration, through the press in Virginia." This was untrue; there were prominent opposition papers in Richmond which simply for the sake of fighting Ritchie's *Enquirer*, if for no other reason, would have published anything Randolph chose to write against Madison. Though Macon was a life-long friend of Randolph and though he often agreed with him, especially about 1820, on leading public issues, he was not now, in 1815-1817, a member of the group of malcontents which Randolph headed and which had led Macon into some political errors in 1807. Virginia was not the object of his anger and jealousy as it was of Randolph; but it was constantly praised by him in private and in public.

Macon's position was a difficult one at this time, the beginning of Monroe's administration. Having favored Monroe, as we have seen, against Madison in 1807, and having lent himself to Randolph's scheme of winning the vote of Virginia for Monroe against Madison, and against Jefferson's wish as well, then having broken away from Monroe and publicly advocated the nomination of Gallatin by North Carolina in 1808, even advising his constituents to prefer De Witt Clinton to Madison, and finally in a characteristic way turning to the support of Madison at the beginning of the war of 1812, sustaining the Administration heartily against all detractors, he had scarce anything left except a stainless reputation as free from charges of intrigue as from over-devotion to any man or cause. He was respected by the new President but apparently was not relied upon as an Administration leader; he was somewhat dissociated from his party and could not play an important part for an administration which was drifting as he thought further and further from the "old Republican doctrines." Occupying such a position relative to the Administra-

---

308 Garland's *Life of Randolph*, II., 53 letter dated Dec. 15, 1814.

tion, he sustained a no less unique one towards the real leaders of Congress. Known for his almost parsimonious policy on the score of public expenditure, Clay and his brilliant but somewhat windy following of young orators could not count on Macon in anything. His interpretation of the Constitution made any agreement with the "young Republicans" impossible. They tried to laugh him down, and they succeeded well enough in giving him the name of "old fogy" — a name which certain classes in his own State delighted after his death to fix in the public memory concerning him. Not in the confidence of the President and out of harmony with the leaders of his own party, but supported almost unanimously in his own State, Macon's position was one of absolute independence, just such as he had always desired to occupy; and his long and varied experience made him one of the most important characters in the Senate.

Monroe's first care after being securely seated in the President's chair, as has been suggested in another connection, was to become head of the whole nation. Any policy looking to this end could not but take prime notice of New England, torn as it was by faction and exasperated by a prolonged exclusion of its representatives from the first places in the national councils. Monroe's original plan was to give each of the four sections of the country, East, Middle, West and South, one representative in his cabinet, New England getting first place, the West coming in for second honors, as custom then arranged things. John Quincy Adams, than whom there was no abler man for the place, was made Secretary of State, thus being placed in line of promotion for the presidency. Smith Thompson, of New York, was given the Navy Department, Clay the War, and Crawford, of Georgia, the Treasury. This gave every section at least one position, leaving the Attorney- and Postmaster-Generals still to be named. This would have made a representative and an exceedingly able cabinet.[309] But Clay's ambition would not admit of his accepting anything but the first place; he was aggrieved at Adams' precedence and he declined all Monroe's overtures. Since the plan of giving Massachusetts what the President's sense of fair play suggested did not please the Kentucky statesman, he preferred the position of Speaker of the House where he felt himself almost absolute, and from which vantage ground he expected to upset the plans of the Administration in regulating the succession in 1824 at the expiration of Monroe's al-

---
309 Schouler, III., 13-14.

lotted two terms. Clay intended to appeal to the people against the President. His means of winning the people was the House of Representatives. There was no reason why the Representatives, going back to their districts every few months to laud to the skies the man whom they elevated to the speakership time after time with almost unanimous vote, should not win or him the desired precedence over Adams. This was a promising scheme in the majority of states, especially since there seemed to be a mutual understanding between the Virginia and Massachusetts politicians that the presidency was an office to which other states need not aspire; and Clay felt that he was just the man to carry it out — a similar game in national politics to that which Andrew Jackson played against Clay in 1832, with results far different for the initiators. It was the selection of issues which decided the contest, not so much the man, though there never was a more popular man than Clay at several periods of his almost wonderful life.

Monroe threw down the gauntlet in December, 1817; it was his open declaration in the annual message that Clay might expect a veto if he brought forward a second time his favorite Internal Improvements bill, rumors of which were thick about Washington before Congress assembled. Henry Clay did not hesitate to accept the challenge. St. George Tucker, of Virginia, whose name meant something for the success of the Speaker's plan, brought in a bill almost identical with the one vetoed by Madison less than a year before.[310] The House was led at once into a long and envenomed debate on a bill which every one knew could not pass over the President's veto, there appearing somewhat to Clay's surprise stronger opposition to internal improvements than had characterized the last Congress. It appears that the Speaker, interpreting the decisions of the Supreme Court, which John Marshall had made popular as well as great in the case of Martin vs. Hunter's Lessee, of the year 1816, and other similar decisions, and the attitude of the young Republicans North and South, to point to latitudinarian construction of the Constitution as the coming popular view, was willing to stake every thing on this fight. It began March 6, 1818, and continued about three weeks. Clay showed himself imperious and overbearing, and though he carried his measure it weakened instead of strengthened him in the nation.[311] He put himself in the same position relative to Monroe's administration that John Randolph

---

310 *cf.* Schurz *Life of Henry Clay*, I., 142 on.
311 Annals of Congress, 15th Cong., 1st Sess., 1114-1402.

placed himself in 1806-'07 towards that of Jefferson and with similar motives.

The North Carolina delegation voted against the Clay-Tucker resolutions ten to two. The erratic Lemuel Sawyer, again in Congress from the Edenton section, made the most sensible and vigorous speech of his life in opposition to the Speaker in this personal war on the Executive. George Mumford, of Rowan, and Jesse Slocum, of Wayne, were the two members who voted for internal improvements.

When the Senate met and organized it showed at once that the President would be supported heartily. No trouble was made about Executive appointments and the standing committees were put under the leadership of men who were friendly to the Administration. James Barbour, of Virginia, became Chairman of the committee on Foreign Relations, with Macon as his first associate; the committee on Finance was headed by George W. Campbell, of Tennessee, Macon being a member of this committee also. Barbour, Campbell and Macon were all decidedly enough opposed to the war in the House. In fact before the standing committees were appointed Barbour introduced a resolution in the Senate calling for an amendment to the Constitution to enable Congress to appropriate funds to public improvements.[312] Barbour had voted for the Internal Improvements bill of the last Congress, believing it to be legitimate and not unconstitutional; but he was unwilling, now that Monroe had expressed openly his scruples as to the constitutionality of such a measure, to embarrass the Administration; "The present Chief Magistrate has very frankly and properly disclosed his opinion, and decided it (the proposed Clay bill) unconstitutional. The impracticability of passing it, with this impediment, through Congress must be palpable. Indeed I do not know that it is desirable that it should be. It is better, perhaps, in all cases of doubt, to recur to the people — the only original and only legitimate fountain of power."[313] This was somewhat strange language for such a progressive young Republican as Barbour had been in the last Congress. If it does not show a change of heart it at least shows that as a leader of the Senate he did not propose to allow that body to be drawn into Clay's contest with the Executive. The resolution which Barbour introduced was referred to a special committee composed of Barbour, Lacock, Macon and Eppes. The committee did no more than submit the origi-

---

[312] Annals of Congress, 15th Cong., Sess., I., 21-22.
[313] Annals of Congress, 15th Cong., I., 22.

nal Barbour resolution again which was indefinitely postponed by a vote of twenty-two to nine, Barbour and Macon voting against postponement.[314] The House Internal Improvements bill, and consequent debate, never reached the Senate. Macon heartily favored the Barbour amendment, thus definitely defining the powers of the National Government on this subject, since so fruitful of public waste and extravagance. He wrote a friend[315] in North Carolina a full exposition of his views on the subject. This paper has been lost, but his accompanying letter contains the following language:[316] "If Congress can make canals they can with more propriety emancipate. Be not deceived. I speak soberly in the fear of God and the love of the Constitution. Let not love of improvements or a thirst for glory blind that sober discretion and sound sense with which the Lord has blessed you. Paul was not more anxious or sincere concerning Timothy than I am for you. Your error in this will injure if not destroy our beloved mother, North Carolina, and all the South country. * * * Be not led astray by grand notions or magnificent opinions; remember you belong to a meek state and just people, who want nothing but to enjoy the fruits of their labor honestly and to lay out their profits in their own way."

These significant statements furnish the key, were one needed, to Macon's policy in 1820. To read into the Constitution powers not specifically granted meant to him to set out on the road which led directly to the emancipation of slaves. It would "ruin North Carolina and all the South country." Yancey was inclined to follow the young Republicans. Macon desired to point out to him the error of his way — an error which most of the brilliant young Southerners, Calhoun for example, freely confessed later in our political history.

The persistent efforts of Clay in keeping up opposition to the Executive in another matter, that of recognizing the South American Republics, only kept the House in a turmoil; the subject was not so much as mentioned in the Senate at this session. This was not true in the country generally. As in all such instances public sympathy ran high, found expression among Representatives and greatly disturbed the President in his cooler, more deliberate policy. Macon's attitude toward all these questions was one of "hands off," except in reference

---

314 Annals of Congress, 15th Cong., Vol. I., 292.
315 Macon to Bartlett Yancey, April 15, 1818.
316 Yancey had been requested to send him his opinion on the subject while the Senate committee was discussing it. Yancey had given an opinion favorable to the constitutionality of Clay's doctrines.

to Florida, which again came to be much discussed because of the Amelia Island controversy. In consequence of a revolt in East Florida Amelia Island had gained the protection of our government; many Americans had gone there seeking what fortune there was to be won. Spain, too feeble to settle her difficulties in South America, was entirely unable to restore order in Florida. A chronic state of anarchy thus existed on our Southern borders, and Adams, with the hearty support of Calhoun, who had accepted the war portfolio which Clay declined, was doing his utmost to bring about annexation and thus close the question. The fear of strengthening the slave-holding States to the disadvantage of the free States did not influence the broad-minded Secretary of State. For Macon the annexation of Florida was an old desire dating back to 1803, when he had advised Jefferson to do whatever lay in his power to purchase Florida along with Louisiana. He shows his insight into the real difficulties of the situation in a letter to Yancey February 8, 1818: "It seems probable that we may find ourselves in possession of all or nearly all Florida without being at war with Spain or having waited on her performing the treaty stipulation[317] concerning the Indians. I am not acquainted with the intentions of the Executive relative to Amelia Island. * * * It is believed that circumstances justified driving the Army and company from Amelia, but this justification may be destroyed by improperly holding possession." This was not very urgent language for one who had long desired to see Florida made an American territory. It shows Macon's disposition to do strict justice or, at least, when this seemed a difficult thing to determine, to proceed very cautiously. So when Jackson a year later presented his *fait accompli*, he heartily disapproved of the General's unwarranted proceedings, and in most characteristic language: "The Constitution gives Congress the sole authority to declare war; war has been waged and every act of sovereign power exercised without the consent of Congress. The constitution has been violated and I am for the Constitution rather than for man."[318] More than a year elapsed before the tardy Spanish Minister could be brought to terms on the Florida question. Adams was hastening matters as much as possible. Macon became impatient: "The Spanish minister had not yesterday (April 18, 1820), I believe, given any proof what he would do or what he expects from the U.S. It is probable he wishes to make a flourish or

---

317 A guarantee that peace among the border Indians and white adventurers should be maintained.
318 Macon to Bartlett Yancey, February 7, 1819.

two before he declares his ultimatum." He was delighted a short while afterwards to see Florida annexed to the "South Country" whose extension he begins now to desire much more warmly than in former years.

Macon began in 1818 to express his fears that a great struggle over slavery was pending. When he wrote Yancey that the passage of a bill granting money for internal improvements made possible a bill for the emancipation of the negroes, he desired to put North Carolinians on their guard, and not simply North Carolinians, but all Southerners. "The South Country will be ruined," was his expression. He wrote a little later: "We have abolition, colonization, Bible and peace societies; their contentions can not be known, but the character and spirit of one may without injustice be considered that of all — it is a character and spirit of perseverance bordering on enthusiasm. And if the general government shall continue to stretch their powers, these societies will undoubtedly push them to try the question of emancipation. I have written very freely to you, and it is intended for you alone. Under a fair and honest construction of the constitution the *negro property* is safe and secure. Besides the subjects before mentioned, we can not forget that the Sedition act was declared constitutional by the U.S. Courts. The states having no slaves may not feel as strongly as the states having slaves about stretching the constitution, because no such interest is to be touched by it. The camp that is not always guarded may be surprised; and the people [who] do not watch their rulers may be enslaved. Too much confidence is the ruin of both."[319]

The fear of a long contest which Macon felt in 1818 proved not unfounded in 1820. In fact, both Northern and Southern leaders began to foresee that the great question before the American people would be that of slavery. The American Colonization Society, for which Macon felt no sympathy, was an expression of the uneasiness of the South. Madison, Monroe and Clay encouraged its work which was to advocate and foster a spirit of emancipation in the South and wherever possible to transport the freed blacks to Liberia in western Africa. Repeated attempts on the part of the Northern border States at ridding themselves of the duty of assisting in the return of fugitive slaves to their masters were made.[320] Since 1808 the African slave trade had nominally ceased; but in fact it was continued in such a

---

319 Macon to Bartlett Yancey, March 8, 1818.
320 Annals of Congress, 15th Cong., Vol. I., 225 on.

bold way that Congress finally (1820) passed a law making the slave trade piracy.[321] The partial closing of the African slave trade and the ever-increasing demand for cotton and tobacco, staple exports of the South, so increased the demand for negro labor that Virginia and in part North Carolina and Maryland became breeding grounds for the more Southern and Southwestern States. Washington, Norfolk and Richmond became important slave markets.[322] And again the method of pairing a slave with a free State whenever the territories were admitted into the Union shows both the determination and ability of the Northern people to limit the spread of slavery. The North had a population six hundred thousand greater than the South; and the next distribution of Representatives would give her an advantage of thirty-six members in the House.

The fight opened in the House in 1818 when a bill for the territorial organization of Arkansas was presented. The partisans of slavery rallied every Southern vote on the question, submitted by Taylor, of New York, whether slavery should not be forever excluded from the new territory; and a bill limiting the extension of slavery was passed and sent to the Senate, which body struck out the anti-slavery clause by a vote of thirty-one to seven. On the next day Burril, of Rhode Island, made an attempt to get a reconsideration favorable to the abolition of slavery but failed by a vote of only nineteen to fourteen — a vote which shows the real strength of the two sections of the country in the Senate as the new anti-slavery clause was to be less aggressive than the former. The pro-slavery party won because of the absence of Van Dyke and Horsey, of Delaware, Hunter, of Rhode Island, and by the votes of Ohio and Indiana. The modified bill was returned to the House just before the close of the session when a motion to reconsider the bill failed by the Speaker's vote.[323] There is no record of a speech on this subject by Macon.

This whole movement was the outcome of the desire on the part of Missouri and the South in general to make a state of the present territory of Missouri, leaving the southern part of the original territory as a basis for still another slave state a few years later. During the ensuing spring and summer public opinion was wrought up to the highest pitch either for or against the admission of Missouri, that is,

---

321 Annals of Congress, 15th Cong., Vol. I., 97 on.
322 See letter of Thomas Ritchie to his brother, *Branch Historical Papers*, II., 153.
323 For the Senate's action in this, see Annals of Congress, 15th Cong., 2nd Sess., 272-274.

for or against the extension of slavery. A grand convention composed of prominent men from all parts of the North assembled in Philadelphia in October; and in the Eastern and Middle States indignation meetings were held, in all of which resolutions were drawn up and passed memorializing the next Congress on the subject of slavery. Going back to pre-revolutionary practices, committees of correspondence were established. Excitement ran so high that party lines could not be maintained; Jeffersonian republicans and Hamilton federalists cooperated now in pushing forward a veritable crusade against Southern expansion.

The South responded with equal determination to this onslaught against one of its fundamental institutions. Crawford, of Georgia, looking to the successorship in the White House, already proposed to lead; but a leadership that would win Northern votes was necessary. He could not therefore speak out his opinion; the South could not elect him to the presidency. Then the Southern States, through their legislatures, following the example of Virginia, took up the burning question. This brought most of the young Republicans who had formerly voted with Clay and enlisted under his banner back to the strict construction doctrines of the old Republicans whom Randolph and Macon led, though only in these particular policies. Pinckney, of Maryland, was the great leader and champion of Missouri on the platform; while the celebrated Thomas Ritchie made the Richmond *Enquirer* the champion of the States' Rights doctrines based on the Virginia and Kentucky resolutions of 1798. Richmond, prophetic of her later destiny, was made the storm-center of the South.

Before Congress came together in December, 1819, Massachusetts, ready now to make great sacrifice in order to regain her former leadership, had arranged a scheme by which to balance once more an additional slave state. Maine was the sacrifice. It was cut off from the old state and, without passing through the territorial probation hitherto customary, a memorial from its representatives was presented to the Senate on the very heels of the President's message, asking admission into the Union. Missouri knocked a second time at the Senate's door on the same day. But two days before the President had submitted the application of Alabama, which was immediately referred to a committee whose report was favorable, and on the 8th of December, the date of the Maine memorial, was admitted into the Union as a slave state. This restored the balance, leaving the new Florida acquisition as a balance in favor of the South in future contests. The House, already won to the anti-slavery influence, hastened through a bill for the admission of Maine; but the Senate, still controlled by pro-slavery men, refused to admit Maine without Missouri. In the discussion which arose over this balancing of the two proposed states, Macon made a longer speech than usual: "The appearance of the Senate today is different from anything I have seen since I became a member of it." He then reviewed the history of the admission of new states and outlined in an able manner what he regarded as absolutely essential to the peace and happiness of the country. "But," said he, "the true reason of the objection to the admission of Missouri is the principle to which gentlemen have alluded and which has made so much noise out of doors. I confess that on this question I have felt more anxiety than on any other lately presented to my view. It may be a matter of philosophy and abstraction with the gentlemen of the East, but it is a different thing with us. They may philosophize and hold town meetings about it as much as they please; but, with great submission, sir, they know nothing about the question."[324] Otis, of Massachusetts followed Macon and referred to him in a way which shows clearly enough the respect accorded him even by the greatest of his opponents, and it also testifies to Macon's own uneasiness of mind on this occasion: "With others (members of the Senate) a longer acquaintance has ripened into real friendship; and for my old friend above me (Macon), I profess a sincere affection and respect (inspired by a long experience of his honorable character), though we have formerly broken together many a political lance, and I am sorry to discern in him symptoms of wounded or excited feelings on the present occasion."[325]

In the midst of the debate, Thomas, of Indiana, who had voted against the slavery clause in the former Missouri bill, proposed a substitute which became famous as the great compromise of 1820. It provided for the admission of Missouri as a slave state stipulating at the same time that slavery was to be forever afterwards prohibited in the Louisiana territory west and north of the new state, that is, north of the parallel 36 degrees 40 seconds north latitude. This fixed a definite line which was to be regarded as the boundary between the two great sections of the country. In the East it was to be the old Mason and Dixon's line between Maryland and Pennsylvania, thence up the

---

324 Annals of Congress, 16th Cong., 1st Sess., I., 97-99.
325 Annals of Congress, 16th Cong., 1st Sess., I, 111.

western boundary of Pennsylvania to the Ohio, thence along that river to the Mississippi, up the Mississippi to the northern boundary of Missouri, then the northern boundary of Missouri to the limits of the state where it dropped directly south to the parallel above mentioned. It might appear at first that this substitute, should it pass, would be a genuine compromise; but viewed more carefully it could only be a great victory for the anti-slavery party. In addition to Missouri it proposed to give the pro-slavery section the small part of the original Louisiana purchase, not quite equivalent to that now embraced in Oklahoma and the Indian Territories, while the anti-slavery section was to get all the public lands now embraced in the State of Kansas, Nebraska, Iowa, Minnesota, South and North Dakota, and about half of Colorado, Wyoming, and Montana. The North was to gain ten times as much as the South.

It is significant that Illinois made this proposition and that the old Northwest voted in the main with the South in this contest. Still public opinion in that section was strongly anti-Southern.[326] But the Thomas substitute was held back for some time in the hope that the Roberts amendment, abolishing slavery in Missouri itself, then under discussion, might pass. There was great excitement in Washington and angry threats were constantly being made.

It was at this stage that Macon made his well-known speech.[327] Only an outline of his argument will be given here. Beginning by repeating the opening remark of a previous speaker, that this was the most important debate ever held in the United States, that it required therefore to be discussed with the utmost coolness and deliberation, yet he had heard a great many hard sayings from gentlemen on the other side: "We have been told by the honorable gentleman from Pennsylvania (Lowrie), that he would prefer disunion rather than slaves should be carried west of the Mississippi. Age may have rendered me timid or education may have caused me to attach greater blessings to the Union and the Constitution than they deserve." (1) He then goes on to show the practical impossibility of ever getting the once severed Union back together again, and to lament the tendency of Senators to speak lightly of disunion. The second point he made was that the passage of the Thomas amendment would produce "geographical parties," against which Washington had warned us, whose

---

326 See speech of Senator Edwards of Illinois, Annals of Congress, 16th Cong., 1st Sess., I., 187.
327 See Peele's *Distinguished North Carolinians*.

council seemed not to avail any thing any longer. "But party and patriotism are not always the same thing. Town meetings and resolutions to inflame one part of the nation against another can never benefit the people, though they may gratify an individual. * * * A child may set the woods on fire, but it requires great exertions to extinguish it. This now very great question was but a spark at the last session." (2) On the question of the rights of the old states in the lands beyond the Mississippi, he said: "All the states now have equal rights and all are content. Deprive one of the least right which it now enjoys in common with the others and it will no longer be content. * * * All the new states have the same rights that the old have; why make Missouri an exception? Why depart in her case from the great American principle that the people can govern themselves? All the country west of the Mississippi was acquired by the same treaty, and on the same terms and the people in every part have the same rights. * * * The amendment will operate unjustly to the people who have gone there from the other states. They carried with them property [slaves] guaranteed by their states, by the Constitution and by treaty; they purchased lands and settled on them without molestation; but now, unfortunately for them, it is discovered that they ought not to have been permitted to carry a single slave. Is this just, in a Government of Law, *supported only by opinion* — for it is not pretended that it is a Government of force? (3) Bad policy: "A wise legislature will always consider the character, condition and feeling of those to be legislated for. * * * In all questions like the present in the United States, the strong may yield to the weak without disgrace even in their own opinion; the weak can not, hence the propriety of not attempting to pass this new condition on the people of Missouri. Let the United States abandon this new scheme; let their magnanimity, and not their power, be felt by the people of Missouri. The attempt to govern too much has produced every civil war that ever has been, and will, probably, every one that ever may be. All governments, whatever their form, want more power and more authority, and all the governed want less government." He then points out the effects of this unwise policy, citing the American Revolution as a parallel to the war which might ensue if Missouri were dealt such a blow as was intended by the Roberts amendment. Good policy demanded that the powerful party deal justly by the apparently weaker party. "Let me not be misunderstood as wishing or intending to create any alarm as to the intentions of the people of Missouri. I know nothing of them. But in examining the question, we ought not to forget our own history, nor the character of those who settle on our frontier. Your easy-going, chimney-corner people, the timid and fearful, never move to them. They stay where there is no danger from an Indian, or any other wild beast. It is the bravest of the brave and the boldest of the bold who venture there" Then follow some paragraphs which show a clear understanding of the character of our backwoodsmen and the importance of the border states.

He then changes the tone of his speech pointing out the dangers towards which this new political road leads: "Why depart from the good old way? Why leave the road of experience to take this new one, of which we have no experience? The way leads to universal emancipation, of which we have no experience. The Eastern and Middle States furnish none. For years before they emancipated they had but few [slaves], and of these a part were sold to the South, before they emancipated. * * * A clause in the Declaration of Independence has been read, declaring that all men are created free and equal. Follow that sentiment, and does it not lead to universal emancipation? If it will justify putting an end to slavery in Missouri, will it not justify it in the old states? Suppose the plan followed, and all the slaves turned loose, and the Union to continue, is it certain that the present Constitution would last long? Because the rich would, in such circumstances, want titles and hereditary distinctions; the negro food and raiment. They would be as much or more degraded, than in their present condition. * * * Take the most favorable [view] which can be supposed, that no convulsion ensue from a liberation of the negroes, also that the whites and the blacks do not marry and produce mulatto states, will not the whites be compelled to move and leave their land and houses, leave the country to the blacks? And are you willing to have black members of Congress? What is the condition of the blacks in the free states, especially in the large cities? Do the whites and the blacks intermarry? If they do, are not the whites degraded by it, are the blacks in the learned professions of law and physic? If they are degraded, where there are so few, what will be the consequence when they are equal in number or nearly so? It may be stated, without fear of contradiction, that *there is no place for the blacks in the United States* — no place where they are not degraded. If there was such a place, the society for colonizing them would not have been formed, their benevolent design never known. A country wanting inhabitants, and a society formed to colonize a part of them, prove there is no place for them." Aside from Macon's defense of slavery as the better condition of an inferior race in the presence of a superior, and from his constant references to the Constitution which guaranteed the South all the rights she claimed, these form the gist of this second ablest of all his addresses in Congress.[328]

After a month's debate and much disagreement between the two Houses the Thomas substitute was passed on March 3, 1820. Macon opposed the bill in all its phases to the last. It was to him what the Alien and Sedition Laws of 1798 had been — violation of the Constitution and a far more dangerous violation than had ever before been sanctioned. He said of its advocates a few days after the compromise passed: "They will, no doubt, push it with a view to form new parties on the principle of slave or no slave. It is the only hope left them by which to get power; and power gives offices which are much in demand, and which members of Congress now ask the President for, at least so I am told, and so I believe."[329] And again to the same correspondent, June 20, 1820, he wrote: "Much electioneering for the presidency ("shy-hogging" he called it) was done and more openly about the Missouri compromise than I ever saw before. I have no doubt, it would not have taken place, had not the Administration and the supposed leaders of those opposed to it, declared in favor of it, after the failure of Stone's motion, which would have given two degrees more to the people of the South. I have no desire for any place and I shall attend the next session of Congress, because the Missouri question may return on the admission of the state into the Union. If Holmes and Hill should be elected Senators from Maine, they will strengthen the Senate on the question, which is now believed to be strong enough for admission; but [their] election may weaken the House."

As was suggested in Macon's letter to Yancey the Missouri question did come up again. While Congress was engaged in the Missouri debate, and during the interval between the passage of the Compromise and the assembling of the Missouri constitutional convention newcomers were arriving in the disputed territory, some from the South determined to have a share in fixing slavery forever in the new state, others from the North hoping by some means to contravene both the will of the majority in Missouri and the acts of Congress.

---

328 Annals of Congress, 16th Cong., 1st Sess., I., 219-232.
I have quoted Macon somewhat freely, making slight changes at one or two points for the sake of clearness. — AUTHOR.
329 Macon to Bartlett Yancey, April 14, 1820.

The Convention met in June and declared that slavery should be established in that state by constitutional provision, and that the State legislature should not have the right to abolish it, and secondly that the legislature should pass a law forbidding all free negroes from settling in the state. The victory was won so far as the new state was concerned.

But when Congress reassembled in November the Missouri constitution was submitted as a final step in the process of admission. The anti-slavery party knew that Maine was now safely in the Union; they had failed in winning their contest in Missouri; there remained the final joint resolution before Missouri — Maine's balance mate, according to the understanding of both sides at the last session — could become a state. Maine's representatives now had the right to vote on Missouri's admission! The pro-slavery party in Missouri had gone a step too far in their victory. They had made it a part of their constitution that free negroes should not be allowed to live as citizens under its operation. This was plainly a violation of the constitution since citizens of some states could thus be denied ordinary civil rights in that part of the country. The anti-slavery party, with King of New York, who hoped to make a party issue of this question and thereby at last "swing" himself into the presidency, prepared to defend their last ditch. Their chances were promising. Clay was not present at the opening of Congress. To win the vacant Speakership became at once the goal of each party in the House. Lowndes, a "compromiser," was made the candidate of the South, since only he could hope to win votes enough at the North necessary for election; Taylor, of New York, became the candidate of the anti-slavery party. After three days balloting, Taylor was elected. This gave assurance that Missouri would not be admitted. Clay came into the House in time to urge adherence to the great Compromise of the last session on condition that the Missouri legislature give a solemn promise that free negroes should not be excluded from the state as citizens. At first he failed; but a month later he succeeded in getting a joint committee of twenty-three members which finally agreed to his plan.

Macon took no part in the Senate debate on the various resolutions presented for the third settlement of the Missouri controversy. When Clay's resolution from the joint committee came before the Senate he was absent and so he did not offer his single protest against it. But when the final vote on the admission according to the joint resolution passed, he voted with thirteen others in the negative. Among these was King, who thus saw the Kentuckian's compromise destroy his hopes for the presidency. Macon had voted against the resolution because he maintained that no restrictions could be placed upon a sovereign state as to what class of men she should admit to citizenship.[330] His old friend Randolph was again in the House where he also voted against the Clay arrangement and on the same grounds.

Macon's dissatisfaction concerning the settlement of this question was evident. It comes to light in his correspondence during the remainder of his life. He believed with Randolph and his school of Southern extremists that the whole of the Louisiana purchase lands should have been left open to settlers from the South, and they were so strongly convinced of the necessity of this Southern expansion that they readily excused the clause of the Missouri constitution which prohibited a citizen of Massachusetts from enjoying what the National Constitution guaranteed him — equal rights with the citizens of other states. This extreme position, however, became the position of the whole South before 1850.

The effect of the Compromise was for the South what Macon had predicted it would be for both sections,[331] consolidation in defence of or opposition to one issue, which consolidation bore its first fruits in 1828 and 1832. It brought Jefferson more actively into politics as a councilor than he had been in some years, and had its influence in giving the country the Democratic party as it is now known.

Macon, it will be remembered, had not been on very intimate terms with Jefferson since their disagreement in 1806, though they kept up friendly relations. In 1815 the Governor of North Carolina (Miller) charged Macon with purchasing a statue of Washington to be erected in the rotunda of the capitol.[332] This commission gave Macon an opportunity to approach the sage of Monticello in a way which could not but be flattering to the latter. Jefferson cheerfully responded and freely gave his advice about having a suitable statue made, which the people of North Carolina gladly followed, and a handsome piece of work by the celebrated Conova was purchased.[333] But no regular correspondence followed until 1819, when the signs of the times were pointing to the Missouri controversy. Macon wrote Jefferson in the early days of the year asking advice on the public

---

330 Annals of Congress, 16th Cong., 2nd Sess., 388.
331 See letter of April 19, 1820.
332 See letter of Macon to Jefferson, Jan. 7, 1816, in Jefferson MSS.
333 See Jefferson's letter of January 22, 1816, in Washington's *Works of Jefferson*.

questions of the day. To which Jefferson responded, still professing great confidence in those who were in power, "I willingly put both soul and body into their hands. While such men as yourself and your worthy colleagues in the legislature and such characters as compose the Executive administration are watching for us all, I slumber without fear and review in my dreams the visions of antiquity." Yet a little further on he joins Macon in his complaint against the manufacturing of paper money, which he called "filching from industry its honest earnings, wherewith to build up palaces and raise gambling stock for swindlers and shavers."[334] And to show Jefferson's increasing anxiety, a letter to John Adams, December 10, 1819, is quoted: "The banks, bankrupt law, manufactures, Spanish treaty, are nothing. These are occurrences, which, like waves in a storm, will pass under the ship. But the Missouri question is a breaker on which we lose the Missouri country by revolt, and what more, God only knows. From the battle of Bunker Hill to the treaty of Paris, we never had so ominous a question. It even damps the joy with which I hear of your high health, and welcomes to me the consequences of my want of it. I thank God that I shall not live to witness its issue. *Sed haec hactenus.*" This despondency characterized Jefferson's correspondence during the years immediately following,[335] and it led to a revival of the former intimacy between him and Macon, whose constant presence in Washington as a member of the Senate was to Jefferson a living link between him and the great days of 1800. Macon wrote Jefferson August 7, 1821, chiefly, as it seems, on the decisions of the United States courts, to which Jefferson replies by sending Macon a copy of a letter to another friend which "I place in your hands as the Depository of old and sound principles and as a record of my protest against this parricide tribunal. There are two measures which if not taken, we are undone. 1st. To check these unconstitutional invasions of state rights by the federal judiciary. 2. To cease borrowing money, and to pay off the national debt." The first he proposed should be done by constantly recurring protests from Congress against the decisions of the Supreme Court, and the second was to be accomplished by reducing the army and by putting the navy out of commission altogether if necessary. November 20, 1821, we have still another expression of his sentiments to Macon: "Our government is now taking so steady a course as to show by what road it will pass to destruction, to-wit, by consolidation

---

334 Jefferson to Macon, January 12, 1819 — unpublished.
335 See Jefferson to Hugh Nelson, March 12, 1820, in Ford's *Writings of Jefferson*.

first, and then by corruption, its necessary consequence. The engine of consolidation will be the Federal judiciary, the two other branches the corrupted and corrupting agencies. I fear an explosion in our state legislature.[336]

At the same time a lively war of pamphlets and speech-making was carried on. John Taylor wrote a book on the Constitution of the United States which was widely circulated in Virginia. But Macon feared; "it is too late for [it] to do the great majority of the people good; too many persons have lived so long and so well on the public debt and bank stock and by bank and other swindling, that it will be almost impossible for the honesty and industry of the nation to get clear of them; the newspapers are generally on the paper and idle side and they are generally as much depreciated as the bank bills. The principles which turned the federalists out of power are not fashionable at Washington, nor is there much probability of their being shortly."[337]

Macon believed it was the deliberate purpose of the Northern states to draw on Southern resources in every way possible, never allowing anything to return thither in the form of National expenditures.

Nearly all the federal taxes collected there (in the South) are paid for the interest of the public debt (owned by Northern capitalists) or laid out to the North of the James River, hence the constant drain of money from these states to the U.S. bank. This is not strictly chargeable to the bank, because, whether that existed or not, the money could still be drawn as it now is. It operates like a balance of trade almost equal to the amount of the national revenue there collected."[338] And it was likewise his opinion that the Supreme Court was committed to the cause of consolidation and corruption already mentioned by Jefferson: "The plan of the federal court seems to keep pace with Congress. The decisions do not go beyond the system of internal improvements, which has often been before the National legislature and received the sanction of both branches. As Congress attempts to get power by stretching the Constitution to fit its views, it is to be expected, if the other departments do not check them, that each of them will use the same means to obtain power and thus destroy any

---
336 Ford's *Writings of Jefferson*, X., 193-194.
337 Macon to Jefferson.
338 Macon to Bartlett Yancey, December 12, 1821.

check that was intended by the division of power into three distinct and separate bodies."[339]

Still another letter from Jefferson, October 10, 1823, introducing a friend, says: "His political principles are yours and mine, and proposing a visit to Washington he naturally wishes to be known to one so long and so prominent in the school of genuine republicanism. It gives me the occasion of recalling myself to your recollection and of assuring you that time has not changed nor ever will change towards you my constant affection and friendly attaint and respect."[340]

---

[339] Macon to Jefferson, February 2, 1822.
[340] From the Macon Papers.

CHAPTER XVIII.
IN THE UNITED STATES SENATE 1820-1828.
II.

Following the plenteous years of 1817-1819 there came, as is customary, years of scarcity. In 1820 the National Government borrowed three million dollars with which to pay current expenses; the next year five million were necessary, and all this in time of peace. The country had been flooded with paper money insufficiently secured. A spirit of speculation, starting from the years when Congress was at its wits end to know what to do with the surplus in the treasury, had continued until individuals, corporations and states all became borrowers for purposes of extravagant speculation. More than twenty-three millions were due the National Government for public lands taken up on the installment plan; the debtors were unable to pay. The demand for Western and new lands had been so great that land in the old states was next to worthless; the accumulated wealth of the country had been squandered to such an extent in uncertain enterprises that the first shock brought financial stagnation. Imports fell off at once; the Government receipts were less than its expenditures, and when a loan was asked a very high rate of interest was demanded.[341] A sad reminder of these distressing times is Jefferson's appeal to the Virginia legislature for the privilege of disposing of Monticello by lottery in order to get something like its value. A comparatively small debt had thus engulfed him.

He said in a letter to a friend that he should have to end his days in a cabin on his small plantation in Bedford County unless his petition were granted. This was not done. Through the generosity of friends in New York the auctioneer's hammer was stayed until a few months after his death when that magnificent estate was sold for less than enough to satisfy pressing creditors.

These alarming conditions caused great uneasiness and had no small influence in the formation of new party lines, particularly in compacting the leaders of the South in a defensive organization directed against all measures looking to internal improvements or high tariffs, for these were associated not unnaturally by the people of that section with the present ills of the country. These ills bore harder, too, on the older Southern states than on any other part of the Union

---

341 Schouler, III., 190-192.

owing to the constant drain on them in the building up of Alabama and the Southwest, and more especially because of the unequal operation of the tariff laws. Retrenchment and reform became the cry of a compact party of Southern congressmen even during the agitation of the Missouri question. Macon and Randolph consistent with the traditions of their party, led the movement in the two Houses: Macon summed up the difficulties confronting Monroe at the end of his first term, charging him with having deserted his party in seeking to gain the support of New England,[342] with having squandered six millions of the public money, with then making an immediate demand on the treasury for twelve millions, with having decreased the public revenues and with having assisted the people at home to get heavily in debt.[343]

Notwithstanding these unfavorable conditions, Monroe need not have exerted himself to secure his second election. The principal aspirants to the office geared their machinery to fit the year 1824 instead of 1820; and the people had long since agreed to give the leader of the "Era of Good Feeling" a second term. So nowhere was there any organized opposition, and Monroe received all the votes of the electoral college save one. The old parties had gone to pieces; the political chieftains all belonging nominally in 1820 to one organization were putting themselves forward in their own ways to gain the public support, and before the adjourning of Congress in 1820 there were four candidates well advanced on the way towards 1824. Macon names them in the following order: "Of the great men at Washington, Crawford, I think, rather stands the highest, though not so high as he has done; Adams has a few warm supporters, a part of them from local considerations and others for his violent defence of the attack of the Spanish forts in Florida;[344] Calhoun stands well with the military, with the manufacturers not so well as formerly, and with those for internal improvements very high; Clay stands high with the two last mentioned [classes]; King has, I think, lost ground with his party — Pinckney's and Smith's replies to him on the Missouri bill lessened his reputation as a statesman, or rather his own speech did it."[345]

---

342 "I suspect that Mr. Monroe begins to feel that he can not safely depend on his new friends and old opponents to support his administration." — Letter to Yancey, April 19, 1820.

343 "Add to that six million dollars he found in the treasury and nearly or quite twice as much wanted at this time and the present means likely to diminish and the people at home generally in debt." *Ibid.*

344 He refers here to Jackson's unauthorized invasion of Florida.

345 Macon to Yancey, June 20, 1820.

Macon had decided whom he should support in this long hurdle race for the Presidency before the meeting of Congress in 1821. On the 12th of December, he wrote Yancey from Washington: "Already there is much talk here about who is to be the next President, and it is frequently asked who N.C. will support. My answer has been, Whoever was thought to be most republican and most economical. Unanimity in the South would give great weight to the man who may be there supported. I have said especially in the South, because nearly all the federal taxes collected there are paid for the interest of the public debt, or laid out north of the James River." He then betrays his decided preference for Crawford, and by March of 1822, he is ferreting out every source of opposition to his candidate in North Carolina: "It is reported here that the Salisbury newspaper is out decidedly against C., and that some of our ex-members of Congress (Pearson, Henderson) are the same way. The opposition to him will be determined and violent; his friends ought not to expect that he will be elected and they be idle. You know all the men whose names have been mentioned for the next President, and that some of them are remarkable for their talents at shy-hogging (scheming), and never lose the opportunity of using them. The General Assembly at which the electors of President and Vice-President are named will be a very important one in North Carolina, and the members ought to be selected with a view to the Presidential electors."[346] Before the end of the session he is again putting his friends in North Carolina on their guard: "Calhoun was last summer in Pennsylvania, and will be this summer in the South. You know his talent by general observation for gaining on strangers. Several of our Representatives here are also for Calhoun, who will be in the Assembly at the proper time to recommend electors." He fears, too, that the Salisbury paper is advancing Calhoun's cause. During the next year Macon is constantly on the watch and directing how to serve Crawford, how to checkmate Adams, Calhoun and Clay. At one time the New England influences seem about to combine with Republican Pennsylvania to give Adams the first place in the race; at another Clay, or Calhoun, seems to be combining the influences favorable to protection and the banks, and thus threatening to defeat Crawford. In February 1823, he fears that an investigation of the Treasury Department, under Crawford, prompted by the enemies of that candidate, may prejudice his cause.[347] This plan of

---

346 Macon to Yancey, March 17, 1822.
347 Annals of Congress, 17th Cong., 2nd Sess., 159-160.

injuring Crawford began by a motion of Eaton, of Tennessee, to demand of the Secretary of the Treasury a statement of the methods of that department in making loans. A branch of the National Bank had been established a short while before at Cumberland, Tennessee, under circumstances which pointed to the improper use of public money. Crawford was suspected of attempting thus to build up a party in that state favorable to himself and opposing Jackson, who begins suddenly to loom above the political horizon. Macon wrote his friend later that Crawford's chances had not been injured by this attack.

At the beginning of the next session, December 1823, Crawford had arranged his plans to have a Congressional caucus assemble early in the next year, and to have himself nominated as the regular candidate for the presidency. Macon had served the scheming Georgian faithfully, but this was too much for him. A caucus was one of the most distasteful of political machines to him. At a great Republican harmony dinner in Philadelphia, December 27, 1823, Crawford was toasted as the *friend of Nathaniel Macon*; but this friendship was not enough to overcome Macon's dislike for the caucus. About this time the North Carolina Legislature held a similar meeting to that now proposed in Washington, and nominated Crawford. It was not unanimous, for the next day a large minority caucus was held in Raleigh, in which Calhoun was nominated.[348] The friends of the latter candidate in that State tried to get a law passed which would give the selection of electors to the districts again. This failed, but only served to increase Calhoun's popularity. Several other State legislatures held partisan caucuses favorable to Crawford, and then came the Congressional caucus in Washington. It was set for February 14, 1824. Great efforts were made to get Macon to attend. Yancey wrote urging him to lay aside his prejudice and give their favorite candidate this last token of his friendship. Gallatin was appealed to use his influence with Macon. Gallatin yielded, and wrote Macon a long letter, but to no avail. Indeed, he seems to have cooled in his ardor for Crawford, for he replied to Yancey's letter: "if I attend [the caucus], might it not, nay would it not, be said that, after having refused more than 20 years, and that too in the troublesome time of war and the Hartford Convention, that now in time of peace the principle or practice is changed, that the master intriguer is the first and only one who has been able to find and touch the chord which produced the change?

---

348 Richmond *Enquirer*, December 30, 1823.

A change at this time would give rise to suspicions that a promise or bargain had been made. If I have the national influence which you suppose, by what means has it been obtained? Not, I am sure, by pursuing the opinions of others."[349] He refused to attend, and a great many other Crawford supporters remained at home that evening. The Richmond *Enquirer* considered this act of Macon's worthy of especial attention in its review of the meeting a few days later: "The venerable Nathaniel Macon, known to be for Crawford, would not attend." The caucus was a lame affair; it was the last of this sort of Congressional usurpation. Macon had been, as he said, hoodwinked into one, but he was never caught a second time. His opinion as to how to get candidates regularly before the voters of one's party was that the people themselves should be consulted by some means. How this should be done, he did not suggest. The nominating conventions and primaries of the present had not been invented.

At this session of Congress, 1823-1824, Jackson's chances grew more and more promising. Adams made efforts to enter into an alliance with the hero of New Orleans, offering him the Vice-Presidency. Jackson was not the man to take second place, so the brave and plucky New Englander was left to plod his difficult path alone. Calhoun, forecasting well the future, and being himself a young man, finally joined hands with the Tennesseean, accepting second place, with an understanding as to the future. This added to Jackson's influence the support of the young Republicans, who, Macon said, began a second time "to be the fashion" in Washington. Macon opposed this alliance as lustily as he had favored Crawford: "It is believed here, and some say known, that Calhoun has withdrawn from the contest, and that his friends will support General Jackson. I have heard that the greatest exertions are to be made for the General in North Carolina; that a meeting was to take place last Saturday in Warrenton to nominate him. When I left home, a great majority in the county appeared to be for Crawford, and I imagine are so yet. A meeting for the same purpose was to take place in Hillsboro."[350] A few weeks later he warns his friends against losing interest, "the Republicans should always be at their posts, power once lost is not easily regained;" and on May 6, he says North Carolina would be canvassed that summer by William R. King, of Alabama, and John H. Eaton, of Tennessee, in favor of the Jackson-Calhoun ticket, which was much to Macon's disliking.

---

349 Macon to Yancey. December 23, 1823.
350 Macon to Yancey, February 24, 1824.

Fate was not favorable to the "old Republicans" who, though they had regained much of their former influence and were excellently organized, were destined to lose in their first fight after the Missouri battle. Crawford's health failed in the summer of 1823; he retired, stricken with paralysis, to a country residence near Washington, where his bosom friends alone were allowed to see him.[351] Macon was one of these, and he constantly gave the public the most hopeful accounts of his friend's health, on which depended the hopes of his party.[352] It was a great disappointment to Macon that Crawford was thus disabled, for it lost him the Presidency. In North Carolina, where such a strong bias for Calhoun as candidate for the first place had been shown, the people now turned readily to the support of the Jackson ticket, on which the great South Carolinian's name appeared second. The party machine with which Macon was somewhat in accord, as has been seen, was set all out of gear when the news spread abroad that Crawford was paralyzed. No resistance could longer be made against the two most popular men in the South, the one for his daring military career, the other on account of his ability and wonderful personal magnetism. What determined Macon in his opposition to Jackson was the assumption of sovereign authority on the part of the latter in Florida a few years before; and what he opposed in Calhoun was his whole creed; Calhoun had voted in 1816 for the second National Bank, he had advocated the passage of the Internal Improvements bill, which Madison had vetoed, and he was in accord with the demands of the Northern manufacturers for a high tariff. These things were enough, in Macon's eyes, to condemn forever any man aspiring to a position of public trust in the National government. But just these features of Calhoun's policy attracted strong support in the North Carolina of 1824, where there were many advocates of the so-called American system, and where the nucleus of the Whig party was already formed. When the election took place, North Carolina cast her full vote for Jackson and Calhoun.[353] No account of Macon's disappointment at the results of this election has been preserved. But it is evident that he was not in harmony with the majority in his State at that time.

The contest was not decided, however, until after a long wrangle in Congress during the winter of 1824-1825, when what appeared to

---

351 Schouler, III., 305-306.
352 Macon to Yancey, March 31, 1824.
353 *cf*, Benton's Abridgment of Debates, VIII., 324.

be a popular verdict was set aside by Clay, and the second highest on the list of candidates was elevated to the first place in the land. Macon failed also to leave on record his opinions on the subject of Adams' election over Jackson in the House of Representatives. But a letter to Yancey, written soon after he reached Washington, and more than a month before the Presidential contest began, shows clearly enough his dissatisfaction with conditions there: "Very soon after getting here, one of the Representatives from N.C. asked me what I thought the friends of Crawford ought to do. This question was put in the presence of two or three others of *our brethren*. The answer was, do nor say nothing; by a union you have been defeated, let the victors decide who shall be President, because you may at any time take your choice, if you think proper, of those you do not approve."[354]

The prevailing sentiment in North Carolina was not in accord with Macon's views; in the nation at large there was little promise of any return to what he called true Republican doctrines; and all the possible candidates for the Presidency were equally distasteful to him; he was now sixty-six years old, and accounted seventy. How could the closing years of his political life be promising? He gave them to earnest, determined opposition, not unlike he had done soon after the beginning of his public career when the elder Adams was in the President's chair.

About the time Crawford's illness upset all his plans for the campaign of 1824, the policy of protective tariff was again revived, with Clay as its champion. Clay knew well the state of American politics at that time. His purpose seems to have been to come out from his two years' retirement, become Speaker of the House, and thus bring to the front his former scheme for "protecting infant industries," and by this means, while Adams, Crawford and Jackson were wrangling over the first place in the dying Republican party, combine the North and West on a new issue and bring himself with one stroke into the Presidency. The great dividing line between North and South which he had done much to fix was to be broken over in the organization of his followers by obscuring the slave question. High tariff was to be the main issue; next to it lavish public expenditure in the form of internal improvements. The tariff was not a new thing in the country, but a purely protective duty for the building up of the manufacturing interests was somewhat novel. On the subject of internal improve-

---

354 Macon to Yancey, December 26, 1824.

ments, Clay had failed twice, yet nothing loth he now made it a part of his American system. The objects of the "system" were to foster all kinds of manufactures at the expense of the vast majority of the people, under the pretense of making the nation independent of foreign countries. Everyone who opposed Clay would thus be made to favor *foreigners*. The tariff bill introduced to meet the demands of the new policy raised the average rate from twenty-five per cents in 1816, to thirty-three and one-third in 1824.[355] More than two months were spent in the debate that followed, in which it was seen that the South had changed grounds since 1816; when its Representatives largely favored a protective tariff. When the vote was taken, New England, the Middle States and the West favored the new issue; the South, from Virginia to Louisiana, except one man, voted solidly against it. When the bill reached the Senate it there underwent another two months of debate. Its friends could count only on a bare majority, even if that much. Southern Senators were unanimous this time in opposition to that kind of National improvement.

Macon spoke against the bill on May 4, expressing surprise that the West should attempt to tax the South for the benefit of Western hemp and wool growers and Northern manufacturers. He called particular attention to the poverty of the Southern States, the States which would have to bear the burden of the tax without the prospect of receiving any of its benefits.[356] Two votes of New Englanders would decide the tariff, said Macon in a letter to Yancey in May, 1824. But these two votes were likely to be won by concessions of one kind or an other from the friends of protection. Again Macon proposed several amendments or exemptions, but, the South being now isolated, these were all, save one, rejected without debate.[357] Then Senator Branch, of North Carolina, with Macon's concurrence, offered to add a new clause to the bill, providing for an appropriation of $500,000 to build canals in Eastern North Carolina, and for removing the obstructions to an outlet to the sea from that State. This was taking the protectionists on their own grounds, for they were all in favor of internal improvements; but the proposition was promptly voted down. On the very last day of the debate, Macon spoke against the tariff, and, significantly enough, Benton, his friend from Missouri, replied to him. The protective policy passed with a majority of five votes on

---

355 Channing: *History of the United States*, 386.
356 Annals of Congress, 18th Cong., 1st Sess., I., 690.
357 Annals of Congress, 18th Cong., 1st Sess., I., 733.

May 19, 1824. Just four years before Missouri and the South, including Kentucky and Illinois, had voted solidly together on the Great Compromise. It was then Thomas of Illinois who came forward with the compromise which Southern congressmen thought gave them the best terms to which the North would submit. Now Missouri, Kentucky and Illinois joined hands with Pennsylvania, New York and the Eastern States to pass a law which everyone knew would constantly draw large taxes from the South without chance of their returning thence in any form, unless that section should change its whole economic structure and become a seat of manufacturing. This was next to impossible under the system of slave labor.

When Clay's first campaign for public improvements failed because of Madison's veto in the closing days of his administration, and when in the following December (1817) Monroe announced that he would veto any similar bill which Congress might pass, De Witt Clinton and the people of New York hastened forward their great Erie Canal to its completion, and gained their object — the trade with the West. At the beginning of Adams' administration in 1825, public attention had become so much occupied with the idea of internal improvements that Congress, having reason to believe the new President would give the assent of the Executive, especially since Clay had become Secretary of State, took up the twice-defeated bill for internal improvements. "The return of prosperity," as the followers of Clay called it, had filled the treasury again; the new tariff and the gradual return of normal conditions in a growing country were really responsible for the new prosperity. At any rate there were three millions lying idle in the treasury. The same conditions had returned which had helped forward Clay's bonus bill more than eight years before, with the advantage that the Executive was now favorable to latitudinarian interpretation of the Constitution. When this bill was about to come up, Macon wrote his friend: "I never think of these claims of power, which appear to me not to be granted, but I shudder for the States where slavery exists. The spirit for emancipation is stronger and more enthusiastic than that for internal improvements. It may sleep, but it never dies. It has been adopted by religious societies with a zeal not likely to tire. He then expresses uneasiness as to the effects in the South of the emancipation of slaves in St. Domingo, and adds: "Many of the State legislatures have passed resolutions against slavery which are published and republished again and again. It is made piracy by the laws of the United States to bring a slave from Africa. What, then, is it to hold one on land, being a descendant of an African? The question with us is not an original question of slavery or no slavery; but what is the power of the Federal government?" This shows the foundation of his dogged opposition to every measure of Congress during the four years just beginning. And the temper of Congress was the cause of his constant mental depression during those years. Nothing shows this more clearly than his speech of February 24, 1825, on the bill for subscribing $150,000 in stock to the Delaware and Chesapeake Canal: "I rise with a full heart to take a last farewell of an old friend which I have always admired and loved — the Constitution of the United States. Gentlemen say it is now unnecessary to enter into the constitutional question on this measure." He then cited the celebrated Virginia and Kentucky resolutions of 1798 as giving the true interpretation of the Constitution. "I can give no other name to my feelings than fears. It is true I have no fears for my personal liberty, but I fear my descendants will be taxed up to the nose so that if they get breath it will be as much as they can do. My fears may be groundless — they may be nothing but suggestions of a worn-out old man, but they are sincere and I am alarmed for the safety of this government." The bill passed by a vote of twenty-four to eighteen.[358]

His last struggle against the American system was made just before he retired from the Senate in the spring of 1828. Clay was still in the Cabinet; the House, as usual on anything which concerned Clay, was opposed to the Senate and favorable to the Administration; another presidential campaign was opening, and the Jackson-Crawford influences, now united, were promising to sweep the country. A plan for raising the tariff rates had been proposed towards the close of the last Congress; it had passed the House, but was promptly vetoed by the Senate. During the following summer, the Pennsylvania society had called a convention of manufacturers to assemble in Harrisburg. This convention, not with out influence in suggesting similar political assemblies for the nation, attended by members of that class of people from Maine to Virginia and from New York to Illinois, petitioned Congress in favor of raising the rate of protection from 33 1/3 percent to a higher average. Whether Clay had anything to do with the introduction and passage of a bill giving 40 to 75 percent is not certain; but it suggests that his hand must have been seen when the House, still friendly to him, although organized to oppose Adams, readily passed

---

358 Beaton's Abridgment, VIII., 180-81.

the required bill. In the Senate changes of a radical nature had taken place; Calhoun, the Vice-President, had now become an opponent of protection, and the Southern members had been steadily coming together into a close organization since 1820. Macon, more influential and more popular now than ever because he had formerly stood almost alone in his advocacy of Southern and State rights, spoke twice, at first not so long, the second time more than two hours. His speeches may be summed up in the following sentences: "I have always considered this system of high duties as the strife of private interests against the public good. It was said to the South a few years ago: Only pass our tariff bill and your cotton will rise, but it has not risen. The full intention of this system seems to be, that we are to have nothing but what is made in this country. Sir, if the Southern States had looked as sharp after their own affairs as the North have, where would the great export trade have come from? In nothing ought equality to be more strictly observed than in taxation. It is an old-fashioned opinion that the maxim, which directs that everybody should be let alone and allowed to do that which he can do best, contains a sound doctrine." The tariff passed both Houses and became a law just before the close of the session, the South voting "solidly" against it. It received the name of "the tariff of abominations," and instead of helping Clay it injured him.[359]

The passage of this bill brings Macon and the other Southern congressmen into still closer affiliation. In Virginia Giles uniting with the mighty Ritchie, and favored by the dying counsels of Jefferson, had built up a boisterous and belligerent Democracy ready to die in the last ditch; in South Carolina Hamilton and the old regime were thinking of secession; in Georgia the warlike Troup who had defied the National Government in the recent Creek Indian controversy, was the leader of the new party. It was the beginning of 1861! North Carolina, like ancient England, returning to her more conservative and aristocratic moorings, occupied a unique position. The Whigs, legitimate offspring of the strong anti-Jefferson party in 1800, were constantly growing, though at the time under cover of a strong wave of Old Hickory enthusiasm, which will be noted presently. The part Macon played in this change of things in the South outside of his own state was significant. It began with his foresight in 1820, increased with his constant reiteration of the fact that all constructive interpretation

---

[359] Schouler, III., 420-427.

of the Constitution pointed to the downfall of slavery, and reached its culmination in his and Randolph's determined and dogged opposition and obstruction to Adams' administration. He was almost without hope while Clay's star continued in the ascendency, and was almost equally distrustful of Jackson.

Thus far Macon's course in the Senate has been viewed chiefly from the standpoint of obstruction and opposition with only here and there a bit of constructive policy cropping out. Let us now trace his advance in personal popularity, in constructive statesmanship and in public confidence during the last eight years of his career in the Senate. His long political life was devoted chiefly to opposition excepting the first six years of Jefferson's administration and the first five years of Madison's when he was an exponent and champion of independent measures. As soon, however, as the war of 1812 closed, the policy of the young republicans, no longer hampered by a most embarrassing war, was made to embrace the fundamental principles of the Federalists; and combining these with the more popular democratic practices of the Jefferson republicans and, adding to this their great talents and exceedingly popular manners, these younger men, especially the Southerners, seized more firmly than ever the reins of power. But Macon, keeping his vision clear as to the true position of his State and section and true in every fiber to the "old Republican" doctrines, could not support the revived policy of the Federalists no matter in how feasible a form. He was again forced into the opposition, where he remained until his final retirement. During this time he was a member of the Senate, which body had become the centre of great debates, the organ, too, of the opposition since it was seldom in accord with the Executive. With Madison it will be remembered, the Senate disagreed on the subject of internal improvements and even talked of passing their bonus bill for that purpose over the President's veto; under Monroe's administration there were even more causes of dispute, and with Adams the Senate was in a state of open war from the very beginning of his term. The Senate, then, was called upon to do more than merely oppose; it was expected to make proposals and outline policies of its own particularly on the subjects of internal improvements and the South American relations. What made this the more necessary was the attitude of the House of Representatives which, under the spell of Clay's influence and popularity, was one of opposition to the Senate and for a great portion of the time of opposition also to the President. The Senate had grown in the respect and esteem of the nation. All which tended to give that body a more important share in the National Government.

To this body Macon had been sent in 1815 to fill the unexpired term of David Stone, resigned. It was not until 1817 that Macon was appointed to membership on important committees. In December of that year, he became second member of the great committee on Foreign Relations and last on the committee on Finance. His principal colleagues on these committees were James Barbour of Virginia, George M. Troup of Georgia, Rufus King of New York, George W. Campbell of Tennessee and John W. Eppes of Virginia, all of whom occupied the very highest rank in the nation, Barbour, Campbell and Eppes having distinguished themselves under previous administrations, King having served eight years as American minister to Great Britain. Macon had held so many conspicuous positions and had been so long in public station that he was scarcely less favorably known to the country than his colleagues.[360]

The committee on Foreign Relations reported, through its chairman, Barbour, early in April of the next year (1818) a navigation bill which included the main features of the famous Macon bill No. 1 of the year 1810, that is, it provided (1) that the harbors of the United States should be closed against every British vessel coming from ports not open to American trade, (2) that every English vessel leaving American ports and bound for harbors closed against the United States should be compelled to give bond that their cargoes should be landed at the designated port under penalty of confiscation of both vessel and cargo in case any evasion were discovered. It is not claimed that Macon was the author of this bill, but that as its co-author and earnest advocate he deserves to receive credit for its preparation and final passage by the Senate, especially since the bill embodies some of the principal features of his great bill of eight years before.[361] At the second session Macon became chairman of the committee on Foreign Relations and as such made an able report on the condition of American-British trade relations in which he insisted on reciprocity between the two countries more especially in the commerce between the United States and the English colonies — a policy which was first realized under the McLane treaty of Jackson's first administration. And as regarded the shipping of the two nations, he said: "It must be placed on a footing of practical and reciprocal equality, both as

---

360 Annals of Congress 15th Cong., 1st Sess., I., 25-26.
361 Annals of Congress, 15th Cong., 1st Sess., I., 312-339.

respects duties and charges, and the equal participation of the trade." The recent navigation law (the measure just described) he reported later as having been "productive of increase of the American shipping engaged in the direct trade between the United States and Great Britain, and the corresponding decrease of that of Great Britain — but sufficient time has not yet been afforded satisfactorily to ascertain this point or to determine other questions that are in a course of solution. Perhaps it would be prudent to allow time for this important experiment, and to suffer the negotiation on this subject to remain where it is for the present. It ought not to be forgotten, that without cutting off the trade with New Brunswick, Nova Scotia and Bermuda, this experiment can not be fairly made. Whether it would be expedient at the present session to adopt this measure is perhaps doubtful."[362] Congress accordingly took no action leaving the subject of foreign commerce in the hands of the committee and our representative in London. Macon's cautious disposition is evident in the report; its language, too, is his.

Macon was a prominent member of this committee until he was elected President *pro tempore* of the Senate to succeed Gailliard in 1826. He was chairman again in 1825-26 when the controversy over the celebrated Panama mission took place. Since this subject was made the basis of a fierce attack on the President, John Quincey Adams, and Macon being a principal party to the attack, it becomes necessary to examine it more closely.

It will be remembered that Adams and Clay had been in accord during Monroe's administration in regard to the policy of the United States towards South America. Clay had warmly advocated the recognition of the new South American republics even before the more prudent Adams could clear the way of pacifying Spain. Adams had written the Monroe doctrine as a reply to the manifesto of the Holy Alliance and, as the advocate of such a doctrine, he could not but favor entering into any plan for establishing closer and more friendly relations with South American states. The Panama Congress, planned by the American states of Spanish origin, was intended to encourage and foster closer friendship among all the American powers. It was to meet on the isthmus in October, 1825. Invitations were sent to the United States. And Clay, smarting under the sting of public criticism for having placed the unpopular Adams in the President's chair,

---

362 Annals of Congress, 15th Cong., 2nd Sess., I., 249-50.

hastened to turn public opinion into another channel. He desired to make a great pan-American demonstration of the Panama Congress and create more interest in inter-American commerce. He took up the invitation with his usual enthusiasm and gusto and urged Adams to accept it and promise to send representatives to Panama without so much as consulting Congress. This was determined upon in May, 1825; and the Administration set to work creating a public sentiment favorable to the proposed mission. When Congress met Adams simply announced to the Senate that he would send proper representatives still leaving out of consideration the fact that the Senate might interpose by refusing to confirm his nominations. The President felt, like his father before him after the X. Y. Z. explosion in 1798, that in view of the hearty public support which had been worked up and was now manifesting itself in meetings and resolutions, the Senate would not make vigorous opposition.

But opposition was made. The debate began with closed doors and the people, always jealous of secret legislation, began to murmur, taking pains to applaud the President. Van Buren proposed to remove this obstacle to public favor on the part of the Senate by opening the doors to the public. Adams looked with disfavor on this maneuver and insinuated in a short message that the Senate desired thus to curry favor with the public. The secret sessions continued and the President outlined more fully in a special message his policy in the Panama business. This message was referred to the committee on Foreign Relations, and Macon, now its chairman, made an elaborate and detailed report: 1. Such a mission was in direct violation of our policy of avoiding entangling alliances. 2. That we had long maintained a strict neutrality in all these Spanish American revolutions. 3. There was no cause for our breaking that neutrality by taking part in this American international Congress. 4. The President proposed to endow our agents there with undefined powers. 5. That those who had invited us to take part had disclosed their real purpose to be to draw the United States into an alliance with them against "their mother country." And 6. In fact, European affairs no longer threatened to become dangerous to American liberty, so that there was no cause for the movement on foot, and that if in the future it should become necessary for such a cooperation of all the American states the Senate would suggest that the United States take the initiative and send out invitations consistent with their own purposes.[363] This cold analysis of

---
363 Schouler, III., 363-64.

the Administration's policy did not please the public any more than it flattered the President. The House sided at once with the Executive, and the Senate yielding to popular influences voted down Macon's report. The ministers to Panama had been appointed, their appointments were confirmed by the Senate, and the sum of forty thousand dollars was voted to pay the expenses of the mission. The Government gained the victory, but the results proved within a year both the correctness and wisdom of Macon's report.

From this report and its cause, President Adams' message on the Panama mission, arose Macon's speech on the powers of the Executive already mentioned and which shows his own personal views to have been in accord with his report which we know he did not write,[364] and which also had much to do with his attempt to limit the scope of the President's powers by special legislation to be related in another connection. In the speech he said first that no other President had ever claimed the power to create offices, but that nearly every other President had either transcended his powers or acted on matters in a way which compelled Congress to act sometimes in opposition to their sentiment, citing the Monroe doctrine as the most notable instance of Executive action which had committed the whole country to a policy not determined by its representatives. The second objection he made to the exercise of liberal powers by the Executive was that it disturbed the balance of power among the several departments in the United States Government. The last point was that the people were generally clamoring against the expansion of the President's functions, and as a representative of the people he stood up to make his and their protest against the evil.[365] And in his private correspondence at the time he was equally outspoken: "The message of the President seems to claim all the powers of the Federal Government which have heretofore produced so much debate and which the election of Mr. Jefferson was supposed to have settled; but so it is, a decision against power in the government is no precedent, while one in favor of it is. Hence all governments are apt to gain power."[366] And again to the same correspondent a year and a half later he employs similar language but extending it to a criticism of the people for allowing each Administration to name its successor by placing the Secretary of State before them as the best trained and most suitable

---

365 Benton's Abridgment, VIII., 550-51.
366 Macon to Yancey, December 6, 1825.
364 Benton's Abridgment, VIII., 421.

candidate. "If this goes on," he continued, "each President will appoint his successor."

Macon's would-be detractors, especially those in his own State, have maintained that he never ran counter to public sentiment, that he never risked his popularity by upholding what the people opposed. It need only be said that in the long Panama contest he constantly opposed the popular view and, from 1823 to 1828, he opposed the election of Jackson though his own constituents met at Warrenton to nominate Jackson and Calhoun.[367] It was not his intention persistently and for long periods to oppose his views to those of his constituents. This would have been contrary to his idea of the meaning of representative government. The people were, in accordance with the tenets of his party, his last resort and final authority; but he understood the meaning of temporary excitement and enthusiasm and so he could set himself strongly against the popular will thus influenced if it seemed necessary.

In connection with his speech on the powers of the Executive some mention of his attitude towards the Administration in its war with Georgia ought to be made. This outbreak on the part of the lower South was the result of two influences at work in the Southern mind: (1) That the bounds of the slave power must be expanded as rapidly as possible, and (2) that the Northern States in accord with their demands in the Missouri compromise, were, with the help of the General Government, rapidly extending their boundaries in the Northwest. The question in dispute in 1825-26 was: How would the United States extinguish the Indian title to lands occupied by the Creek nation within the limits of the State of Georgia? In 1802 the National Government had agreed to do this for the State of Georgia in consideration of the cession by that State of the territory out of which the States of Alabama and Mississippi had been carved. The National Government, as is usual with all governments, was slow to execute the conditions of the contract and the Georgians, face to face with the Indians, whose lands they coveted, kept up a state of intermittent warfare on their western borders. In 1824 the Cherokees and Creeks, the tribes then occupying the disputed territory, declared they would never give up their lands. The advancing plantation builders accused the National Government of instigating this declaration on the part of the Indians, "because," said they, "the Administration is

---

367 See letter quoted on p. 243.

desirous to check the expansion of the slave power." A treaty was soon negotiated between the United States and the Chief of the Creeks, General McIntosh, by which the two tribes yielded their claim to large areas of land in Georgia and Alabama. As soon as the news of the treaty was published the Indians fell upon McIntosh and killed him. They refused to recognize the McIntosh treaty, and the United States Government, seeing Georgia going forward as though the recent treaty were entirely valid, called on the Governor of Georgia to have the surveying of the lands in question suspended until further notice. A United States officer, General Gaines, was ordered to the scene. Governor Troup had already taken measures to remove the Indians beyond the bounds of the State according to the terms of the repudiated treaty; the United States could not assent to this. Gaines and Troup were about to bring on a war between the National and State governments. All Georgia was aflame and the Governor called on the people to "stand to their arms." Troup finally agreed to wait till another treaty could be agreed upon and, after a year or two more of bloodshed on the Georgia border and of harassing delay in the negotiations which were being conducted in Washington, the Indians were removed to lands beyond the Mississippi — an event remembered and talked of today by the oldest inhabitants of the section as the most important event after the Revolution in the development of the lower South.

What made the subject so difficult and at the same time so important was the spirit already referred to, the spirit of rapid expansion on the part of the slave States, which was even then casting longing eyes towards the fertile plains of Texas, and which, distrusting all the professions of the General Government, was determined to work out its own destiny under the sanction of State authority. Macon shared this spirit already, as appears in the following brief comment: "It seems somewhat strange that the Federal Government should be able to acquire so much land from the Indians to the West and Northwest and so little to the South and Southwest. Georgia claims of her to fulfil the bar gains made many years since and no other State or territory has a bargain by which to claim the extinction of the Indian title."[368]

There remain two other lines of study in Macon's life in the Senate — his advocacy of constitutional amendments and his standing with the public. Monroe's first message to Congress in December,

---

368 Macon to Yancey, December, 1823.

1817, had earnestly recommended adequate amendments of the Constitution in order to enable the Government to carry on internal improvements. Though Macon opposed on principle the expenditure of public money in this way, except through the State governments, he favored the proposition of Monroe as the best method of settling definitely the theory of interpretation. This plan was generally approved in the Southern States. There was another complaint which came very much into public notice during the following year: the election of presidential electors by popular vote in districts. The North Carolina Legislature petitioned Congress in January, 1818, through Macon, for such an arrangement. Only a few years before the change from the district to the general ticket method had been made in that State. The change was not satisfactory. Many other States followed this method of election by general ticket in the legislature; but there was no uniformity. The proposition of North Carolina in some form or other was discussed at length at different times until in 1824 other amendments to the Constitution for allowing internal improvements, for restricting the term of service in the Presidency to eight years, for the election of the President by popular vote and for limiting the Executive patronage were added and all submitted to a special committee, which reported back to the Senate, but no action was taken. In 1825 Macon moved that a second committee be appointed. Benton, Macon, Van Buren and others, all favoring amendments of some kind to the National Constitution, were selected as members. Their report recommended the present plan of electing the President and Vice-President, with the exception that Congress should convene every fourth year to receive the reports of the election immediately, and if it appeared that no choice had been made then a new election should be set for the first Thursday and Friday of December following. It is evident that dissatisfaction with the late election in the House of Representatives entered largely into this proposition. Years before Macon had favored popular elections for all officers, both State and National. He stated openly in the Senate at this time that he had changed his mind with reference to the President and that he favored some indirect method. Benton seems to have favored a popular election of President; but he yielded to the indirect method which Macon advocated.

But this committee made a better recommendation than this. From the beginning of the War of 1812 when Madison appointed so many members of Congress to office, Macon had repeatedly by speech and by private correspondence proposed and urged an amendment to the National Constitution prohibiting the President from appointing to office any member of Congress until the expiration of the presidential term in which such person shall have served as a Senator or Representative." The evil which he meant to remedy was, and is, quite patent. Macon now brought forward his reform and secured for it the endorsement of the special committee. The plan was reported to the Senate but was never debated[369] and of course never passed either branch of Congress.

In December, 1825, John Randolph of Roanoke joined Macon in the Senate and the two old friends now more closely united in politics and representing a "solid South" waged a ceaseless war on everything Northern, commercial or anti-slavery. Randolph made his and Macon's attitude towards the Missouri Compromise a sort of political platform to which they adhered most rigidly and on which they were uniting all Southern congressmen. Slavery was endangered, they thought, in every attempt to extend the powers of the Executive, in the seeming lethargy of the government in extinguishing the title of the Creek Indians to Georgia lands. Randolph, as he had done so often before in their earlier comradeship in the House, made a parade of Macon's friendship by referring to him in nearly every speech as his "honored" or "venerable friend from North Carolina."

They lived in the same "mess" in Washington spending "whole hours together, in the long winter nights, keeping each other company."[370] Garland says: "In silence they sat and mused as the fire burned. Each had his own private sorrows and domestic cares to brood over; both felt the weight of years pressing upon them, and still more, the wasting hand of disease. They had long since learned to look upon the honors of the world as empty shadows. * * * Nothing but the purest patriotism, and ardent devotion to their country and her noble institutions, could hold them to the discharge of their unpleasant duties, while every admonition of nature warned them to lay aside the harness of battle and be at rest. * * * They meditated with awe and trembling on the many difficulties that now beset their path. What a treasure of wisdom could those meditations have been embodied in words, and handed down for our instruction!" Whether their united wisdom was so great or their path of duty so thorny need not be dis-

---

369 Benton's Abridgment, VIII., 375, 400.
370 See Garland's *Life of Randolph*, II., 275-76.

cussed here; but it is certain their long political careers were drawing to a close in the most peaceful bonds of friendship and happiness so far as they were concerned. As to the future of the country they were filled with misgivings and, fearing the worst, they had decided what the duty of Southerners was: to stand for their States.

The creed of these founders of the second school of States' rights was well expressed by Randolph: "Myself and my colleague, who with another gentleman whom I shall not refer to, though near me, were the only persons whom I have heard of, belonging to the Southern interest, who determined to have no compromise (the Missouri bill) at all on this subject. They determined to cavil on the nineteenth part of a hair in a matter of sheer right — touching the dearest interests — the life-blood of the Southern States."[371] And again the same kind of principles were advanced in the debate on the Executive Powers, to which reference has been made: "I trust that it will turn out in the end — whether our adversaries be born to consume the fruits of the earth, whether or not they belong to the caterpillars of the Treasury or of the law that our name, too, is Legion, for, sir, we belong to the cause and the party of the people; we do claim to belong to the majority of this — 'nation?' No, sir, I acknowledge no nation — of this Confederate Republic. For I, too, disclaim any master, save that ancient Commonwealth whose feeble and unprofitable servant I am.[372] I know there are gentlemen, not only from the Northern, but from the Southern States, who think that this unhappy question — for such it is — of negro slavery, which the Constitution has vainly attempted to blink, by not using the term, should never be brought into public notice, more especially into that of Congress, and most especially here. Sir, with every due respect for the gentlemen who think so, I differ from them *toto coelo*. Sir, it is a thing which can not be hid — it is not a dry-rot that you can cover with the carpet, until the house tumbles about your ears — you might as well try to hide a volcano in full operation it can not be hid; it is a cancer in your face, and must be treated *secundum artem*."[373]

These were the ideas for which these two friends stood. They spoke of Senators from Northern States as *our adversaries* and of their colleagues from Southern States as *our brethren*. And they had succeeded by the help of events, and especially by the help of Henry

---

371 Benton's Abridgment, VIII., 475.
372 Benton's Abridgment, VIII., 475.
373 Speech of March 2, 1826.

Clay, in converting John C. Calhoun and his fellow South Carolinians, William R. King and others of the far South to their views. And outside of Congress there was rapidly maturing under the leadership of the Richmond *Enquirer* in Virginia, of Troup and others in Georgia, a school of politicians who were returning to the Virginia and Kentucky resolutions as their chart and compass. These celebrated resolutions were resurrected and brought into the public prints; their author, Jefferson, was called on to express himself on public affairs. His advice looked backwards, too, to the days of his own great struggle. It is needless to say that Macon, a living representative of the rigid and austere democracy which won that contest and regarded Jefferson as the first, the truest and greatest American, was looked up to by this younger school in Virginia with esteem and veneration. Jefferson himself wrote him in one of his last letters, dated February 24, 1826: "I am particularly happy to perceive that you retain health and spirits still manfully to maintain our good old principle of cherishing and fortifying the rights and authorities of the people in opposition to those who fear them, who wish to take all power from them and transfer all to Washington. The latter may call themselves republicans if they please, but the school of Venice and all of this principle I call tories; for consolidation is but toryism in disguise, its object being to withdraw their acts as far as possible from the ken of the people. God bless you and preserve you many and long years."[374] This letter, written when dissatisfaction with the Administration was running high, was significant, and had without doubt some circulation among "good republicans" in Congress during the debate on the Panama Mission then in progress.

But Macon was already popular in Virginia. His influence there had been great in the Crawford campaign. The Democrats in the Virginia Legislature held a caucus in February, 1824, for the purpose of nominating candidates for President and Vice-President. Macon received six votes for the first place on the ticket and eleven for the second.[375] And when the electoral vote was finally cast Macon received the whole vote of Virginia for the Vice-Presidency.[376] And in June, 1824, when it was seen that Crawford's ill health was likely to prove fatal, or at least to defeat his election, George M. Troup, the militant governor of Georgia and ardent Southerner, wrote Macon: "In this

---

374 *Jefferson's Writings* (Ford), X., 378.
375 Richmond *Enquirer*, February 17, 1824.
376 Benton's Abridgment, VIII., 324.

unfortunate event I know of no person who would unite so extensively the public sentiments of the Southern Country in his favor as yourself. In such an unhappy result therefore, unless you forbid it I will take the liberty to propagate my opinion as diffusively as I can. In the administration of the General Government we want virtue, virtue, virtue." This shows clearly enough that Macon was not the recipient of a merely complimentary vote for the Vice-Presidency, as has been so often contended; that the South was completing that consolidation which began in 1820, was interrupted by the Jackson campaigns and the premature Nullification contest in South Carolina, set in again when the Texas question was up, and culminated in 1861. Macon was voted for in real earnest in the Virginia caucus and the hot-headed Georgia Governor advocated him for the Vice-Presidency, believing that the proposed candidate for the Presidency would be incapacitated by ill health for the office. It was not claimed that Macon was a great man, but a virtuous one, on whom the " South Country" could rely. And it will have been noted more than once in these pages that Macon was addressed as the friend of the "South Country." He and Randolph spoke constantly of their only masters — North Carolina and Virginia. From the three or four men in 1820 who "would hear of no compromise on the slavery question," the small group had grown to be a great party in 1824-28 — a party which claimed that slavery or no slavery was at bottom the only question in national politics. That they did not keep together in 1828, 1832 and 1840, was due to causes not within the scope of this study to discuss.

Not the least remarkable plan of that intriguing day was that which proposed that Macon should become Adams' running mate in 1828. Adams knew that Calhoun and Clay, and even Webster, were all intriguing against him; and day after day brought new proofs of the hostility of the Senate. Randolph was allowed to harangue that dignified body five hours at a time on the President's dishonesty and incapacity. The President was ambitious above all others to be re-elected. His only hope of success lay in a combination with some of his opponents from the South. His great competitor and political foe was Jackson; and Jackson's nominal friend was Calhoun, but every one knew the great South Carolinian was very ambitious to be come head of the ticket instead of second, as he had been in 1824. Macon opposed Jackson vigorously until very late in the administration. Randolph, Adams' bitterest political enemy, disliked Jackson and neither Macon nor Randolph were friendly to Calhoun because of his earlier career.

Under these circumstances the President made overtures to Macon's friends that he should become candidate for the Vice-Presidency. Macon was popular at the far South for his uncompromising attitude on the slavery question since 1820; his own State was ready to do him honor; and Virginia, coming more and more under the influence of strictest States' rights ideas, was ready to vote for him a second time for the Vice-Presidency. Such a combination might, so it was thought, break Jackson's hold on the South and bring Adams to his much coveted goal.

Just how Macon received the proposition can not be determined from our sources of information. In all probability he paid little heed to it, seeing how utterly inconsistent such a position would be for him. Had he not been chief among the opponents of the President? The plan is only to be viewed as one of the many made during that stormy administration. Yet the President honored Macon and Macon, unlike Randolph, believed in the uprightness of Adams. Nothing came of the scheme. It deserves attention here only as evidence of Macon's standing at the time and of the desperate shifts of the time for gaming the Presidency.

The last honor conferred on Macon while in the Senate was his election to succeed John Gailliard of South Carolina as President *pro tempore* of that body. It was not without a struggle on the part of his friends that he was successful. Seventeen ballots were required before they could secure a majority of the votes.[377] But Macon's service in the Speaker's chair during the two years following was small, for Calhoun was almost invariably present.

As another presidential campaign drew near, Macon began to cast about for a suitable man. North Carolina would be influenced by his decision, not withstanding the popularity of Jackson. The following cautious language appears in a letter of March 31, 1826: "The next presidential contest will probably be between A. and J. I have often been asked which I shall support if only these two were up. I answered it was time enough to decide; that unless A. changed his measures, I should not support him and that I did not wish to see J. president, and that I did not mean at this time to commit myself." In the same letter he gives expression to a fear that Jackson would, if elected, introduce the practice of rotation in office. He was disgusted at the idea and always vigorously opposed the use of patronage by

---

377 Benton's Abridgment, VIII., 593.

the Executive. Indeed it was one of his favorite doctrines that all patronage should be taken from the President and lodged in some unpartisan board, not in Congress and not even open to members of Congress, so jealous was he of the abuse of the powers of office. But notwithstanding this, after Calhoun's partial conversion to strict construction principles, his vote on the tariff bill and his quarrel with the Administration in 1827, Macon inclined to give his support to Jackson, who meanwhile had renewed his political friendship with Calhoun. About this time the *National Intelligencer*, the most powerful newspaper in the country, came out for Adams. Macon wrote Yancey: "The *National Intelligencer* has certainly changed its character. The *Raleigh Register* follows the *Intelligencer* as truly as the big wheel of a wagon follows the little one. Neither the *Intelligencer* nor the *Register* are calculated for the interest of North Carolina, though they may suit Washington City and the Administration." By December, 1827, he had given Jackson his support,[378] and appeared to think the candidate would be elected. The reasons for his change were strictly sectional.

He thought Jackson would be able to unite Pennsylvania and New York with the Southerners in national politics, though he feared his military habits. With Calhoun, however, he became content, and, tempered by the influence of the latter, Macon hoped that Jackson would become a *constitutional* President, that is, a strict constructionist and State rights man. Yet he said: "It is only a scuffle for the Presidency, rather a scuffle for men than principles, but this ought not to prevent our trying to get the one we prefer, hence I go for Jackson." He was then under the shadow of the "tariff of abominations," and no matter how hopeful as to the success of his candidate, he felt that the great economic struggle was going once more against the South.

After the passage of the tariff bill of 1828, in one of his last letters from Washington, Macon wrote, giving the James and the Mississippi Rivers, the Atlantic Ocean, the Gulf of Mexico, and the Alleghany mountains as the true boundaries of the South: "The Southern country is nearly ruined. They must save themselves by not buying what is not obliged to be bought; do as they did in the war of the Revolution." The tariff and paper money systems, he thought, had wrought the ruin; and if ever that section should become prosperous again, it would be by means of manufacturing, for which there was ample water power. To show how closely he and Randolph agreed on this sub-

---

378 Garland's *Life of Randolph*, II., 294.

ject, a quotation of one of Randolph's letters written a year later from Washington says: "The operation of the present government, like a debt at usurious interest, must destroy the whole South. It eats like a canker into our very core. South Carolina must become bankrupt and depopulated. * * * I am too old to move, or the end of this year should not find me a resident of Virginia."

Such were the feelings of these two ardent Southerners and lifelong companions, worn out in the service of their States, when Macon, before the reassembling of Congress in December, 1828, wrote the following characteristic letter to the General Assembly of North Carolina: "Age and infirmity render it proper for me to retire from public service. I therefore resign the appointment of Senator to the Senate of the U.S., that of Trustee of the University of the State, and that of Justice of the Peace for the county of Warren.

"In retiring from the service of the State, I want words to convey to the Legislature, and through them to the people, my thanks and gratitude for their kindness and confidence reposed in me. There are feelings which words can not express. Mine are of this kind. I may, however, be permitted to add that no person can be under more obligations to a State than I am to North Carolina, nor feel them more strongly, and that duty alone has induced me to resign."[379]

On the back of the letter to the Legislature appears his own sketch of his life: "While at Princeton, New Jersey, in 1776, I served a short tour of militia duty. After the fall of Charleston, S.C. (12 May, 1780), I served in the militia till the preliminary articles of peace were signed (30 November, 1782), and never received or charged a cent for militia duty anywhere. I never solicited any man to vote for me, or hinted to him that I wished him to do so. Nor did I ever solicit any person to make interest for me to be elected to any place. When elected to the U.S. Senate, I did not receive double pay for traveling."[380]

"Twice offered the office of Postmaster-General — Speaker of the House of R. 3 times successively, 1801-1807."

This short letter and postscript make a true commentary on the character of the man. Thus ended his active political life with the close of his sixty-ninth year. He had been in Congress thirty-seven years without interruption, and forty-two in public life. He had grown

---

379 Letter dated Buck Spring, Nov. 14, 1828.
380 An abuse of the mileage privilege which then prevailed and is not yet quite obsolete.

to be exceedingly popular in the South; his later years in Congress had witnessed the formation of the extreme States' Rights party, of which he was a foremost leader, and to which Calhoun had already given his allegiance. But it was his hope now that he might have ten years of quiet retirement at his home in Warren county, some miles from the nearest town or post office, and he resolutely withdrew from the public service.

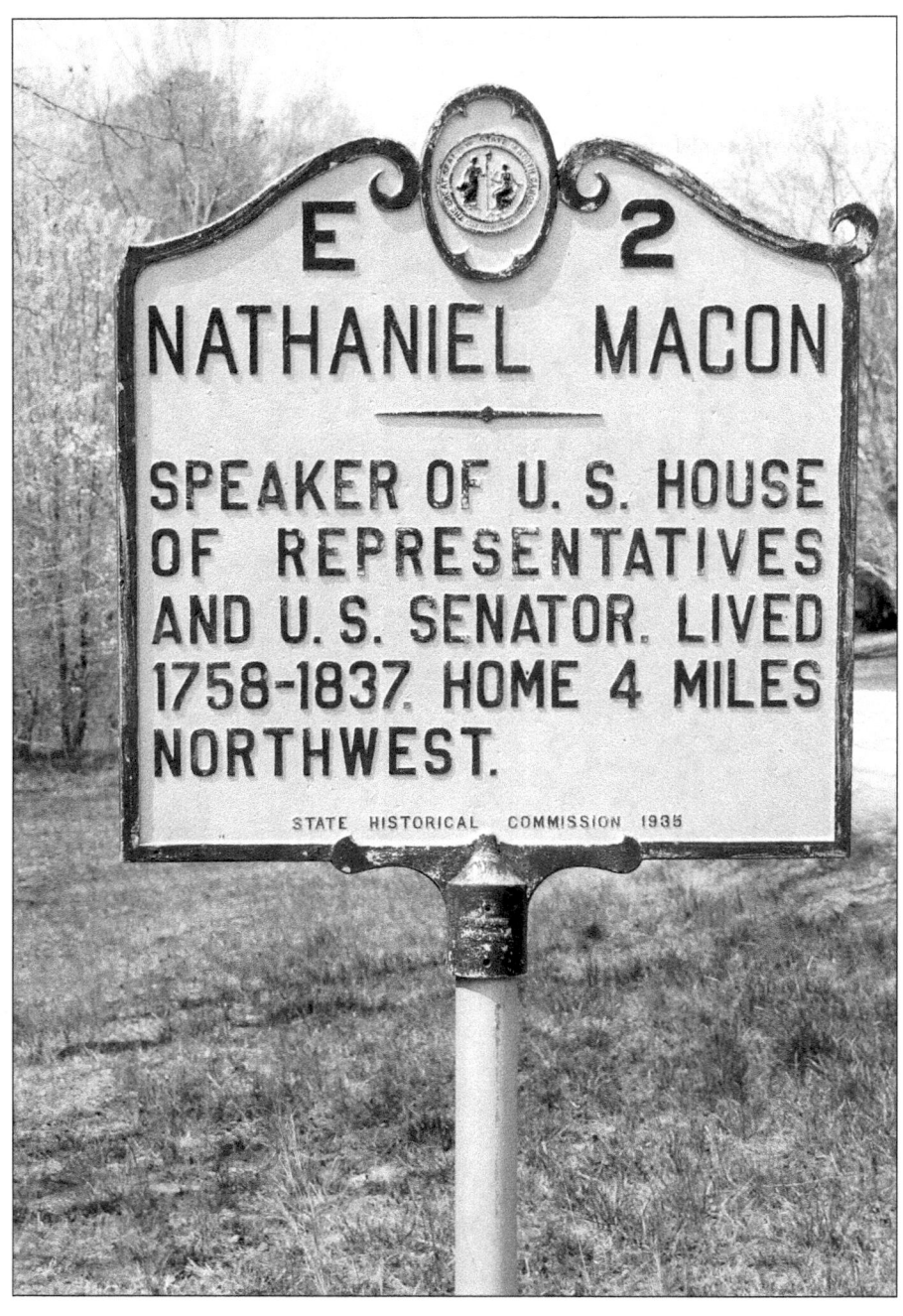

CHAPTER XIX.
Macon's LAST YEARS.

The last years of Macon's life, with the exception of his activity in the Convention of 1835 and his share in the election of Van Buren, were spent in a quiet and peaceful retirement at his plantation near the Roanoke, Buck Spring. Like Washington and Jefferson, he thought the most fitting close to a long political career was on a plantation far removed from the centres of life and turmoil. His post office was twelve miles distant, and he did not get his mail oftener than once a week, and many times two weeks passed without his receiving a word from the outside world.

Of the manner of this life on the Roanoke, not much is to be said, because we know so little of the man except where he touched the public life of his State and Nation. He had divided his property into three equal shares soon after the marriage of his youngest daughter in 1807, giving each child a third of his estate and reserving for himself a third. This, he said, was the just and true policy of a father, since it would give help to the younger generation at the time it was most needed. Before 1830 Macon's share had grown again to considerable proportions. His estate embraced two thousand acres of land, well improved and cultivated by about seventy negroes.[381] For his pastime and pleasure he kept ten thoroughbred horses, though not so many were ready for the saddle at any one time, since he raised his own stock. His extraordinary love for thoroughbreds is manifested in his keeping the record of their births on the fly-leaf of the family Bible.[382] The fox chase, in which he engaged up to the very last year of his life, was one of his special delights, and many a time Congressmen going to and from the National capital turned aside to spend a day or two with Macon and to engage with him in this popular Southern sport. Like Jefferson and the other older gentlemen of the old regime of that day, Macon furnished his guests with well-groomed horses on each occasion, and it was oft-times with great difficulty that the gentleman of the younger generation could keep his seat on a steed that leaped fences and hillside gullies with almost as much ease as the fox himself.

---

381 Macon's will in Warren County Records.
382 This Bible, now in the possession of Miss Laura Alston of Warrenton, shows a record of the births of his horses from 1800 to 1837.

Buck Spring was a sort of Mecca in upper North Carolina, where its sage discoursed of men and things a half century old with amazing accuracy. National and State politics since 1776 was his theme. He knew nearly every man who sat in the North Carolina Constitutional Convention which met at Halifax,[383] and he had known every prominent man in National politics since 1789. He made a point of relating accurately the course of events leading up to the great contest of 1800-1801, and of giving the attitude, without animosity or feeling, of the principal actors in that struggle.[384] A good instance of this was his account of the mock serenades given Vice-President Jefferson by the young aristocrats of Philadelphia in 1799-1800, in which the rogue's march and other pieces of Jacobin music were played under his window. So thorough was this knowledge of the past that the members of the North Carolina Constitutional Convention, which met a few years later, called on him repeatedly for precedents in the early policy of his party.

His home had not changed with his growth into a national character, but had remained the same as when he first built it. In fact, he lived alone, except when visitors called, with his slave cabins clustering around and the pickaninnies frolicking about the great shady grove. No extravagance was indulged; his table was supplied from his own pantry and garden, and the fare was simple, indeed. Yet his large cellar for wines and liquors was kept well stocked. His favorite drink was corn whiskey, which he took at the beginning of each meal; but he never offered it to anyone else, on the ground that it might be a temptation. He regretted his appetite for drink, saying that the drink habit was a great and unfortunate evil. Wine was kept, however, for the benefit of his friends, who called for it when they desired; and Macon's wine was noted for its age and flavor. His demeanor in the home was easy, and his manners affable; the stranger, says Govan, a South Carolina Congressman who visited him in 1825, was made to feel himself at home and under a hospitable roof. His personal magnetism and dignity were not disproportionate to his rank in the State and Nation. An excellent illustration of this has been handed down by tradition in Halifax County.[385] An important lawsuit was to come before the Court of Quarter Sessions in Halifax about 1830. The point at issue was the validity of a will. The suit depended on Macon's evi-

---

383 See his speech in the North Carolina Convention of 1835 — Debates, 176.
384 Southern History Association Publications, IV., 11-12.
385 Related by Hon. Josephus Daniels of Raleigh.

dence. Gavin Hogg, a prominent lawyer of the day, declared in bold braggadocio that he would examine Macon in such a way as to break down his evidence, and thus destroy the will. Hogg was to receive a fee of five hundred dollars if he discredited Macon's testimony — a large fee at that time. But when the suit was called, and Macon appeared in the courtroom, Hogg began to feel uneasy; he went to the witness, who received him so suavely and so overcame him by his personality that the lawyer gave up his plan, and declined to cross-question Nathaniel Macon, deciding to accept his statements as given, though this meant the loss of the suit.

The relations of the retired Sage of Buck Spring, despite the homely name, with his neighbors were such as few men and communities have ever enjoyed. Everyone, high and low, visited him without ceremony. And he returned their visits, thus keeping in close contact with all classes of people for miles around. An aged man who used to work on Macon's plantation tells of instances of Macon's going to his father's house and upbraiding him for not keeping up his visits as of old. At a country dance young Joseph Jones, of Shocco, made some blunder, and Macon, who, even at his advanced age, sometimes attended such meetings of the young, called Jones attention to his error on the ground that the young man was "a kinsman," and as such should know the right thing. In dealing with his relatives, as well as with his neighbors, he was most careful to require them to keep engagements to the letter. One of his fears for the dignity of public life was the apparent decline in the character of the Justices of the Peace. He was almost severe in his reprimand of a young neighbor, Drake,[386] who declined an appointment as Justice by the Legislature. Drake reconsidered and accepted the honor.

Macon took the greatest interest in the training of young men. On one occasion he advised a young relative to go to the University of Virginia after graduating at Chapel Hill, his idea being that at Charlottesville the young man would come into contact with men from the various sections of the United States. Macon gave him a letter to Jefferson, even though the latter was then in his eighty-third year. A letter has recently come to light[387] which still better illustrates this side of Macon's character, and which at the same time shows something of the author's range of reading. It was written from Washington City, October 20, 1814, to Mr. Frank A. Thompson:

---
386 The father of Caswell Drake of Warren County.
387 The letter is now in the Hall of History, Raleigh, N.C.

"I could not, were I to try, tell you how much I have been pleased with reading your letter. Go on in your good determination and make yourself an honor to your parents and an ornament to the country. I am so pleased with your letter that I shall send it to your mother, unless you object to it. I feel no hesitation in saying to you that I approve your determination to study law, in preference to Physic; besides this, I think it right in all persons, whether parents or guardians, to consult the inclination of young persons as to the learned profession they wish to study. If you should hereafter change your opinion and wish to practice, the law is quite as profitable as medicine, and as you prefer the law, let me advise you, while you are young, to make yourself perfectly acquainted with the history of England. When reading it pay particular attention to the changes made in the Judiciary and observe well the causes which induced Parliament to pass the laws which made the change; you will also notice with attention the anxiety of Mr. Hume to excuse the kings in every tyrannical act. Next, be well acquainted with the history of our own country; we ought to be well acquainted with the history of England, because our laws and customs are in a very great measure derived from her. The history of Charles the Fifth contains the best account that I ever saw of the feudal system, and is well worth reading. The study of Physic, if the lectures in any large city are attended, is much more costly than the study of law, and without attending the lectures no great advantage can be derived from the study. I repeat to you that I approve your choice. It is true, as you state, that the law is the road to eminence in the United States, and it is equally true that a man must be well acquainted with the laws in any other country to make a figure in it in public life. After reading the before-mentioned books, I would advise you to read the histories of Greece and Rome, and do not forget the Bible and New Testament. With them every one ought to be well acquainted. A very good plan to improve yourself would be to read a paper in the *Spectator* or *Guardian*, and then write one as near like it as you can. After writing, compare yours and the original together. This is the plan which Dr. Franklin, when young, adopted to improve himself and his style, and no man has written in a more easy and elegant style than the Doctor. The reading recommended ought not to interfere in your school studies, when you begin Euclid. Be assured that it will always give me great pleasure to render you any service in my power, and believe that I am your friend, and that no one, not even your dear mother, is more anxious for you to do well and to make yourself a man of first-rate talents and respectability than I am, and that you may be so is the sincere wish of

"Yr. friend & relation,

"NATH. MACON."

Macon's treatment of his slaves was characteristic of the man. Each Sunday morning, when the weather permitted, they were all required to assemble "in clean clothes" in front of the "Great House" and hear their master read to them from the Bible. After the reading and a talk from Macon himself, one of the older negroes was called on to lead in prayer. If any boy disregarded this regulation of the plantation or failed to come in his best clothes, he was promptly flogged. And so careful was Macon in his observance of religious exercises, that he took all his "field hands" with him to church on Saturdays. It was a custom in the country then, and even now in North Carolina, to hold church services once a month on Saturday. Hence, when simple "Brother Hudgins," the Baptist pastor near Macon's home, met his flock, he had the honor of preaching to the distinguished man whose negroes almost filled the gallery. Macon did not believe in emancipation. He held out no hope of freedom, no matter how faithful the slave. Emancipation meant to him the ruin both of the negro and of the Southern country; colonization was to him a humbug with which politicians hoped to catch votes. Kindly treatment, steady work and ample food and clothing were all the negro could expect. As to the negro ever becoming a citizen, he never admitted such a possibility. In the Constitutional Convention already referred to, he declared that free negroes had no place in the State, that he could never be allowed to vote under any circumstances. He admitted that some of them had fought in the Revolution for American liberty, but this did not entitle them to vote, as it did not entitle many white men to exercise the same privilege. The negro was the white man's property, pure and simple, and if by chance, or otherwise, he acquired his freedom, good policy demanded that he should enjoy no rank whatever in society. It would incite the main body of slaves to insurrection, which was so much feared in those days.

One might be led by the attitude of Macon towards religious matters to think him a strict church man. He was not a member of any church, though he professed to be of "the Baptist persuasion," and he attended that church regularly. His family before him had been Episcopalians, and his neighbors when a boy were chiefly of that denomination. The cause of his change was doubtless the hierarchical character and aristocratic organization of that church. The Baptists were then, as they are still, in tensely democratic in polity and in practice; their simple and unpretentious lives were in accord with his principles of life. He was a constant and close reader of the Bible, especially of the Jewish history and of Paul's writings. His Bible shows signs of much use, and his letters during the last thirty years of his life bear testimony to his familiarity with the Holy Scriptures; he cited book, chapter and verse from memory. His speeches, too, were often interspersed with quotations from the Mosaic writings. No other book was read half so much by him, and no other, except the book of human nature, supplied him with so many illustrations and practical truths.

The most signal honor ever given a North Carolinian came to Macon in the naming of Randolph-Macon College, Virginia, in the year 1830.

This institution, famous throughout the South for its sound educational policy and for the men whom it has graduated, was chartered under the laws of the State of Virginia in February, 1830. It was given the name of Randolph and Macon, according to the custom of the time, in honor of the two life-long friends and popular public characters of the Roanoke valley. The college was located at Boydton, in Virginia, about halfway between the homes of the men whose names it bore. Randolph-Macon was thus placed near the boundary line of Virginia and North Carolina, because it was to be the "seminary of learning" for the Methodist Episcopal Church of these two States. It was for a long time, how ever, the Methodist college for the whole South; it was liberally supported, and remained *the college* for the whole of upper Carolina and lower Virginia up to the outbreak of the War Between the States. There was nowhere a better territory for such an institution; the wealth and culture of the section, based essentially on slavery and planting, supplied a background to the new school, so that it was not simply a fitting school for young clergymen, but a favorite resort for the rollicking sons of a fox-hunting gentry.

Why this institution, founded specially for the purpose of advancing Christian education, was named for men neither of whom openly professed faith in the Nazarene, is a pertinent question here. The popularity of Randolph and of Macon, first of all, and second, the desire to perpetuate the names of these extraordinary men, were the motives. It was, moreover, the custom in Virginia to give educational institutions the names of popular leaders. And there may have been a lurking hope in the minds of the founders of the College that the two old gentlemen, then nearing the end of life, the one without direct heirs, the other having no children then alive and no grandchildren who were not reasonably wealthy, might possibly remember the young institution in their wills. If this was their hope, it was a vain one. Neither Randolph nor Macon ever gave the school which bears their names any financial aid whatever, so far as the records show. No written evidence of Macon's opinion of the College and its mission has been found; but tradition in and about Warrenton says he was sensible of the honor conferred, and his love of education and plans for better public schools, which were expressed in 1835, vouch for the correctness of this view. It became the fashion in a few years with the youth of Warrenton and the surrounding country to go to *the College*, and a graduate of the institution of the year 1844[388] says that Virginia and North Carolina used to vie with each other as to which could send the most beautiful girls to the Boydton commencements. Randolph's religious preferences were with the Church of England, not with the Episcopal Church of Virginia. So he leaned rather towards the Presbyterian college Hampden-Sydney of his own county, but made it no gift. The statement that Randolph-Macon, a Christian college, was named in honor of an infidel and for a politician who cared nothing for the Christian church, is not correct. Macon, as has been seen, was careful enough to contradict any such assertion by his actions; and Randolph's letters, recently discovered by the author, show him to have been a believer in the Christ, though not according to any of the particular faiths then prevalent in the South.

Notwithstanding the seeming incongruity and the failure on the part of Randolph and Macon to leave the College any legacies, the Randolph-Macon trustees have never changed its name; and it is today the best and only monument of any importance ever erected to their memories.

For such a man as Macon to retire absolutely from public life in such times as those of 1828 to 1837 was not to be expected. He did retire officially, and he never again accepted emoluments for any service he rendered the public. For example, there is a receipt from every member of the Constitutional Convention of North Carolina of 1835 in the State Department at Raleigh, except from Macon. He wished to

---

388 Captain Richard Irby of Nottaway, Va., now deceased.

give that service to the public, it appears, and so refused to accept any pay, either for expenses or services rendered.

The first great question that agitated the country after Macon's retirement was the breaking up of Jackson's first Cabinet and of Calhoun's secession from the party of the President. Macon had supported Jackson and Calhoun in 1828, but only as a lesser evil than Adams and Rush. The Jackson and Calhoun followings had joined hands with the aim of getting a Southern President. Calhoun himself had expected to get Jackson's support for the successorship; but soon after the new Administration went into operation, the great South Carolinian saw clearly enough that the President was not disposed to do this, that he was not even hasty in securing a reduction in the tariff, which was so burdensome to South Carolina. Consequently, Calhoun severed all connection with the President and wrote his famous Nullification manifesto — a document based on Jefferson's Virginia and Kentucky resolutions.[389] This breach came in 1831. Before matters drew to a crisis in Washington, the democratic Republicans of Virginia and North Carolina had developed John Randolph's and Macon's dogma of absolute States' rights to the point of instructing both Representatives and Senators in Congress how to vote. In the event that a member of the Senate refused to recognize this claim of his legislature, his resignation was to be loudly called for; the Representative would be dealt with at the next election. Thomas Ritchie, the editor of the *Richmond Enquirer*, was a champion of this school in Virginia. In North Carolina, Bedford Brown, Macon's preferred successor in the Senate after the death of Bartlett Yancey, was its best exponent. But the State was equally divided in 1828, and ex-Governor Iredell, a quasi-opponent of Macon's, was sent to the United States Senate to fill out the unexpired term. A little later Bedford Brown was elected to succeed John Branch, who had been called to a seat in Jackson's Cabinet. This divided the strength of North Carolina in the Senate.

The question of instructing Senators by the State was a paramount issue in North Carolina's politics from the time of Macon's retirement until 1846. In 1831 Willie P. Mangum was elected to succeed Iredell. Mangum and Brown were the standard bearers of the two factions of the old Republican party, Brown being the strict constructionist and Mangum the latitudinarian, anti-Jackson man. These factions soon joined in a fierce contest for supremacy. It was in this fight that

---

389 Schouler, IV., 36-37.

the line of demarcation was drawn between the Democrats and the Whigs, both claiming, at first, Jefferson as their political teacher. At this time there were two political papers of importance published in Raleigh: the old *Raleigh Register*, whose proprietors, the Gales family, had grown rich in the service of the Republican party, had been anti-Republican since 1828;[390] the more ancient *Raleigh Star*, formerly a violent opponent of everything the *Register* favored, was now a hearty supporter of Jackson. Of course Macon sided with the Jackson party and with Brown, and we have proof of this in a letter of Macon's to Brown, April 10, 1830, in which he urges his correspondent to stand out for a payment of the National debt, reduction of the tariff, and the abandonment of Clay's internal improvement schemes. Brown replies that if the Clay policy continues "it cannot but be looked on with dismay and apprehension by those who are friendly to preserving the limitations which the framers of the Constitution designed to impose on the Federal government."[391] He then brands as "selfish politicians" those who have combined to establish the "American system by which extortions are to be practised on a portion of the people of the Confederacy, a system more false to the prosperity of the Southern portion of America, better calculated to annihilate the sovereignty of the States, could not have been devised." By this exchange of letters it is seen that both Macon and Brown were supporting Jackson.

In June of the same year Macon writes Gallatin, then a bank president in New York, that he expects to make a public attack on the Bank of the United States, and asks Gallatin's assistance. A long letter and a magazine article favorable to the bank were the responses of Gallatin. Why Macon made this move can not be determined. There is some reason to believe that Jackson's special friends approached Macon, the life-long opponent of the bank, and secured his promise to attack it. Nothing could have been more natural than for him to oppose the bank, and in view of his continued cordial support of Jackson, the Administration seems to have worked up this opposition nearly two years before Clay began his right in Congress for re-chartering the National Bank.[392] The attack was not made general, but there was a continuous stream of opposition to the bank and its friends in North

---

390 See last chapter, p. 366.
391 Bedford Brown to Macon, April 29, 1830.
392 See Gallatin's letter of Dec. 3, 1830, in *The Nation*, Jan. 15, 1903.

Carolina until the re-charter failed, until Benton's expunging resolution was passed in 1836."[393]

When Congress came together in 1831, Henry Clay returned to the Senate to oppose Jackson, as he had opposed Monroe in 1817-1820. He adopted a similar policy to that waged against Monroe, except that he was now in the Senate with Webster and Calhoun, both enemies of Jackson, supporting him. There was never a stronger coalition than this. It was soon perfectly organized, and a majority of both Houses was gained for its support. Clay selected the bank question as the issue of the next year a Presidential year. Jackson's influence was at this time at its lowest ebb as a result of the dissolution of his Cabinet.

In North Carolina the United States Bank had always been unpopular; Macon had fought it at every turn for forty years. But under the leadership of Mangum, Judge Gaston, and others of the same political faith, the National Bank was gaining rapidly on the popular mind in 1830. Branch banks were established in all the large towns, and these, in violation of the National banking laws, were issuing notes in competition with those of the State banks. Since the National bank secured these notes, it was an easy thing for them to outstrip the State institutions. Party alliances in the old South of 1830 were arranged strangely enough. Calhoun having revolted from Jackson and assumed the position and politics of John Randolph, was looking about for support from any and all parties. In North Carolina and Virginia he allied with the pro-bank and anti-instructing party, that is, with Mangum and Benjamin W. Leigh, with the Whigs who in the nation opposed most violently all that South Carolina favored. Macon, who from 1824 to 1827 opposed both Jackson and Calhoun, now became an ardent Jackson man, and most determined opponent of Calhoun, though, as we shall see, Calhoun was the best representative of Macon's own life-long political creed, and in a few years he became its recognized champion before the world.

Calhoun had favored the bank and internal improvements for twenty years, and Macon had not understood the change of heart, and so did not support the South Carolinian. Until the end of the war on the bank, Macon fought for the Administration, saying that no one could have convinced him in 1824 that Jackson would ever do

---

[393] Jackson was severely censured by the Senate in 1834 for removing the Government deposits from the U.S. bank. Benton began immediately his long fight for his expunging resolution, which was finally carried two years later.

the people so great a service as he had done. And what caused Macon to give his support the more gladly was the steady reduction of the National debt, the extinction of which had been his fondest hope ever since the foundation of the government. This forlorn hope of his for so many years was realized two years before Macon's death, and almost contemporary with this glad news came the final dissolution of the bank.

Parallel to these gratifying deeds of Jackson came others which were as displeasing as they were perplexing to Macon. Calhoun's withdrawal from Jackson's party already described, and his famous manifesto on nullification, raised "a storm in the South," as Ritchie's *Enquirer* termed it, which quieted down only when the whole South lay prostrate at the feet of the National government in 1865. The foundation of the grievance was the "tariff of abominations," passed in 1828, through Clay's instrumentality, and which Jackson gave no promise of reducing after he was made President. In fact, the President was not then strong enough in the face of Clay's coalition against him to remedy the evils which bore so heavily on the South. Nullification was Calhoun's remedy. Macon admitted the right to nullify, but said the State so doing would have to secede from the Union: "I have never believed a State could nullify and stay in the Union, but have always believed that a State might secede when she pleased, provided she would pay her proportion of the public debt, and this right I have considered the best guard to public liberty and to public justice that could be desired."[394]

While he thus justified in a manner the move of South Carolina, he criticized severely the President's proclamation against nullification: "The proclamation contains principles as contrary to what was the Constitution as nullification. It is the great error of the Administration, which, except that, has been satisfactory in a high degree to the people who elected the President."[395] Then calling to mind the Whiskey Insurrection in Pennsylvania, which he had approved, he said that South Carolina's case was as different as it could be. It was with feelings of great despondency he contemplated the situation, yet Calhoun's position was exactly what both Randolph and Macon had advocated from 1820 to 1828, and one which both would have approved but for the past career of the man who now took it. Macon dreaded war, however, with all the earnestness of his soul, and most

---

394 Macon to Samuel P. Carson, February 9, 1833.
395 *Ibid.*

of all a civil war, which, he said, would bring the final downfall of our free institutions.

Macon received letters from his former political associates urging him to use his influence with the President to avert the calamity which seemed about to fall upon the Nation. He wrote, August 26, to Jackson condemning his attitude towards South Carolina, especially the threat to send troops to that State. Macon held that the Government could not legally use force to maintain the Union. This was a government of opinion, a confederacy of independent states, which could be peacefully dissolved whenever any member of it saw fit. Jackson replied to Macon in a six-page letter of great force, in which he justifies his position, declaring that the National government has authority over every individual in the United States — authority, too, which each State had given and guaranteed on entering the Union. Macon's doctrine that a man was a citizen of his individual State and not of the United States received no credence with Jackson. The President closes with the following words: "I send you herewith the proclamation, the report from the department by which it was seconded, and the law passed consummating them. I hope you will receive them as an earnest of the high respect I bear you, and if, on comparing them, you find the principles I have advanced and the measures I have recommended, the same in effect with those which were proclaimed and carried out by Mr. Jefferson, yourself and other fathers of the school of 1798, I hope you will do me the justice to believe that we follow the precedents of such high authority and which have been sanctioned by almost universal approbation of the country from that time to this."[396] Macon had referred to the proposed plan of enforcing the embargo against New England in 1807, which Jefferson outlined and he, Macon, approved, confessing that, perhaps, they had gone too far in "those hot times." Jackson cited their proposition as a precedent, and reminded Macon of his former position.[397] Macon was worsted in this tilt with old Hickory, though in the most friendly and courteous way possible, and, though there is only circumstantial proof of it, it is fairly certain that from this time on he ceased to criticise the President. He certainly gave him his open support in all things else to the close of his second term.

---

396 Macon Papers.
397 *American Historical Review*, July, 1901. This is one of the most interesting letters in the Macon Papers, and it deserves to be read by all who would understand Jackson's attitude at this crisis.

In 1835 Macon was elected a member from Warren county to the North Carolina Constitutional Convention. There had been pretty steady and increasing complaints against the Constitution formed at Halifax because of its discrimination against the West, which was now much more important than ever before. Macon had been identified with the East; he did not desire any radical change, but simply amendments which should satisfy the West and meet the changed conditions. The Convention met in Raleigh early in June, 1835, and continued its sessions until July 11. Macon was made president by unanimous vote, the word unanimous being italicized by all the papers which gave accounts of the proceedings.

Macon's life-long political creed may be summed up here, since it was at this time he had most to do in shaping the organic law of his native State : (1) Suffrage based on maturity of judgment and not on property holding; but this was to be limited once for all to the white race, no matter what the condition of the negro be or become. (2) Public education supported by general taxation. (3) Annual legislatures. (4) The *viva voce* method of voting, because every citizen had the right to know how his representative voted in the Assembly; and "no man should be ashamed," said he, "to let his neighbors know how he cast his vote in all elections." (5) Religious liberty. (6) County integrity. (7) All officers, judges not excepted, should be elected for stated terms, and not during good behavior. With the great fads of that day, advancement of commercial and internal improvements, he had little patience. North Carolina was an agricultural community, not a commercial, and if her people could not become wealthy and great, they could remain happy and be virtuous.[398] His proposal for public education applied to free schools for white children, and included the State University, which he said should be moved to Raleigh, "education in cloisters," according to his judgment, "not being suitable for young men in a free country where knowledge of men and affairs is absolutely necessary to a successful career." Annual legislatures, the rule of the past, he could not persuade the Convention to maintain; but *viva voce* voting in the legislature and short terms of office he did succeed in getting established, and North Carolina has remained faithful to his ideas on these subjects till the present time. Religious liberty was not a difficult thing to establish in a State where such a man as Judge Gaston was about the only person discriminated

---

398 Debates of the Convention; to letter Jefferson, February 2, 1822.

against; and the county system remained the same until after the deluge of 1861-1865. The final result was that the old Constitution was amended and not made anew. These amendments, in addition to the changes already indicated, provided for senatorial districts arranged according to population, maintained the old property qualifications for holding office, and for voting, and prohibited all free negroes from participating in any way in the affairs of government. The election of Governor was to be by popular vote and not by the legislature, as under the old Constitution. The new features mark a spirit of liberality towards the West, in giving them their due voice in the law-making body and in the election of Governor; but there was also manifest a much greater jealousy of the free negro than had characterized the former Constitutional convention. Slavery had grown to be an institution of threatening mien.

It will hardly be surprising that Macon made a speech against accepting the work of the Convention, or of submitting it to the people for ratification, because of the failure of his plan for annual elections, and because the election of Governor was to be by popular vote, for he based everything on yearly elections, and often quoted Jefferson's dictum that when these cease, public liberty dies. He could not sacrifice this principle for any other advantage whatever, and he carried this point so far that some of the newspapers, particularly the *Raleigh Register* and *Raleigh Star*, were disposed to ridicule him. On the election of the chief magistrate by the people he was not so inveterate in his opposition; though he opposed, he did not give his reasons in his speech of protest. It was probably due to his sense of the dignity of the office and his conservative inclinations in all matters pertaining to the State. Twenty members voted against accepting the work of the Convention as a whole.

Macon made a short farewell speech in which he referred very gracefully to the harmony of the Convention and the mutual forbearance of its members in the sometimes warm debates which had taken place. He closed with very simple but characteristic language: "This, I expect, will be the last scene of my public life. We are about to separate; and it is my fervent prayer that you may, each of you, reach home in safety, and have a happy meeting with your families and friends, and that your days may be long, honorable and happy. While life is spared, if any of you should pass through the country in which I live, I should be glad to see you."

But this was not the last scene of his public life. Already a most acrimonious Presidential campaign was beginning in North Carolina. The bank controversy, nullification and the instruction of Senators were the questions which engaged the attention of the people. The bank question was involved in the Benton expunging resolution which the Legislature had instructed Mangum to support. Mangum refused to recognize the instructions and voted against expunging. Bedford Brown, his colleague, was waging a bitter warfare on the man "who refused to be instructed by his State." Nullification was a white elephant on the hands of the Whigs, for strange as it may seem, Calhoun was supporting Mangum and his followers in North Carolina, while both Mangum and Brown were particularly anxious to repudiate nullification in all its forms. Each party in the Van Buren campaign charged the other with being milliners and each with some degree of justice, for the ideas of Macon and Brown which culminated in instructing Senators naturally led to nullification, while the alliance of Calhoun and Mangum for a purpose, could not be kept strictly secret. Again the very candidates for the presidency complicated matters; Van Buren, the ablest of our public men of the second order, was the regular Jackson nominee, and to him not much objection could be made; but Richard M. Johnson of Kentucky, his running mate, had begun his career in Congress by engineering a tariff measure through the House. Since Henry Clay's rise to supremacy he had been forced into the opposition in that State, and had always been known for his obliging politics. It was not without difficulty that such a man as Macon could be brought to support him. Hugh L. White, a former supporter of Jackson, but who, on account of some real or imaginary slight, had taken up the role of an opponent of the President in his own State, was now the Whig candidate for the presidency. White was born in North Carolina and this gave him a claim on the votes of the State. John Tyler of Virginia was White's associate on the anti-Jackson ticket. This was giving both offices to the South, and for that reason the ticket appealed strongly for sectional support. All the candidates had supported Jackson in 1828.

There were now three enterprising newspapers published in Raleigh, all of which entered heartily into the fight for or against Van Buren. Both the old papers, the *Star* and the *Register*, had made unceasing war on the President since the beginning of the bank controversy. In 1835, at the opening of the Presidential campaign, both these papers were likewise violent opponents of Jackson's protégé, Van

Buren, of the advocates of the right of instruction and of the expunging resolution, which was still the issue of the day in Washington. The third paper had been established in 1834 as an organ of the Administration, receiving the public printing for the National Government at the very start. It was known as the *Raleigh Standard*, and was edited by Philo White, who in 1837 had the distinction of carrying the Van Buren electoral vote to Washington. White was an able editor, and, it appears, a good politician; his ablest successor was the celebrated W. W. Holden.

The Van Buren campaign had been on a full year before Macon announced himself. When he did "come out" the *Standard* announced in an editorial that "Van Buren's political friends and supporters in North Carolina could have no stronger evidence than the approval of so distinguished a patriot of Republicanism (Nathaniel Macon), that theirs is the cause of Democracy and of the people."[399] Long before this, however, Macon had decided to give Van Buren his vote and influence. In the early days of the year he wrote a letter to Van Buren commending his course and endorsing Jackson's administration. This letter also bore the news that Macon had given one of his grandchildren the name of the Vice-President. Both Jackson and Van Buren responded warmly to this apparently much appreciated letter and the candidate for the successorship took special pains to announce to Macon his policy of non-interference with slavery. [400] There were other reasons for Macon's supporting Van Buren. They had worked long and hard together in the Senate against most of the schemes of John Quincey Adams. They had agreed in everything. And again, when Van Buren was candidate for Vice-President in 1832, he had received Macon's earnest support. There was no other man in the Union for whom Macon would have preferred to vote for the Presidency in 1836.

The Congressional elections held in August, 1835, had resulted in the choice of seven anti-Jackson men out of a total of thirteen. Macon's district remained Democratic, and Warren County gave only seventy votes out of five hundred to the Whig candidate. Still, North Carolina had been lost to the Democrats, though by only a small majority. At the same election, Virginia "had gone" Democratic by a very small margin. So both parties began to put forth their utmost efforts

---

399 *Raleigh Standard*, August 3, 1836.
400 VanBuren to Macon, February 13, 1836.

to win in 1836. Great excitement was worked up on the subject of abolition. A citizens' mass-meeting was held in Warrenton in September, 1835, at which a committee of vigilance was appointed to keep the people informed on the subject of Northern encroachments on the rights of the slave-holding States. The best citizens of the county took part, a relative of Macon presiding.[401] Similar meetings were held in other counties. In March, 1836, a second Warren County meeting gave enthusiastic endorsement to Van Buren for President.

April 9 General Henry Blount, of Nash County, as a representative man from the tenth district, wrote Macon asking him to offer himself as a Van Buren elector. Macon declined, but at the same time he stated positively that he should vote for a Van Buren elector, and added: "If the wisest man living had have predicted that Jackson would have done half the good he has for the people, no one would have believed him. His doings are known to everybody, and need not be repeated. He was manfully abused, because France would not execute the treaty, but the people have manfully supported him, and will, I hope, elect a successor who will do like him."[402] As a result of this and other overtures, Macon formally announced his willingness to become a Democratic elector in June. This decision became known throughout the State during July, and, as already mentioned, the *Raleigh Standard* made much of it.

On the second Thursday in August, 1836, the first Governor under the new Constitution was to be chosen. Edward B. Dudley, president of the Wilmington and Weldon Railroad, was the Whig candidate; Richard Dobbs Speight, son of a former Governor and the present incumbent, was the Democratic nominee. An exciting campaign, in which public dinners and long toasts were the main features, was waged all through the summer until election day, when Dudley won by a majority of four thousand. The Whig politicians took this as an earnest of how the Presidential campaign would terminate; the Democrats, especially their organ, the *Standard*, declared that the vote for Dudley was largely dependent on personal preference and local conditions. At any rate, it served as a spur to Van Buren's friends. Redoubled energy was injected into the Democratic fight; Macon's name was kept constantly before the people at the head of the electoral ticket, which appeared in the first editorial column of all the Administration papers. September 22 the *Raleigh Standard* appealed

---
401 *Raleigh Standard*, September 10, 1836.
402 Macon to Henry Blount, May 7, 1836.

to the public to vote for Van Buren as follows: "People of the good old North State! Friends and supporters of the principles of Jefferson! Inhabitants of the land of Macon, the well-tried, the wise, the honest, the consistent Republican, vote the Van Buren ticket." And two weeks later the same paper said, "Even now men of the purest patriotism, such as NAT. MACON and his political associates, are reviled by this *sectional party* of Judge White." A favorite appeal of the Whigs for public support was the fact that both White and Tyler were Southern men, and this advantage was used with great effect to counteract the influence of the name of Macon.

In the very thickest of the fight, William Henry Harrison was brought forward by the Whigs of the North in the hope of carrying the election of President into the House of Representatives, where that party had a majority. It was believed in North Carolina that Henry Clay was the author of this project. The Democrats bent every energy to beat their opponents by trying to show that Harrison was an abolitionist. Letters of Harrison and Van Buren, declaring the attitude of the former to be that of an uncompromising opponent of slavery, that of the latter to be friendly to "the dread institution," were freely circulated in the State. There is no doubt that this appearance of a third ticket and the accompanying fear of another contest in the House of Representatives, injured the cause of the Whigs. The Brown-Mangum fight helped the Democrats because the Whigs suffered Brown to be reviled as a man of "common manners, a man of the lower classes." Macon's name now appears in every Democratic paper in bold capitals, attracting attention the moment the eye fell upon the paper. "If you would chase away the poisonous heresy of *Nullification*" said they, "or avert the horrors of *Disunion*, go to the polls. Republicans, and vote the Democratic ticket; if you would cling to the Union, if you would cherish your liberties, and if you love your country, go to the election and vote the Van Buren Republican ticket, headed by our venerable Father in Democracy, the HON. NAT. MACON." The Tennessee papers took up the strain, calling attention to the position of "the *Father of Democracy*. When such a man as old NAT. MACON supports Mr. Van Buren, how idle is it for the mush-room politicians of the present day to charge him with a want of attachment to Republican principles. We mention this fact be cause every man now of age knows the character of Macon for devotion to the Republican party — and because we know that the opinion of such a man must weigh with the Republicans of Tennessee."[403] Macon's name was a tower of strength to the Democratic party throughout the South.

Towards the end of October came the news that Pennsylvania, in the State election held October 11, had given a large majority for the Democratic cause. Calhoun had been strong there, and the interests of the ever-growing manufactures in that section caused the Whigs to expect the vote of Pennsylvania. The State elections there, said the Democrats, pointed to Van Buren's success.[404] The Whigs of North Carolina were now as much disheartened as their opponents had been two months before. There never was a more hotly contested campaign conducted in North Carolina than this first great battle of the Whigs and Democrats. The result, tardily announced, showed a majority of 3,284 for Van Buren. It was not until November 30 that both parties accepted the count. It can scarce be doubted that Macon's influence turned the tide. The *Standard* announced the vote of the "old thirteen States" as follows: "North Carolina, Virginia, Pennsylvania, New York, Connecticut and New Hampshire for Martin Van Buren; the other six went for Harrison, Webster, Old Nick & Co." It was a curious breaking up of the old political boundaries. Only two Southern States gave majorities for the Democrats, the others voting because of widely varying reasons for the Whigs. Clay had gained the South; Calhoun had as yet effected nothing in his great scheme of united opposition; the vote of South Carolina, which he was said to "carry in his vest pocket," was given to Willie P. Mangum for President. This fulfilled the prophecy of the Democrats that the Whigs of North Carolina had entered into a corrupt bargain with the great Nullifier. Mangum resigned his seat in the United States Senate, as did also his friend, Benjamin W. Leigh, of Virginia, both rightly interpreting the election a condemnation of their refusing to vote for Benton's famous resolution.

When the electoral college met in Raleigh, December 7, Macon consented to an interview, the first and only one on record against him. It runs as follows: "The Hon. Nathaniel Macon, president of the college. — Mr. Macon appeared at a loss for language to express his patriotic emotions at the success of those pure principles of Democracy of which he had been the devoted champion during the whole period of his political life declares it is his opinion that the election of Mr. Van Buren is a far more important triumph to *Southern Repub-*

---

403 *Tennessee Democrat*, October, 1836.
404 *Raleigh Standard*, October 20, 1836.

licans than even the success of Mr. Jefferson in 1801. Both were triumphs of *principle*; but Mr. Jefferson's nativity and residence were calculated to concentrate the whole South in his favor, while *State* pride, Southern feeling, and every local consideration were arrayed against Mr. Van Buren in North Carolina; and that the Republicans should have succeeded in this embittered contest, with such odds against them, was," as Mr. Macon sincerely believed, "the best evidence in the world of the indomitable democracy of our people."[405] Casting his vote in and presiding over this electoral college was the last public act of Macon's life, and his "interview" the last message of his to the people of his "beloved Mother," North Carolina. There is probably no student of American history who agrees with him that the campaign of 1836 was as momentous as that of 1800; but no one will dispute with him the indomitable democracy of our people."

Macon retired to his home again, where he died June 29, 1837. Death came rather suddenly in his seventy-ninth year, though it was not unexpected to him. He died as he had lived, remarkably: when he felt that the hour was drawing near, which was early on the morning of the 29th, "he shaved himself," says the only authority we have on the subject (Edward R. Cotten), "dressed and lay down." Then sending for the physician, he inquired what his bill was, for Macon had been unwell some days, and paid it; the undertaker was likewise paid for his work. About twelve o' clock he passed away without a struggle. He had provided in his will, according to an old English and colonial custom, that all who attended his funeral should be furnished with "dinner and grog." Fifteen hundred people attended, and an eyewitness says, "No one, white or black, went away hungry." Macon's remains were buried beside those of his wife and son on a barren knoll not far from the house, and the graves were covered, according to his directions, with a great heap of flint rock. The explanation of this was given by himself: no one would desire to use these stones for building purposes, neither would any one consider it worth while to "remove them in order to cultivate such a poor piece of land." He gave explicit directions that no other monument should mark his grave and the people of North Carolina, according to their custom with most of their other leaders, have taken him at his word. The heap of stones remains undisturbed; broom-sedge and scrubby post-oaks surround

---

405 *Raleigh Standard*, December 14, 1836.

the place; and only within the last year has the spot been enclosed by any sort of fencing.

The news of Macon's death spread fast over the State, and the public prints vied with each other in paying their tributes of respect. The *Raleigh Register*, the paper which he had done much to establish, said of him: "He has filled a large space in the history of the State, and doubtless some one competent to the task will do justice to his memory in a biographical sketch." The greatest Democratic paper in the country, the *Enquirer*, announced his death to the world on July 4 in the following characteristic language: "The whole nation will sincerely share in this deep regret. Mr. Macon was one of those patriots who fill a vast space in the nation's eye. No one ever more completely exemplified the elevated character of the Roman poet: *Justam et tenacem propositi virum*. But we forbear. We leave it to abler pens to do justice to Nathaniel Macon."[406]

Time enough has elapsed for candid students to assign to Nathaniel Macon his rightful place in the history of North Carolina and of the United States.

---

[406] Despite these predictions, no one rose to do him justice: and North Carolina, falling into the hands of his political opponents, knows very little of this most typical, if not greatest, of her sons.

The grave of Nathaniel Macon

From a militia volunteer in the Camden campaign, he rose to the position of an influential political leader of the Willie Jones school in North Carolina, to that of Speaker of the National House of Representatives, leader of the Madison administration in 1810, member of the United States Senate, and president of the North Carolina Constitutional Convention of 1835. In all of these stations he enjoyed the satisfaction of having distinguished himself, and above all of knowing that his State and the "South Country" approved of his course. In fact, his place in history must be determined by his relations to the South as a distinct section of the nation. He believed with Jefferson, and more especially "with Jones, that the State was the centre of power in this country, and that next to the State the South had the first demands on his service; he was among the first to suggest the annexation of Florida, and, with John Randolph, he first laid down the dictum, which the South accepted and clung to until 1865, that no compromise on the slave question should be admitted by the South. In fact, Macon must be regarded as Randolph's counterpart in founding the creed of the secessionists; he was a stronger and more influential man than "his brilliant but flighty friend of Roanoke." In the Senate he ranked very high, and in North Carolina he was the idol of the people. The question has often been asked, "Was he a statesman?" He was a Southern statesman in the sectional sense; and the giving of his name to counties and towns all over the South shows that he was so recognized. That is all that this very imperfect, yet somewhat painstaking, study of his life justifies the author in claiming for him. As such he opposed every encroachment on the rights of his section, and pleaded to the last moment of his political life for the simple, straightforward interpretation of the National Constitution. His life was a continued protest against everything Henry Clay advocated, against every principle the realization of which brought civil war and frightful bloodshed, against every extravagance for which the name of the National government has since become synonymous. He was no great man in the ordinary sense of the word, but no taint of corruption ever touched his garments, and he served his constituents, the people of North Carolina, more faithfully and more satisfactorily by far than any other man who ever represented them. *He actually believed in democracy.*

FINIS.

APPENDIX.

A. DEBATE IN THE HOUSE OF REPRESENTATIVES ON THE REPEAL OF THE FEDERAL JUDICIARY ACT, FEBRUARY, 1802.

In February when the debate on the Judiciary bill was at its height, Henderson, of the Salisbury district, delivered the ablest speech from the Federalist point of view that had ever been offered by a North Carolinian on the floor of Congress. He outlined the opinions of his party leaders in general and especially of those from his State — men who had gone into office by means of the Federalist victory of 1799. The General Assembly of North Carolina had passed resolutions of instruction to its delegates in Congress calling on them to do all in their power to have the Federal Judiciary act of the last session repealed. It was indeed the custom of all the states at that time to vote similar resolutions on most important questions. It has already been shown that North Carolina's first representatives in the United States Senate were not re-elected at the expiration of their terms because they refused to be instructed." On this particular occasion the State had *instructed* its Senators and *recommended* to its Representatives how to vote.[407] Henderson announced that he refused to be instructed, that he did not pray "thy will, not mine be done" to the North Carolina Assembly. Henderson's position was that of his party, his arguments were along the line of Bayard's and Griswold's. His closing remarks were worthy of Fisher Ames, "if the doctrine contended for by gentlemen on the other side of the House should become the settled construction of the Constitution, and enlightened America acquiesce with that construction, I declare for myself, and for myself alone, I would not heave a sigh, nor shed a tear over its total dissolution. The wound you are about to give it will be mortal; it may languish out a miserable existence for a few years, but it will surely die. It will neither serve to protect its friends nor defend itself from the omnipotent energies of its enemies. Better at once to bury it with all our hopes."[408]

John Stanly, of New Berne, followed his leader in a speech of greater length but less declamation. His position with reference to

---

407 Annals of Congress, 7th Cong., 1st Sess., 523.
408 Annals of Congress, 7th Cong., 1st Sess., 530.

the right of the State to instruct delegates in Congress was the same as Henderson's. Independence of the Judiciary was his theme and his closing prediction was: "Should this measure pass, it will be the first link in that chain of measures which will add the name of America to the melancholy catalogue of fallen Republics." The Federalist party in North Carolina never was better represented than at this time nor more numerously. In addition to Henderson and Stanly, William B. Grove, of Fayetteville, and William H. Hill, of Wilmington, ardently supported its policy.

Following Stanly's address came an exciting and impassioned debate between Giles, of Virginia, and Bayard, of Delaware, in which the latter reviewed Jefferson's appointments claiming that Charles Pinckney was sent as minister to Madrid, W. C. C. Claiborne appointed Governor of Mississippi in reward for campaign services in 1800; that Linn, of New Jersey, "the man who secured the President the vote of his State," Lyon, of Vermont, and Edward Livingston, of New York, were all helped into lucrative offices in reward for faithful party work. Every kind of corruption and political trickery was charged against the President and most of the leaders of both parties made set speeches. It was at this point that Macon made the longest and most characteristic speech of his congressional career.

B. Macon's SPEECH ON THE REPEAL OF THE JUDICIARY ACT, FEBRUARY 23, 1802.[409]

"MR. SPEAKER: I should not, I believe, have spoken on this question, had not my colleagues, who differ with me in opinion, thought proper to bring into view a vote of the Legislature of the State, instructing her Senators and recommending it to the Representatives to use their best endeavors to obtain a repeal of the last Judiciary Act. On this resolution of the State legislature they made some extraordinary remarks, which I mean to notice; but first permit me to inform the Committee, that it has been the constant practice of the Legislature of the State, from the commencement of the general government to the present day, to instruct her Senators and to recommend to her Representatives, to pursue such measures on all the great national questions that have occurred, as the Legislature judged the interest of the State required, and this

---

409 See above, pages 125, 126.

proceeding has never been considered improper. I shall endeavor to answer the gentlemen in the order they spoke, beginning with my colleague, (Henderson), who was first on the floor. If I understood him rightly, (and if I do not he will correct me, because it is not my desire to mistake a single word), he said that the Legislature of the State might have adopted the resolutions in consequence of the message of the President; but, upon examination of the dates, this will be found to be impossible. The message could not have reached the Legislature before the question on the resolutions was taken and decided; and on no important questions was that body more unanimous; and though my colleague has said the question was there viewed but on one side, and decided in a manner *ex parte*, yet I will be bold to say, if there were any member in that Legislature who thought on this subject as he does, he enjoys the same right there that my colleague does here, to deliver his sentiments.

"Knowing, as I do, the great talents and integrity of my colleague, and I believe no one on this floor knows them better, I was surprised when he charged others with being under the influence of passion, when his conduct must convince them that he was guided by the very same passion which he attributes to others. He quoted the Constitution of North Carolina; let us examine it and see whether his arguments can be aided by the practice under that instrument. The thirteenth article is in the following words, that the General Assembly shall, by joint ballot of both Houses, appoint judges of the Supreme Court of law and equity, judges of admiralty, and attorney-general, who shall be commissioned by the Governor, and hold their offices during good behavior. On this clause he quoted the independence of the State judiciary; and they are independent so long as the law creating their office is in force, and no longer; and it is worthy of notice that in this section no mention is made of salary, and yet the judges have been considered as independent as the judges of the United States. Soon after the adoption of the Constitution, the Legislature of the State established courts in conformity thereto; first county courts, and then superior, and afterwards, by a legislative act, without electing a single new judge, gave the superior courts the additional jurisdiction of a court of equity, and never a solitary complaint that this law was unconstitutional; and it must be acknowledged, that if you can make the court of law also a court of equity by legislative act, you can, by the same power, take away; and what becomes in this case, of the commission which is to be held during good behavior? It is, according to my construction, to last no longer than the law which created the office remains in force, and this is long enough to make the judges independent. As to the salaries of the judges of North Carolina, the twenty-first section of the Constitution says, they shall have adequate salaries during their continuance in office, and yet with this clear right in the Legislature, to lessen as well as to add to their salaries, the judges, it is agreed, are independent. My colleague well knows that many attempts have been made to deprive the Superior Courts of exercising any jurisdiction in cases of equity; and he also knows that attempts have been made to establish a court of appeals, which should revise the decisions of the Superior Courts now in being; and by the Constitution of the State any Supreme Court may on presentment of a grand jury, try the Governor for maladministration, etc., and I believe the present courts are authorized to do this. I have not at this place been able to see the act which gives this authority, but no doubt is entertained of the fact.

"It is clear, then, that in North Carolina, all parties have thought that 'during good behavior' only meant so long as the office existed; because, by establishing a court of appeals the judges now in being would not be supreme judges, and in all these various attempts no one ever charged either of them to be unconstitutional. On examination of the Constitution of North Carolina it will be found that it makes provision for the appointment of other officers of the Legislature, but says nothing about adequate compensation, except in the section last read, and if you take the office away, what is an adequate compensation for doing nothing? Another proof might be drawn from the Constitution of North Carolina, in favor of the opinion I hold, which is taken from the twenty-ninth section, that no judge of a Supreme Court shall have a seat in the General Assembly, because they are supreme. And he also knows that no one ever doubted the constitutional right of the Legislature to establish the courts before mentioned; and it seems to me this, on his construction, would be a violation of the Constitution, because, having once made a Supreme Court it must always remain so, to secure what he calls the independence of the judges.

"Sir, I was astounded when my colleague said that the judges should hold their offices, whether useful or not, and that their independence was necessary, as he emphatically said, *to protect the people against their worst enemies, themselves;* their usefulness is the only true test of their necessity, and if there is no use for them they ought not to be continued. I will ask my colleague whether, since the year 1783, he has heard any disorder in the State we represent, or whether any act has been done there which can warrant or justify such an opinion, that it is necessary to have the judges to protect the people from their worst enemies, themselves. I had thought we, the people, formed this government, and might be trusted with it. My colleague never could have uttered this sentence had he not been governed by that passion which he supposes governs others. It is true that we are not a rich and wealthy State, but it is equally true that there is no State in the Union more attached to order and law; and my colleague himself would not say that it was necessary to have judges for this purpose in the country we represent; the people there behave decently without having Federal judges or standing armies to protect them against themselves. Is it not strange that the people should have sense enough to pay their taxes without being driven to it by superior force, and not have sense to take care of themselves without this new Judiciary? They certainly contrived to do this before the act establishing this Judiciary passed.

"Another expression of his equally astonished me; he said that on the 7th day of December a spirit which had spread discord and destruction in other countries, made its entry into this House. What! are we to be told, because at the last election the people thought proper to change some of their representatives and put out some of those who had heretofore been in power, and to put others in power of different opinions, that a destroying spirit entered into all the public functionaries? For what, sir, are elections held, if it be not that the people should change their representatives when they do not like them ? And are we to be told from the housetops that the only use of elections is to promote, not public good, but public mischief? We are also told that this Constitution was to be destroyed by the all-devouring energies of its enemies. Who are its enemies? We are not, nor do I think there are any in this House; but there are parties as well in this House as out of doors, and no man wishes more sincerely than I do that they were amalgamated, that we might get rid of all party gall, and free ourselves from improper reflections hereafter. But by what energy is the Constitution to be destroyed? The only energy heretofore used, and which made the change so much complained of, was the energy of election. Sir, I scarcely know what to say when I hear such uncommon sentiments uttered from a head so correct, and a heart so pure; it is the effect of a passion of which he is unconscious. Again he says if you repeal the law the rich will oppress the poor. Nothing but too much law can anywhere put in the power of the rich to oppress the poor. Suppose you had no law at all, could the rich oppress the poor? Could they get six, eight or ten percent for money from the poor without law? If you destroy all law and government can the few oppress the many or will the many oppress the few? But the passing of the bill will neither put it in the power of the rich to oppress the poor, nor the poor to oppress the rich. There will then be law enough in the country to prevent the one from oppressing the other. But while the elective principle remains free, no great danger of lasting oppression, can be really apprehended; as long as this continues the people will know who to trust.

"He has also brought into view the repeal of internal taxes, and the naturalization law, and these are some of the measures which this destructive spirit approves; and will they oppress the poor; will the repeal of taxes oppress the poor, or will it oppress anybody? If it will, the people will cry out with the gentleman from Virginia (Randolph), give us more oppression. You can not give us too much of this kind of oppression, provided you pay our debts and protect us at home and abroad. One word respecting the naturalization law — observe the danger apprehended by North Carolina on this head; the fortieth section of her Constitution is in the following words, 'that every foreigner who comes to settle in this State, having first taken an oath of allegiance to the same, may purchase, or by other just means, acquire, hold and transfer land or other real estate, and after one year's residence shall be deemed a free citizen.' After this can we believe the people of the State have any fear of the few aliens that may wish to settle among them?

"It is asked, will you abolish the mint, that splendid attribute of sovereignty? Yes, sir; I would abolish the mint; that splendid attribute of sovereignty, because it is only a splendid attribute of sovereignty, and nothing else; it is one of those splendid establishments which takes money from our pockets without being of any use to us. In the State that we represent I do not believe there are as many cents in circulation as there are counties. This splendid attribute of sovereignty has not made money more plenty; it has only made more places for spending money.

"My colleague next said, what I sincerely wish he had not said, that if you pass the bill, he would neither shed a tear nor heave a sigh over the Constitution. If we pass the bill, and the people should think we did wrong in so doing, nay, that it violates the Constitution in their opinion, have they not the power to bring it back to its original stamina, by a peaceable corrective, which they can exercise every two years at the elections? Suppose this done, would not the Constitution then be worth some thing, even in his estimation? Would it not be better to cherish this expectation than to destroy the Constitution and put everything afloat? Would not this be much better than confusion, anarchy, and the sword of brother drawn against brother? As to myself, I confide in the people, firmly believing they are able to take care of themselves, without the aid or protection of any set of men paid by them to defend them from their worst enemies, themselves.

"Permit me here, sir, to advert to the resolutions of North Carolina. (Macon read the instructing resolutions.) In commenting upon these resolutions my colleague certainly used very complaisant language towards the Legislature of that State; but it seemed to me that he gave them a back handed compliment when he said they passed these resolutions without a fair hearing. But, sir, is there anything indecent in them? Have they expressed a sentiment which they had not a perfect right to express? They wish the law repealed, because they believe the old system adequate. They wish the law repealed because it produces a useless expense. This, perhaps, they more sensibly felt from being in the habit of conducting their public affairs with the greatest economy; and, finally, they wish the law repealed, because it is an useless extension of executive patronage; and they, at the same time, declare that they have due confidence in the Chief Magistrate of the Union. Yet they do not wish offices continued merely that persons may be appointed to fill them. I perfectly agree with them in every particular.

"We have heard much about the judges, and the necessity of their independence. I will state one fact, to show that they have power as well as independence. Soon after the establishment of the Federal courts they issued a writ — not being a professional man I shall not undertake to give its name — to the Supreme Court of North Carolina, directing a case then pending in the State Court to be brought into the Federal Court. The State judges refused to obey the summons, and laid the whole proceedings before the Legislature, who opposed their conduct, and, as well as I remember, unanimously; and this in that day was not called disorganizing.

"As so much has been said about the resolutions of North Carolina I will repeat again, that it is no uncommon thing for the Legislature to express their opinion on great National subjects, and will ask my colleagues whether they ever heard any complaint of the resolutions about the Western land? And whether none of them in the Legislature ever voted for the resolutions about the Western land, nor about post offices and post roads? The Legislature surely had as much right to give an opinion as the Chamber of Commerce of New York; but, put it upon what footing you please, it is entitled to respect as the uninfluenced opinion of so many respectable individuals; and the Legislature never intended nor wished that the recommendation to the representatives should be binding on them at all events; and if I believed the bill to be unconstitutional, I should not vote for it, but as I do not, I hope the gentleman will pardon me for pursuing my own sentiments, and voting for it. I hope no man will ascribe to me a disposition to produce anarchy in my native country. Although poor myself I feel as strong a desire as any one on this floor for the preservation of good order and good government.

"If it has been asked by the gentleman from Delaware (Mr. Bayard) will the gentleman from Virginia (Mr. Giles) say the assuming of the State debts was improper? I have no hesitation to say it was done at an improper time; and, in showing that it was I hope I shall be pardoned for traveling over topics that really have nothing to do with the merits of the present question. The act is now done, and, by what I say, it is not to be understood that I wish Congress should put their hands upon it. It will be noticed that Congress is authorized to establish post offices and post roads for the general and equal dissemination of information throughout the United States; and it is not known that no act was passed on that subject before the assumption of the State debts, and that there was only one post road which runs near the sea coast? Of course, the people in the interior country had no communication with those in the government, nor had they any knowledge of what was doing. But the rich speculator, who was on the spot, by going into the country where the people were ignorant of what had been done purchased up their certificates — the only reward they had received for their toil and wounds — at about one-tenth of their value. And it is possible that many of these purchases may have been made with public money.[410] And it is clear to me that if a proper number of post roads had been established before the act was passed for assuming the State debts the war-worn soldier would

---

410 See Macon's resolution on this subject, p, 49.

not have lost half as much as he did by the speculation on his certificates.

"The gentleman from Delaware says we drove them to the direct tax. This is the first time I ever heard of a minority driving a majority. Is such a thing possible? Did we drive them to the measures that made such immense expenditures of the public money necessary? No sir; we opposed those measures as useless; and the true ground of the direct tax is this: the public money was expended; public credit was stretched, until to preserve it, it became necessary to provide for paying, and the means adopted were the direct tax.

"The same gentleman tells us there is nothing sacred in the eyes of infidels. We know our opponents. The allusion here is too plain not to be understood; and evidently is that those who differ with him in opinion are infidels. This is a strong expression; it would have seemed that his love of Americans ought to have prevented the use of it. I shall make no answer to it, except to remind him that in a book the truth of which he will not deny, he will find these words, Judge not, lest ye be judged. He also said that gentlemen might look to the Executive for victims and not to the judges. Notwithstanding this remark and without condemning or approving the appointments made by the late President, I hope I may be permitted to express my own ideas, without being considered under the influence of the present President. Prior to the fourth of last March, all, or nearly all, the offices in the gift of the Executive were in the hands of men of one political opinion. On that day the people changed the President because they did not like measures that had been pursued. But, to those who had attended to the debates in this House it must appear strange, indeed, to hear gentlemen complain of the President for having in office those who agree with him in opinion, when we were formerly told that the President would do wrong if he appointed to office those who differed from him in political opinion; and whenever he had done it he had cause to repent of it. Was that opinion then correct, and now false, in the estimation of gentlemen? For my part, I did not think the opinion correct when I first heard it, nor have I since been convinced of its propriety. Indeed, before I can think so I must have a worse opinion of human nature than I now have, and think of men as they pretend to think of us, which God forbid! But, taking things as they are what course, on this point, is most fair and tolerant? The community, as well as this House, is divided into two parties. It seems to me that all the most tolerant could wish would be an equal division of the offices between the parties and thus you might fix a reciprocal check on each other. But I ask gentlemen to be candid, and tell me whether they are at this time equally divided? Sir, they know that there are many more persons who now fill offices who agree with them in opinion than agree with us. As to myself, I care not who fill offices, provided they act honestly and faithfully in them. I can with truth say so little party attachment have I on this head that I never solicited to have any man discharged from office. Knowing that a large majority of those now in office agree with those gentlemen in political opinion I am at a loss for the cause of all this clamor. They have no doubt some reason for it which has not been declared. The fact is they have a majority of the offices and a majority of the people are with us. I am contented it should be so.

"The gentleman has dwelt much on a subject which, from my habits of life, I am not enabled fully to notice; I must decide for myself, and, judging with the small share of information I possess I can not agree with him. I do not pretend to understand the subject as well as he does, but certainly he was not so perspicuous as might have been expected. I mean, sir, his opinion on the common law. He told us that the judges only adopted such parts of the common law of England as suited the people and that he apprehended no danger from this. Sir, I do apprehend danger from this, because I can not find any authority given them in the Constitution to do it, and I suppose it is not an inherent right. Without pretending to know the extent of this common law, it has always appeared to me to be extremely dangerous to the right of the people, for any person not elected by them to undertake to exercise the power of legislating for them, and this adopting the common law is only another name for legislation. He also told us, that the States had adopted it. If the States adopted it, it became a law of the State and not of the United States; but the adoption of it by the individual States could not give the judges a right to adopt it for the United States. The judges have no powers but what are given by the Constitution or by statute and this power can not be found in either. He even told us that the Constitution was a dead letter without it. I do not believe this was the opinion of the Convention that formed it and by an examination of the debates of the State conventions that ratified it, it will not be found to be their opinion; nor is it, I believe, the opinion of all the judges of the Supreme Court, that the Constitution would be a dead letter without the common law of England. I have understood, that one of them has given it as his opinion, that the common law was not in force in the United States. The gentleman told us that the Sedition law was constitutional, and that the judges had so determined. This we have been told before; but, in my opinion, the contrary is the fact. I firmly believe there is no authority given in the Constitution to pass that law, and although the judges agree with him in opinion, I believe the people agree with me. He, like my colleague, did not pretend to say that the judges under the old system had too much business, but too much riding. The whole burden of the song seems to be riding and salary, salary and riding; you may destroy the office, but the officer must have his salary, and this, I suppose, without riding. The old system was, in my opinion, equal to every object of justice contemplated by its establishment.

"The gentleman has ascribed to us the wish to have the courts viciously framed. Is it possible, that he can have so degrading an idea of the American people, as to suppose they would send men here to legislate on their dearest interests, so base and corrupt, as to wish their courts so formed that vice and not virtue should prevail in them? I am happy to say that gentleman is the only one who has uttered a sentiment so abhorrent to human nature. He also said, if you permit the State courts to execute your laws, you would have no Constitution in ten years. I have not heard anyone express a desire that you should have no courts, or that the State courts should execute your laws; but I do not believe, that, if the State courts were to execute your laws, that they would destroy the Constitution which they are sworn to support. He has told us that we paid millions for an army which might be useless, and refused thousands to a judiciary which was useful. As to the army, those who agree with me in sentiment are as clear of it as it is possible for men to be of any political sin whatever; we always considered them useless, except in a small degree and voted against them.

"But," says he, this is the President's measure; he may prevent it. This is indeed a bad assertion. Are a majority of this House so degraded, so mean, so destitute of honor or morality, as to act at the nod of a President? What the majority may here after do, I can not tell; but I can say, as yet they have done nothing which even the eye of criticism can find fault with. But are we to infer from these charges, that it has heretofore been the practice for the President to give the tone to the majority of the House, and to wield them about as he pleased? I had before a better opinion of our adversaries. I had thought, and still think, that no man can wield a majority of this House; that the House is, and has been, too independent for this; to think otherwise, would be degrading to my country. Sir, I do not believe the gentleman from Delaware himself, with all his talents, can wield those with whom he votes, at his will and pleasure.

"Much has been said about the manner in which the late law was passed (the Judiciary Act of 1801), and the purpose for which it was done. I hope I shall be pardoned for saying nothing on this subject; enough, if not too much, has already been said on it; nor can I conceive that it has anything to do with the question.

"The question is, were there courts enough under the old system to do the business of the nation? In my opinion there were. We had no complaints that suits multiplied, or that business was generally delayed; and when gentlemen talk about Federal courts to do the business of the people, they seem to forget that there are State courts, and that the State courts have done, and will continue to do, almost the whole of the people's business in every part of the Union; that but very few suits can be brought into the Federal Courts, compared with those that may be brought into the State Courts. They will be convinced that under the old system we had Federal judges and courts enough; besides, sir, I believe each State knows best what courts they need, and if they have not enough, they have the power and can easily make more. I am sure the old system answered every purpose for the State I live in as well as the new.

Until the present session, the people have not presented a single petition to this House on the subject of courts, and now, I believe, there are a majority of the petitioners in favor of the repeal; but their not having heretofore petitioned, is conclusive in my mind, that they were perfectly satisfied with the old system. They know that they have the right to petition, and we know that they have exercised it whenever they pleased, and if they wanted these new courts, they would have told you so by petition.

"The gentleman said he would forgive the gentleman from Virginia (Mr. Giles) for everything he said, except disturbing the ashes of the venerable dead. I did not understand the gentleman from Virginia to say a word about the illustrious Washington. It is needless for me to say what I think of him; I have said before what my opinion was; I sincerely regret that ever his name should be mentioned in this House in such debates as these, respect for his memory ought to forbid it.

"He also told us, that we attempt to do indirectly what we can not do directly. I do not know of any such attempts. The bill is certainly a direct attempt to repeal the act of last session; but I have seen things done indirectly which I believe could not have been done directly; such was the army of volunteers; it surely was an indirect attempt to officer and get possession of the militia. The same gentleman challenges us to say there are any in the United States who prefer monarchy. In answer to this I say, there were such during the American Revolutionary War, and I have not heard that they had changed their opinions; but as he has told us there are jacobins in the country, it is not unfair to suppose there are monarchists, they being the two extremes. We are also charged with a design to destroy the whole Judiciary. If there is such a design, this is the first time I ever heard it; no attempt of the kind is yet made. But what is the fact? We only propose to repeal the act of the last session, and to restore the Judiciary exactly to what it was for twelve years, and this is called destroying the Judiciary.

"The same gentleman told us that under the new system you would have an uniformity of decision in each circuit, and that it was not very desirable to have it uniform in every circuit. I differ with him; I think uniformity of decision desirable, for this reason, that a person knowing a decision of the Federal court on any given point in any part of the Union, may know that the same decision would prevail in every other court of the United States; and unless there is an uniformity of decision, you may have a different one in each circuit; a determination one way in Delaware, another in Maryland. But, sir, from the very nature of the courts, you must have an uniform decision in either system; because, if different courts should decide differently, appeals would soon be carried to the Supreme Court, where the question would finally be settled.

"Another curious principle was advanced by the gentleman, which was this, that the judges received their pay from the date of their commissions. If they do, I am confident they are the only officers appointed by Government that do. I had always before understood, that the pay of officers did not commence until they accepted their appointments. On this idea a judge might have pay as a circuit judge, while he was holding court as a district judge, because he might be a district judge, and appointed a circuit judge without his knowledge; and before he was informed of his new appointment, might hold the court under the old, and the gentleman himself would not pretend to say that the proceedings of the court in such case would be illegal or irregular. The salary of the President is brought into view. I have never heard these gentlemen before complain that it was too high;

if it is, I am perfectly willing to join them, and diminish it to what shall be deemed only an adequate compensation for services actually rendered, for the next Presidential term; sooner, the Constitution will not authorize its reduction.

"To complete the scene, we are told of the sword of civil discord, and of the sword of brother drawn against brother. Why such declamation? Why do we hear of such things on this floor? It is for them to tell who use the expressions; to me they are too horrid to think of. Do gentlemen appeal to our fears rather than our understandings? Are we never to be clear of these alarms? They have often been tried without producing any effect. Every instrument of death is dragged into this question; sword, bayonet, hatchet, and tomahawk; and then we are told that the passing this bill may be attended with fatal consequences to the women and children.

Can it be possible, sir, that the gentleman was really serious when he talked about an injury to women and children? He also told us, if you pass the bill and it should produce a civil war, not only himself but many enlightened citizens would support the judges. And have we already come to this, that enlightened citizens have determined on their side in case of a civil war, and that it is talked of in this assembly with deliberation and coolness? We certainly were not sent here to talk on such topics, but to take care of the affairs of the nation, and prevent such evils. In fact it is our duty to take care of the nation, and not destroy it. Compare this with the conduct of the former minority. I challenge them to show anything like it in all their proceedings. Whenever we supposed the Constitution violated, did we talk of civil war? No, sir; we depended on elections as the main cornerstone of our safety; and supposed, whatever injury the State machine might receive from a violation of the Constitution, that at the next election the people would elect those who would repair the injury, and set it right again; and this in my opinion ought to be the doctrine of us all; and when we differ about Constitutional points, and the question shall be decided against us, we ought to consider it a temporary evil, remembering that the people possess the means of rectifying any error that may be committed by us.

"Is the idea of the separation of these States so light and trifling an affair as to be uttered with calmness in this assembly? At the very idea, I shudder, and it seems to me that every man ought to look on such a scene with horror, and shrink from it with dismay. Yet some gentlemen appear to be prepared for such an event, and have determined on their sides in case it should happen. For my part, sir, I deplore such an event too much to make up my mind on it until it shall really happen, and then it must be done with great hesitation indeed. To my imagination the idea of disunion conveys the most painful sensation; how much more painful then would be the reality! Who shall fix the boundaries of these new empires, when the fatal separation shall take place? Is it to be done with those cruel engines of death that we have heard of, the sword, the bayonet, and the more savage instruments of tomahawk and hatchet? And is the arm of the brother to plunge them into the breast of brother, and citizen to be put in battle array against citizen; to make this separation which would ruin this whole country? And why is all this to be done? Because we can not all think alike on political topics. As well might it be said, because we can not all agree in the tenets embraced by each particular sect of our holy religion, because one is a Calvinist and another a Lutheran, that each should be employed in plunging the dagger into the heart of the other. But suppose, sir, you agree to divide these States, where is the boundary to be? Is it to be a river, or a line of marked trees? Be it which it may, both sides must be fortified, to keep the one from intruding on the other; both the new Governments will have regular soldiers to guard their fortified places, and the people on both sides must be oppressed with taxes to support these fortifications and soldiers. What would become, in such a state of things, of the national debt, and all the banks in the United States? If we do wrong by adopting measures which the public good does not require, the injury can not be very lasting; because at the next election the people will let us stay at home, and send others who will manage their common concerns more to their satisfaction. And if we feel power and forget right, it is proper that they should withdraw their confidence from us; but let us have no civil war; instead of the arguments of bayonets, etc., let us rely on such as are drawn from truth and reason.

"Another topic has been introduced, which I very much regret: it is the naming of persons who have received appointments from the late or the present President. I hope I shall be pardoned for not following their example. And one gentleman is named as having been an important member during the election of President by the late House of Representatives. It ought to be remembered there were others as important as the gentleman named. In talking about the late or the present President, it ought not to be forgotten that they both signed the Declaration of Independence, that they both have been Ministers in Europe, and both Presidents of the United States. Although they may differ in political opinion, as many of us do, is that any reason we should attempt to destroy their reputations? Is American character worth nothing, that we should thus, in my judgment improperly, attempt to destroy it on this floor? The people of this country will remember that British gold could not corrupt nor British power dismay these men. I have differed in opinion with the former President, but no man ever heard me say, that he was either corrupt or dishonest; and sooner than attempt to destroy the fame of these worthies, to whose talents and exertions we owe our independence, I would cease to be an American; nor will I undertake to say that all who differ from me in opinion are disorganizers or jacobins.

"We have heard much about the document No. 8, sent to this House by the President, and are told that it is not correct. Admit everything which has been said about it, and does it amount to anything like the least invalidating it? No, it only shows a clerical error of no importance, and it must be agreed to be sufficiently correct to prove the inutility of the late system. The gentleman from South Carolina told us, that many learned men who agreed with us generally in politics, differed with us on the present question. This I never heard before; but, suppose the fact to be so, it unquestionably proves that with us each man makes up his own opinion for himself. He told us of one, who had lately held a high office under the Federal Government, who had, when in office, made a report, a part of which was directly against our opinion, and that he was high in the ranks of the opposition. The opinion of that gentleman formerly given is nothing more than this, that he at that time thought the then Judiciary system might be amended. From the rank which he assigned to the author of the report, he is certainly much better acquainted with the opposition than I am. He included, among those who differed with us on the question, and who generally agreed with us, all the judges of Virginia. I am acquainted with but few of these gentlemen, and do not know anything of the political sentiments of those with whom I am not acquainted; but if the few with whom I am not acquainted differed with us in opinion, they would not esteem us the more for relinquishing an opinion before we were convinced it was erroneous. But, sir, judging from a pamphlet which has been read during this debate, and said to contain their opinion, it is clear to my mind, that we perfectly agree. The same gentleman read to the Committee a part of a lecture of one of the judges of Virginia, which, if it strengthened his opinion on the present questions, ought to convince him that the Sedition law was unconstitutional. And what will he say to the opinion of the same judge, on the favorite doctrine that the common law of England is in force in the United States? He told us, by passing the bill we shall not save more than the small sum of $5,000. Here he and my colleague (Mr. Stanly) differ a little in opinion. My colleague thinks the saving will be somewhere about $40,000, though not a dust in the balance. Sir, I would vote for the bill, on the principle of economy, if it would only save the useless expenditure of $1,000 of the public money. Let it be remembered that the public money in all countries is drawn from the sweat of the people.

"The same gentleman told us that we ought to keep up these courts to convince the nations of Europe of the stability of our Government, to look respectable abroad. Sir, the public good alone shall be the principle by which I will govern myself, with out considering what the people of Europe may think. I will never consent to keep up what I deem useless and expensive establishments, merely be cause it may make us look respectable abroad, or to convince the people of Europe of the stability of our Government. Nor can I believe the passing the bill, which is altogether an internal regulation, can affect our national character in Europe; it is one of those internal regulations that the governments of Europe care nothing about. All that independent nations require of each other is, that they govern themselves with honesty and equity toward other nations.

"The gentleman asked us to show him the clauses in the Constitution which authorize the repeal of the Judiciary act. I will answer this question, by asking another: Can he show any clause in the Constitution which gives express and direct authority to repeal any law? He can not; there is no such clause. But the authority given to pass laws, gives also the authority to repeal, except in cases named, where you are expressly forbid, and this is not a forbidden case. The whole authority to repeal is an implied one; you may establish post offices and post roads, you may establish courts, and if you can repeal the one, you may repeal the other.

"The gentleman says, if you pass the bill, you make the Judiciary dependent on a faction. Who is the faction, sir, the majority or the minority? Formerly, I have heard it said in this House, the majority was the nation, and the minority a faction; and has the meaning of these words changed ? This the gentleman did not tell us.

"He also told us, there were but two ways of governing; one by the Judiciary and the other by the bayonet. Sir, we are so daily in the habit of hearing of all the instruments of death, that a stranger would suppose no other articles were manufactured or used in the United States, and that it was a standing order of the day to be told of them; and it is a little extraordinary, that most of the gentlemen who have spoken on the other side, have reminded us of them. Power, says the gentleman, in whatever hands it may fall, will be abused. I hope that he is mistaken, and that time will convince him of his error; but if it should be so, no one in the country will hold power long, because there is a peaceable corrective in the nation, the application of which is perfectly well understood, and is, in my opinion, a sovereign antidote to prevent this abuse. I mean a remedy to which I have often already refer red the gentleman; it is an answer of itself to almost everything that has been said — I mean elections. These gentlemen seem to depend on threats and bayonets. We always had a better dependence; it was elections and the good sense of the people; and these, it seems to me, are what every true republican ought to depend on, in a country where the people would as soon change a President as a constable for doing wrong.

"Do gentlemen expect to affright us by the constant cry of terror, or do they intend to prepare the nation for civil war, and all the evils consequent to such a state of things? If such be their object, let me tell them they will find themselves mistaken in both respects; they will not deter us from doing what we think ought to be done; and if all Congress were to join, they could not produce a separation of the States; the people would laugh to scorn all those who should wickedly make the attempt; they would say to them, in language not to be misunderstood, We gave you no authority to divide us from our brethren, we are determined never to fight them, let you determine what you may. Instead of fighting our neighbors, we will hold elections, and send more faithful men to fill the places you have dis graced.

"It is rung in our ears from all quarters, that we shall destroy the constitutional divisions of the departments by passing this bill. The Legislative, the Executive, and the Judicial, will all be unhinged by keeping them in exactly the same condition they have been for twelve years; and to add to all the other mighty charges, we are told, that we are about to repeal the law because the judges do not agree with us in political opinion. This could scarcely be thought to have much weight, if the gentleman will reflect that six judges are quite enough to sound the tocsin, whenever there shall be danger that the other departments are about to invade the liberty of the people; or is it necessary to keep up these new judges to prepare the people for this terrible work of plunging the bayonet into the breast of their nearest kinsman or neighbor? Whatever may be the opinion of the judges lately appointed in other States, I hope I may be permitted to state, that the judge appointed in North Carolina does not disagree with us in politics (Sitgreaves, of Halifax); and if a sincere and disinterested friendship for a worthy man, whom I have known from his infancy, and who left a lucrative practice, when he took a seat on the bench, could influence my vote, I should certainly vote against the passage of the bill. But, sir, shall friendship, shall respect for a worthy man, induce us to give a vote which we know to be wrong? Were it possible we should not only despise ourselves, but every man of worth and candor would also despise us.

"Mr. Chairman, it was my intention when I rose, to have examined more particularly the Constitutional ground which the gentlemen on the other side have taken; but as I most cordially agree in the opinion delivered on this subject, by a very respectable member from Massachusetts (Mr. Bacon), and as I also agree with the gentleman from Virginia (Mr. Giles), it would be needless to take up the time of the Committee in repeating arguments which have been some days delivered and remain yet to be answered.

"I beg pardon of the Committee for the time I have occupied. I did not expect to have detained them so long, but the importance of the subject, and the wide field into which it has been branched by those who preceded me, will be my apology."

INDEX.

Abolitionists, 59.
Academy, Davidson, 40; Granville, 40; Hillsboro, 40.
Adams, John, 51, 58, 64, 67, 72, 79, 80, 94, 95-97, 100-103, 113.
Adams, John Quincy, 135, 201, 221.
Adams, Samuel, 114.
Adet, French minister to the United States, 60, 77.
Alabama, admitted into the Union, 228, 255.
Alexander, Evan, 161.
Alliances, strange party, in the South in 1832, 276.
Alien and Sedition laws passed, 93, 94, 97, 99, 100, 103, 114, 171, 216, 233.
Alston, Willis, 127, 129, 161, 193, 198.
Amelia Island, 225.
Ames, Fisher, 64.
Anson, county of, 17.
Anti-Federalists, 41.
Arkansas, territory applies for admission into the Union, 227.
Army, Regular, 15, 17, 18, 204, 207.
Army, standing, 60, 73, 114, 176, 191, 207.
Ashe, Samuel, judge of North Carolina superior courts impeached, 138.
Ashe, Colonel of Wilmington, 65, 128.
Assumption bill, 52, 69.
Aurora, newspaper, 77, 89, 90, 103, 179, 185.

Bank, National, 48, 75, 166, 193, 212, 215, 216, 242, 244, 275, 276.
Barbour, James, U.S. Senator from Virginia, 212, 215, 223, 251.
Barron, Commodore, James, and the "*Chesapeake* affair," 157.
Bayard, James A., 109, 118, 126, 201, 291, 292, 298.
Benbury, Thomas, of North Carolina, 38.
Benton, Jesse, of North Carolina, 24.
Benton, Thomas H., 20, 246, 257, 276, 281, 285.
Betts, William, of Wake county, North Carolina, 18.
Bloodworth, Thomas, 66.
Bloodworth, Timothy, 28, 29, 38, 57, 94.
Blount, Henry, of Nash county, North Carolina, 283.
Blount, Thomas, M. C. from North Carolina, 59, 161.
Blount, William, U.S. Senator from Tennessee, convicted of treason, 77.
Bourne, Benjamin, M. C. from Rhode Island, 45.
Boylan, William, editor of the Raleigh *Minerva*, 114, 128.
Branch, John, U.S. Senator from North Carolina. 274.
Breckenridge, John, leader in Kentucky politics, 113, 125.
Brown, Bedford, U.S. Senator from North Carolina, 274, 281.
Bryan, Nathan, M.C. from North Carolina, 59.
Buck Spring, home of Nathaniel Macon, 32, 34, 66, 72, 120, 127, 128, 147, 158, 267, 268, 269.
Buford, A. S., Colonel in Revolutionary war, 17.
Burges, Dempsey, M. C. from North Carolina, speech of, on Assumption bill, 69.

Burgoyne, General John, 19.
Burke, Edmund, 44.
Burnet, staff officer to General Nathaniel Greene, 47.
Burr, Aaron, 6, 7, 52, 113, 117, 118, 119, 120, 137, 190.
Burril, James, U.S. Senator from Rhode Island, 227.
Bute, county of, 2, 5, 7, 8, 9, 14.
Butler, of South Carolina, colonel in Revolutionary war; 19.

Calhoun, John C., 198, 199, 202, 206, 207, 212, 214, 219, 224, 225, 240, 241, 242, 243, 244, 249, 255, 259, 261, 262, 263, 265, 274, 276, 277, 281, 285.
Campbell, G. W., 158, 268, 169, 212, 213, 216, 223, 251.
Campbelltown, battle of, 13, 17.
Canada, 162, 194, 199, 200, 202, 204, 207.
Cape Fear river, 6, 19.
Capital, National, proposal to remove, 165.
Carriage tax, 54.
Caswell, Richard, militia general in the Revolution, 17, 26, 29.
Caswell, William, militia general in the Revolution, 17.
Catawba river, 130.
Caucus, Congressional, dissatisfaction with, 242.
Chase, Samuel, Supreme Court Judge, 138, 139, 144, 147.
Charleston, South Carolina, 17, 18, 20, 28, 46, 47, 52, 58, 113, 152, 264.
Charlotte, North Carolina, 17, 18, 20, 104, 208.
Cheves, Langdon, 198, 200.
Chowan, county of, 17, 24, 38.
Civil service, Jefferson makes changes in, 141.
Clay, Henry, 39, 113, 179, 204, 222, 259, 276, 281, 284, 289.
Clay, Joseph, M. C. from Pennsylvania, 150.
Cleveland, Benjamin, militia colonel in the Revolution, 20.
Clinton, De Witt, of New York, 202, 203, 215, 220, 247.
Congressmen, 47, 217, 218, 219, 240, 247, 249, 258, 267.
Connecticut, 9, 37, 44, 45, 58, 69, 75, 78, 81, 89, 103, 113, 114, 135, 175, 180, 211, 285.
Constitution, National, 25, 27, 29, 35, 38, 39, 40, 41, 43, 59, 74, 84, 85, 88, 89, 90, 91, 92, 93, 97, 100, 110, 127, 130, 131, 133, 136, 147, 148, 153, 171, 177, 178, 179, 193, 194, 195, 215, 216, 218, 221, 222, 223, 224, 225, 226, 230, 231, 232, 233, 234, 235, 237, 247, 248, 250, 257, 258, 259, 275, 277, 279, 280, 283, 289, 291, 293, 294, 295, 296, 297, 300, 301, 304, 307
Convention, Constitutional, of North Carolina, 25, 27, 41, 268, 273, 279, 280, 289, vi; Philadelphia, 35, 38, 39, 44, 153.
Cooper, Doctor Thomas, 86.
Cornwallis, Lord, 17, 18, 19, 20, 27.
Cotten, Edward K., 3, 4, 5, 20, 286.
Cotton-growing, 50.
Crawford, William H., 221, 228, 240, 241, 242, 243, 244, 245, 248, 260.
Credit, American, 36, 37
Creek Indian controversy, 249.
Crisis, financial, of 1820, 239,

Cross Creek, battle of, 17.
Culpeper. John, 161.
Cumberland, county of, 12, 17, 51.

Dana, Samuel, 81, 84, 179, 180, 211.
Dandridge, Martha, 1.
Davidson, William L., 19.
Davie, William R., 19, 20, 39, 94, 95, 102, 115, 116, 122, 123, 127, 128, 129, 130.
Dayton, Jonathan, 58, 100.
de Armond, legion of, 18.
Debt, 29, 36, 48, 141, 236, 275, 277, 305.
Declaration of Independence, 44, 232, 305.
D'Estiang, 17.
Deficit, National, 212.
De Grasse, Count, 55, 56.
Democracy, The Western, 39.
Democrats, 59, 198, 213, 214, 260, 275, 282, 283, 284, 285.
Dickson, Joseph, 117, 120.
Dissenters, English and Scotch, 6.
Duane, William, editor of the *Aurora*, 103, 128, 149, 179, 185, 192.
Dudley, Edward B., 283.
Duvall, 55, 64.

Eaton, John H., of Tennessee, 242, 243.
Edenton, 3, 6, 24, 35, 50, 122, 128, 198, 206, 223.
Edgecombe, county of, 17, 18.
Edinburg, University of, 6.
Education, public, 279.
Edwards, Weldon N., 5.
Ellsworth, Oliver, 102, 103.
Embargo, 57, 147, 157, 161, 162, 167, 168, 169, 170, 172, 173, 175, 176, 177, 178, 183, 185, 186, 189, 200, 201, 204, 278.
England, 6, 13, 35, 36, 62, 63, 74, 75, 77, 81, 83, 86, 87, 91, 96, 102, 114, 146, 157, 158, 159, 161, 162, 170, 176, 179, 181, 182, 183, 186, 191, 192, 197, 198, 199, 201, 203, 204, 205, 208, 249, 270, 273, 300, 307.
Enquirer, Richmond, 192, 212, 220, 228, 243, 260, 274, 277, 287.
Eppes, John W., 186, 188, 189, 212, 223, 251.
"Era of Good Feeling," The, 217, 240.
Erskine, British minister to the United States, 176, 179.
Essex Junto, 158.
Excise law, 51, 52, 53, 54, 79.
Expansion of the slave power, 256.

Fasting and Prayer, day of, ordered by the Government, 93
Fayetteville, 13, 44, 117, 128, 130, 138, 161, 198, 292.
Federalists, 41, 48, 51, 53-54, 57, 61-65, 67, 72-73, 77-81, 84-85, 88-90, 92-96, 99, 102-104, 106-108, 110-111, 112, 115-121, 125-126, 128, 130-131, 135, 138, 148, 150-151, 157, 166-167, 175, 178, 180, 182, 188, 198, 200-203, 207, 211, 213, 228,

237, 250.
Federal courts, 113, 139, 297, 302.
Fithian, Philip, 6.
Florida, 96, 135, 145, 194, 207, 225-226, 228, 240, 244, 289.
Foreign affairs, 44, 192.
Forsyth, staff officer to General Greene, 47.
France, 1, 75, 77, 80-81, 84, 86-87, 89, 93-96, 98, 100-103, 115-116, 131, 138, 162, 170, 172, 178-179, 181, 183-184, 186-187, 191, 201, 283.
Franklin, Meshack. 161, 198.
Frederick the Great, 9.
Freneau, Philip, 44.

Gailliard, John, 212, 252, 262.
Gaines, General E. P., 256.
Gales, Joseph, founds the Raleigh *Register*, 114, 117, 127-128.
Gallatin, Albert, 66, 70-71, 78, 81-82, 84-86, 88, 93, 99, 111, 124, 144, 149, 154-155, 164, 167-169, 172, 175-177, 181, 184-185, 187-188, 191-193, 200, 203, 212, 220, 242, 275.
Garnett, James 151.
Gaston, William, 198, 203, 205, 219, 276, 279.
Gates, General Horatio, 18-20.
Gazette, United States National, 77.
George III, 2, 62, 114.
Georgia, 143-144, 148, 180, 203, 218, 221, 228, 249, 251, 255-256, 258, 260-261.
Gerry, Elbridge, 89, 95, 100-101, 113, 202.
Giles, William B., 51-52, 62, 66, 68, 135, 180-182, 185, 249, 292, 298, 302, 309.
Govan, A. R., 268.
Government, National, 28, 38, 78, 90, 92, 108, 132, 193, 215-216, 224, 239, 244, 249, 251, 255, 277-278, 282, 289.
Granville, county of, 12, 24, 38-39, 43.
Greene, General Nathaniel, 21, 27, 46-48.
Greene, Mrs. Nathaniel, claim of, 46-48.
Griffith, David, 12.
Griswold, Roger, 51, 78-79, 97, 99, 291.
Grove, W. B., 51, 56-57, 64, 120, 128, 130, 292.
Grundy, Felix, 198-199, 201.
Guerard, Governor of South Carolina, 47.
Guilford, county of, 12, 17.
Guilford Court House, 14, 26-27.

Hagner, Peter, second auditor of the U.S. Treasury, 109.
Halifax, 9, 18-21, 24, 27, 38, 41, 94, 127-129, 198, 268, 279, 309.
Hamilton, Alexander, 7, 43-44, 46, 48-49, 51-54, 75, 77, 80, 82, 95-96, 100-103, 117, 125, 131, 166, 168, 178, 192, 213-214, 228.
Hamilton, Paul, 190, 249.
Harper, Robert Goodloe, 85, 87, 90, 93, 96-97, 139.
Harrington, Colonel, 19.
Harrison, Carter B., 89.

Harrison, William H., 284-285.
Hawkins, Benjamin, 3, 45, 7, 15, 25, 39, 51, 57, 84, 123.
Hawkins, Joseph, 3, 5, 39.
Hawkins, Philemon, 1, 3.
Henderson, Archibald, 117, 120, 128, 130, 241, 291-293.
Henry, Patrick, 41, 102, 104, 106, 115.
Hill, M. C. from Maine, 233.
Hill, William, 130.
Hillsboro, 10, 13, 18, 20, 24-25, 40-41, 43, 91, 114, 127-128, 243.
Hogg, Gavin, 269.
Holden, W. W., editor *Raleigh Standard*. 282.
Holland, 9, 37, 86, 102.
Holmes, M. C. from Maine, 233.
Hooper, George, 28.
Hooper, William, 110, 11, 13, 25, 28-29, 40, 51, 59, 138.
Horsey, U.S. Senator from Delaware, 227.
Hubquarter creek, 2, 31.
Hudson river, 9, 37, 44, 162.
Huger, Daniel, 50.
Hunter, Banks & Co., 46.
Hunter, U.S. Senator from Rhode Island, 227.

Instructing U.S. Senators, policy of, 274.
Internal Improvements in North Carolina, 279.
Iredell, James, 10-11, 29, 36, 59, 67, 91.
Iredell, James, Jr., U.S. Senator from North Carolina, 274.
Iron, mining and manufacture of, 75.
Irving, Washington, 20.

Jackson, Andrew, 67, 193, 206, 214, 222, 225, 242-245, 248, 250-251, 255, 261-263, 274-276, 278, 281-283.
Jackson, British minister in Washington, 179, 200.
James River, 237, 241.
James II, of England; 12.
Jay, John, 44, 58, 62-63, 117-118.
Jay treaty, 58, 62-65, 79, 113.
Jefferson, Thomas, 3, 4, 6-7, 13, 15, 27+28, 33, 36, 40, 43-44, 52-53, 62, 65-67, 70, 77, 79-80, 82, 93, 95, 97-100, 106, 110-111, 113-125, 127-131, 133-141, 143, 145-151, 153-158, 160-161, 166-169, 172-173, 175-177, 183, 188, 194, 200, 202-203, 211-213, 216-218, 220, 223, 225, 235-239, 249-250, 254, 260, 267-269, 274-275, 278, 280, 284, 286, 289, 292.
Johnson, Richard M., candidate for the Vice-Presidency, 281.
Johnston, Charles, 24, 25.
Johnston, county of, 17.
Johnston, Samuel, 3, 10, 13, 25, 29, 37, 51, 57, 94.
Jones, Joseph, 269.
Jones, Willie, 26-27, 33, 38, 66, 94, 122, 123, 289.
Judiciary bill, 125, 291; Judiciary act, 130, 291-292, 302, 307.

Kalbe, Baron Von, 18, 19.
Kenan, Thomas, 161.
Kentucky resolutions, 113, 171, 228, 248, 260, 274.
King, William R., 198, 199, 243, 260.
King, Rufus, 96, 168, 211, 251.
King's Mountain, battle of, 24.

Leigh, Benjamin W., 276, 285.
Leopard, war vessel, engagement with the *Chesapeake*, 157.
Lincoln, Benjamin, 17, 18.
Livingston, Brockhoist, and the Louisiana Purchase, 131.
Livingston, Edward, 292.
Locke, Matthew, 38, 59, 87.
Logan, Doctor George, 95, 97-99.
Louisiana Purchase, 130, 135-136, 143, 145, 230, 235.
Lowndes, William, 137, 198-199, 219, 234.
Lyon, Matthew, 78-79, 103, 178, 188, 292.

MacFarland, Duncan, 161.
MacLaine, Alexander, 28, 37, 51, 138.
Macon, family, The, 1; Macon Manor, 2.
Macon, Betsey, daughter of Nathaniel Macon, 33-34,
Macon, Gideon, 1-2.
Macon, John, 15, 18, 24, 38, 41, 57, 66, 94.
Macon, Priscilla, wife of Gideon Macon, 2-3.
Macon, Seignora, daughter of Nathaniel Macon, 33-34.
Madison, James, 1, 5, 44, 51-52, 54, 56, 65-66, 68, 81-82, 100, 113, 117-118, 131-133, 143-144, 146-147, 149-150, 154-155, 160, 167, 169, 172, 175-179, 181, 184, 191-192, 197-198, 200-20204, 216, 220, 222, 226, 244, 247, 250, 257, 289.
Maine, 228-229, 233-234, 248.
Mangum, Willie P., 274, 276, 281, 284-285.
Marbury, 131-133.
Mark, Jacob, 70.
Martin, Alexander, 29, 54, 94.
Martin, Josiah, 9, 12, 39.
Maryland, 18, 37, 55, 64, 80, 118, 133, 175, 185, 191, 204, 218, 227-229, 303.
Massachusetts, 43, 52, 64, 73-74, 103, 106, 113-114, 117, 135, 146, 153, 158, 166, 169, 171, 182, 200-201, 204, 206, 222, 228-229, 235, 309.
McBryde, Archibald, 175, 193, 198, 201.
McDowell, Colonel Joseph, 20, 73.
McIntosh, leader of Creek Indians, 256.
McKean, Governor of Pennsylvania, 113, 132.
Mecklenburg, county of, 14, 161.
Mercer, from Maryland, 55.
Mercer, Hugh, from Virginia, a "Quid," 149, 219.
Mifflin, of Pennsylvania, 113.
Militia of New Jersey, 7; of Connecticut, 9; militia bill in Congress, 53; bill for amending, 159.

Miranda, John, South American revolutionist, 96, 103, 168.
Missouri compromise, 211, 233, 255, 258.
"Mobocrats," 53, 59.
Monroe, James, 5-6, 15-16, 77, 113, 118, 130-131, 143, 146-147, 149-150, 154-155, 165, 167, 197, 214, 216-217, 220-223, 226, 240, 247, 250, 252, 254, 256-257, 276.
Moore, county of, 13, 95.
Moore, Colonel John, 17, 127-128.
Moore, J. W., the historian, 23.
Moore's Creek Bridge, battle of, 13, 51.
Morris, Robert, 78, 118.
Muhlenberg, Speaker of the National House of Representatives, 45.
Mumford, George, 223.
Murfree, William H., 206.
Mutiny of Halifax (North Carolina) regiment, 18.

Napoleon, 130, 179, 191.
Nash, Abner, Governor of North Carolina, 25.
Nash, county of, 17-18, 283.
Nationalists, 36-37.
National Intelligencer, 148, 263.
New Bern, 23, 27, 38, 128, 198, 291.
New England, 35, 44-45, 75, 77, 83, 86, 100, 103, 118, 140, 145, 152-153, 157-158, 162, 167-168, 171-173, 176, 179, 188, 195, 200-202, 204, 212, 220-221, 240-241, 246, 278.
New Hampshire, 19, 64, 72, 132, 213, 285.
New Jersey, College of, 3, 5-6, 39.
New York, 11, 37, 39, 46, 52, 58, 62-63, 66, 68-69, 84, 87, 90, 99, 113, 117, 122, 125, 137, 152, 155, 183, 191, 198, 202-203, 211, 213, 215, 221, 227, 234, 239, 247, 248, 251, 263, 275, 285, 292, 298.
Nicholas, W. P., 54, 79-80, 106, 172.
Nicholson, of Kentucky, a Jefferson leader, 157.
Nicholson, Joseph H., 113, 124, 133-135, 138-140, 144, 146-147, 149-151, 157, 163, 168, 172, 177, 186, 197, 217.
Non-importation, 137, 150-152, 157, 161, 177, 181, 186, 191-192, 204.
Northampton, county of, 18.
Northern Neck of Virginia, 6.

Orange, county of, 12, 43.
Otis, Harrison G., 85, 89-90, 93, 100, 173, 211, 229.
Oxford, University of, 6.

Page, John, 50.
Page, Thomas J., 119.
Paine, Thomas, 44.
Parker, Josiah, 83.
Patriots, The, 11, 13-14.
Patton, John, 64.
Pearson, Joseph, 193, 198, 201, 203, 205, 241.

Pennsylvania, 11, 44, 50, 52-53, 64, 66, 75, 77, 82, 92, 99, 103, 106, 113, 116-117, 120, 132, 146, 149-150, 175, 183, 185, 188, 191, 203, 230, 241, 247-248, 263, 277, 285.
People, right of, to instruct Congressmen, 84.
Person, Thomas, 24, 38, 55.
Petersburg, 2, 172.
Pettigrew, Charles, 3, 5.
Peyton, Francis, 119-120.
Philadelphia, 33, 36-37, 39, 48-49, 52, 57-59, 63, 66, 70, 77-79, 82, 84, 86, 89, 93, 95-96, 102-103, 114, 152, 165-166, 228, 242, 268.
Pickering, John, 132.
Pickering, Timothy, 95-96, 100-101, 103, 139, 168, 201, 207.
Pinckney, Charles C., 114, 292.
Pinckney, William, 228.
Pittman, Thomas M., 32.
Plummer, Miss Hannah, 31.
Potomac River, 6, 124, 165, 203.
Porter, Peter B., 198.
Porterfield, militia colonel in Revolution, 17, 19.
Portsmouth, militia of, 83.
Powell, Leven, 11, 119.
Presbyterians, 6, 40.
Princeton, 3, 5-7, 44, 165, 264.
Prosperity, return of, 247.
Prussia, 9, 79.

"Quids," The, 143, 146, 149, 150, 155.
Quincy, Josiah, 170, 194, 201.

Radicals, in North Carolina, 44, 61, 67.
Raleigh, 21, 114-116, 123, 127-128, 242, 273, 275, 279, 281, 285.
Raleigh Register, 114, 128, 263, 275, 280, 287.
Raleigh Standard, 282-283.
Raleigh Star, 275, 280.
Ramsour's Mill, 19.
Randolph, John, 104, 124, 138-139, 151, 160, 222, 258, 274, 276, 289.
Ransom, James, 2.
Records, North Carolina, Colonial and State, 11-12.
Regulars, Delaware, 18; Maryland, 18.
Regulation, war of, 11.
Regulators, 12-14.
Republics, South American, 95-96, 224, 250, 252.
Republicans, democratic, 26, 274.
Representatives, National House of, 41, 117, 289.
Revolution, American, 44, 96, 231, 303.
Revolution of 1800, 113-114.
Revolution in Congress, 197.
Rhode Island, 45, 227.

LIFE OF NATHANIEL MACON 319

Richmond, 18, 120, 133, 220, 227-228.
Ritchie, Thomas, editor of the *Richmond Enquirer*, 228, 274.
Roanoke River, 1-2, 31.
Roosevelt, Nicholas J., 70.
Rowan, county of, 12, 223.
Royalists, Scotch, 11-12, 17, 19, 26, 35, 39, 47.
Rutledge, Edward, 114.
Rutledge, John, 113.

Salisbury, 10, 17-18, 20, 48, 67, 117, 128, 198, 241, 291.
Saratoga, battle of, 10, 18-19.
Saunders, Colonel, W. L., 12.
Savannah, 6, 10, 14, 17, 206.
Sawyer, Lemuel, 161, 175, 182, 198, 223.
Schouler, James, 48, 123, 148, 172, 185.
Scotch, in North Carolina, 11-14.
Seawell, Major Benjamin, 18-21.
Sedgwick, Theodore, 43, 52, 54-55, 63, 71, 102-104.
Sedition law, 92-94, 97, 99, 103, 108-110, 113-114, 133, 171, 216, 233, 301, 307.
Senate, U.S., 223, 264.
Sewall, Samuel, 74-75, 86.
Shocco Creek, 1-2.
Slave holders, 35.
Slavery question, 46, 136, 261-262.
Slocum, Jesse, 223.
Smallwood, Colonel of militia in the Revolution, 19
Sitgreaves, Samuel, 71, 84, 86-87, 97.
Smith, Jeremiah, from New Hampshire, 72.
Smith, Robert, 175, 184.
Smith, William, 50.
Society, American, Colonization, 226.
South, The, begins to become "solid," 258.
South Carolina, 9-10, 12-14, 17-18, 47, 52, 85, 87, 92, 96, 113, 117-118, 129-130, 137, 139, 153, 180, 203, 212, 219, 249, 26-262, 264, 268, 274, 276-278, 285, 306.
Southern Puritans, 59.
Southside of Roanoke, 1-2, 14, 28.
Speight, Richard D., 283.
Spriggs, Richard, 80.
Stanford, Richard, 150, 160-161, 191, 193, 197-199, 201, 209, 219.
Stanly, John, 130, 175, 193, 291-292, 307.
State rights, 37, 43, 64, 68, 73, 100, 137, 145, 153, 155, 203, 228, 236, 249, 262-263, 265, 274.
Steele, General John, 48, 50, 56, 128-130, 132.
Stevens, militia general in Revolution, 18.
Stone, David, 208, 251.
Stuart, House of, 12.
Sumner, General Jethro, 10, 14, 19-20.
Sumpter, General, of South Carolina, 19, 87.

Supreme Court, 27, 64, 91-92, 113, 115, 131-133, 138-140, 143, 166, 222, 236-237, 293-294, 297, 300, 303.

Talleyrand, burned in effigy, 80, 95.
Tarleton, Colonel, 17.
Tariff, 37, 50, 70, 75, 188-189, 195, 204, 211, 239-240, 244-248, 263, 274-275, 277, 281.
Tatom, Absalom, 59.
Taylor, John, of Caroline county, Virginia, book of, on State rights, 237.
Taylor, John W., 227, 234.
Tennessee, 55, 65, 67, 77, 97, 158, 199, 212, 216, 218, 223, 242-243, 251, 284-285.
Texas, The South and, 256, 261.
Thanksgiving, day of, voted by Congress, 208.
Thatcher, George, 106.
Thomas, J. B., 229, 233.
Thompson, Charles, 36.
Thompson, Frank A., 269.
Thompson, Smith, 221.
Tories, 14, 17, 19, 25, 27-29, 35, 38, 59, 115, 141, 260.
Trade, National, Macon's view of, 29; The American carrying, 86.
Treaties: with Algiers, Indians, Spain, 63, 123.
Troup, George M., 249, 251, 256, 260.
Trumbull, Jonathan, 45.
Tryon, county of, 17.
Tryon, British governor of North Carolina, 2, 11-12.
Tucker, St. George, 219, 222.
Turner, James, 213.

Union, The National, 29, 38, 43.
United States frigates: *Constitution, Constellation, United States*, 74.
University, National, 68, 192.

Valley Forge, 15, 18.
Van Allen, John E., 89-90, 93.
Van Buren, Martin, 253, 257, 267, 281-286.
Van Cortlandt, Philip, 87.
Van Dyke, Nicholas, 227.
Vans Murray, William, minister to Holland, 102.
Varnum, Joseph, 64, 146, 158-159, 175, 181.
Venable, Abraham, 68.
Vermont, 19, 78, 118, 292.
Virginia, 1-2, 5-6, 9, 25, 27-28, 32, 37, 40-41, 44, 47, 50, 52, 54, 60, 62-63, 67-68, 75, 79, 82-83, 103-104, 106, 110, 113, 118-120, 124, 126, 131-132, 135, 139, 143, 148, 155, 157-158, 164, 166, 171, 173, 175, 177, 185, 188, 191, 197, 199, 203, 206, 212, 214-215, 218-220, 222-223, 227-228, 237, 239, 246, 248-249, 251, 260-262, 264, 269, 272-274, 276, 281-282, 285, 292, 296, 298, 302, 306, 309.
Volney, French scientist, 86.

Wake, County of, 18, 43; Court House, 24, 26.
War of 1812, 74, 197, 211, 215, 219-220, 250, 257.
Warren, county of, 10, 15, 18, 20-21, 23, 31, 33, 43, 94, 208, 264-265, 279, 282-283.
Warrenton, 31-33, 208, 243, 255, 273, 283.
Washington and Lee University, 68.
Washington, George, 7, 9, 14, 18, 29, 37-38, 40-41, 49, 51-52, 55, 57-58, 61-63, 66-68, 71, 75, 79, 94-96, 102, 109-113, 113-114, 129, 164, 169, 173, 176, 183, 188, 192, 217, 230, 235, 267, 302.
Webster, Daniel, 212, 214, 219, 261, 276, 285.
Wheeler, John H., 12, 23, 161.
Whigs, 13-14, 17, 26, 36, 59, 249, 275-276, 281, 284-285.
Whiskey insurrection, 277.
White, Hugh L., 281.
White, Philo, editor of the *Raleigh Standard*, 282.
Wilkinson, General James, 189-190.
William and Mary College, 5-6.
Williamson, Doctor Hugh, 46, 50.
Wilmington, 13, 28, 35, 57, 66, 94, 128, 283, 292.
Winston, Joseph, 150, 154.
Wirt, William, 147.
Witherspoon, Doctor, 6-7.
Wyoming Valley, 44.
Wythe, George, 6.

X Y Z correspondence, 81.

Yadkin, River, 19-21, 24.
Yancey, Bartlett, 224-226, 233, 241-242, 245-246, 263, 274.
Yankees, 75, 158.
Yazoo, The, land frauds, 143-144, 148.
Yorktown, 27.

www.ingramcontent.com/pod-product-compliance
Lightning Source LLC
Chambersburg PA
CBHW070041230426
43661CB00034B/1454/J